# DRUG TESTING
## IN THE WORKPLACE

# DRUG TESTING

**Robert P. Decresce, MD, MBA**
Department of Pathology
Michael Reese Hospital
Chicago

**Mark S. Lifshitz, MD**
Clinical Assistant Professor of Pathology
New York University
School of Medicine
New York

*Assisted by*
**John Ambre, MD, PhD**
Associate Professor, Internal Medicine
Northwestern University Medical School
Chicago

ASCP Press
American Society of Clinical Pathologists
Chicago

# IN THE WORKPLACE

**Adrianne C. Mazura, JD**
Member; Pope, Ballard,
Shepard & Fowle, Ltd.
Chicago

**Joseph E. Tilson, JD**
Member; Pope, Ballard,
Shepard & Fowle, Ltd.
Chicago

*Assisted by*
**Kathryn M. Cochran, JD**
Associate; Pope, Ballard,
Shepard & Fowle, Ltd.
Chicago

 The Bureau of National Affairs, Inc.
Washington, D.C.

*Library of Congress Cataloging-in-Publication Data*

Drug testing in the workplace / Robert P. DeCresce . . . [et al.]:
  assisted by John Ambre, Kathryn M. Cochran.
    p. 292
    Includes bibliographies and index.
    1. Drug testing—Law and legislation—United States.    2. Drug testing—
United States.    I. DeCresce, Robert P.    [DNLM: 1. Civil Rights.
    2. Personnel Management—methods.    3. Substance Abuse—diagnosis.
WM 270 D795003]
KF3540.D778    1989
658.3'822—dc19
DNLM/DLC
for Library of Congress                                    88-39191
                                                              CIP

    ISBN: 0-89189-260-5 (ASCP)
    ISBN: 0-87179-588-4 (BNA)

Printed in the United States of America.

93  92  91  90  89        5  4  3  2  1

# CONTENTS

v

# FIGURES

# TABLES

# FOREWORD

In the first half of the '70s when I was Chairman of the National Labor Relations Board, drug abuse was just beginning to be recognized as a potentially serious employment problem. I do not recall a single NLRB case among the over 4,000 cases in which I participated as a decision-maker in which any major issue centered around the use or abuse of drugs by employees.

As to arbitration decisions of that vintage, one can count on the fingers of one hand the number of discharge or discipline cases growing out of drug problems, with the possible exception of alcohol-related matters.

Employers, even those with sophisticated Human Resource departments, had very little knowledge about drug use, testing for drugs, or any of the topics which are now commonplace at virtually every seminar on personnel practices or employment law.

Nor did union conventions or union executive conferences include in their agendas any serious discussion of drug-related issues. Today, these are important and even sometimes divisive matters in union circles.

As we near the end of the '80s, we have encountered a proliferation of drug-related employment problems. They have had to be dealt with by employers, unions, arbitrators, government agencies and courts. Yet, unfortunately, many of the persons called upon to deal with these issues still have essentially superficial knowledge of the medical, legal, and factual foundations which should undergird intelligent coping with drug-related problems at the workplace. Too many employers, unions, and even prestigious public decision makers are still acting on the basis of only the sketchiest of information as to both the medical facts and the legal principles involved.

It is timely then, and terribly important, in my view, for there to be available a source book which goes deeper than the surface, which is fully documented and referenced, and which is nevertheless readable and understandable by persons who may be neither lawyers nor medical experts. This book is fully responsive to that crying need. Human Resources executives, union officials, legal and medical practitioners, and governmental decision makers will all find this comprehensive and comprehensible reference desk book an invaluable tool.

Edward B. Miller

# FOREWORD

A drug is any chemical which when administered to a living thing produces an effect. Drug abuse is the use of a drug in a manner that may be calculated as likely to cause harm. In all of recorded history there has been drug abuse and drug abusers and there is no reason to believe there won't always be such as long as drugs are available and humans are unstable. Psychoactive drugs—those which affect the way you think, feel, or behave—will probably always have a strong appeal.

In addition to their pleasant and useful effects, psychoactive drugs do awful things. They generate psychological dependence, tolerance, physical dependence, withdrawal, addiction, overdose, and toxicologic physical disease; and are closely associated with problems such as AIDS infection, trauma caused by resultant automobile accidents and fire deaths, sociologic problems like divorce and child abuse, and economic problems like work-related inefficiency and large hospital bills.

We easily forget that they pervade all society, making jobs for bartenders, tobacco farmers, analytical toxicologists, and litigation attorneys. Virtually everyone uses psychoactive drugs, whether illegal or legal.

The current epidemic of abuse has produced many "strategic interventions," occurring in homes, schools, the media, streets or public areas, the doctor's office, and (increasingly) the workplace. In this age of high technology and high litigation, urine testing for substance abuse has become a favored method of strategic intervention. When first proposed 15 years ago, technology was too error-prone to justify this approach. The technology has improved to the point that only human factors, ie, positive specimen identification, chain of custody, and contaminated specimens continue to be persistent problems.

This book from the ASCP Press should help substantially in applying technology for the social good in the area of drug abuse, diagnosis, treatment and prevention. It points out that such testing is both medically sound and often legal and provides great detail on the scientific, clinical, managerial, and legal considerations. As the reader threads his or her way through "probable cause," "random unannounced," "clinically indicated," "legal" and "illegal," I hope he or she will remember the quote of Wilson Riles, who says "Don't ever do anything just because you can." Remember that in our country one is still innocent until proven guilty, and, finally, when one identifies a drug user one should be redemptive and not punitive.

George D. Lundberg, M.D.

# DRUG TESTING
## IN THE WORKPLACE

# 1

# INTRODUCTION

## —— SCOPE OF DRUG ABUSE

Substance abuse costs American society more than $135 billion annually. Disturbingly, this is considered a conservative estimate of the hardship actually inflicted upon families, communities, and workplaces. And studies indicate that while the cost of alcohol abuse is declining, the cost of other drug abuse has increased to $46.9 billion per year.[1]

In an economy that many perceive to be unsteady, plagued by deficits, increased foreign competition, renewed inflationary pressures, and low productivity, the cost of drug abuse can be viewed as a singularly intolerable area of waste. For both economic and social reasons then, increasing numbers of employers have turned to a consideration of drug testing in the workplace; likewise the federal government.

Laws regarding testing for illegal drugs by workers in the American workplace are "in the making" now, and are anything but firmly in place. Judges and arbitrators dealing with these issues have taken many divergent views. In September, 1986, the Reagan administration made its position clear when it issued Executive Order 12564.

This executive order requires that federal employees "refrain from the use of illegal drugs, whether on or off duty," and calls for testing. It reads ". . . The Federal government, as the largest employer in the Nation, can and should show the way towards achieving drug-free workplaces through a program designed to offer drug users a helping hand and, at

1

the same time, demonstrating to drug users that drugs will not be tolerated in the Federal workplace. . . ." This Executive Order and the guidelines concerning it that were subsequently issued by the U.S. Department of Health and Human Services are discussed in Chapter 2.

## Areas of Increased Cost

Losses from decreased productivity and lower profits result from behaviors that are sometimes hard to quantify: reduction in normal work capacity, poor workmanship, and mistakes or damage to company property. Businesses or agencies who have a significant number of drug-impaired workers, however, soon show losses to which dollar amounts can be attached. Such workers have increased tardiness and absenteeism as well as health problems in general, some of which result from higher-than-average accident and injury rates. More sick benefits are requested, the costs of health care and treatment rise—and so do insurance rates. In this downward productivity spiral, businesses notice more requests for time off, more grievances and worker-compensation claims, and, finally, increased costs for replacement and retraining of lost workers. In a workplace plagued by these problems, workers who do not abuse drugs may also experience lowered morale, which leads to lower productivity.

Some evidence is starting to accumulate that drug testing of employees can reduce the costs associated with drug abuse. Illinois Bell Telephone Company showed a savings of $459,000 in reduced absences, accidents, and medical and disability benefits resulting from a rehabilitation program in which 309 employees were enrolled.

Workers are understandably concerned about the erosion of their rights in the workplace, but they may also see the merits of removing threats to their own safety. In a first-ever request by an industrial group for intervention via drug testing by the Occupational Safety & Health Association (OSHA), the National-American Wholesale Grocers' Association asked OSHA to mandate drug tests for workers employed in warehouses storing harmful chemicals. The request was aimed at barring employees or job applicants from operating potentially dangerous equipment, such as forklifts, if they tested positive for certain drugs. (OSHA itself announced in November 1987 plans to fund research efforts—up to $1.5 million in grants—to identify ways of fighting drug abuse in the workplace.)

In addition to minimizing workers' compensation claims and employer's liability, management needs to give special consideration to employees who have access to valuable company property or actual funds or control of funds. In the December 1986 issue of *Digital Review*, a bank's systems manager reported a loss of well over a million dollars as a result of mistakes by a computer programmer who, under the influence of drugs, caused one of the bank's systems to "crash."

## Distribution of Abuse

The largest single source of income for organized crime is the profit derived from the sale of illegal drugs. An International Labor Organization report[2] has confirmed that drug and alcohol abuse in the workplace is increasing in the United States and Western Europe. The United Nations released a report in January 1988 indicating that heroin and cocaine abuse continue to increase worldwide. Cocaine is more widely available and of greatest concern, owing largely to the increased use of "crack," the most addictive form. Marijuana, however, remains the most widely abused drug (other than alcohol) worldwide.

But statistics may be difficult to interpret and the wrong conclusions may be drawn from them. The National Institute of Drug Abuse (NIDA) for instance reported the first significant decline in cocaine use among American youth in its 1985–86 annual survey of high school seniors. The report also showed a drop in overall drug use among high school seniors, college students, and young adults, continuing a decline from the previous year. In addition to the NIDA survey showing specific declines in cocaine, marijuana, heroin, amphetamine and sedative use, the Alcohol, Drug Abuse, and Mental Health Administration (ADAMHA) found an 8.2% decrease from 1977 to 85 in the number of 18- to 25-year-olds who used marijuana frequently. The same group, however, showed an increase of 0.8% in frequent use of other drugs, which ADAMHA attributes to the concentration of cocaine users in that age group. Nonetheless, researchers warn that the United States still has the highest rates of drug abuse among the world's industrialized nations.

Federal experts believe that between 10% and 23% of all U.S. workers use dangerous drugs on the job, and that regular users are likely not only to use them on the job but also to come to work impaired, at least occasionally. Counselors on the 800-COCAINE hotline who conducted a survey in 1986 found that 75% of callers reported they sometimes used drugs on the job; 69% regularly worked under the influence of cocaine; and 25% used cocaine at work every day.

Since the late 1960s, when the growing popularity of psychoactive drug use became apparent, illegal drug use has become more widespread in all socioeconomic strata, hence in all ranks of the work force. As evidence of this phenomenon, a 1987 publication,[3] citing a Harvard Medical School study, reported that one-third of all doctors under 40 years of age admitted continuing use of "recreational drugs."

Once rare, studies of drug abuse in the workplace and work-related environments now are published regularly by official agencies. One such study reported early this year[4] on a six-month-long investigation of drug abuse among commercial truck drivers in California. State undercover agents arrested 130 truck-stop drug dealers in what the state's attorney general called a "huge, rolling drug connection." Impetus for the investigation was an increase in truck accidents and concern for public safety on the highways.

Unfortunately, the outlook for the next generation of workers is uncertain, for as the use of illegal drugs has spread in the work force, it has also spread to schoolchildren. Accordingly, the U.S. Department of Education, in conjunction with the U.S. Department of Health and Human Services, was mandated by the Drug-Free Schools & Communities Act of 1986 to study the effectiveness of federal, state, and local drug prevention and education programs. The department's report to Congress recommended that schools design a broad-based antidrug initiative, including not only curriculum but also such elements as parent education and consistent enforcement of school antidrug policies. Another recommendation was the strengthening of prevention programs in order to deter initial drug experimentation and reduce the number of users.

## Reasons for Abuse

If we really knew why people use drugs, diagnosis and treatment could be more focused and less costly. However, as with many other human problems, root causes must be inferred from our world as we know it.

Mankind has a long history of using any available herbs and medicaments to alter awareness or dull pain. Opium was used in Greece and Cyprus as early as 2,000 B.C. In fact, opium was legal in the United States as late as 1909 (in which year import was banned because of an obvious increase in drug abuse and addiction).

During Prohibition, many Americans became accustomed to purchasing alcoholic beverages illegally. With law enforcement focused on alcohol, the use of opium and cocaine was ignored. Again, little public attention was paid to the use of illegal drugs until the late 1950s. And the attention that was directed toward the subject often was misguided. Little was known about the effects of several increasingly popular drugs, and "experts" frequently overdramatized their potential harm. When people sampled marijuana and learned that it did not drive them into a frenzy, so-called authorities lost their credibility.

Dr. Arnold Washton, a director of research for the National Cocaine Hotline, gave this perspective on the more recent increase in recreational drug use: "In the 1960s, the 'baby boomers' got fooled into thinking, just like people in the 1890s, that you could use drugs recreationally and not get addicted to them. Marijuana had a meaning beyond just getting high. It was the source of shared identity among people who had a common point of view, notably that their parents were stupid, that government was immoral, and that the war in Viet Nam was wrong."

The drug of choice has changed with changing times. The "Beat Generation," of the 1950s was known for the passivity associated with smoking marijuana. A more performance-oriented generation in the 1970s was attracted to cocaine, which seemed nearly a "designer drug"—chic, or at least expensive—but with no telltale odor. But cocaine has proven to be far more addicting than was previously believed, and it has been made more available, in a new and cheaper form—crack—a smokable preparation that may cause addiction after a single use in a vulnerable person. Our times have also seen an increase of synthetic drugs in the illegal marketplace, some of which have led to unforeseen and long-term consequences.

In general, people experiment with drugs to alter their mood: to speed up, slow down, tune out, or tune in to sights and sounds not available in an ordinary conscious state. Thus, most of the drugs described in this handbook are classified as stimulants, sedatives or hypnotics, and hallucinogenics.

Drugs are usually consumed for purposes thought to be relatively short-term and harmless. In fact, many unwanted and dangerous side effects occur, such as trembling, decrease in motor skills, seizures, cardiac arrhythmia, anxiety, distortions in reality and paranoia, psychoses, and unconsciousness.

Most drug testing is concerned with these classes of drugs: cocaine, marijuana/cannabinoids, opiates, amphetamine and methamphetamine, barbiturates, benzodiazepines, methaqualone, and phencyclidine (PCP). However, drug testing can also be designed to detect most prescription and over-the-counter drugs. Most commonly misused drugs and their effects are described in Chapters 3 and 4.

## —— TESTING PROGRAMS

### Trends

Testing for the use of illegal drugs in the workplace is becoming increasingly common, even though a body of law governing the legality of such testing is not in place. Faced with the urgent need for a reliable, competent work force, employers are gearing up to test job applicants as well as current employees in ways they hope will be deemed legal in the courts. For their part, the courts are handing down decisions on drug testing on a case-by-case basis almost daily.

Fully 30% of all Fortune 500 companies were using some tests for drugs in 1986, with many more planning to implement programs. In a poll reported in February 1988, Fortune 500 companies were asked to name the single most important disqualifier of otherwise qualified applicants. According to the 252 personnel directors who responded, suspected marijuana use was the most important disqualifier. Two-thirds of respondents said they believed that smoking marijuana after work decreases on-the-job productivity. Fewer than 10% listed physical appearance, weight, schools attended, or whether or not a candidate smokes tobacco as important criteria.

College Placement Council, Inc., surveyed 1,200 employers: nearly 30% of the 497 companies who responded who employ new college graduates screen for drug use; another 20% plan to begin testing soon. More than 88% who test said they would not hire a graduate who failed, and only 38% said they would retest an applicant who failed.

## Impetus

President Reagan, in a followup letter to his September 1986 executive order on establishing a drug-free workplace, said. "There is no reason to believe that there is a greater incidence of illegal drug use in the Federal workforce than in the private workforce. However, as the Nation's largest employer, the Federal government and its two million civilian employees must be in the forefront of our national effort to eliminate illegal drugs from the American workplace." Among the first groups of civilian employees affected were railroad workers. In the mobile society of the 1980s, with greater masses of people traveling faster and farther, safety in the transportation industry is paramount. On January 4, 1987, a single train accident—the worst in Amtrak's history—killed 16 people and left 175 injured. By the end of January, then Transportation Secretary Elizabeth Dole announced plans for a sweeping, random drug-testing program, and two bills were introduced in Congress requiring drug testing in the transportation field.

In the accident's aftermath, both the engineer and brakeman admitted to smoking marijuana in the engine cab shortly before the accident, and blood and urine samples from both employees tested positive for marijuana. The National Transportation Safety Board concluded that marijuana use was the primary cause of the disaster. Testifying before the Senate Commerce Committee in February 1988, the engineer said he believed that from 10% to 20% of rail workers drink or use drugs on duty; the brakeman said that usage was nearer 40% to 50%.

In another Amtrak accident about a year later—on January 29, 1988— the switch operator fled his post after a derailment that injured 25 passengers. He did not reappear to submit to blood or urine testing until more than 72 hours after the accident. He then tested positive for marijuana and at least one other drug.

 Certain regulations covering drug tests for employees involved in on-the-job accidents took effect in 1986. According to the Federal Railroad Administration, which released a report of 175 accidents that occurred from February 10, 1986, to January 15, 1987, in which 759 railway employees were tested nine, or 1.2%, tested positive for alcohol, and twenty-nine, or 3.8%, tested positive for drugs, including marijuana, cocaine, and methamphetamine. (Fourteen, or 1.8%, were found to have taken controlled substances that might have been included in prescription medicine.)

## Breaking Ground

As the nation's first employer to use drug testing on a routine basis, the U.S. Department of Defense (DOD) began testing in the 1970s in order to identify drug abusers, especially among Viet Nam war veterans addicted to heroin. It was intended that treatment be provided before sending them home. In the summer of 1981, an accident occurred aboard the aircraft carrier *U.S.S. Nimitz*. A Marine Prowler jet crashed into the flight deck of the carrier, killing all three airmen aboard the jet. The resulting explosion killed eleven others, injured forty-eight, and destroyed three fighter planes, at a cost to the Pentagon of $300 million. In the investigation that followed, widespread drug use among sailors was documented, although drug use was not found to have caused the fatal accident.

By the next year, the DOD had implemented mandatory urine-testing programs in every branch of the military. The Navy claims its testing program has shown a dramatic decrease in positive tests for drugs in personnel under 25 years of age: in 1981, 47%; 1982, 22%; 1984, 10%; and 1986, 4%. The DOD has developed a comprehensive testing program in which an employee can be temporarily removed from duty when an initial test is positive; no final action can be taken toward the employee unless the test is confirmed positive by another test; and the employee must be returned to duty if the initial test is not confirmed positive.

The railroads, airlines and aerospace companies were the first private industries to use drug testing.

## Sampling Materials

Until five years ago, almost all drug testing in the United States was done by the military, corrections agencies, and drug treatment programs. The military still conducts about half of all drug testing, mostly by checking urine samples. Drug testing of urine, however, has now become commonplace throughout public and private industry.

Several kinds of materials from the human body can be used for drug testing, but each has its drawbacks. A blood sample provides the best information concerning the potential effect on behavior of the drug consumed, because most drugs are distributed through the body by blood. Therefore, the concentration of a drug (or its breakdown products) in the blood would seem to provide a meaningful yardstick. However, since levels in blood plasma that clearly indicate impairment have not been established for most drugs, the result of a blood test is not always meaningful, especially from a legal standpoint. In fact, testing the blood for drugs is inconvenient and expensive due to the special equipment and trained personnel involved. It is also an invasive procedure carrying some risk. As a sample, blood also requires more particular handling than urine.

Urine, on the other hand, is easily available, easily collected during a natural bodily function, and can be analyzed and transported cheaply with some special care. The material itself is aqueous and therefore lends itself easily to laboratory manipulation. The technology for accurate testing of urine for drugs is already available, but there remains a need for properly accredited laboratories and personnel to do competent testing and for acceptance by the public of the idea that drug testing serves the common good. Guidelines for methods of urine collection, analysis, and storage have been recommended by NIDA. The guidelines are contained in Chapter 7.

Samples of skin, saliva, hair, and some other body tissues can also be tested for the presence of drugs but with greater difficulty. Some of the tests are discussed in Chapter 3.

## Cost Factors

We have seen that the cost to society of drug abuse—for our purposes, drug abuse in the workplace—is high enough to warrant a serious effort to curb it. At the same time, it would be possible to react so hastily that vast sums are spent wastefully in trying to attack the problem. Processing large numbers of urine samples, cheap and abundant as that material is, is extremely expensive. A urine sample that tests positive and then is confirmed by a second test may cost about $100 in the laboratory alone, with the administrative costs of handling the specimen (collecting and labeling), administering the program, and taking legal action adding to the expense. If, as President Reagan's executive order allows, the 2.8 million federal employees were each tested just once a year, the government's bill could come to $300 million!

The current cost to the military of specimen collection, transportation, analysis, and reporting amounts to $90 to $100 per sample—not including time lost from work of the person being tested. If each employee in the nation's work force were tested once a year, society's bill would come to $8 to $10 billion! Obviously, a decision on how much money can and should be spent to rid the workplace of drug abusers must be arrived at with intelligence. Sufficient data have not yet been collected to point toward exactly what kind of testing and how much is truly cost efficient.

## —— AREAS OF PUBLIC CONCERN

The rapid rise in popularity of workplace drug screening programs has prompted concerns on the part of employees and the public. These concerns have centered around the accuracy and legality of drug testing. In general, tests are accurate and legal when performed under carefully controlled conditions. For this reason, drug testing cannot be addressed without first having a fundamental understanding of testing theory and legal doctrines. These topics are discussed at length in the chapters that follow; an overview is presented here.

## Accuracy

The public is rightfully concerned about the accuracy of drug tests. After all, an individual may face disciplinary action, dismissal, or denial of employment based upon a positive test result. The concept of accuracy is one that depends upon the sensitivity, specificity, and predictive value model for a given test. Screening tests are not 100% accurate; sometimes they give false positive results and sometimes false negative ones. It is important to understand the circumstances under which this occurs.

In populations where the prevalence of drug abuse is very low, most positive test results are apt to be false positives. As the prevalence of drug abuse increases, the tests are apt to be more accurate in that most positives are true positives. For this reason, all presumptive positives should be confirmed by another method before they can be considered positive. Adverse employment decisions based on drug tests are more likely to pass legal scrutiny when confirmatory tests are used.

In addition to the scientific definition of accuracy, there are also practical considerations. Strictly speaking, the purpose of a drug test is to identify those individuals who are abusing illegal drugs. However, in certain circumstances, though a test result is confirmed positive, the individual may not be abusing drugs. These circumstances occur because it is not always possible to differentiate active from passive drug use or legal drugs from illegal ones. For instance, positive results for marijuana can occur due to the passive inhalation of smoke, and eating poppy seed cake can cause a positive test for opiates. Similarly, a legal prescription for codeine can mask heroin abuse, since both drugs produce the same byproduct, which is then detected by immunoassays.

On the other hand, it is not always possible to detect the presence of a drug even though it is there. This may be because the urine specimen is adulterated, the drug is present in concentration below the cutoff point, or the drug cannot be detected by the method used. For example, flurazepam (a commonly prescribed sedative) is not detected by the EMIT assay for benzodiazepines, but it is detected by FPIA. Likewise, methadone and meperidine are not easily detected by opiate immunoassays, although they may be identified by other techniques. Some drugs cannot be detected by any of the generally available methods.

Thus, it is important to understand the basic concepts of test accuracy as well as the scientific principles involved in test methods as they relate to specific drugs. As demonstrated above, the method used can determine the "accuracy" of the test. Also, medical knowledge of the drug excretion pattern is important in interpreting results, eg, drug presence in blood can indicate more recent abuse than drug presence in urine. Clearly, limitations in testing provide insight into the legal defensibility of a test result.

## Legality

Is testing legal? The answer to that question depends on many factors including the type of employee being tested, the workplace involved, and the kind of program being implemented. When drug testing is confined to job applicants, as opposed to current employees, employers face fewer legal challenges. Many Fortune 500 companies have opted to test all applicants but have shied completely away from testing current employees to avoid the delicate employee relations and legal issues. Even testing of job applicants is not without legal pitfalls, however. State and local legislation in a growing number of jurisdictions prescribe detailed procedures that must be followed in testing applicants and employees; employers with unionized work forces may be obligated to bargain with the union before testing even applicants; and applicants who are rejected following a positive test result may bring handicap discrimination suits under liberal interpretations of state and federal discrimination laws. Imaginative lawyers also try to persuade courts to accept novel tort theories whenever the spectre of mandatory drug testing is raised, and they have enjoyed some success.

Drug testing of current employees poses more legal and practical problems, especially mandatory testing "without cause," testing without any evidence that employees tested are using illegal drugs on the job. Of course, unannounced random testing has drawn the most vocal and vitriolic criticism from employees and labor unions. Testing may also take place "without cause" in connection with annual physical examinations or upon return from leaves of absence or layoffs.

Absent compelling public safety considerations, however, most employers have confined testing to "for cause" situations, where there is reason to believe that employees tested are using drugs on the job or reporting to work under the influence. Mandatory testing after industrial accidents, even absent evidence of drug use, has also become a popular but controversial form of testing.

The many different types and permutations of "for cause" testing policies have received varying degrees of approval when challenged, depending upon the nature of the employer, the duties of the employees, safety considerations, and the forum of the challenge. Employees who work for state or federal governments (like police officers or air traffic controllers) and employees subject to intensive governmental regulation (like jockeys and air traffic controllers) possess important constitutional rights including, among others, the right to be free from unreasonable searches. Similarly, unionized employees in the private sector have certain rights under collective bargaining agreements. Thus, public and unionized employers are subject to more legal challenges—and greater legal constraints—when testing for drug use.

*Private, nonunion employees have fewer protections. Indeed, the sole recourse for most private nonunion employees is to take advantage of the newly emerging common-law protections against such things as defamation, invasion of privacy, and intentional infliction of emotional distress.

Because the legality of drug testing depends on so many factors, many employers have adopted hybrid policies, incorporating different approaches toward different groups of employees. The wide variety of testing options and relevant legal and practical considerations for selecting an appropriate testing program are discussed in detail in the chapters that follow.

## Future Trends

Drug testing is not a medical test, it is a forensic one. Therefore, in the future, we will continue to see a merging of scientific principles with legal issues. This will determine who can be tested, how tests should be done, and the type of quality control and proficiency testing that is required to maintain accurate results.

# —— NOTES

1. *Economic Cost to Society of Alcohol and Drug Abuse, and Mental Illness*, Research Triangle Institute, 1984.
2. *Biweekly Reporter*, March 15, 1987.
3. *Biweekly Reporter*, Feb. 15, 1987.
4. *The National Report on Substance Abuse*, Feb. 3, 1988.

# 2

# LEGAL CONSIDERATIONS— AN OVERVIEW

## ───── PUBLIC VERSUS PRIVATE EMPLOYMENT: CONSTITUTIONAL ISSUES

The Fourth Amendment to the U.S. Constitution provides:

> "The right of the people to be secure in their persons, houses, papers, and effects, against unreasonable searches and seizures, shall not be violated, and no Warrants shall issue, but upon probable cause, supported by Oath or affirmation, and particularly describing the place to be searched, and the persons or things to be seized."

The Fifth Amendment provides that "No person shall . . . be deprived of life, liberty, or property, without due process of law." These amendments are part of what is commonly known as the Bill of Rights.

Virtually every court that has considered the validity of a testing program in the public sector has found a urinalysis test to be a search and seizure within the meaning of the Fourth Amendment. Some courts have found that the Fifth Amendment's guarantee of due process of law is implicated by the implementation of a drug testing policy in governmental employment. Still others have considered the constitutional "right to privacy" and the concept of "equal protection of the laws" when discussing testing programs in the public sector.

Contrary to popular belief, federal constitutional protections apply only to state and governmental employees[1] and employees subject to intensive governmental regulations in industries such as railroads, nuclear power, and horseracing.[2] Persons employed in private industry generally do not enjoy such constitutional safeguards,[3] although the concepts underlying these protections have been adopted in one form or another by arbitrators reviewing drug testing policies under collective bargaining agreements and by judges reviewing testing programs in the context of wrongful discharge suits.

Constitutional challenges to drug testing in the public sector are reaching the federal and state courts with increasing frequency. In fact, most decisions in this area have been rendered in only the past two years. This section will review the decisions in this area and outline the constitutional principles that regulate testing in the public sector.

## Search and Seizure

Finding that there are few activities in our society more personal or private than the act of urination, courts uniformly have held that drug screening by urinalysis infringes the employee's reasonable expectation of privacy and thus constitutes a search and seizure within the meaning of the Fourth Amendment.[4]

The next inquiry, therefore, is whether such a search and seizure is reasonable as required by the Fourth Amendment. In cases involving searches of public employees, the determination of reasonableness usually involves a balancing of the individual's expectation of privacy against the government's right as an employer to investigate employee misconduct.[5]

Most courts have found that this balance requires a public employee to submit to a urinalysis test only upon a showing of cause, or at the very least, a "reasonable suspicion" of drug use.[6] Under these standards, testing must be precipitated by circumstances such as actual observation of drug use or behavior indicating drug use. Thus, testing has been deemed lawful after undercover agents observed the employee smoking marijuana on the job[7] and after a bus driver was involved in a serious on-the-job accident.[8] Performance problems that suggest drug use also have been recognized as creating enough of a reasonable suspicion of drug use to support testing of public employees.[9] A mere "feeling" that an employee may be using drugs because a drug problem exists within the employee's particular department or within this country, however, has not been enough to support testing.[10]

Testing of public employees absent cause or individualized suspicion of drug use has been closely scrutinized. Such testing has been upheld when the individual's privacy interests have been minimal, the government's interests were substantial, and safeguards were provided to ensure that any reasonable expectation of privacy was not subjected to unregulated discretion.[11]

These standards have been met in only a few instances. For example, the Federal Aviation Administration has been permitted to require urine testing of flight service specialists (who perform air traffic controller duties with regard to private aircraft) as part of their annual medical exams because of the pervasive regulation of and strong public interest in air traffic safety.[12] Similarly, a federal court has upheld the U.S. Customs Service requirement of scheduled drug screening tests for employees who seek positions involving the interception of illicit drugs.[13] According to the court, the rule was justified because "an employee's use of the substances he has been hired to interdict casts substantial doubt upon his ability to carry out his duties honestly and vigorously, and undermines public confidence in the integrity of the Service."[14]

The courts have been most reluctant to uphold truly random, unscheduled drug tests of public employees. Indeed, such tests have been upheld only for certain private employees in highly regulated industries (such as jockeys)[15] or where public safety is a great concern (such as in prisons[16] or in nuclear power plants).[17] Absent such circumstances, random, unscheduled testing will be held in violation of the Constitution.[18]

## Due Process

On May 26, 1986, all firefighters and fire officers employed by the City of Plainfield, New Jersey, were ordered to submit to a surprise urinalysis test. The Fire Chief and Director of Public Affairs entered the city fire station, locked the station doors, and awakened the firefighters present on the premises. Each employee was required to submit a urine sample under the surveillance and supervision of bonded testing agents employed by the city. This procedure was repeated until all of the department's employees were tested. The firefighters had no notice of the intention to conduct the mass urinalysis. In fact, there was never a written directive, order, departmental policy, or regulation promulgated establishing the basis for such testing and prescribing appropriate standards and procedures for collecting, testing, and utilizing the information derived. Sixteen firefighters were advised that their tests proved positive for controlled substances. They were terminated immediately without pay. Further, they were not told of the particular substance found in their urine. Shortly after their termination they were served with written complaints charging them with numerous violations including the "commission" of a criminal act.

These employees filed suit against the city seeking reinstatement and enjoining the city from further standardless, department-wide testing. They won. In *Capua v. City of Plainfield*,[19] the court granted a permanent injunction banning further testing, based on the city's violation of the Fourth and Fourteenth Amendments.

The court held that the plaintiffs had a constitutionally recognized liberty and property interest in their individual reputations and in the honor and integrity of their good names. According to the court, defendants' discharge of the plaintiffs on what were essentially charges of drug abuse impermissibly violated these protected liberty and property interests without due process of law. The court ruled that the mass urinalysis was completely lacking in procedural safeguards because it was unilaterally imposed as a condition of employment without prior notice to plaintiffs and without an opportunity for plaintiffs to voice objection or seek the advice of counsel.

Moreover, the court stated that because the reliability of urinalysis tests was questionable, the defendants' refusal to afford the plaintiffs a full opportunity to evaluate and review their personal test results or to have their own specimens retested by a technician of their choice offended traditional notions of fundamental fairness and due process. Apparently, the enzyme multiplied immunoassay test (EMIT) was used to test the Plainfield firefighters.[20]

Plainfield's testing program illustrates how *not* to conduct urinalysis of public sector employees. The testing procedure used by the U.S. Customs Service and found lawful[21] stands in marked contrast. Testing in the Customs Service has been required only of employees seeking promotion into specified positions such as those involving the interdiction of illicit drugs. The test is scheduled in advance. The initial screening test is an EMIT; employees testing positive are tested again using the gas chromotography/mass spectrometry (GC/MS) method. Elaborate chain-of-custody and quality control procedures are employed. Moreover, customs workers can resubmit a positive test to a laboratory of their own choosing for retesting.

These cases illustrate the importance of notice, chain of custody, quality control, and procedural guidelines in the implementation of a testing procedure in the public sector. Reliable confirmatory tests also are critical.[22] Without such safeguards, a drug testing program will not pass constitutional muster.[23]

## The Constitutional Right of Personal Privacy

Drug testing programs also have been challenged, albeit less frequently, on the grounds that they invade the public employee's constitutional right to personal privacy. Although the Constitution does not specifically mention any right to personal privacy, the U.S. Supreme Court has held that part of the "liberty" protected by the Fourteenth Amendment is "a right of personal privacy, or a guarantee of certain areas or zones of privacy."[24] The constitutional right of personal privacy has been defined by the Court as the right to make certain "important" personal decisions without unjustified governmental interference.[25] Decisions recognized by the Court to be protected include decisions relating to marriage,[26] procreation,[27] contraception,[28] family relationships,[29] and child rearing and education.[30] Currently the courts are split on whether drug testing violates a public employee's right to personal privacy.

One court has ruled that the urinalysis tests detract from the dignity of public employees and invade the zone of privacy they possess under the Constitution.[31] According to this court, "excreting bodily wastes [is] a very personal bodily function normally done in private; it is accompanied by a legitimate expectation of privacy in both the process and the product."[32] On this basis the court held that the tests interfere with certain public employees' constitutional privacy rights.

In contrast, the court in *National Association of Air Traffic Specialists v. Dole*[33] held that the Federal Aviation Administration's drug testing program did not implicate any right to privacy. Interpreting this right narrowly, the court ruled that the constitutional right of personal privacy falls only within the areas of family and procreation. Accordingly, the court concluded that the constitutional right to privacy did not include the right to be free from a drug test.

## Equal Protection

The Fourteenth Amendment to the Constitution prohibits states from denying "equal protection of the laws." Courts have faced arguments that drug testing programs violate this constitutional provision when testing is required of some but not all similarly situated persons.

To date, equal protection arguments have met with little success, either because no unequal treatment was proved or because any differences in treatment were supported by valid reasons. Thus, in *Everett v. Napper*[34] the court held that Atlanta's drug testing program for city firefighters did not violate the equal protection clause of the Constitution since all other employees suspected of drug use were required to take drug screening tests. And in *Shoemaker v. Handel*,[35] the court held that the random testing of jockeys but not of officials, trainers, and grooms was lawful because substance abuse by jockeys could affect the integrity of horseracing, since they are the most visible human participants in the sport.[36]

# ——— DRUG TESTING LAWS

## Federal Laws and Regulations Relating to Drug Testing

At the time of this writing, there is no federal statute that directly prescribes or regulates the testing of employees for substance abuse. However, in

September 1986, President Reagan, in keeping with his well publicized stand against drug use, issued an executive order designed to make the federal government a drug-free workplace. Executive Order 12564[37] states that "[p]ersons who use illegal drugs are not suitable for Federal employment" and requires the head of each federal agency to develop a plan to achieve a drug-free workplace "with due consideration of the rights of the government, the employee and the general public."[38]

The executive order mandates that the head of each agency establish a program for voluntary testing and a testing program for the use of illegal drugs by employees in "sensitive" positions. Employees in such positions include those so designated by the agency, employees who have been granted access to classified information, individuals serving under Presidential appointments, law enforcement officers, and "[o]ther positions that the agency head determines involve law enforcement, national security, the protection of life and property, public health or safety or other functions requiring a high degree of trust and confidence."[39]

The order also authorizes the testing of other current federal agency employees under the following circumstances:

"(1) When there is reasonable suspicion that any employee uses illegal drugs;

(2) In an examination authorized by the agency regarding an accident or unsafe practice; or

(3) As part of or as a follow-up to counseling or rehabilitation for illegal drug use through an Employee Assistance Program."[40]

Under the order, applicants also are allowed to be tested.

Executive Order 12564 requires that agencies instituting drug testing programs give employees 60 days' notice of the program.[41] It further mandates that test results be kept confidential and that the privacy rights of individuals providing urine specimens be protected. Agencies are authorized to discipline employees testing positive for illegal drug use and to refer such employees to employee assistance programs. Pursuant to the order, the determination that a federal employee uses illegal drugs can be made on the basis of direct observation, criminal conviction, administrative inquiry, or solely on the results of an authorized testing program.

Two months after Executive Order 12564 was issued, Federal Personnel Manual (FPM) Letter 792–16 was published, expanding upon the guidelines set forth in President Reagan's executive order. This letter, among other things, specifies random testing of employees in "sensitive" positions. It also identifies when "reasonable suspicion" testing can take place by defining "reasonable suspicion" as "an articulable belief that an employee uses drugs drawn from specific and particularized facts and reasonable inferences from those facts."[42] According to FPM Letter 792–

16, a reasonable suspicion that an employee uses illegal drugs may be based upon the following circumstances:

"(a) observable phenomena, such as direct observation of drug use and/or the physical symptoms of being under the influence of a drug;

(b) a pattern of abnormal conduct or erratic behavior;

(c) arrest or conviction for a drug related offense; or the identification of an employee as the focus of a criminal investigation into illegal drug possession, use, or trafficking;

(d) information provided either by reliable and credible sources or independently corroborated;

(e) newly discovered evidence that the employee has tampered with a previous drug test.[43]

In April 1988, the Department of Health and Human Services issued final guidelines for drug testing of federal employees.[44] These guidelines require agency applicant and random drug testing programs to test for marijuana and cocaine at a minimum. They also allow applicant and random drug testing programs to test for opiates, amphetamines, and phencyclidine (PCP). Reasonable suspicion, accident, or unsafe practices testing may be performed for any drug listed in Schedule I or II of the Controlled Substances Act.[45] In addition, an agency can petition the Secretary of Health and Human Services for approval to include additional drugs in the agency's testing protocol.[46]

The collection procedures set forth in the guidelines require the use of a bluing agent in toilet bowls to prevent the employee being tested from adulterating the urine sample with toilet water.[47] They also allow for the use of a private stall or other partitioned area to protect the individual's privacy.[48]

The guidelines further mandate both an initial test and a confirmatory test. The initial test must use an immunoassay technique meeting the requirements of the Food and Drug Administration for commercial distribution.[49] All specimens identified as positive must be confirmed using GC/MS methods.[50] The guidelines set forth additional testing standards and establish certification and review procedures for laboratories.[51]

Executive Order 12564 and its implementing letters and guidelines could eventually affect up to 1.1 million federal employees. Not surprisingly, these measures have been controversial.

Soon after its issuance, a coalition of federal employee unions challenged the executive order and the FPM letter in *National Treasury Employees Union v. Reagan*.[52] The court dismissed the constitutional claims but ruled that the guidelines in the FPM violated the Administrative Procedure Act because they had not been made subject to the notice and comment procedures of the Act. Four days after the federal drug testing guidelines were first announced in January 1987, the American Federation of Government Employees filed suit to halt their implementation.[53] Whether and in what form Executive Order 12564 and the Health and Human Services guidelines will withstand such challenges remains to be seen.

## State and Municipal Legislation Regulating Drug Testing

The few states and one municipality that have enacted drug testing laws have taken an opposite approach to that of the federal government. Rather than encouraging drug testing, state and local governments have sought to place limits on all employers' rights to test employees. As of this writing, nine states—Connecticut, Iowa, Louisiana, Minnesota, Montana, Nebraska, Rhode Island, Utah, and Vermont—and the city of San Francisco have passed laws regulating drug testing in both the private and public sectors.

**Connecticut.** In Connecticut, employers are prohibited from making personnel decisions, including hiring decisions, on the basis of a positive urinalysis drug test unless an initial result is confirmed by two confirmatory tests.[54] The initial test must utilize "reliable methodology"; the final test must use GC/MS or a methodology determined by the state commission of health services to be as reliable or more reliable than GC/MS.[55] In addition, the employer is prohibited from directly observing the employee or prospective employee in the process of producing the urine specimen.[56]

A current employee cannot be subjected to drug testing unless the employer has a "reasonable suspicion" that the employee is "under the influence of drugs . . . which adversely affects or could adversely affect such employee's job performance."[57] Random testing of current employees is allowed only if (1) authorized by federal law, (2) the employee serves in a high-risk or safety-sensitive position, or (3) the employee is a voluntary participant in an employee assistance program.[58] Applicants can be tested only upon written notice and must be given a copy of the results.[59]

The statute prohibits collective bargaining agreements from contravening the act "so as to infringe the privacy rights of any employee."[60] It also subjects employers, laboratories and medical facilities that violate the act to special and general damages, attorneys' fees, and costs.[61]

**Iowa.** The Iowa testing statute completely prohibits random testing of applicants and employees.[62] Applicants and employees can be tested for substance abuse as part of a preemployment or regularly scheduled physical only upon notice.[63] Applicants must be informed personally and in writing as part of the application or job advertisement that they will be tested for drugs; current employees must receive 30 days' notice.[64]

The law allows an employer to test when there is probable cause to believe that an employee is impaired on the job.[65] In addition, the employee's impairment must present a danger to himself, others, or the employer's property or violate a known work rule.[66]

The test sample must be analyzed by a laboratory or testing facility that has been approved under rules adopted by the state department of health.[67] If a test result is positive for drug use, a second test using an alternative method of analysis must be conducted.[68] When "possible and practical," the second test must use a portion of the same test sample withdrawn from the employee for the first test.[69] Furthermore, an employee must be allowed an opportunity to rebut or explain the results of a drug test.[70]

A testing employer must provide substance abuse evaluation and treatment with costs apportioned by an employee benefit plan or, if there is no plan, at the employer's expense.[71] An employee who consents to evaluation and successfully completes treatment for substance abuse cannot be disciplined at the time of the first positive test. However, an employer can discipline an employee up to and including discharge if the employee fails to undergo evaluation or treatment when recommended by an evaluation.

An employer who violates the statute is guilty of a misdemeanor and may be liable in a civil suit for back pay, attorneys' fees, and costs.[72]

**Louisiana.** Louisiana's regulation of drug testing is contained in the state's unemployment compensation law.[73] The law disqualifies individuals for benefits who have been discharged for either on- or off-the-job use of a non-prescribed controlled substance and provides that an employer need only prove such fact by a "preponderance of the evidence."[74] In meeting this burden, only the results of drug testing performed pursuant to a written and promulgated substance abuse rule or policy is admissible.[75] Discharge for refusal to submit to a test under such a rule or policy is presumed to be misconduct.[76]

Testing under this law is allowed for investigation of possible impairment, accidents, or theft; for safety or security reasons; and for "maintenance of productivity [or] quality of products."[77] Drug testing laboratories must be located in and licensed to do business in Louisiana.[78] Collection of samples and testing must (1) be performed under "reasonably sanitary conditions," (2) be done with due regard for an individual's privacy and in a manner reasonably calculated to prevent substitutions or interference with the collection or testing of reliable samples, (3) include labeling of samples and an opportunity for an employee to submit relevant information, (4) be performed so as to preclude the probability of sample contamination or adulteration, and (5) include a verification of positive testing using GC/MS.[79]

Information obtained as a result of a drug testing program is confidential.[80] The law further prohibits defamation claims against employers who have established programs in accordance with the statute unless test results were disclosed to third parties, the information disclosed was based on false test results, and all elements of defamation are satisfied.[81]

**Minnesota.**    Minnesota law limits random drug and alcohol testing of current employees to "safety-sensitive" jobs, defined by the law as supervisory or management positions in which impairment caused by drug use would threaten the health or safety of any person.[82] Other employees can be tested when there is a reasonable suspicion that an employee is under the influence of drugs, when an employee has violated written work rules on drugs or has caused an accident or injury, or as part of an annual physical exam upon two weeks notice.[83] Employees undergoing chemical dependency treatment may be tested without notice for two years after completion of the treatment program.[84]

Applicants can be tested only after a job offer is made.[85] In addition, the same test must be required of all applicants who have been given conditional job offers. If the job offer is withdrawn, the employer must inform the applicant of the reasons.

In order to test, an employer must have a written testing policy which identifies (1) the employees or applicants subject to testing, (2) the circumstances under which testing may be required, (3) the right of the person to refuse to be tested and consequences of refusal, (4) the disciplinary or other action that may be taken as a result of the test, (5) the right of the person to explain a positive test result and pay for a retest, and (6) available appeal procedures.[86] The employer must notify all affected persons of a testing policy in writing and conspicuously post a notice that such a policy has been adopted.

An employer who tests must use a laboratory licensed by the state Commissioner of Health.[87] Under the law a testing laboratory is required to perform a confirmatory test on all samples that produce a positive test result.[88]

An employer cannot discharge an employee as a result of a positive confirmatory test without giving the employee an opportunity to participate in a rehabilitation program.[89] Violation of the Minnesota law exposes an employer or laboratory to a civil action for damages and attorneys' fees.[90]

**Montana.**    The Montana statute limits testing of applicants to those who work in hazardous work environments or in a job "the primary responsibility of which is security, public safety or fiduciary responsibility."[91] It allows testing of current employees only upon "reasonable belief" of on-the-job impairment.

The law requires employers to adopt a written policy for testing procedures that must include, among other things, a confirmatory test different from the initial testing procedure. The law further requires that the employee testing positive be given an opportunity to obtain a confirmatory test at the employer's expense at a laboratory of the employee's own choosing. The law forbids discipline if the person tested presents a "reasonable explanation" or medical opinion indicating that the results were not caused by illegal drugs. A person violating the statute is guilty of a misdemeanor.

**Nebraska.** The Nebraska drug testing law applies to governmental employers and private employers who employ six or more employees.[92] It prohibits drug testing of current employees unless all positive results are later confirmed using GC/MS.[93] Samples must be refrigerated and preserved in sufficient quantity for retesting for a period of 180 days, and a written record of the chain of custody must be kept.[94] Test results may only be disclosed as required by law or to the employee tested and other employees "who need to know the information for reasons connected with their employment."[95]

Employees who refuse the test may be lawfully subjected to discharge.[96] Persons who alter test results or tamper with bodily fluids may be discharged and are guilty of a misdemeanor.[97]

**Rhode Island.** Rhode Island law prohibits urine, blood, or bodily fluid testing unless an employer has "reasonable grounds to believe based on specific objective facts that an employee's use of controlled substances is impairing his ability to perform his job."[98] Employees tested must provide the sample in private, outside the presence of any person. Testing must be conducted "in conjunction with" a bona fide rehabilitation program and positive tests must be confirmed by means of GC/MS or "technology recognized as being at least as scientifically accurate."[99] In addition the employer must provide the employee, at the employer's expense, the opportunity to have the sample tested at an independent testing facility and must allow the employee to rebut or explain the results.

Any employer who violates the statute is guilty of a misdemeanor punishable by a fine of not more than $1,000 or not more than one year in jail or both. In addition, the employee can bring a civil action against violating employers for actual and punitive damages, attorneys' fees, and costs and injunctive relief.

**Utah.** Utah's law is perhaps the most comprehensive statute to date. It protects employers from liability for failure to test, for false test results, and for defamation.[100] To obtain such protection, employers must follow written drug testing policies that include privacy protection, specimen labeling, and a second confirmatory test if the first test is positive.[101] The law requires that employers and management must also submit themselves to periodic testing.[102] The Utah act allows employers to test for drugs in the absence of reasonable suspicion where such tests are used to "maintain safety for employees or the general public or maintain productivity, quality of products or services or security of property or information."[103] In this regard, the Utah statute is far broader than those of other states.

**Vermont.**    The Vermont statute allows testing of applicants only after a conditional offer is made, and upon a 10-day notice that lists the drugs to be tested.[104] Current employees can be tested only if there is probable cause to believe the employee is using or is under the influence of a drug on the job and the employer has a bona fide rehabilitation program available to the employee.[105] An employee testing positive cannot be terminated if that employee agrees to participate in, and successfully completes, a rehabilitation program.

The statute prohibits employers from requiring blood tests for drug use.[106] Positive urine tests must be confirmed by the GC/MS method or its equivalent. In addition, the applicant or employee must be allowed an opportunity to explain the results and for a retest at an independent laboratory at the employee's expense.[107]

An applicant or employee aggrieved by a violation of the statute may bring a civil action for injunctive relief, damages, court costs, and attorneys' fees.[108] The statute places the burden of proof of compliance on the employer. In addition, the state can seek both civil and criminal penalties for violation of the statute.

**San Francisco.**    The City of San Francisco prohibits both public and private sector mandatory urinalysis and blood and encephalographic testing for drugs unless the employer has reason to believe that the employee is impaired and that such impairment presents a clear and present danger to safety.[109] The ordinance exempts police, sheriffs, firefighters, and certain other emergency personnel.

**Summary.**    As of this writing, there are numerous bills pending before various other state legislatures and city councils that would restrict a public and/or private employer's right to conduct drug tests. Any employer who is testing is well advised to monitor these developments closely.

# —— DISCRIMINATION LAWS

In addition to knowing which, if any, federal or state laws limit drug testing, employers planning to test for drug use should familiarize themselves with the basic employment discrimination laws. Various federal and state statutes prohibit employment discrimination on the basis of race, color, religion, sex, national origin, and handicap. These prohibitions apply whether the employer is a federal agency, a state agency, or a privately owned company. Before embarking on any testing program, employers must keep in mind the requirements of these laws.

## Civil Rights Statutes and Their Prohibitions

Following the Civil War, Congress enacted a series of civil rights statutes to remedy employment discrimination. The Civil Rights Act of 1866,[110] better known as Section 1981, prohibits intentional race and alienage discrimination by private employers.[111] The Civil Rights Act of 1871[112] similarly proscribes intentional race and alienage discrimination in the public sector.

A more recently enacted civil rights statute, Title VII of the Civil Rights Act of 1964, forbids discrimination on the basis of race, color, religion, sex, and national origin.[113] Title VII applies to both private and public sector employees.[114] In addition, most states have human rights laws that parallel Title VII and similarly outlaw race, color, religion, sex, and national origin discrimination.[115]

When enforcing these civil rights laws, courts look for discriminatory treatment of or adverse impact on employees protected by these laws.[116] To determine the existence of unlawful discriminatory treatment, courts examine whether employees have been treated in the same manner as those outside the protected class.[117] The employer defends a disparate treatment case by producing evidence that the reasons for its actions were legitimate and non-discriminatory.[118]

Courts will find adverse impact on a protected class when a high percentage of minorities, women, or employees of the same ethnic background are affected by a drug testing policy. In such a case, discriminatory intent need not be proven.[119] The employer defends such a case by demonstrating that the policy is justified by business necessity.[120]

No cases have yet been brought challenging drug testing under the civil rights laws. However, such suits could arise if the testing program is administered in a discriminatory manner. Accordingly, women who test positive for drugs should not be treated differently than men because of a belief that drug use by women is less socially tolerable. Nor should minority employees or employees of one ethnic background be targeted for testing because of a belief that such groups are more likely to use drugs.

It is also important for an employer to monitor the results of a drug testing program to see if the program is affecting employees[121] in protected classes more severely than other employees. If such an adverse impact is found, the employer must be prepared to justify the program. Thus far, only public safety has been deemed a business necessity sufficient to justify a drug policy that unlawfully impacts on protected classes.[122]

## Prohibitions Against Handicap Discrimination

The Rehabilitation Act of 1973[123] prohibits the federal government, federal contractors, and employers receiving federal financial aid from discriminating against "otherwise qualified" handicapped individuals. Under the Act, a handicapped person is defined as any individual who:

"(i) has a physical or mental impairment which substantially limits one or more of such person's major life activities;

(ii) has a record of such impairment; or

(iii) is regarded as having such impairment.[124]

Most states also have laws that prohibit discrimination against handicapped persons by public and private employers.[125] Many states define a handicapped individual in the same manner as the federal Rehabilitation Act.[126] Other states define handicapped individual differently but include in the definition those persons who have "a record of such impairment" or those "regarded as having such an impairment."[127]

Under both the federal and state laws an employer is required to "reasonably accommodate" handicapped persons unless to do so would create "undue hardship."[128] What constitutes reasonable accommodation and undue hardship are factual questions that depend upon the "unique circumstances of the individual employer-employee relationship."[129]

The laws protecting handicapped employees do not prohibit drug testing. However, these laws do come into play when employees or potential employees test positive for drug use. Whether drug users are protected by these laws is a question that has been explored by a number of courts.

Most courts have acknowledged that former drug abusers who have a record of impairment that substantially limited their major life activities are persons protected under the federal Rehabilitation Act.[130] Such protected drug abusers include former and recovering addicts who, according to one court, should be encouraged and supported in overcoming drug addiction as a matter of public policy.[131]

On the other hand, current recreational drug users are probably not protected by these laws. At least one court has held that occasional users of marijuana are not handicapped under federal law because they were unable to show substantial impairment of a major life activity. Under the Rehabilitation Act, major life activities include such things as caring for oneself, performing manual tasks, walking, seeing, hearing, speaking, learning, and working.[132] According to the court in *McLeod v. City of Detroit*,[133] there was no evidence that any of these activities were affected by the plaintiffs' recreational use of marijuana.

The status of current addicts under the handicapped laws is less clear. The federal Rehabilitation Act[134] and some state laws[135] seem to imply that current addicts who can satisfactorily perform their jobs and who do not pose safety risks are handicapped. One state court has so held. In *Hazlett v. Martin Chevrolet*,[136] the Supreme Court of Ohio held that a current drug addict who satisfactorily performed his job as finance and insurance manager for a car dealer was handicapped under state law.[137] Federal courts, however, have faced the issue of current addicts under the Rehabilitation Act only where public safety was involved. These courts have uniformly held that drug users were not qualified for jobs such as police work and fire fighting.[138]

It appears that when a drug test uncovers a recreational user, the employer will be free to discharge or refuse to hire that individual. Ironically, when a drug test reveals an employee or applicant who is addicted to drugs, the employer may be required to accommodate that person if he or she is otherwise qualified.

The courts have not yet defined the scope of an employer's duty to reasonably accommodate drug abusers who fall within the definition of handicapped. However, a few courts have reviewed the federal government's duty to accommodate the alcoholism of its employees.[139] In *Walker v. Weinberger*,[140] the Department of Defense (DOD) allowed an alcoholic employee who had had absenteeism problems to undergo treatment. Following this, the employee was absent for reasons unrelated to his alcoholism. Taking into account both pre- and post-treatment absences, DOD terminated the employee for excessive absenteeism. The court held that the employer failed to accommodate the plaintiff's handicap. According to the court, "[i]n a disciplinary context . . . 'reasonable accommodation' of an alcoholic employee requires forgiveness of his past alcohol-induced misconduct in proportion to his willingness to undergo and favorable response to treatment."[141]

Similarly, the court in *Whitlock v. Donovan*[142] held that the United States Department of Labor (DOL) did not reasonably accommodate an alcoholic employee. Upon hearing of his alcoholism, DOL offered to transfer the employee to a less stressful job or to reduce his working hours. Over a four-year period, DOL counseled him and referred him to several rehabilitation programs. When the employee dropped out of his treatment program and his performance problems continued, DOL gave him a final warning and discharged him. The court found fault with the Department's "indecision" in handling the employee's alcoholism problem and stated that the employee should have been given the "firm choice" between rehabilitation and discipline immediately after the employee dropped out of the treatment program.[143]

These cases illustrate that choosing the right accommodation is not always easy. An employer implementing a drug testing program should decide in advance what it will do if an employee who tests positive for drug use acknowledges a chemical dependency. The employer will probably be required to allow such an employee at least one clearly stated opportunity to rehabilitate himself or herself. It has also been suggested that such an employee should be allowed to use accumulated sick days or to take advantage of any leave of absence.[144] Other accommodations could include changes in job duties or transfers to a different position.[145]

## ⸺ COMMON LAW PRINCIPLES

There are a number of civil wrongs for which the courts rather than the legislature have created remedies. Certain of these judge-made or "common law" causes of action have been or could be asserted by employees subjected to drug testing. These include classic tort claims like defamation, invasion of privacy, intentional infliction of emotional distress, and false imprisonment, as well as the newly developed causes of action related to wrongful discharge and breach of employment contract.

Cases brought under common law principles are usually decided by juries. Jury trials often result in large monetary awards to aggrieved employees. As a result, these common law cases of action are of particular importance to every employer contemplating drug testing.

### Tort Claims

**Defamation (Libel and Slander).** Defamation occurs when an untrue statement is communicated to a third party that "tends to harm the reputation of another so as to lower him in the estimation of the community or to deter third persons from dealing with him."[146] Libel is a written statement; slander is an oral statement.[147]

An employer can be accused of defamation whenever the employer transmits information about an employee. This is especially true when the information transmitted relates to an employee's drug test results. Not surprisingly, defamation is the most frequently alleged claim in a suit involving drug testing.

For example, in *O'Brien v. Papa Gino's of America*,[148] a jury found that the employer's statement that "plaintiff was terminated for drug use" was not completely true. Although the jury found that the plaintiff was terminated for drug use, it also found that the employer had retaliatory reasons for discharging the plaintiff—specifically the plaintiff's failure to promote the son of one of his superiors who also happened to be the godson of the company president. The jury awarded the plaintiff $448,200.

Similarly, in *Houston Belt & Terminal Railway Co. v. Wherry*,[149] an employee was terminated after a drug test (which later proved incorrect) revealed a trace of methadone in his urine. The company's labor relations director wrote a letter to DOL stating that the methadone trace constituted grounds for the plaintiff's discharge. The employee sued the labor relations director, the safety supervisor, and the company for defamation. The jury awarded $200,000 in compensatory and punitive damages.

In contrast, the court in *Rosemond v. National Railroad Passenger Corp.*[150] held that plaintiff had no claim for defamation. The court found an Amtrak official's statement that minute quantities of drugs were detected in the plaintiff's system to be true.[151]

Truth is an absolute defense in a defamation action.[152] Consent to a disclosure also protects an employer from a defamation suit.[153] In addition, certain circumstances give rise to a qualified privilege which protects employers.

Generally, employers will not be liable for defamation if they have a duty to communicate information to those with a need to know.[154] This privilege has been applied when information is communicated during arbitration,[155] in the course of disciplinary proceedings,[156] in response to reference requests,[157] in performance evaluations,[158] or to public officials such as the police[159] and state unemployment compensation agencies.[160] A qualified privilege, however, can be lost if the employer knows the information is false or recklessly disregards the falsity of the information, acts with malice or ill will, or is guilty of excessive publication.[161]

Usually an employee who communicates false information only to the affected employee is not liable for defamation. However, some recent (rather questionable) state court decisions have sustained defamation cases against employers when employees communicated false reasons for termination to prospective employers. In *Lewis v. Equitable Life Assurance Society of U.S.*,[162] the Court of Appeals of Minnesota sustained a jury verdict of $900,000 in favor of four plaintiffs when they informed prospective employers that they were terminated for gross insubordination. The jury found the reason for their discharges to be false. According to the court, the plaintiffs were forced to accomplish the defamation themselves or lie.[163] The court further held that it was reasonably foreseeable to the guilty employer that such republication would occur, particularly since the employer had a policy of refusing to discuss former employees with potential employers. The appeals court, therefore, upheld the jury's verdict.[164]

Defamation suits and their potential for large monetary awards present a real risk to employers testing for drugs. They can be guarded against when the test results are communicated only to those with a need to know and, according to recent decisions, only when testing results are correct. Because of these recent developments in the law of defamation, reliable collection procedures, accurate testing programs, and reputable laboratories are critical to any drug testing program.

**Invasion of Privacy.** The notion that people have a right to privacy has grown up alongside of cases interpreting the Constitution's right to privacy. This common law right to privacy has been defined as "the right to be let alone."[165] Although courts often borrow constitutional concepts in defining common law privacy rights, such protections exist separate and apart from the Fourth Amendment. Accordingly, the common law right to privacy protects both public and private sector employees from unwarranted invasions of privacy by employers.

Four types of common law privacy claims have been recognized: appropriation of another's name or likeness; intrusion into another's seclusion; public disclosure of true, private facts; and placing another in a false light in the public eye. Appropriation of another's name or likeness usually occurs when employers use photographs of employees in advertising; however, the three other privacy claims are applicable to employees subjected to drug testing. Although no appellate courts have interpreted these claims in the context of drug testing, such causes of action are being alleged with increasing frequency.

*Intrusion into an Employee's Seclusion.* Liability for invasion of privacy can arise when a person intentionally intrudes upon the solitude or seclusion of another in a manner that is highly offensive to a reasonable person.[166] Some courts have required intrusion into a private geographical space such as a home or hotel room for liability to attach under this theory.[167] Recent cases, however, have dispensed with this requirement and acknowledged that employees possess certain privacy rights in the workplace.

In *K-Mart v. Trotti*,[168] the court held that a search of a workplace locker could constitute an invasion of privacy if an employee purchased and used her own lock on the locker. According to the court, a jury "is justified in concluding that the employee manifested, and the employer recognized, an expectation that the locker and its contents would be free from intrusion and interference."[169]

Similarly, one court held that an employer violated an employee's reasonable expectation of privacy when, contrary to its policy that information concerning an employee's physical or mental condition could only come through the company's medical director, a supervisor communicated directly with the employee's psychiatrist.[170] Another court considered a supervisor's coercive sexual demands to constitute intrusion into an employee's seclusion in the psychological sense.[171]

In light of these cases, drug testing can give rise to a claim of intrusion into seclusion. In suits involving drug testing of public employees, the courts have acknowledged that urination is considered to be a private act in our society.[172] When an employee is required to urinate in a bottle while a supervisor looks on, the privacy rights of the employee are very definitely implicated. An intrusion into seclusion claim could also be based on disclosure of medical information in connection with a drug test or the involuntary disclosure of private off-the-job drug use, which might result from a drug test.

Recently, a number of cases have been filed attacking drug testing under such theories.[173] Thus, before implementing a drug testing program, employers should assess potential liability in this area by examining the reasonableness of the employees' expectation of privacy and the means used to conduct the test. Applicants probably have a smaller privacy expectation than do current employees. Similarly, employees in high-risk industries and those subjected to testing for "cause" or upon "reasonable suspicion" have less expectation of privacy than do those who have jobs where safety is not a factor or where testing is random. A written, published drug testing policy that takes steps to conduct testing in the least offensive manner possible would also be helpful in obviating employees' privacy expectations and in preserving the dignity of the employee.

*Public Disclosure of Private Facts.* This privacy claim arises when an employer widely disseminates truthful information about an employee that would be highly offensive to a reasonable person and is not of legitimate concern to the person receiving the information.[174] Although cases have been brought alleging this form of invasion of privacy in the area of drug testing,[175] none has yet been adjudicated.

Employers implementing testing programs can reduce exposure to liability from this kind of privacy claim by handling test results and employees who test positive with strict regard for confidentiality. The number of employees who have access to such information should be limited to those with a need to know.[176] In addition, employees with access to drug testing information should be made aware of the importance of confidentiality in this area. Under no circumstances should test results be disseminated company-wide.

*False Light in the Public Eye.* The final form of privacy invasion applicable to drug testing involves disclosure of information that places the employee in a false light in the public eye.[177] This cause of action is very much like defamation except that the information need not be inaccurate. According to one authority, protection against "false light" invasion of privacy implies the right to prevent both inaccurate portrayals of private facts, and accurate portrayals where disclosure would be highly objectionable to the ordinary person under the circumstances.[178]

Like public disclosure of private facts, however, dissemination must be widespread. For example, communication of the reasons for termination to unemployment compensation officials and potential employers may not be widespread enough to support a claim for false light invasion of privacy.[179]

Only one decision discusses this theory in the context of drug testing. In *Rosemond v. National Railroad Passenger Corp.*,[180] the plaintiff, who was a signal operator for Amtrak, alleged that he was placed in a false light when he was forced to submit to drug testing after a train accident and this fact was published in newspapers nationwide. The federal court refused to recognize such a cause of action because New York law, which was applicable to the case, had not recognized false light as an actionable claim.

For employers in states that do recognize false light as a cause of action, claims can be protected against in the same manner as claims of public disclosure of private facts; that is, by dealing with testing results and employees who test positively on a confidential basis, and by limiting the number of employees with access to this information to those with a need to know.

**Intentional Infliction of Emotional Distress.** Liability for the tort of intentional infliction of emotional distress arises as a result of extreme and outrageous conduct that intentionally or recklessly causes severe emotional distress to another.[181] Although malice is not an element of the claim, the tort is made out "only where the conduct has been so outrageous in character, and so extreme in degree, as to go beyond all possible bounds of decency, and to be regarded as atrocious and utterly intolerable in a civilized community."[182]

No reported decisions discuss this tort in the context of employee drug testing. However, employees have brought a number of intentional infliction of emotional distress suits in the analogous area of polygraph testing. Most of these suits have been unsuccessful.[183] In all of these cases, the employee was tested as part of an employer's investigation of theft, serious inventory loss, or unacceptable business practices. In addition, no aggravating circumstances existed that could characterize the employer's actions as outrageous or extreme. Employees have succeeded in challenging polygraph testing under the theory of intentional infliction of emotional distress only when the employer, in addition to requiring polygraph testing, abused or humiliated the employee. Thus, in *Tandy Corporation v. Bone*,[184] the Supreme Court of Arkansas upheld a jury verdict for intentional infliction of emotional distress where the employee being tested begged to take a tranquilizer but was not allowed to do so. Because of his highly agitated condition, the employee hyperventilated and had to be taken to the hospital. He returned to work but could not finish the day. He called his psychiatrist, was hospitalized for a week, and never returned to work.

Similarly, in *M.B.M. Company v. Ounce*,[185] the same court found an actionable claim for intentional infliction of emotional distress where an employee was forced to submit to a polygraph exam in connection with a money shortage. The exam was given to her after she was terminated for reasons having nothing to do with the shortage and as a condition of receiving her final paycheck. She passed the exam, but $36.00 was deducted from her check. This deduction was later explained to be her share of the shortage. Her final paycheck amounted to only 81 cents, and she was required to go to the state labor department to recoup the unauthorized deduction.[186]

Polygraph testing cases seem to indicate that "for cause" or "reasonable suspicion" testing by itself will not be deemed outrageous, indecent, or atrocious enough to support a claim for intentional infliction of emotional distress. However, these cases further illustrate that even "for cause" testing may prove vulnerable under this theory when coupled with abusive or humiliating tactics. Such tactics should be avoided when testing for drug use.

Whether random testing is sufficiently intolerable in and of itself to support a claim of intentional infliction of emotional distress is not addressed by these cases. Such a determination regarding drug testing will probably depend on such factors as the nature of the industry and the seriousness of the drug problem in the workplace.

**False Imprisonment.** False imprisonment occurs when a person is confined within fixed boundaries.[187] Confinement may occur as a result of submission to threats of physical force or other duress "where such duress is sufficient to make the consent given ineffective."[188]

A number of employees have brought actions against their employers alleging false imprisonment. For example, an employee who was forced by supervisors to remain in a room during a theft investigation filed suit against his employer for false imprisonment.[189] In the area of drug testing, an employee transported to a doctor's office for testing brought a similar claim.[190] A California employee also has claimed false imprisonment as a result of his confinement to a rehabilitation program after testing positive for drug use.[191]

None of the courts have held that a claim of false imprisonment can be brought against an employer. The first two cases were dismissed on other grounds;[192] the case brought by the California employee is still pending. Thus, whether a claim of false imprisonment can be brought successfully against a drug testing employer remains to be seen.

## Wrongful Discharge and Breach of Contract Claims

**Wrongful Discharge.** It has long been held that in the absence of an employment contract, an employer or employee may terminate an employment relationship at any time for a good reason, a bad reason, or any reason at all. This concept is commonly referred to as the "employment at will" doctrine. In recent years, however, the courts have been vigorously carving out exceptions to the employment at will doctrine and have created a new body of law regarding wrongful discharge.

One of the first and most widely accepted exceptions to the employment at will doctrine was the "public policy" exception. This exception established the existence of a cognizable claim when an employee's termination violates public policy. This usually occurs when an employee is terminated for refusing to commit an unlawful act or for performing an act that is protected by a public policy.[193] The public policy exception is often referred to as the tort of retaliatory discharge.[194]

Courts have recognized such a cause of action when an employee is terminated in retaliation for such actions as filing a workers' compensation claim,[195] voicing safety concerns,[196] performing jury duty,[197] reporting a crime to the police,[198] or refusing to violate the law.[199]

To date, there is only one reported decision addressing a public policy challenge in the drug testing context. In *Greco v. Halliburton Co.*,[200] a federal court in Wyoming held that termination for refusal to submit to urinalysis did not violate the state's public policy.

A number of reported cases challenge discharges in an area similar to drug testing—polygraph testing. The majority of these cases have been unsuccessful.[201] In the few successful challenges to lie detector tests on these grounds, courts primarily have relied upon the existence of state statutes prohibiting the use of polygraph tests.[202] However, in *Cordle v. General Hugh Mercer Corp.*,[203] the court held that plaintiffs terminated for refusing to take a polygraph test had a cause of action for retaliatory discharge even though no statute prohibiting polygraph testing existed. Indeed, such a statute was not enacted by the West Virginia legislature until after the test in question was refused. Despite this, the Supreme Court of Appeals of West Virginia held that requiring a polygraph test violated an individual's interest in privacy and, therefore, the public policy of West Virginia.

In states with laws prohibiting or restricting drug testing, employees will be able to claim retaliatory discharge as a result of or for refusing to take a drug test. In states without such statutes, the *Cordle* case may well provide a means to challenge drug testing on public policy grounds. Before implementing drug testing, employers should familiarize themselves with any applicable drug testing laws and privacy rights created by the courts in their respective states.

**Breach of Employment Contract.**    Courts in a growing number of states have shown a tendency to imply a contractual commitment on the part of an employer not to discharge employees in the absence of good and sufficient cause. Some courts have held that a personnel manual may form the basis of an employment contract that can only be terminated for just cause.[204] Other courts have inferred contracts from such things as longevity of employment, regular raises, and the absence of criticism.[205] Some courts have gone a step further by holding that an implied covenant of good faith and fair dealing exists in every employment relationship, and it would be violated if the employer discharged an employee without cause.[206]

Only one reported case has challenged a drug testing program asserting a violation of a company's personnel policy and an implied covenant of good faith and fair dealing.[207] Both claims were rejected.

Thus, employers may well find themselves defending discharges as a result of drug testing programs from such "just cause" challenges. Because few cases have been decided, employers probably will find themselves drawing guidance from the principles articulated by the courts and arbitrators in interpreting collective bargaining agreements. These principles, developed in response to union challenges to drug testing, are discussed elsewhere in this book.

# —— COLLECTIVE BARGAINING CONSIDERATIONS

## The Duty to Bargain

The National Labor Relations Act (NLRA) requires private sector employers to bargain in good faith with unions over all proposed management actions which affect "wages, hours, and other terms and conditions of employment."[208] The duty to bargain extends only to "mandatory" subjects of bargaining: those proposals which are "germane to the 'working environment' " and are not among " 'managerial decisions . . . which lie at the core of entrepreneurial control.' "[209] Section 8(a)(5) of the NLRA makes it unlawful to refuse to bargain in good faith.[210] The National Labor Relations Board (NLRB) has not yet decided whether the imposition of a drug testing program, or changes in work rules prohibiting drug use or requiring physical exams, constitute mandatory subjects of bargaining.

Employers may expect that the NLRB will decide that a decision to implement drug testing of current employees requires bargaining.[211] The NLRB has held that other sorts of programs designed to enforce work rules or to ensure that employees are fit for duty are mandatory subjects of bargaining. Thus, the NLRB has held that employers must bargain over the implementation of polygraph testing.[212] Similarly, the NLRB has held that imposing physical exams to determine fitness for duty, or expanding the scope of physical exams, is a mandatory subject of bargaining.[213]

The NLRB's General Counsel, in reliance on these cases, has issued a guideline memorandum instructing the NLRB's regional offices to handle charges alleging that an employer failed in its duty to bargain over drug testing, as though drug testing was a mandatory subject of bargaining.[214] Until the NLRB can rule on drug testing issues, the General Counsel has taken the position that drug testing for job applicants, as well as for current employees, requires an employer to bargain. The obligation to bargain, the General Counsel has determined, extends not only to the decision to implement a testing program or to change an existing program, but to decisions about the validity and integrity of the testing procedure, the breadth of the test, the qualifications of persons who devise and administer the test, and the impact the test results will have on an employee's or a job applicant's employment status. In pursuit of the General Counsel's policy, the Board has been instructed that there is a presumption that reinstatement and back pay are the appropriate remedies for employees discharged *solely* because of a positive test result under a unilaterally implemented policy. Employers may still show that this remedy is inappropriate by showing that the employee is in fact a drug or alcohol user, and that his position is incompatible with drug or alcohol use, based on the kind and level of drug detected.[215]

Even if the drug testing proposal is determined to be a mandatory subject of bargaining, there are certain circumstances which release an employer from the obligation to bargain. When an employer can establish that a union "clearly and unmistakably waived its right to bargain," the employer has a defense against the claim that it violated Section 8(a)(5) of the NLRA.[216] A union may waive its right to bargain by something as simple as failing to request in a timely way that the employer bargain over the new proposal.[217] For a defense of this type to prevail, an employer must demonstrate that it gave the union adequate notice that the proposal would be implemented, so that the union had a meaningful chance to request bargaining.[218]

The NLRA protects a union from this sort of defense if the employer seeks to make a change during the term of an existing contract in an item which is embodied in the contract. A union may fail to discuss a proposed unilateral modification under these circumstances without waiving a right to bargain, because the law does not require it to bargain away what has been already agreed to for a fixed term.[219] The employer can attempt to prove a waiver by demonstrating that the union's inaction is part of a pattern of allowing similar unilateral changes to go unchallenged in the past.[220] The General Counsel has taken the position that the proof of a past practice of unilateral changes must concern drug testing specifically, not merely unilateral implementation of similar, but not exactly equivalent, proposals.[221]

Certain kinds of contract language may constitute a waiver of the right to bargain. In cases not involving drug testing, the NLRB occasionally has held that language, such as a management rights clause, which expressly permits the employer to change work rules, amend safety policies, or implement physical exams, gives the employer the right to make changes without bargaining over them during the term of the contract.[222] General language in a management rights clause allowing discretion to implement "rules" or manage the business may be insufficient to constitute a defense to a failure to bargain charge involving drug testing.[223] Under the weight of NLRB authority and the General Counsel's guidelines, employers should bargain over the implementation of a drug testing program unless the contract between the employer and the union *specifically* provides that the employer retains the right to implement drug testing procedures.[224]

Likewise, the NLRB will narrowly construe contract language which "zippers" closed all discussions of any subject not specifically mentioned in the contract. Unless a "zipper" clause is very broad and clearly covers the disputed change, the NLRB will normally require that the parties bargain over any mandatory subjects which have not been treated in the contract and which the parties have never discussed.[225]

Under circumstances where the employer has refused to bargain over the implementation of a drug testing program in good faith reliance on existing work rules and contractual authority to implement the testing program, the NLRB will dismiss complaints alleging Section 8(a)(5) violations in deference to the arbitration process. The Board will not defer to arbitration if the union can show that the employer relied on existing written authority in bad faith in an attempt to undermine the union, or out of anti-union animus.[226]

Assuming that an employer is required to bargain over the implementation of a drug testing program, the National Labor Relations Act imposes the legal requirement that the employer and the union "meet at reasonable times and confer in good faith with respect to . . . the negotiation of an agreement."[227] In general terms, "good faith" requires both sides to participate in negotiations with an intent to find a basis for agreement,[228] but it does not require that the parties do in fact reach an agreement.[229] To avoid a charge that it failed to bargain in good faith, the employer must be attentive to the "totality" of its conduct in bargaining from the time the union makes the demand to bargain.[230]

The NLRB has identified several factors which, taken in combination, are evidence that an employer has bargained in bad faith in violation of the requirements of the NLRA. Especially where no drug testing program existed before, employers should avoid proposing a drug testing policy with features which are predictably unacceptable to a union and might be called outrageous. This type of proposal, in conjunction with other factors, could induce the NLRB to find a violation of Section 8(a)(5) of the NLRA.[231] The NLRB will conclude that an employer has engaged in "surface bargaining," in avoidance of its duty to bargain in good faith, when it finds various combinations of factors such as failure to schedule meetings that the union can attend,[232] delaying negotiations,[233] failing to provide a negotiator with authority to conduct talks,[234] indicating from the start that there is no room for discussion,[235] or imposing conditions necessary to progress at the bargaining table.[236] In addition, the employer should be prepared to offer information relative to its decision to test.[237] If the parties do agree to any proposals at the bargaining table, the employer should avoid withdrawing proposals, continually substituting new points, and any other action which step-by-step frustrates compromise on the original proposal.[238] At the same time, the employer is not legally required to make concessions, avoid "hard" bargaining, or back down from a "firm, fair" offer.[239]

In the event that the parties have bargained, and the employer and the union are unable to reach an agreement, the employer may declare an impasse and implement its last offer concerning the drug testing program.[240] If the employer bargains with the union during the term of an existing contract, the union might consider whether the arbitration clause in its contract is broad enough to require the parties to submit the dispute over the drug testing program to arbitration before the employer unilaterally implements its last offer. If the clause is broad enough, the union may bring suit under Section 301 of the Labor Management Relations Act (LMRA)[241] for breach of the labor agreement's arbitration provision and compel arbitration and enjoin implementation of the drug testing program pending the arbitrator's decision.

## Preemption of State Law Claim

The relationship between federal labor statutes dealing with collective bargaining and the sorts of common law claims previously discussed adds a wrinkle to litigation over drug testing programs. That wrinkle, the doctrine of "preemption," takes two forms. One, more properly called "primary jurisdiction," prevents a state or federal court from asserting its jurisdiction to hear a suit when the employee makes claims concerning any conduct encompassed in the protections or prohibitions of the National Labor Relations Act.[242] The other prevents individuals with employment rights defined under a collective bargaining agreement from suing in state court for damages, when the claims they raise—under whatever legal name—are really claims for a breach of the collective bargaining agreement, or involve interpretation of the agreement. These types of claims are more properly raised in a suit for breach of an agreement under Section 301 of the Labor Management Relations Act.

**Primary Jurisdiction of the NLRB.**    On occasion an employee will file suit in either state or federal court to seek a remedy for some employer action which restrains, threatens, or coerces the employee in the exercise of his rights under the NLRA, or to otherwise protect those rights from invasion by an unfair labor practice. The United States Supreme Court has determined that when the actions in question "are protected by §7 of the National Labor Relations Act, or constitute an unfair labor practice under §8, due regard for the federal enactment requires that state jurisdiction must yield."[243] In other words, the Court's long-standing concern for safeguarding uniform federal labor law policy[244] ensures that the National Labor Relations Board has "primary jurisdiction" over claims which arise under the Act the Board administers. Employees who complain of conduct within the scope of the NLRA must therefore seek a remedy first at the NLRB. This principle applies whether the employee seeks a remedy at common law (for instance, for damages arising out of a strike situation), or under a statute, such as one awarding damages for economic injuries from peaceful picketing.[245]

Only when the conduct the employee complains of is an activity which is a "merely peripheral concern of the Labor Management Relations Act," or where it "touch[es] interests so deeply rooted in local feeling and responsibility that, in the absence of compelling Congressional direction, [the Court] could not infer that Congress had deprived the States of the power to act," can the employee bring suit in state or federal court without first filing a charge at the NLRB.[246] The courts have recognized several types of conduct falling into this exception. In the drug testing context, an employee concerned that he has been defamed by an employer's circulation of reports about his drug use might be able to file a suit which the NLRB's primary jurisdiction does not preempt.[247] Such a suit may be preempted for other reasons, however. For instance, as discussed below, if a lawsuit involves the interpretation of a collective bargaining agreement, or if the plaintiff did not take advantage of a contractual grievance/arbitration procedure, the employee who goes to court may find himself without a remedy.[248]

A plaintiff could bring suit regarding conduct other than defamation which might fall outside the primary jurisdiction of the NLRB. The Supreme Court has allowed suits to recover damages for violent wrongful activity, on the grounds that the federal labor laws do not protect violent conduct.[249] An employee might be able to avoid preemption and sue for violent conduct surrounding any aspect of the drug testing procedure. Likewise, an employee could sue for damages resulting from the employer's intentional infliction of emotional distress by means of "outrageous" conduct stemming from the drug testing scheme. As the Supreme Court noted in *Farmer v. United Brotherhood of Carpenters & Joiners of America, Local 25*, there is no federal labor law protection for that kind of conduct, and the states have a "substantial interest in protecting . . . citizens from th[at] kind of abuse."[250] Such a suit will still fall prey to preemption unless the suit can be "adjudicated without resolution of the 'merits' of the underlying labor dispute."[251] If the plaintiff seeks damages for the abusive *manner* in which an employer treated him discriminatorily or unlawfully, courts generally will find that a suit is not preempted, even though the underlying discriminatory treatment could be the subject of an NLRB charge.[252]

Invasion of privacy suits that do not involve drug testing have not been found preempted in favor of the NLRB's primary jurisdiction, when the claims are based on "the particularly abusive manner" in which a plan to fire an employee was carried out.[253] Thus it appears that plaintiffs may successfully sue for defamation, intentional infliction of emotional distress, and invasion of privacy if their claims are sufficiently unrelated to the coercion and discrimination the NLRA prohibits.

**Preemptive Effect of Section 301 of the LMRA.** Most drug-related cases to date have addressed privacy claims under state tort law as an issue of preemption under Section 301 of the Labor Management Relations Act (LMRA), still the biggest hurdle to leap for a plaintiff covered by a collective bargaining agreement wishing to sue in court instead of pursuing a grievance or filing an NLRB charge. Section 301 of the Labor Management Relations Act of 1947 provides that suits for violation of a contract between "an employee and a labor organization" or between labor organizations may be brought in federal court when the industry involved affects commerce.[254] When a union represents an individual employee as his exclusive bargaining representative, the employee may sue the union for breaching its duty to represent him fairly and file a "hybrid" suit against the union under Section 301 for a breach of the collective bargaining agreement[255] and a breach of the duty of fair representation. In the same suit, the employee may also sue the employer under Section 301 as a third-party beneficiary of the labor agreement, for a breach of the agreement's provisions.[256]

However, when tort claims are "inextricably intertwined with consideration of the terms of the labor contract," Section 301 preempts them, and the suit must be considered as one under Section 301.[257] That is, any time a federal or state court must interpret a contract in order to determine finally the merits of the plaintiff's claim, the claim cannot be heard as a tort claim. Instead, the employee must bring a suit for breach of a labor contract under Section 301, and fulfill that section's jurisdictional requirements, including the obligation, in many cases, to exhaust grievance/arbitration remedies before looking to the courts for help. Only when the employment contract involved is an individual contract rather than a collective bargaining agreement will a unionized plaintiff's tort or breach of contract claims avoid the effect of the preemption doctrine.[258] The idea behind the preemption doctrine is the protection of the integrity of the body of federal law Congress authorized the courts to develop for interpreting and enforcing labor agreements, consistent with the policy of the federal labor laws.[259] As the Supreme Court explained,

> "questions relating to what the parties to a labor agreement agreed, and what legal consequences were intended to flow from breaches of that agreement, must be resolved by reference to uniform federal law, whether such questions arise in the context of a suit for breach of contract or in a suit alleging liability in tort."[260]

The courts have been vigilant in preventing plaintiffs' attempts to sneak contract claims into state or federal court under other names. Dressing the claim up as a tort claim against a union for failing to provide a safe workplace, for instance, will not protect the suit from the effect of the preemption doctrine when the real duty alleged to have been breached is a duty the employer owes under a collective bargaining agreement.[261]

Where drug testing is concerned, claims which are related to investigation, disciplinary procedures, or damages stemming from termination will most probably be preempted just as wrongful termination claims are preempted in other contexts. For instance, the court in *Strachan v. Union Oil Company*[262] found preempted a wide range of claims concerning a company's temporary suspension and investigation of two employees suspected of drug use while on duty. The court held their state law claims challenging the medical exams and blood and urine tests preempted, as well as their claims concerning false arrest (stemming from a mandatory cab ride to the doctor's office) and invasion of privacy (arising from a search of one plaintiff's person, car, and locker). The court found that the plaintiff's allegations of malice and defamation were unfounded based on their depositions. It granted the company summary judgment, explaining that any mistakes the company made were subject to the grievance/arbitration procedure under the collective bargaining agreement.[263] The *Strachan* court forcefully summed up the rationale for preemption:

> "These various claims . . . demonstrate clearly an attempt to create major state court claims out of matters which are all part of a company claim of right under a collective bargaining agreement, and the employee's right to challenge such claims through grievance procedure ending in binding arbitration. To hold otherwise in this case would subject thousands of grievance procedures involving disciplinary investigations and disciplinary actions including such matters as careless destruction of production, chronic tardiness, drinking on duty, insubordination to lawsuits asserting state court claims. The conclusion that such claims are preempted . . . reveals the wisdom and necessity of the established legal principle. Otherwise, the critically important aspect of collective bargaining which is involved in the establishment of the grievance procedure to protest breaches of labor contracts would be destroyed.[264]

A similar result obtained in a case in which a federal court faced ten state tort claims spun out of a situation in which a vehicle search on company premises disclosed alcohol and a gun in violation of company rules. In *Penrith v. Lockheed*[265] the court dismissed on preemption grounds a wrongful discharge claim and six other tort claims in their entirety, because they alleged wrongful conduct which was a part of or which flowed from the investigatory procedure and could be remedied via a grievance under the contract.[266] With respect to two other claims, both for tortious intentional infliction of emotional distress, the court found that those portions of the claims which did not relate to the investigation, but related instead to conduct undertaken "in a 'particularly abusive manner' " were not preempted. The conduct in question was the alleged pointing of a shotgun, and malicious disclosure of confidential information with the intent of causing emotional distress.[267]

Claims alleging a violation of state common law privacy rights have likewise been held preempted under Section 301. Despite the particularly emotional content of many of these claims, courts firmly hold that privacy claims on behalf of unionized employees are no more than claims that a drug testing program is *unreasonable* and must be addressed as matters of contract. One court held that a claim of invasion of privacy, stemming from a body search of an employee who resigned after refusing to allow his car to be searched, "would require a decision as to whether the employer could require such a search under the labor contract."[268] This involved "reference to, and interpretation of, the collective bargaining agreement," and justified dismissal of the claim on the ground that it was preempted.[269]

Another court dismissed a union's challenge on privacy grounds to a unilaterally implemented testing program which mandated testing, with or without cause, for all employees requiring medical attention after accidents.[270] The court in *Association of Western Pulp and Paper Workers v. Boise Cascade Corp.*[271] noted that in order to establish the tort of invasion of privacy, the union would have to show that the testing policy was offensive or objectionable to a reasonable person. The court then reasoned that this standard was the same as that an arbitrator would apply to review a challenge to the program under the bargaining agreement: "whether the rules are reasonable."[272] Thus, because an arbitrator could have resolved the issue by reference to the contract, Section 301 preempted the tort law claim.

If the right to privacy an employee asserts is statutory or constitutional, and not grounded in the common law of tort, there is some authority indicating that Section 301 would not preempt a claim based on this right. The Supreme Court made it clear that with respect to preemption issues arising over a claim other than a breach of contract claim, Congress did not intend "to preempt state rules that proscribe conduct, or establish rights and obligations, independent of a labor contract."[273] The court in *Cronan v. New England Telephone and Telegraph*[274] characterized a statutory right of privacy as a non-negotiable state law right independent of contractual rights, and refused to dismiss on preemption grounds a suit an employee filed after his employer revealed his affliction with AIDS-Related Complex. The labor agreement before the court contained no privacy protections, and the court rejected the argument that the words "any complaint" in the grievance procedure included all claims for breach of privacy.[275] The court concluded that "since the privacy claim . . . need not be resolved through contractual interpretation of the Agreement, and since a right to privacy is exactly the type of individual right that need not be subject to collective processes and is independent of private agreements," the privacy claim was not preempted.[276] However, the Ninth Circuit Court of Appeals recently held that Federal law preempted a claim that a random drug testing policy violated employees' rights to privacy and freedom from unreasonable search and seizure under the California constitution.[277]

**Conclusion.** When unionized employees file suit in state court alleging the various torts discussed above, in most cases they actually make claims for a violation of the NLRA or a breach of the collective bargaining agreement covering the terms of their employment. In either case, employers may, and probably will, attempt to have the state law suits heard—and dismissed—in federal court, by resorting to federal law allowing the removal to federal court of suits involving claims arising under the Constitution, treaties, or laws of the United States.[279] When a suit alleges facts which state a violation of the NLRA, such as discrimination on the basis of union adherence, it is likely to be dismissed on grounds that the claim should properly be brought in the first instance before the NLRB. When a suit alleges facts which state a claim involving a matter of contract interpretation, the suit will be treated as a suit for breach of contract under Section 301 of the LMRA. If the claim is redressable under the grievance/arbitration procedure, and the plaintiff has not resorted to that procedure and has no excuse for not doing so, the suit is likely to be dismissed. Only when the plaintiff alleges conduct such as defamation, intentional tortious conduct involving a particularly abusive method of handling matters subject to the contract, or a state statutory claim of right, is a suit likely to survive a challenge on preemption grounds.

# ——— NOTES

1. *Rendell & Baker v. Kohn*, 457 U.S. 830 (1982); *Flagg-Bros., Inc. v. Brooks*, 436 U.S. 149 (1973). *See also Greco v. Halliburton Co.*, 674 F. Supp. 1447, 2 IER 1281, 1283 (D. Wy. 1987) (constitutional proscriptions against drug testing apply only to governmental employees).

2. *Railway Labor Executives' Ass'n v. Burnley*, 839 F.2d 575 (9th Cir. 1988) (railroads); *Rushton v. Nebraska Public Power District*, No. 87–1441, 3 IER Cases 257 (8th Cir. April 14, 1988) (nuclear power); *Shoemaker v. Handel*, 795 F.2d 1136, 1 IER Cases 814 (3d Cir.), *cert. denied*, ___ U.S. ___, 1 IER Cases 1136 (1986) (horseracing).

3. Twelve state constitutions—Alaska, Arizona, California, Florida, Hawaii, Illinois, Louisiana, Massachusetts, Montana, Rhode Island, South Carolina, and

Washington—provide for their respective citizens' rights to privacy. The courts have interpreted the California Constitution's guaranty of privacy broadly. *E.g., White v. Davis*, 13 Cal. 3d 757, 533 P.2d 222 (1975). California's privacy right may well apply to private as well as public action. *See, e.g., Rulon-Miller v. IBM*, 162 Cal. App. 3d 241, 1 IER Cases 405 (1984).

4. *See, e.g., Railway Labor Executives Ass'n v. Burnley*, 839 F.2d 575, 580 (9th Cir. 1988) (citing cases).

5. *Allen v. City of Marietta*, 601 F. Supp. 482, 489 (N.D. Ga. 1985).

6. *National Federation of Federal Employees v. Weinberger*, 818 F.2d 935, 2 IER Cases 145 (D.C. Cir. 1987); *Feliciano v. City of Cleveland*, 661 F. Supp. 578, 2 IER Cases 419 (N.D. Ohio 1987); *American Federation of Government Employees v. Weinberger*, 651 F. Supp. 726, 1 IER Cases 1137 (S.D. Ga. 1986); *Penny v. Kennedy*, 648 F. Supp. 815, 1 IER Cases 1047 (E.D. Tenn. 1986); *Lovvorn v. City of Chattanooga*, 647 F. Supp. 875, 1 IER Cases 1041 (E.D. Tenn. 1986); *Capua v. City of Plainfield*, 643 F. Supp. 1507, 1 IER Cases 625 (D. N.J. 1986); *Jones v. McKenzie*, 628 F. Supp. 1500, 1 IER Cases 1076 (D.D.C. 1986), *rev'd, vacated in part*, 833 F.2d 335, 2 IER Cases 1121 (D.C. Cir. 1987); *Caruso v. Ward*, 133 Misc. 2d 544, 506 N.Y.S.2d 789, 2 IER Cases 238 (N.Y. Sup. Ct. 1986), *aff'd*, ___ N.Y.2d ___; 2 IER Cases 1057 (N.Y. App. Div. 1987); *Patchogue-Medford Congress of Teachers v. Board of Education of the Patchogue-Medford Union Free School District*, 510 N.E.2d 325, 2 IER Cases 198 (N.Y. 1987); *Fraternal Order of Police, Newark Lodge 12 v. City of Newark*, 216 N.J. Super. 461, 524 A.2d 430, 2 IER Cases 437 (1987); *King v. McMickens*, 120 A.D. 2d 351, 501 N.Y.S.2d 679 (N.Y. App. Div. 1986); *City of Palm Bay v. Bauman*, 475 So. 2d 1322 (Fla. Dist. Ct. App. 1985).

7. *Allen v. City of Marietta*, 601 F. Supp. 482 (N.D. Ga. 1985); *See also Everett v. Napper*, 833 F.2d 1509, 2 IER Cases 1377 (11th Cir. 1987) (firefighter implicated as buyer of marijuana).

8. *Division 241 Amalgamated Transit Union v. Sucsy*, 538 F.2d 1264 (7th Cir.), *cert. denied*, 429 U.S. 1029 (1976). *Compare Brotherhood of Maintenance of Way Employees, Lodge 16 v. Burlington Northern R.R. Co.*, 802 F.2d 1016, 123 LRRM 593 (8th Cir. 1986) (upholding post-accident drug testing of railroad employees) *with Railway Labor Executives' Ass'n v. Burnley*, 839 F.2d 575 (9th Cir. 1988) (railroad accidents do not create reasonable suspicion of drug use).

9. *Lovvorn v. City of Chattanooga*, 647 F. Supp. 875, 1 IER Cases 1041 (E.D. Tenn. 1986).

10. *Guiney v. Roache*, 654 F. Supp. 1287 (D. Mass.), *vacated and remanded*, 2 IER Cases 1225 (1st Cir. 1987); *Capua v. City of Plainfield*, 643 F. Supp. 1507, 1 IER Cases 625 (D.N.J. 1986); *Caruso v. Ward*, 133 Misc. 2d 544, 506 N.Y.S.2d 789, 2 IER Cases 238 (N.Y. Sup. Ct. 1986), *aff'd, 520* N.Y.2d *551*, 2 IER Cases 1057 (N.Y. App. Div. 1987). *But see City of East Point v. Smith*, 3 IER Cases (S.Ct. Ga. March 10, 1988) (upholding constitutionality of drug testing based upon reports that some police seen smoking in public).

11. *Patchogue-Medford Congress of Teachers v. Board of Education of Patchogue-Medford, supra* note 6.

12. *National Association of Air Traffic Specialists v. Dole,* ___ F. Supp. ___, 2 IER Cases 68 (D. Alaska 1987).

13. *National Treasury Employees Union v. Van Raab,* 816 F.2d 170, 2 IER Cases 15 (5th Cir. 1987), *cert. granted,* ___ U.S. ___ (March 1, 1988).

14. *Id.* at 178, 2 IER Cases at 20. *See also Jones v. McKenzie,* 833 F.2d 335, 2 IER Cases 1121 (D.C. Cir. 1987) (drug testing of school transportation employees lawful).

15. *Shoemaker v. Handel,* 795 F.2d 1136, 1 IER Cases 814 (3d Cir.), *cert. denied,* ___ U.S. ___. 1 IER Cases 1136 (1986). *But see Serpas v. Schmidt,* 808 F.2d 601, 2 IER Cases 647 (7th Cir. 1986) (holding that pervasive state regulation of the Illinois racing industry did not justify warrantless searches of race track employees' dormitories).

16. *McDonnell v. Hunter,* 809 F.2d 1302, 1 IER Cases 1297 (8th Cir. 1987).

17. *Rushton v. Nebraska Public Power Dist.,* No. 87–1441, slip op. 3 IER Cases 257 (8th Cir., April 14, 1988). *See also, Mulholland v. Department of Army,* 660 F. Supp. 1565 2 IER Cases 868 (E.D. Va. 1987) (upholding random testing of mechanics who service Defense Department helicopters); *Transport Workers Local Union 234 v. SEPTA,* 678 F. Supp. 543, 127 LRRM 2835 (E.D. Pa., 1988).

18. *Thomson v. Weinberger,* 682 F. Supp. 829, 3 IER Cases 7 (D.Md. 1988); *National Federation of Federal Employees v. Carlucci,* 680 F. Supp. 416, 2 IER Cases 1709 (D.D.C. 1988); *American Federation of Government Employees v. Weinberger,* 651 F. Supp. 726, 1 IER Cases 1137 (S.D. Ga. 1986); *Lovvorn v. City of Chattanooga, supra* note 9; *Patchogue-Medford Congress of Teachers v. Board of Education of Patchogue-Medford,* 510 N.E.2d 325, 2 IER Cases 198 (N.Y. 1987).

19. 643 F. Supp. 1507, 1 IER Cases 625 (D.N.J. 1986).

20. *Id.* at 1521.

21. *National Treasury Employees Union v. Von Raab, supra* note 13.

22. Courts generally have recognized that while an immunoassay test like EMIT may have a high rate of false positive readings, the GC/MS method is almost always accurate, assuming proper storage, handling and measurement techniques. They have approved its use as a confirmatory test. *See National Treasury Employees Union v. Van Raab,* 816 F.2d at 170, 2 IER Cases at 23; *National Assoc. of Air Traffic Specialists v. Dole,* ___ F. Supp. ___, 2 IER Cases 68 (D. Alaska 1987); *Rushton v. Nebraska Public Power Dist.,* 653 F. Supp. 1510 (D. Neb. 1987). Only one court has gone so far as to find that the requirements of due process are satisfied even without the use of subsequent GC/MS testing as long as an EMIT test is confirmed by a second test which simply may be another EMIT test. *McDonnell v. Hunter,* 809 F.2d 1302, 1309, 1 IER Cases 1297 (8th Cir. 1987).

23. *See, e.g., Jones v. McKenzie,* 628 F. Supp. 1500, 1 IER Cases 1076 (D.D.C. 1986), *rev'd on other grounds,* 833 F.2d 335, 2 IER Cases 1121 (D.C. Cir. 1987) (employee's termination on the basis of unconfirmed EMIT test was arbitrary and capricious and a violation of due process).

24. *Roe v. Wade*, 410 U.S. 113, 152 (1973).

25. *Whalen v. Roe*, 429 U.S. 589, 599–600 (1977).

26. *Loving v. Virginia*, 388 U.S. 1, 12 (1967).

27. *Planned Parenthood of Central Missouri v. Danforth*, 428 U.S. 52 (1976); *Roe v. Wade*, 410 U.S. 113, 152 (1973); *Griswold v. Connecticut*, 381 U.S. 479, 481 (1965); *Skinner v. Oklahoma ex rel Williamson*, 316 U.S. 535, 541–42 (1942).

28. *Eisenstadt v. Baird*, 405 U.S. 438, 453–54 (1972).

29. *Prince v. Massachusetts*, 321 U.S. 158, 166 (1944).

30. *Pierce v. Society of Sisters*, 268 U.S. 510, 535 (1925); *Meyer v. Nebraska*, 262 U.S. 390, 399 (1928).

31. *National Treasury Employees Union v. Von Raab*, 649 F. Supp. 380, 389 (1976), *rev'd on other grounds*, 816 F.2d 170 (5th Cir. 1987), *cert. granted*, ___ U.S. ___ (March 1, 1988).

32. *Id.*

33. ___ F. Supp. ___, 2 IER Cases 68 (D. Alaska 1987).

34. 833 F.2d 1509, 1513–14, 2 IER Cases 1377, 1381–82 (11th Cir. 1987).

35. 795 F.2d 1136, 1 IER Cases 814 (3d Cir.), *cert. denied*, ___ U.S. ___, 1 IER Cases 1136 (1986).

36. *See also New York City Transit Authority v. Beazer*, 440 U.S. 568 (1979) (disparate treatment of class of methadone users rationally based); *Copeland v. Philadelphia Police Department*, 840 F.2d 1139 (3d Cir. 1988) (difference in treatment of drug users and alcoholics justified by lawfulness of liquor).

37. 51 Fed. Reg. 32889 (1986).

38. *Id.* at 32890.

39. *Id.* at 32892.

40. *Id.* at 32890.

41. Agencies with programs already existing before the effective date of the Order are exempted from this requirement. *Id.*

42. FPM Letter 792–16 (November 1986), p.3.

43. *Id.* at 4.

44. Alcohol, Drug Abuse and Mental Health Administration, Department of Health and Human Services, *Mandatory Guidelines for Federal Workplace Drug Testing Programs*, 53 Fed. Reg. 11970 (April 11, 1988).

45. 53 Fed. Reg. at 11980.

46. *Id.*

47. *Id.*

48. *Id.* at 11981.

49. *Id.* at 11983.

50. *Id.*

51. *Id.* at 11980–11989.

52. Case No. 86–4058 (E.D. La. April 29, 1988).

53. *AFGE, AFL-CIO and AFGE, Local 2062 v. Bowen*, No. 87–0779 (E.D. La. 1987). Pursuant to the agreement of the parties, the case is stayed.

54. Conn. Acts 551, L 1987, §2 (Effective October 1, 1987).

55. *Id.*

56. *Id.* at §4.

57. *Id.* at §6.

58. *Id.* at §7.

59. *Id.* at §3.

60. *Id* at §12.

61. *Id.* at §11.

62. Iowa Code, §730.5.2 (effective July 1, 1987). The statute, however, exempts drug tests authorized for state peace and correctional officers, drug tests required under federal statutes, drug tests conducted under nuclear regulation commission policy and drug tests conducted to determine if an employee is ineligible to receive workers' compensation. *Id.*

63. *Id.* at §750.5.7.

64. *Id.*

65. *Id.* at §750.5.3(a).

66. *Id.* at §750.5.3(b).

67. *Id.* at §750.5.3(c).

68. *Id.* at §750.5.3(d).

69. *Id.*

70. *Id.* at §750.5.3(r).

71. *Id.*

72. *Id.* at §750.5.9.

73. La. Rev. Stat. Ann. §23:1601(10)(A)(1987).

74. *Id.*

75. *Id.*

76. *Id.*

77. *Id.* at §23:1601(10)(D).

78. *Id.* at §23:1601(10)(B).

79. *Id.* at §23:1601(10)(C).

80. *Id.* at §23:1601(10)(E).

81. *Id.* at §23:1601(10)(F).

82. Minn. Stat. §§181.93(13), 181.94(4) (effective September 1, 1987). The law, however, exempts applicants and employees who are subject to drug and alcohol testing under certain federal regulations and contracts and state agency rules that adopt federal regulations applicable to industrial companies. *Id.* §181.995.

83. *Id.* at §181.94.

84. *Id.* at §181.94(6).

85. *Id.* at §181.94(2).

86. *Id.* at §181.95.

87. *Id.* at §181.96(1). Under the law the Commissioner is required to adopt licensing rules by January 1, 1985. *Id.* The law does allow employers to use laboratories who meet certain requirements until the licensing rules are promulgated. *Id.* at §181.96(2).

88. *Id.* at §181.96(3).

89. *Id.* at §181.96(10).

90. *Id.* at §181.99(2).

91. Mont. Rev. Code Ann. §39–2–304.

92. Neb. Laws Sec. 2(8), L.B. 582, L.1988 (effective three months after adjournment).

93. *Id.* Sec. 3.

94. *Id.* Sec. 4.

95. *Id.* Sec. 6.

96. *Id.* Sec. 10.

97. *Id.* Sec. 8 and 9.

98. R. I. Gen Laws §28–6.6–1(A-G) (effective July 1, 1987).

99. *Id.* at §28–6.5–1(C) & (D).

100. Utah Code Ann. §§34–38–9, 10 & 11.

101. *Id.* at §34–38–6 & 7.

102. *Id.* at §34–38–3.

103. *Id.* at §34–38–7(2).

104. 21 V.S.A. §512 (effective September 1, 1987).

105. *Id.* at §513. Random testing is prohibited except when such testing is required by federal law or regulation.

106. *Id.* at §513.

107. *Id.* at §515.

108. *Id.* at §519.

109. S.F. Mun. Code Sec. 3300 A.1.

110. 42 U.S.C. §1981.

111. *Saint Francis College v. Magid Ghardan Al-Khazraji,* ___ U.S. ___, 41 FEP Cases 1712 (1986); *Johnson v. Ry. Express Agency, Inc.,* 421 U.S. 454 (1975).

112. 42 U.S.C. §1983.

113. 42 U.S.C. §2000e-2(a).

114. 42 U.S.C. §2000e(b).

115. *See, e.g.,* Ill. Rev. Stat., c.68 ¶¶1–101 *et seq.*

116. An adverse impact case cannot be brought under 42 U.S.C. §1981 or 42 U.S.C. §1983. *Washington v. Davis*, 426 U.S. 229 (1976); *General Building Contractors Ass'n. v. Pennsylvania*, 457 U.S. 375 (1982).

117. *See Smith v. American Service Co. of Atlanta*, 611 F. Supp. 321 (N.D. Ga. 1984) (unlawful discrimination where a black female failed a polygraph test but, unlike a white female, was denied opportunity to explain her answer).

118. *Texas Dept. of Community Affairs v. Burdine*, 450 U.S. 248 (1981).

119. *Griggs v. Duke Power Co.*, 401 U.S. 424, 432 (1971).

120. *Id.* at 426.

121. Assertions have been made that dark skin color may give rise to false positives on drug tests. *Employment Testing: A National Report on Polygraph, Drug, AIDS and Genetic Testing* at D:23 (1987); Chaney v. Southern Railway Co., ___ F.2d ___, 46 EPD ¶38,054 (1988).

122. *See New York City Transit Authority v. Beazer*, 440 U.S. 568 (1979) (rule barring methadone users justified because of safety reasons).

123. 29 U.S.C. §701 *et seq.*

124. 29 U.S.C. §706(6).

125. Delaware and Wyoming do not prohibit discrimination against handicapped persons in their state antidiscrimination laws. *See* Del. Code Tit. 19, §17, subchap. II; Wyo. Stat. §§27-a-101 *et seq.* Alabama, Arkansas, Idaho and Mississippi prohibit handicap discrimination only in the public sector. *See* Ala. Code Tit. 21, §7; Ark. Stat. Ann. §29; Idaho Code of Fair Employment Practices, Executive Order No. 78–4; Miss. Code, Ann. §25–9–103.

126. *See* Haw. Rev. Stat., Tit. 21, ch. 378, §§378–1 *et seq.*; La. Rev. Stat. Ann. §2112 (West); Mass. Ann. Laws, ch. 368, §1(17); Minn. Stat. Ann., §363.01.25; Okla. Stat. Tit. 25, ch. 388, §1301(4); R.I. Gen. Laws §28–5–6(I); Vt. Stat. Ann. tit. 21 §495 at (5); Wis. Stat. §111.32(8).

127. For example, under the Illinois Human Rights Act, handicap is defined as a "[d]eterminable physical or mental characteristic of a person . . . the history of such characteristic or the perception of such characteristic." Ill. Rev. Stat., ch. 68 §1–103(I). *See also*, N.M. Stat. Ann. §28–1–2(M); N.Y. Exec. Law Art. 15 §292(21).

128. B. Schlei & P. Grossman, Employment Discrimination Law, 287–88 (2d ed.) (BNA Books 1983).

129. *Redmond v. GAF Corp.*, 574 F.2d 897, 902–03 (7th Cir. 1978) (interpreting Title VII's duty to accommodate religious beliefs).

130. *See Wallace v. Veterans Administration*, 683 F. Supp. 758 (D. Kan., April 14, 1988); *Simpson v. Reynolds Metal Co.*, 629 F.2d 1226, 1231 n.8 (7th Cir. 1978) (dictum); *Davis v. Bucher*, 451 F. Supp. 791, 796 (E.D. Pa. 1978).

131. *Davis v. Bucher*, 451 F. Supp. at 796.

132. 29 C.F.R. §1613, 702(c) (1985).

133. 39 FEP Cases 225, 228 (E.D. Mich. 1985).

134. The Act excludes from coverage "any individual who is an alcoholic or drug

abuser whose current use of alcohol or drugs prevents such individual from performing the duties of the job in question or whose employment, by reason of such current alcohol or drug use, would constitute a direct threat to property or safety of others." 29 U.S.C. §706(7)(B).

135. *See, e.g.*, South Carolina Human Affairs Commission Rules and Regulations, Article 7; Illinois Interpretive Rules on Handicap Discrimination, ILL. ADMIN. CODE, tit. 56, §2500.20(e) and (d).

136. 25 Ohio St. 3d 279, 496 N.E.2d 478 (1986).

137. Alcoholism also has been held to be a disease protected under state law. *E.g., Consolidated Freightways, Inc. v. Cedar Rapids Civil Rights Comm.*, 366 N.W.2d 522 (Iowa 1985). *But see Habinka v. Lake River Corp. Terminals Div.*, ALS No. 1267 (Feb. 13, 1987) in which the Illinois Human Rights Commission held that plaintiff had not shown that his methadone use arose or constituted a functional disorder or disease.

138. *Heron v. McGuire*, 803 F.2d 67, 68–69 (2d Cir. 1986) (drug habit rendered policeman unfit for duty); *McLeod v. City of Detroit*, 39 FEP Cases 225, 228 (E.D. Mich. 1985) (individuals rejected for firefighter jobs after drug screening not qualified).

139. These cases were brought under Section 501 of the Rehabilitation Act as opposed to Sections 503 and 504 which apply to private employers. Although not directly applicable, they are illustrative of the way courts have dealt with the accommodation issue in substance abuse cases.

140. 600 F. Supp. 757 (D.D.C. 1985).

141. *Id.* at 762.

142. 598 F. Supp. 126 (D.D.C. 1984).

143. *But see, Robinson v. Devine*, 37 FEP Cases 728 (D.D.C. 1985) (no duty to further accommodate where employee was repeatedly intoxicated on the job and where employee was granted sick leave and counseled).

144. T. Geidt, *Drug and Alcohol Abuse in the Work Place: Balancing Employer and Employee Rights*, 11 EMPL. REL. L.J. 181, 186 (Autumn 1985). California law requires that employees be allowed to use accrued sick leave to attend a rehabilitation program. CAL. LAB. CODE §1027 (West App. 1986).

145. *Id.*

146. RESTATEMENT (SECOND) OF TORTS (hereinafter "RESTATEMENT") §559, comment e.

147. *Id.* at §568.

148. 780 F.2d 1067, 1 IER Cases 458 (1st Cir. 1986).

149. 548 S.W.2d 743 (Texas Ct. App. 1977), *cert. denied*, 434 U.S. 962 (1977).

150. No. 85 Civ. 5661 (S.D.N.Y. 1986).

151. *See also Shamley v. City of Chicago*, 516 N.E.2d 646, 2 IER Cases 1237, 1239 (1987) (liberty interests of police officers who failed random drug tests and were reassigned as a result were not implicated because purported harm to reputation was not defamation).

152. RESTATEMENT at §581A.

153. *Merritt v. Detroit Memorial Hospital*, 265 N.W.2d 124 (Mich. Ct. App. 1978).

154. *See* Annot., *Libel and Slander: Privileged Nature of Communication to Other Employees or Employees' Union of Reason for Plaintiff's Discharge*, 60 A.L.R. 2d 1080, 1090–91 (1974).

155. *Joftus v. Kaufman*, 324 F. Supp. 660 (D.D.C. 1971); *Hawthorn v. Western M.R. Co.*, 226 Md. 499, 174 A.2d 175 (1961).

156. *Munsell v. Ideal Food Stores*, 208 Kan. 909, 494 P.2d 1063 (1972).

157. *Arsenault v. Alleghany Airlines, Inc.*, 485 F. Supp. 1373 (D. Mass. 1980), *aff'd*, 636 F.2d 1199 (1st Cir. 1986), *cert. denied*, 456 U.S. 821 (1981).

158. *Caslin v. General Electric Co.*, 608 S.W.2d 69 (Ky. 1980).

159. *Cleveland v. Greenqard*, 162 Ga. App. 201, 290 S.E.2d 545 (1982).

160. *See, e.g.*, ILL. REV. STAT. ch. 48, ¶640. In some states an employer's communications to the state unemployment compensation agency are absolutely privileged. *See, e.g., Aur v. Black*, 163 Ga. App. 787, 294 S.E.2d 616 (1982).

161. RESTATEMENT at §§599, 600, 604.

162. 361 N.W.2d 875, 1 IER Cases 1269 (Minn. 1985).

163. *Id.* at 881.

164. *Accord McKinney v. County of Santa Clara*, 110 Cal. App. 3d 787, 167 Cal. Rptr. 89 (1980).

165. RESTATEMENT §652A, comment a.

166. *Id.* at §652B.

167. *See, e.g., Kobeck v. Nabisco*, 166 Ga. App. 652, 1 IER Cases 200 (1983) (employer's disclosure of employee's attendance record to her husband held not to establish tort because of lack of physical intrusion).

168. 677 S.W.2d 632 (Tex. App. 1984), *aff'd per curiam*, 686 S.W.2d 593 (Tex. 1985).

169. *Id.* at ____. *See also O'Connor v. Ortega*, ____ U.S. ____, 1 IER Cases 1617 (March 31, 1987) (Fourth Amendment case in which court held that employee had reasonable expectation of privacy as to his desk and file cabinets where employee did not share desk or cabinets and where this furniture contained personal items).

170. *Bratt v. International Business Machines*, 785 F.2d 352 (1st Cir. 1986).

171. *Phillips v. Smalley Maintenance Service, Inc.*, 711 F.2d 1524, 1 IER Cases 221 (11th Cir. 1983).

172. See note 6 and accompanying text, *supra*.

173. *Price v. Pacific Refining*, Superior Ct. No. 292000 (Contra Costa County, Cal.) (attacking random mandatory testing); *Luck v. Southern Pacific*, Superior Ct. No. 843230 (San Francisco County, Cal.) (challenge to termination of clerical employee refusing to take a test); *Pettigrew v. Southern Pacific*, Superior Ct. No. 849343 (San Francisco County, Cal.) (challenge to coerced rehabilitation

of employee who tested positive for drug use). The jury in the *Luck* case returned a verdict for $485,000. National L.J., December 7, 1987.

174. RESTATEMENT §652D.

175. *See* case cited in note 6, *supra*.

176. *See, e.g., Hudson v. S.D. Warren Co.*, 608 F. Supp. 477 (D. Maine 1985) (disclosure of employee's drinking on the job to five supervisors is not sufficient disclosure to support claim of public disclosure of private facts).

177. RESTATEMENT §652E.

178. PROSSER & KEETON, TORTS §117 (5th ed. 1984).

179. *See Ledl v. Quik Pik Food Stores*, 133 Mich. App. 585, 349 N.W.2d 529 (1984).

180. No. 85 Civ. 5661 (S.D.N.Y. 1986).

181. RESTATEMENT §46(1).

182. *Id.*, comment d.

183. *See Buffolino v. Long Island Savings Bank*, 126 A.D.2d 508, 510 N.Y.S. 2d 628, 2 IER Cases 894 (N.Y. App. Div. 1987); *Gibson v. Hummel*, 668 S.W.2d 4, 118 LRRM 2943 (Mo. Ct. App. 1985); *Bridges v. Winn-Dixie Atlanta*, 176 Ga. App. 227, 335 S.E.2d 445 (1985); *Todd v. South Carolina Farm Bureau Mutual Ins. Co.*, 283 S.C. 155, 328 S.E.2d 602 (1984); *Food Fair, Inc. v. Anderson*, 382 So. 2d 150 (Fla. Dist. Ct. App. 1980).

184. 283 Ark. 399, 678 S.W.2d 312 (1984).

185. 268 Ark. 269, 596 S.W.2d 681 (1980).

186. *See also Moniodis v. Cook*, 64 Md. App. 1, 494 A.2d 212, 1 IER Cases 441 (Md. Ct. Spec. App. 1985) (upholding claim of intentional infliction of emotional distress where, in addition to polygraph test, employer's conduct amounted to a complete denial of plaintiff's dignity as a person).

187. RESTATEMENT §35.

188. *Id.* at 40A.

189. *Magers v. U.S. Air, Inc.*, 525 F. Supp. 853 (D. Md. 1981).

190. *Strachan v. Union Oil Co.*, 768 F.2d 703, 1 IER Cases 1844 (5th Cir. 1985) (alleging false arrest).

191. *Pettigrew v. Southern Pacific*, Superior Court No. 849343 (San Francisco County, Cal.).

192. In both cases, the court decided that the state claims were preempted by federal labor laws.

193. *See Garibaldi v. Lucky Food Stores*, 726 F.2d 1367, 1 IER Cases 354 (9th Cir. 1984), *cert. denied*, 471 U.S. 1099, 1 IER Cases 848 (1985); *Palmateer v. International Harvester Co.*, 85 Ill. 2d 124, 421 N.E.2d 876, 115 LRRM 4165 (1981).

194. *E.g., Kelsay v. Motorola*, 74 Ill. 2d 172, 384 N.E.2d 353, 115 LRRM 4371 (1978).

195. *Kelsay v. Motorola*, 74 Ill. 2d 172, 384 N.E.2d 253, 115 LRRM 4371 (1978).

196. *Wheeler v. Caterpillar Tractor Co.*, 108 Ill. 2d 502, 485 N.E.2d 372, 121 LRRM 3186 (1985), *cert. denied*, 475 U.S. 1122, 122 LRRM 1080 (1986).

197. *Nees v. Hock*, 536 P.2d 512, 115 LRRM 4571 (Or. Sup. Ct. 1975).

198. *Palmateer v. International Harvester Co.*, *supra*, note 193.

199. *Garibaldi v. Lucky Food Stores*, *supra*, note 193. *See also Johnson v. World Color Press, Inc.*, 147 Ill. App. 3d 746, 498 N.E.2d 575, 1 IER Cases 1446 (5th Dist. 1986) (employee discharged for opposition to accounting practices which employee claimed violated federal security laws state claim for retaliatory discharge).

200. 674 F.2d 1447, 2 IER Cases 1281, 1283 (D. Wyo. 1987).

201. *O'Brien v. Papa Gino's of America, Inc.*, 780 F.2d 1067, 1 IER Cases 458 (1st Cir. 1986); *Walden v. General Mills Restaurant Group, Inc.*, 31 Ohio App. 3d 11, 508 N.E.2d 168 (1986); *Cipou v. International Harvester*, 134 Ill. App. 3d 522, 481 N.E.2d 22 (Ill. App. Ct. 1985); *Hablin v. Damers, Inc.*, 478 N.E.2d 926 (Ind. App. 1985).

202. *Perks v. Firestone Tire & Rubber Co.*, 611 F.2d 1363, 115 LRRM 4592 (3d Cir. 1979); *Moniodis v. Cook*, 64 Md. App. 1, 494 A.2d 212, 1 IER Cases 441, (Md. Ct. Spec. App. 1985), *cert. denied*, 304 Md. 631 (1985).

203. 325 S.E.2d 111, 116 LRRM 3447 (W. Va. 1984).

204. *See, e.g., Duldulao v. St. Mary of Nazareth Hospital Center*, 136 Ill. App. 3d 763, 505 N.E.2d 314, 1 IER Cases 1428 (1986).

205. *See, e.g., Pugh v. See's Candies, Inc.*, 171 Cal. Rptr. 917, 115 LRRM 4002 (Ct. App. 1981).

206. *See, e.g., Clearly v. American Airlines*, 11 Cal. App. 3d. 443, 168 Cal. Rptr. 722, 115 LRRM 3030 (Ct. App. 1980).

207. *Greco v. Halliburton Co.*, 674 F. Supp. 1447, 2 IER Cases 1281, 1283 (D. Wyo. 1987).

208. NLRA §8(d), 29 U.S.C. §158(d). The section reads in pertinent part: "To bargain collectively is the performance of the mutual obligation of the employer and the representative of the employees to meet at reasonable times and confer in good faith with respect to wages, hours and other terms and conditions of employment . . . "

209. *Ford Motor Co. v. NLRB*, 441 U.S. 488, 498 (1979), quoting from *Fibreboard Paper Products Corp. v. NLRB*, 379 U.S. 203, 222–23 (1964) (Stewart, J. concurring).

210. 29 U.S.C. §158(a)(5).

211. The Railway Labor Act, regulating labor relations in the rail and air transport industries, imposes similar obligations to bargain over mandatory subjects concerning "conditions of employment." 45 U.S.C. §152. The Ninth Circuit Court of Appeals recently held that a railway employer must bargain before it unilaterally imposed a drug testing policy requiring after-accident testing of all train crew members, as a means of enforcing a 40-year-old work rule prohibiting the use or possession of drugs or alcohol on duty or reporting for work "under the influence." *Brotherhood of Locomotive Engineers v. Bur-*

*lington Northern R.R. Co.*, 838 F.2d 1087, 127 LRRM 2812, 2816–17 (9th Cir. 1988). *See also Brotherhood of Locomotive Engineers v. Burlington Northern R.R. Co.*, 838 F.2d 1102 (9th Cir. 1988) (use of drug-detecting dogs is a "major dispute" requiring bargaining); *Railway Labor Executives' Ass'n v. Consolidated Rail Corp.*, ___ F.2d ___, ___ LRRM ___, No. 87–1289 (3d Cir., April 25, 1988) (unilateral addition of drug screening to medical exams is not justified in the contract, and is thus a "major dispute" requiring bargaining); *International Brotherhood of Teamsters v. Southwest Airlines Co.*, 842 F.2d 794, 128 LRRM 2225, (5th Cir. 1988) (mandatory testing for drug and alcohol use is a "major" dispute not arguably justified by the collective bargaining agreement, and must be bargained over prior to implementation); *Transport Workers' Union of Philadelphia, Local 234 v. Southeastern Pennsylvania Transportation Authority*, 678 F. Supp. 543, 127 LRRM 2835 (E.D. Pa. 1988) (implementation of random urinalysis testing as to railway employees was a "major dispute" requiring bargaining). *But see Brotherhood of Maintenance of Way Employees, Lodge 16 v. Burlington Northern R.R.*, 802 F.2d 1016, 123 LRRM 593 (8th Cir. 1986) (imposing urinalysis on individual crew member with responsibility for triggering accident is a "minor dispute" not requiring bargaining; court divided on whether use of drug screen as part of periodic and return-to-work physical exams required bargaining; *Railway Labor Executives' Ass'n v. Norfolk & Western Ry. Co.*, 833 F.2d 700 (7th Cir. 1987) (drug screen added to routine urinalysis as part of a medical exam does not require bargaining).

212. *See, e.g., MediCenter, Mid-South Hospital*, 221 NLRB 670 (1975).

213. *Lockheed Shipbuilding and Construction Co.*, 273 NLRB 171 (1984); *LeRoy Machine Co.*, 147 NLRB 1431 (1964).

214. NLRB Office of the General Counsel, Guideline Memorandum GC 87–5 (September 8, 1987).

215. National Labor Relations Board, General Counsel Quarterly Report (April, 1988) (reported in No. 79 DAILY LAB. REP. D-1 (BNA, April 25, 1988).

216. *See, e.g., Metropolitan Edison Co. v. NLRB*, 460 U.S. 693 (1983). *Owens-Corning Fiberglass Corp.*, 86 LA 1026 (Nicholas, 1986).

217. *See, e.g., NLRB v. Healy Vogt Machine Co.*, 728 F.2d 802 (6th Cir. 1983); *Rochester Inst. of Technology*, 264 NLRB 1020 (1982), *enforcement denied on other grounds*, 724 F.2d 9 (2d Cir. 1983).

218. *Kay Fries, Inc.*, 265 NLRB 1077, 112 LRRM 1377 (1982) (company action was a *fait accompli*); *Gulf States Mfg. v. NLRB*, 704 F.2d 1390, 113 LRRM 2789 (5th Cir. 1983) (union got 5 minutes' notice of proposed layoffs).

219. Section 8(d) provides that the duty to bargain "shall not be construed as requiring either party to discuss or agree to any modification of the terms and conditions contained in a contract for a fixed period, if such modification is to become effective before such terms and conditions can be reopened under the provisions of the contract." 29 U.S.C. §158(d). The issue for the NLRB is thus whether the unilateral change the company proposes is a change in an existing term of a contract, or a proposed new term or condition of employment.

220. *See, e.g., Continental Telephone Co.*, 274 NLRB 1452, 118 LRRM 1598 (1985); *Leeds & Northrup Co. v. NLRB*, 391 F.2d 874 (3d Cir. 1968).

221. G.C. Mem. 87–5, *supra* note 214.

222. *See, e.g., Norris Industries*, 231 NLRB 50 (1977) (language in a letter of understanding); *LeRoy Machine Co.*, Inc., 147 NLRB 1431 (1964) (management rights clause giving company sole right to determine employee qualifications held to be a waiver of right to bargain over physical exams prior to the agreement's expiration).

223. *See, e.g., Ciba-Geigy Pharmaceuticals Div.*, 264 NLRB 1013, 111 LRRM 1460 (1982), *enforced*, 722 F.2d 1120, 114 LRRM 3650 (3d Cir. 1983). Even a fairly specific reservation of management rights which does not include the particular action at issue has been held insufficient to meet the "clear and unmistakable" standard for waiver. *Bay Shipbuilding Corp.*, 263 NLRB 1133, 111 LRRM 1375 (1982), *enforced*, 721 F.2d 187, 114 LRRM 3437 (7th Cir. 1983).

224. G.C. Mem. 87–5, *supra* note 190.

225. *Compare Rockwell International Corp.*, 260 NLRB 1346 (1982) (zipper clause did not expressly waive right to bargain over cafeteria food prices) *and GTE Automatic Electric, Inc.*, 261 NLRB 1491, 110 LRRM 1193 (1982). *See Radiocar Corp.*, 214 NLRB 362 (1974) (contractual waiver may be found by examination of contract provisions, bargaining history, and past practice).

226. *California Cedar Products Co.*, NLRB *Advice mem.*, 123 LRRM 1355 (October 10, 1986).

227. NLRA §8(d), 29 U.S.C. §158(d).

228. *See, e.g., NLRB v. Montgomery Ward & Co.*, 133 F.2d 676 (9th Cir. 1943).

229. *First National Maintenance Corp. v. NLRB*, 452 U.S. 666 (1987); *NLRB v. Burns Int'l Security Services, Inc.*, 406 U.S. 272, 80 LRRM 2225 (1972).

230. *See, e.g., Seattle-First National Bank v. NLRB*, 638 F.2d 1221 (9th Cir. 1980), *denying enforcement to* 241 NLRB 753 (1979); *Continental Ins. Co. v. NLRB*, 495 F.2d 44 (2d Cir. 1974).

231. *See, e.g., NLRB v. Wright Motors, Inc.*, 603 F.2d 604 (7th Cir. 1979); *Chevron Chemical Co.*, 261 NLRB 44 (1982), *enforced*, 701 F.2d 172 (5th Cir. 1983). *Compare NLRB v. Tomco Communications*, Inc., 567 F.2d 871 (9th Cir. 1978), *denying enforcement to* 220 NLRB 636 (1975) (predictably unacceptable proposals, without other factors indicating bad faith in bargaining, are not sufficient to warrant a finding that the employer failed to bargain in good faith).

232. *See, e.g., Washington Steel Brass & Iron Foundry, Inc.*, 268 NLRB 338 (1983); *Moore Drop Forging Co.*, 144 NLRB 165 (1963).

233. *See, e.g., Schnelli Enterprises, Inc., d/b/a Cellar Restaurant*, 262 NLRB 796 (1982).

234. *See, e.g., Penntech Papers*, Inc., 263 NLRB 264 (1982), *enforced*, 706 F.2d 18 (1st Cir.), *cert. denied*, 464 U.S. 892 (1983).

235. *General Electric Co.*, 150 NLRB 192 (1964), *enforced*, 418 F.2d 736 (2d Cir. 1969), *cert. denied*, 397 U.S. 965 (1970).

236. *See, e.g., L. & M Mfg. Co.*, 165 NLRB 663 (1967) (unlawful to insist on same-day acceptance of proposal before it was submitted); *Crusader Lancer Corp.*, 144 NLRB 1309 (1963) (requirement that union waive right to bargain during term of agreement held unlawful).

237. *See NLRB v. Tonitt Mfg. Co.*, 351 U.S. 149 (1956).

238. *See, e.g., NLRB v. Cable Vision, Inc.*, 660 F.2d 1, 108 LRRM 2357 (1st Cir. 1981), *enforcing* 249 NLRB 412, 104 LRRM 1322 (1980) (employer bargained in bad faith when it caused delay, tended to defer union proposals for indefinite "study," and remained immovable in key areas without justification); *NLRB v. Industrial Use Prod. Corp.*, 455 F.2d 673 (9th Cir. 1972), *enforcing* 177 NLRB 328 (1969) (rejection of proposals previously accepted); *MRA Associates, Inc.*, 245 NLRB 676 (1979) (introduction of new proposals after months of bargaining).

239. *See, e.g., Atlas Metal Parts Co., Inc., v. NLRB*, 660 F.2d 304 (7th Cir. 1981), *denying enforcement in rel. part to* 252 NLRB 205 (1980); *Gehnrich & Gehnrich, Inc.*, 258 NLRB 528 (1981).

240. *NLRB v. Katz*, 362 U.S. 736 (1962).

241. 29 U.S.C. §185.

242. Another federal labor statute has been held to preempt state law suits. Matters constituting a "minor dispute" under the Railway Labor Act, 45 U.S.C. §151–88, 153 (1)(i), are properly within the exclusive primary jurisdiction of the National Railway Adjustment Board. *Gregory v. Burlington Northern R.R. Co.*, 638 F. Supp. 538, 542 (D. Minn. 1986). *See also, Jackson v. Consolidated Rail Corp.*, 717 F.2d 1045, 114 LRRM 2682 (7th Cir. 1983). The courts have defined "minor disputes" to be disputes relating to the interpretation, meaning or application of an existing collective bargaining agreement. *Gregory*, at 541. The court in *Gregory* found that the plaintiff's claims of wrongful discharge, negligence in administering a pre-employment physical drug test, and intentional infliction of emotional distress were all claims concerning the application of the contract. They were thus minor disputes subject to the jurisdiction of the NRAB. The court reasoned:

"To permit railroad employees to initiate discharge disputes in the federal courts, thereby bypassing orderly arbitration procedures, would frustrate congressional purpose and would precipitate interruptions in the nation's transportation industry. Concern for stability is particularly important where drug testing of railroad employees is involved—given the public's reliance on the services of transportation carriers, substance abuse by employees in the industry raises a potentially grave threat to public safety and welfare. A drug-testing policy designed to meet these concerns would be robbed of its efficacy if employees who tested positively were routinely permitted access to the federal courts."

*Id.* at 547.

243. *San Diego Building Trades Council v. Garmon*, 359 U.S. 236, 244 (1959).

244. *Id.* at 242.

245. *Id.* at 246–47.

246. *Id.* at 243–44.

247. *See Linn v. Plant Guard Workers*, 383 U.S. 53 (1966). In *Linn*, the Supreme Court held that the NLRB did not have primary jurisdiction over state law libel suits as long as the suits were limited to defamatory statements published with knowledge or reckless disregard of falsity, and as long as the plaintiff could prove actual injury from the statements. *Id.*

248. *See, e.g., Johnson v. Hydraulic Research & Mfg. Co.*, 96 LRRM 2466 (Cal. Ct. App. 1977). The court affirmed the trial court's order granting summary judgment, on grounds that plaintiff abandoned the arbitration procedure after filing a grievance to redress injury from his employer's statement that he was involved in drug abuse. The employer had told a state department that the plaintiff was discharged for being under the influence of drugs, and discussed the charges with the union, a company nurse and doctor, and the employee's superiors. The court found that the plaintiff could have remedied the harm to him by pursuing his grievance through arbitration to demonstrate that he was unjustly discharged. His failure to do so meant he could not sue in state court. *Id.* at 2470.

249. *See, e.g., Construction Workers v. Laburnum Constr. Corp.*, 347 U.S. 656, 666 (1954).

250. 430 U.S. 290, 302 (1977). *See also, Keehr v. Consolidated Freightways of Delaware, Inc.*, 825 F.2d. 133, 2 IER Cases 565 (7th Cir. 1987).

251. *Farmer v. United Bhd. of Carpenters & Joiners, supra* note 250, at 304.

252. *Keehr v. Consolidated Freightways of Delaware, Inc., supra,* n. 250, at ___.

253. *Id.* at 137.

254. 29 U.S.C. §185(a).

255. *Vaca v. Sipes*, 386 U.S. 171 (1967).

256. *Smith v. Evening News Ass'n.*, 371 U.S. 195 (1962).

257. *Allis-Chalmers Corp. v. Lueck*, 471 U.S. 202, 213 (1985).

258. *Caterpillar, Inc. v. Williams,* ___ U.S. ___, 2 IER Cases 193 (1987) (employees' claims that employer's implied individual employment contracts with them, made after they assumed managerial positions, *held* not preempted by §301; employees relied on these individual contracts and not on the collective bargaining agreement when they sued for breach of contract after they were downgraded to bargaining unit jobs and then laid off).

259. *See International Bhd. of Electrical Workers. v. Hechler,* ___ U.S. ___, 2 IER Cases 129, on remand, 834 F.2d 942, 3 IER Cases 331 (11th Cir. 1987), *discussing Textile Workers v. Lincoln Mills*, 353 U.S. 448 (1957).

260. *Allis-Chalmers, supra* note 157, 471 U.S. at 211.

261. *International Bhd. of Electrical Workers v. Hechler, supra* note 259.

262. *Strachan v. Union Oil Co.*, 768 F.2d 703, 1 IER Cases 1844 (5th Cir. 1985).

263. *Id.* at 706–07.

264. *Id.* at 705.

265. ___ F. Supp. ___, 1 IER Cases 760 (C.D. Cal. 1986).

266. *Id.*, 1 IER Cases at 762. The court also dismissed a claim alleging breach of fiduciary duty with respect to administration of an EAP program, on grounds the issue was grievable under the contract and was therefore preempted. *Id.*

267. *Id.* at 762.

268. *Kirby v. Allegheny Beverage Corp.*, 811 F.2d. 253, 1 IER Cases 1580, 1582 (4th Cir. 1987).

269. *Id.*

270. *Association of Western Pulp and Paper Workers, Local I v. Boise Cascade Corp.*, 644 F. Supp. 183, 1 IER Cases 1072 (D. Or. 1986).

271. *Id.*, 1 IER Cases at 1075.

272. *Id.*

273. *Allis-Chalmers Corp. v. Lueck*, 471 U.S. 202, 1 IER Cases 541 (1985).

274. ___ F. Supp. ___, 1 IER Cases 658 (D. Mass. 1986).

275. *Id.*, 1 IER Cases at 661–62.

276. *Id.* at 662.

277. *Utility Workers of America Local No. 246 v. Southern California Edison Co.*, ___ F.2d ___, 128 LRRM 2317, (9th Cir. 1988).

278. 28 U.S.C. §1441. The statute provides in part:

> "(a) Except as otherwise expressly provided by Act of Congress, any civil action brought in a State court of which the district courts of the United States have original jurisdiction, may be removed by the defendant or the defendants, to the district court of the United States for the district and division embracing the place where such action is pending.

> (b) Any civil action of which the district courts have original jurisdiction founded on a claim or right arising under the Constitution, treaties or laws of the United States shall be removable without regard to the citizenship or residence of the parties. Any other such action shall be removable only if none of the parties in interest properly joined and served as defendants is a citizen of the State in which such action is brought."

# — 3 ————————————————

# TESTING FOR DRUGS

## —— SAMPLE SELECTION

### Urine

Urine is the preferred sample in almost all cases. Obtaining urine is easy and is not an invasive procedure. This is an important consideration since samples are collected in a variety of manners. Some corporations use their medical departments to collect specimens, while others use medical offices and clinics in remote sites. In some cases, samples are collected at the job site or in other nonmedical settings where untrained individuals are usually present.

Urine is preferred as a sample for another equally important reason. The various drugs of abuse are excreted from the body in the urine in varying degrees. Although each specific drug differs, the concentration of the drug or metabolite is often many times higher in the urine than in plasma. The drug may be present in the bloodstream for only a very short period of time, but the drug and its metabolites remain in the urine for extended periods. Although the detection time in urine after the last dose varies greatly depending upon the drug ingested and other factors, it is many times longer than if blood were tested. It is important to note that the presence of a drug or its metabolite in the urine does not necessarily imply that a person is under the influence of the drug or impaired to any extent.

Quantitation of random urine samples offers additional information which is of little value in evaluating a person's consumption habits, possible state of impairment, or the time from the last dose. It is of technical value, however, since it clearly establishes levels of detectability, and in some cases, is required by employers who have set arbitrary limits for disciplinary action. Quantitation is most commonly requested for tetrahydrocannabinol (THC) since the drug remains in the urine for variable periods of time and passive ingestion can be raised in some cases as a defense. Quantitation should be based on the results of confirmatory assays and not the use of semiquantitative immunoassays.

## Blood

Blood samples are rarely if ever used in routine screening of individuals for drugs of abuse for a number of reasons. First, drawing blood is an invasive procedure which requires a certain degree of skill and an appropriate setting. As with any invasive procedure, there is a small, but nonetheless real chance of untoward reactions, including fainting and the development of hematomas at the drawing site, regardless of the skill of the individual obtaining the blood. These incidents could later form the basis for legal action against a company. Perhaps most importantly, blood samples provide little valuable information since, unless the person has consumed the drug a short time before blood is drawn, the tests are unlikely to detect anything. Chapter 4 reviews the specific kinetics of each commonly abused compound and illustrates that the compounds can be detected in the blood for a much shorter time than in the urine.

The presence of a drug in the blood is an indication of very recent use. Depending on the drug or drug metabolite detected, the time from most recent use can often be approximated within hours or days. Although this information may not be conclusive enough to determine driving impairment, it can be of some value to companies with so called "hour rules," which prohibit the use of alcohol and other drugs for a period of time before reporting to work. In addition, the presence of a drug in the blood can be used as evidence substantiating behavior that may have been inappropriate for a job setting.

Blood samples are typically tested for drugs that have been found in the process of performing the urine drug screen. A combination of simultaneous blood and urine tests allows for more accurate laboratory testing. If no drug or metabolite is found in the urine, the blood sample is not tested (except in cases of alcohol use, where blood is the preferred sample). This is because the amount of sample is generally limited and the detection of drugs in blood is optimized by testing for the particular analyte. However, when a drug or its metabolite is found, the blood is then tested for either the metabolite or, as is usually the case, the parent compound. Quantitation is usually performed on blood samples. The levels can indicate a likelihood of impairment (not impairment *per se*) at a given time, and can also be useful in determining recency of use.

A combination of blood and urine tests are valuable in testing individuals who have been involved in incidents or accidents (for cause testing). A consensus panel convened by the National Safety Council (NSC) was unable to agree on what level in the blood or urine of a variety of drugs would constitute evidence of impairment when driving. NSC's position contradicts the widespread adoption of blood alcohol levels that are presumptive proof of intoxication for driving purposes.

Blood testing, as noted above, is reserved for "for cause" situations in which there is a high likelihood that an accident or untoward event was caused by drugs or alcohol. It is not appropriate for preemployment or random screening of employees, or to determine patterns of use or past behavior of individuals.

**Sample Integrity.** Sample integrity is a crucial issue especially when using immunoassays. Adulteration of samples can be accomplished in a number of ways, including but not limited to (1) dilution with water or by physiological means via diuretics; (2) addition of strong acids or bases; and (3) addition of compounds which affect the ionic strength of the urine, such as sodium chloride, bleach, and other oxidizing or reducing agents. The simplest method, however, involves switching specimens among individuals or substituting a prepackaged urine sample for the real specimen.

Avoiding sample adulteration is a difficult problem. One nearly foolproof method is direct observation of the individual. This requires monitors of each sex and is viewed as most undesirable by employees.

## Saliva

Saliva testing was used in the horse racing industry for a number of years to detect the use of illicit drugs. It has certain attractions for use in employee drug testing. The sample can be obtained in a noninvasive manner, it is difficult to tamper with since collection can be readily observed, and a number of drugs can be detected from a sample. However, a number of problems have prevented widespread use. Since the pH of blood and saliva differ, concentrations of free versus bound drug would differ. Therefore, correlation with blood levels is difficult. In addition, in the case of marijuana, the drug is present as a result of adsorption to the oral mucosa during smoking and not from the formation of saliva. The salivary levels do not correlate with blood levels in this case since the values reflect the amount of drug outside the bloodstream rather than within it. Salivary testing cannot demonstrate impairment since the values are not directly related to blood levels. As noted previously, blood levels are also unable to absolutely prove impairment.

**TABLE 3-1**
Classification of Patients by Test Result

| | Test Result | | |
| | Positive | Negative | Total |
| --- | --- | --- | --- |
| Disease | TP | FN | TP + FN |
| Healthy | FP | TN | FP + TN |
| Total | TP + FP | FN + TN | TP + FP + TN + FN |

## —— ACCURACY OF RESULTS

In drug testing, as in other laboratory methods, not all results are correct. A perfect assay does not exist. Because the implications of a positive drug screen can be so far-reaching, it is imperative that one understand the diagnostic capability of a laboratory test. The accuracy of a test is measured by its sensitivity, specificity, efficiency, and predictive value.[1,2]

A diagnostic test is useful only if its results allow one to discriminate between what is normal and what is abnormal; that is, if it can detect patients with disease and exclude patients who are healthy. (The term "disease" is used loosely and refers to any abnormality such as drug usage.) Based on test results, a population of diseased and healthy people can be separated into four groups as shown in Table 3-1. Patients correctly classified as diseased by a positive test result are called true positives (TP); patients correctly classified as healthy by a negative test result are called true negatives (TN). Diseased patients misclassified as normal are termed false negatives (FN); normal patients misclassified as diseased are called false positives (FP). In the context of drug screening, a false negative is failing to find a drug that is present; a false positive is finding a drug that is not there.

### Sensitivity
Sensitivity refers to the likelihood that a test will give a positive result when disease is present. It is expressed as a percentage of the total number of diseased patients and is calculated as follows:

$$TP/(TP + FN) \times 100.$$

Thus, a drug screen with a sensitivity of 80% will correctly identify 80% of drug users (TPs), but will yield negative results for the remaining 20% (FNs).

## FIGURE 3–1
Overlap of populations of normals and abnormals.

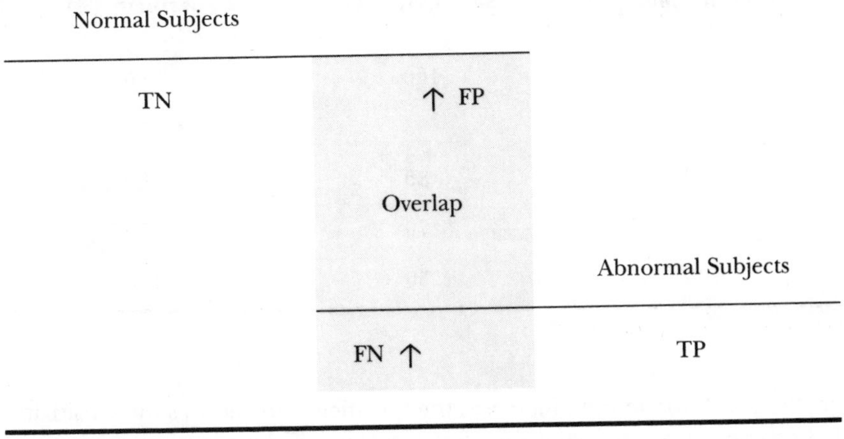

Normal Subjects

TN

↑ FP

Overlap

Abnormal Subjects

FN ↑

TP

## Specificity

The likelihood that a test will give a negative result when disease is absent is termed specificity. It is expressed as a percentage of the total number of healthy patients and is calculated as follows:

$$TN/(TN + FP) \times 100.$$

Thus, a test with a specificity of 80% will give negative results in 80% of people who have not taken any drugs (TNs), and will give positive results in the remaining 20% (FPs).

An abnormal laboratory value is one that falls outside the established "normal" or reference range. If one establishes the "cutoff" as the upper limit of normal, then all values below the cutoff are considered "normal" and all values above it are considered "abnormal." In a "perfect" test, the cutoff value would easily separate healthy subjects from those with disease. A distribution of test values would show no overlap between the two groups; that is, there would be no diseased subjects with test values in the normal range and vice versa. In this hypothetical situation, both the sensitivity and the specificity of the test would be 100%.

Unfortunately, ideal tests do not exist and test values do overlap. Some subjects with disease will have values in the "normal" range (FN) and some subjects without disease will have values in the "abnormal" range (FP).

By empirically selecting a cutoff point for the upper limit of normal, it is possible to alter the sensitivity and specificity of a particular test. For instance, in Figure 3–1, shifting the cutoff to the left increases the sensitivity of the test (fewer FNs) but reduces the specificity (more FPs). Shift-

**TABLE 3-2**
Effect of Altering Cutoff Value

| Cutoff Value | Sensitivity (%) | Specificity (%) |
|---|---|---|
| 20 | 100 | 60 |
| 40 | 95 | 75 |
| 60 | 85 | 85 |
| 80 | 70 | 95 |
| 100 | 50 | 100 |

ing the cutoff to the right increases the specificity but reduces the sensitivity. It becomes clear that there is always a tradeoff between sensitivity and specificity. Tests are not sensitive and specific at the same time. Table 3–2 demonstrates this principle (cutoff values are arbitrary).

In drug screening, the tradeoffs between sensitivity and specificity become more apparent. A test with high sensitivity and low specificity indicates most cases of drug abuse. However, there will also be a large number of false positives, all of which will require confirmation by a different assay; this may result in excessive costs. Alternatively, a test with lower sensitivity but higher specificity may be of limited value since it cannot reveal many nonsymptomatic users of illicit drugs. On the other hand, it may be adequate to detect drug use in symptomatic patients who have taken overdoses.

## Efficiency
Although drug and/or metabolite may be present in the blood and urine simultaneously, the result of a urine test alone can only be used to establish prior use. Although drug levels can be quantitated in the urine with considerable accuracy, these numeric values do not provide the information necessary to prove impairment. Factors such as the type of drug consumed, the purity of the mixture ingested, the route of administration, and the time of use all affect the level detected. These factors will be discussed in detail in Chapter 4, in sections on individual drugs.

## Predictive Value
Sensitivity and specificity are useful parameters, identifying the ability of a test to give positive or negative results in diseased or healthy patients. However, one also needs to know the ability of a positive test to predict

**TABLE 3-3**
Predictive Value as a Function of Disease Prevalence

| Prevalence of Disease (%) | Predictive Value (%) |
|:---:|:---:|
| 1 | 16.1 |
| 2 | 27.9 |
| 5 | 50.0 |
| 10 | 67.9 |
| 15 | 77.0 |
| 20 | 82.6 |
| 25 | 86.4 |
| 50 | 95.0 |

disease and the ability of a negative test to exclude disease. These parameters are defined by the predictive value model shown in Table 3-3.

The predictive value of a positive test result indicates the prevalence of diseased patients in a population of patients with positive test results. The predictive value of a negative test result indicates the prevalence of healthy patients in a population of patients with negative test results. Positive and negative predictive values (PV) are calculated according to the following formulas:

$$\text{PV Positive Result (\%)} = \frac{TP}{TP + FP}.$$

$$\text{PV Negative Result (\%)} = \frac{TN}{TN + FN}.$$

For purposes of this discussion, predictive value refers to a positive test result unless specified otherwise. For instance, a drug screen with a predictive value of 60% indicates that 60% of all positive results are from drug abusers and 40% are from nonabusers.

The efficiency of a test is measured by the percentage of patients correctly classified as diseased or healthy. It is calculated as follows:

$$\frac{TP + TN}{TP + FP + FN + TN} \times 100.$$

The predictive value of a test varies with the prevalence of disease, meaning the total number of diseased individuals within a given population. The following examples illustrate this very important concept. The examples assume a test sensitivity and specificity of 90%.

## Low Prevalence (1%)

In a population of 1,000 employees, 1% are drug abusers; that is, 10 employees abuse drugs and 990 do not. Since test sensitivity is 90%, nine drug users will test positive and one will test negative. With a test specificity of 90%, 891 nonabusers (990 × 0.9) will test negative, and 99 will test positive. The predictive value of a positive result is calculated as follows:

$$\frac{TP}{TP + FP} = \frac{9}{9 + 99} = 8.3\%.$$

## High Prevalence (20%)

In a population of 1,000 employees, 20% are drug abusers; that is, 200 abuse drugs and 800 do not. With a test sensitivity of 90%, 180 will test positive and 20 will test negative. With a specificity of 90%, 720 (800 × 0.9) will test negative and 80 will test positive. The predictive value of a positive result is:

$$\frac{TP}{TP + FP} = \frac{180}{180 + 80} = 69.2\%.$$

As the prevalence of a disease increases, so does the predictive value of a positive test result, regardless of the relationship between sensitivity and specificity. A positive drug screen is much more useful as an indicator of drug abuse in a high-prevalence setting than it is in a low-prevalence one. In fact, even if a test has a sensitivity and specificity of 99%, it may still be a poor predictor if the rate of drug use is low enough. By using the predictive value model, one can identify areas that would benefit most from a drug screening program—areas where a positive screen is most likely to be confirmed as positive. Predictive values also illustrate that a less sensitive and specific test might be a useful diagnostic tool in a high-prevalence setting, but it might be of little value in a low-prevalence one. For instance, a test with 70% sensitivity and specificity will have a predictive value of 50% if the prevalence is 30%; however, its predictive value drops to 2% with a prevalence of 1%. Table 3–3 shows the predictive value as a function of disease prevalence for a test with 95% sensitivity and specificity.

At a given prevalence, an increase in specificity results in a greater increase in the predictive value of a positive result than does the same increase in sensitivity. Similarly, at a given prevalence, an increase in sensitivity results in a greater increase in the predictive value of a negative result than does the same increase in specificity.

The predictive value of a test is also altered by the selection of a cutoff value. Raising the cutoff level increases the predictive value of a positive test but decreases the predictive value of a negative one. For instance, in one study of the (EMIT) assay for opiates, the effect of raising the cutoff from 0.5 µg/mL to 1.0 µg/mL would have increased the predictive value from 72% to 87% in a population with a drug use prevalence of 10%.

## Other Methods of Analyzing Test Performance

From the above discussion it is clear that the selection of a cutoff point for a diagnostic test is not an easy task. Receiver (or relative) operating characteristic (ROC) curves are used to help assess the differences between diagnostic tests at individual points.[3] A ROC curve is a graph of the range of tradeoffs possible between increased sensitivity and increased false positives. It is a plot of a test's sensitivity on the y axis versus the false-positive fraction (1 − specificity) on the x axis over their entire range of values, rather than a single cutoff point (Figure 3–2). The ideal test is located in the upper left portion of the graph. Tests in that area have the highest sensitivity and the lowest number of false positives. It is represented by point B. The line at a 45 degree angle represents a worthless test—one generating false-positive results at the same rate as true positive ones. Any reasonably good diagnostic test should yield a curve that is bowed into the upper left portion of the graph.

Another useful measure for evaluating diagnostic test results is the likelihood ratio.[4] This is the ratio of two probabilities, the probability of a given test result when disease is present (true positives) divided by the probability of the same test result when disease is absent (false positives). In other words, the calculation gives the odds or likelihood of a test result occurring in a diseased patient as opposed to in a healthy patient. The likelihood result can be determined for multiple test result levels. For example, a test result of 400 with a likelihood ratio of 9 would indicate that a level of 400 was 9 times more likely to be found in a patient with disease than in one without. Thus, by generating likelihood ratios for multiple test levels, the degree of abnormality of a test can be taken into account and the number of false negative and false positive results can be reduced.

## Combination Testing

Thus far, this discussion has centered on the sensitivity, specificity, and predictive value of a single test, such as a drug screen. However, in practice, all positive drug screens need to be confirmed by a second, different method. It is, therefore, important to understand how the combination of both tests and the manner in which they are performed affects sensitivity, specificity, and predictive value.

**FIGURE 3-2**
Likelihood ratio plot.

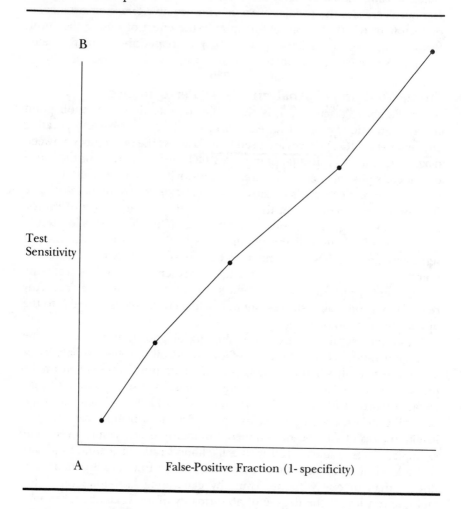

Consider two tests, A and B. The tests can be performed in the following three ways:

1. Test A is done first and all positive results are retested with Test B.

2. Test B is done first and all positive results are retested with Test A.

3. Tests A and B are performed simultaneously.

   Choices 1 and 2 represent a serial approach to testing—first one test is done and then the other. Tests are considered positive only if both A and B are positive ($A+B+$ = positive; $B+A+$ = positive; $A-B+$ =

**TABLE 3-4**
Serial Combination Testing

| Drug | T+ E− | T− E+ | T+ E+ | T− E− | Totals |
|---|---|---|---|---|---|
| Present | 40 | 190 | 760 | 10 | 1,000 |
| Absent | 18,900 | 6,000 | 100 | 74,000 | 99,000 |
| Total | 18,940 | 6,190 | 860 | 74,010 | 100,000 |

Abbreviations: T = TLC  E = EMIT

negative; A−B− = negative; A+B− = negative). Choice 3 represents a parallel testing approach. Tests are considered positive if either or both tests are positive (A+B− = positive; A+B+ = positive; A−B+ = positive; A−B− = negative).

In order to further examine these relationships, consider the hypothetical data from two drug screening methods, TLC and EMIT, performed in a population of 100,000. For purposes of Table 3-4, the prevalence of disease has been arbitrarily selected as 1%. Thus, 1,000 individuals in the population have drug present and 99,000 have drug absent.

The sensitivity of TLC is (40 + 760)/1000, or 80%. The sensitivity of EMIT is (190 + 760)/1000, or 95%. When the tests are performed in series, the combined sensitivity of TLC and EMIT (both positive) is 760/1000, or 76%. However, with a parallel testing combination (TLC or EMIT positive), the sensitivity is (40 + 190 + 760)/1000, or 99%. Thus, series testing in series, the combined sensitivity is less than the sensitivity of either test alone, whereas in parallel testing, the combined sensitivity is greater than the sensitivity of either test alone.

The specificity of TLC is (6000 + 74,000)/99,000, or 81%. The specificity of EMIT is (18,900 + 74,000)/99,000, or 94%. When performed in series, the combined specificity of both tests is (18,900 + 6,000 + 74,000)/99,000 or 99%. However, in a parallel combination, the specificity is 74,000/99,000, or 75%. Thus, in series, the combined specificity is greater than either test alone, and in combination, the specificity is less than either test.

From this discussion of combination testing, it is apparent that series testing results in the lowest sensitivity and highest specificity, and parallel testing offers the highest sensitivity but the lowest specificity. This concept is illustrated hypothetically in Table 3-5.

**TABLE 3-5**
Test Sensitivity and Specificity

|  | Sensitivity (%) | Specificity (%) |
|---|---|---|
| TLC alone | 80 | 81 |
| EMIT alone | 95 | 94 |
| Series | 76 | 99 |
| Parallel | 99 | 75 |

In a drug screening program, it is more important to keep false positive results at a minimum than to identify every drug abuser. For this reason, tests are performed in series. That is, positive tests require confirmation by a method other than the first one.

## Reliability of Urine Screening

Thus far, this discussion has focused on the theory of drug testing. In practice, how reliable is urine drug screening? Unfortunately, its accuracy is not at an acceptable level. A recent study analyzed results from 13 laboratories participating in the proficiency testing program of the Centers for Disease Control.[5] Each laboratory received 100 samples for blind testing. There was a marked discrepancy between the performance on the blind study and a mailed proficiency testing survey, probably because extra care was taken when survey specimens were analyzed. For instance, the average correct response rate on positive samples was 31% to 88% for blind specimens but 89% to 100% for survey specimens. Similarly, correct responses on negative samples were significantly greater for survey specimens that for blind ones.

There were also disturbing results in a review of toxicology survey data from the College of American Pathologists.[6] Although there was an accuracy rate of 75% to 95% for many analytes, for some drugs, accuracy rates were only 30% to 60%. Also, many false positive results occurred despite their confirmation by a second method. Since these studies were not conducted blindly, one can only conclude that these data are the best a laboratory can produce.

This study shows the variability in performance among different laboratories and demonstrates the need for stricter and more comprehensive quality-control procedures.

# SCREENING TESTS

Screening tests are typically used to detect potential users of drugs. As such, they must have a number of essential characteristics to be effective tools. The tests must have low detection limits, be relatively specific and sensitive, detect a broad range of compounds, and be easy to perform on a mass basis. In addition, they must be relatively inexpensive to be cost effective. Not all methods currently in use meet the above requirements. Before discussing individual aspects of screening tests, a clear definition of terms is necessary.

## Definition

The detection limit of a test is the smallest amount of drug that the test can determine in a sample. The higher the detection limit of a test, the less likely it is that the test will find a given drug in a urine specimen. The cutoff value, as compared to the detection limit, is the basis upon which positive and negative results are assigned. It is the level at which the test can reliably and reproducibly discriminate between the presence or absence of a compound. Values above the cutoff value will be considered positive for the presence of the drug while values below the cutoff value are negative. A test result can be above the detection limit yet be below the cutoff and therefore be considered negative. A better term to use in this situation is nondetected, since that is what the result of the test actually demonstrates. Since no tests in use have a detection limit of zero, it is possible that drugs are actually present in many samples but at levels below the detection limit. The use of the term nondetected should, in most cases, eliminate the problem of samples called negative by one method or laboratory and positive by another. Therefore, in discussing the relative merits of different screening tests, the level of detection is important information. In general, a test with a low limit of detection (and a low cutoff value) will detect a compound for longer periods of time after the last dose than one with a higher detection limit (Figure 3-3). There are, however, tradeoffs as one moves to lower levels of detection.

## Sensitivity and Specificity

The concepts of sensitivity and specificity have been described in this chapter. However, it is important to note that different types of screening tests vary greatly in this area. Tests which exhibit high sensitivity but low specificity may actually be less valuable than tests with somewhat lower sensitivity but greater specificity. This is because a great number of false-positive results can be eliminated by using more specific tests. However, the tradeoff is that potentially positive results are being classified as negative for the presence of the drug. This may have certain legal ramifications

**FIGURE 3–3**
Cutoff value versus time of detection.

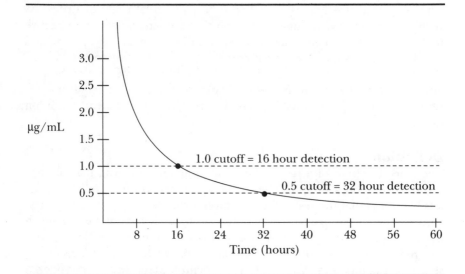

if, in fact, the testing program is proven to be so lax that it is of limited value.

The number of drugs detected by a screening method is extremely important. Since there is no prior knowledge of the compound potentially consumed, the ideal screening test would test for the presence of all known compounds. This is both impossible and quite impractical; therefore, a decision must be made about which drugs will be screened for and which will be eliminated from consideration. Employers and law enforcement officials should but rarely do give much thought to this decision. If a compound is not screened for, it cannot be detected. Since no program can afford to be totally comprehensive, a rational decision should be made based on (1) the prevalence of the various drugs in the local area (there are great regional differences) (2) the age of the individuals being tested (different age groups may use different compounds) and (3) the type of position for which the individuals are applying. In many ways, a comprehensive screen may enable a company or agency to focus attention to areas where the greatest abuse exists. However, the parties doing the testing must consider what substances are and are not being tested for.

## Cost Effectiveness

The cost effectiveness of any screening program depends on a number of important factors. If the initial screening test is not going to be confirmed by any other method, then the screening test that is the most comprehensive for the least amount of money will be the most cost effective. If, however, the results of the screening test will be confirmed by another method, either screening or definitive, then it is more difficult to determine which test is most cost effective.

The cost effectiveness of a given screening test depends on the following factors: 1) the prevalence of drug use in the tested population, 2) the detection limit of the test, 3) the sensitivity and specificity of the given test, 4) the predictive value of positive results, 5) the cost of the confirmation tests, and 6) the actual cost of the screening test that will be employed.

In part, the cost of screening tests depends on the prevalence of drug use in a population. The prevalence of drug use will determine the number of potentially positive individuals, and the higher the prevalence, the more likely it is that positive tests will be confirmed regardless of the method used. However, in typical employer testing settings where the prevalence is in the range of 10% to 15% of the work force, the predictive value model should help determine the relative efficiency of the various methods. In general, tests with high sensitivity and low predictive value generate large numbers of false-positive tests that must be confirmed. If a second screening method is then employed to eliminate these false-positive tests, added expense will be incurred, but the greatest expense of a definitive confirmation will be avoided for most false positives (see the section on combination testing in the section on predictive value). A simple economic model for evaluating the relative costs of alternative methods is shown below (Figure 3-4).

There are two basic methods for screening urine for drugs of abuse on a mass basis, thin-layer chromatography (TLC) and immunological techniques. The following sections will discuss the scientific principles behind these tests, the range of drugs detected, and the detection limits generally achieved. In addition, the relative sensitivity and specificity of the methods in general will be discussed along with the costs. Finally, comments concerning the application of the methods to employee drug screening will be made.

## Thin-Layer Chromatography
The term chromatography dates to the Russian botanist Tswett[7] who performed a rather simple experiment. Plant material was ground up and extracted and placed on a sorbent column. The various compounds in the mixture separated into different bands which had a variety of colors. The term chromatography was then applied since the method was useful in separating different compounds which had different colors. He termed the resulting separation a chromatogram, a descriptive name that has remained. In current applications, chromatography does not necessarily rely

**FIGURE 3–4**

Economic model for evaluating the relative costs of alternative testing methods.

Population: 10,000
Presumed Prevalence: 10%

| Test A = 95% sensitivity, 95% specificity | Test B = 95% sensitivity, 80% specificity |
|---|---|
| Predictive Value (+) = 67% | Predictive Value (+) = 34.5% |
| Confirmation Ratio $\dfrac{1}{PV}$ $= \dfrac{1}{.67} = 1.45$ | Confirmation Ratio $\dfrac{1}{PV}$ $= \dfrac{1}{.345} = 2.90$ |
| True positives = 950 | True positives = 950 |
| **Test A** | **Test B** |
| Screening Cost 2.5 × 10,000 = 25,000 <br> Confirmation <br> Cost $30 × 950 × 1.45  41,895 <br> $66,895 <br> Confirmation Cost × True Positive × Confirmation Ratio | Screening Cost $1.0 × 10,000 = 10,000 <br> Confirmation <br> Cost $30 × 950 × 2.90  82,650 <br> $92,630 <br> Confirmation Cost × True Positive × Confirmation Ratio |

on the separation of compounds of different colors, but the terminology has persisted despite enormous changes in the technology.

Chromatography is based on the partitioning of various compounds between liquid, solid, and/or gaseous phases. The exact technique used depends on the interaction between the phases that yields the closest thing to the desired result. Once the compound(s) are separated, a method of detection must then be employed to identify the compound of interest. A number of chemical sprays are used to stain the spots; they can be viewed under a variety of light sources. Identification of the compound is based on staining characteristics, distance of migration, and comparison with known standards.

Thin-layer chromatography is a method in which a solid support matrix has a stationary separation phase attached to it. In routine practice, the support matrix is glass and the stationary separation phase is silica. The thickness and uniformity of the application of the separation phase to the support matrix has great impact on the reproducibility of any analyses performed.

The first step in using thin-layer chromatography to screen urine for drugs of abuse is the extraction step. Since many drugs and their metabolites are more soluble in organic than polar solvents (such as urine), they can be removed from the urine and separated from potentially interfering substances. In addition, the solvent can then be evaporated easily, yielding an increased concentration of the compound originally extracted. Extractions can be performed at either a single pH, removing all drugs in a single fraction, or at multiple pHs, yielding multiple extraction fractions (acid, basic, and neutral).

Single pH extractions have the advantage of being rapid and easy to perform. However, since most drugs and their metabolites are either weak acids or bases, they are best extracted into solvent in their nonionic form. Using a single pH extraction provides speed and cost effectiveness but sacrifices recovery to some degree. This is because single pH extractions will remove some of most drugs but will not yield the recovery that is achievable with multiple pH extractions. Therefore, the sensitivity of single pH methods will be less for certain classes of drugs.[8] Most single pH extractions are performed in an alkaline medium (pH range of 8.5 to 9.5), optimizing the recovery of many drugs of abuse. Hydrolysis steps increase recovery of certain drugs such as morphine.[9]

Multiple pH extractions involve a sequence of pH changes, each followed by an extraction into an organic solvent. This has the advantage of optimizing the conditions for the removal of the maximum amount of a given drug at the appropriate pH. Recoveries of compounds from urine are higher and therefore the sensitivity of the tests is improved. However, the technique is more time consuming and thus, more expensive. Nevertheless, multiple pH extraction methods are preferable since they permit the identification of a wider range of drugs at lower levels of concentration.[10]

After the drug has been extracted into the solvent from the urine, the solvent is evaporated to dryness. This creates higher concentrations of the drugs that are present by placing them in a much smaller amount of liquid. The extract is then ready for spotting on the plate(s). The extract is resuspended in a small amount of solvent. It is then placed in the TLC plate at approximately 2 cm from the bottom. In addition to other unknown samples, known positive- and negative-control urines are added along with sample(s) containing the primary drugs of interest. The plate is then placed in a developing tank which contains a small amount of the mobile phase. Over time, the mobile phase moves up the plate, carrying with it the different compounds originally present in the urine. A compound's solubility in the mobile phase will determine how far it will move up the plate. Various compounds move characteristic distances. The entire migration phase requires approximately 40 minutes and allows for the maximum separation of the compounds present. It should be noted that single pH extractions will use one plate while multiple pH extractions will use two or more plates. Difficulties in reproducibility can often be traced to the development step since differential wetting of the plate and irregularities in the solid phase contribute to variation.

Once the migration phase has been completed, the detection phase begins. The plate is airdried and first examined under ultraviolet light. Any spots are noted and their distance from the application point measured. A series of compounds are sprayed on the plate and characteristic color patterns form if certain drugs are present. Spots are then compared to the known standards that were run at the same time. In some cases the relative migration distance and color are compared to previously known standards. Following detection, the plate is often photographed for future reference and then destroyed. Thin-layer chromatography can be used as a preparative stage to a further analysis. For example, a spot can be scraped from a plate, resuspended in solvent, and injected directly into another device such as a gas chromatograph. The TLC step provides preliminary identification and separation from potentially interfering substances. In this manner, it is a nondestructive form of testing.

The interpretation of thin-layer chromatography plates is difficult and can be inexact. If a spot on a plate does not match the color and migration distance of a known standard, the compounds are not the same. However, just because two spots appear to be similar and in the same position does not mean that they are the same. More than one compound can have the same migration and color characteristics. Therefore, thin-layer chromatography results can only be presumptive and should not be considered definitive.[11]

**Advantages.**    Thin-layer chromatography has a number of advantages when used for screening normal individuals for the presence of illicit drugs. The major advantage is that the method can detect a wide variety of unknown compounds. Because of the wide range of drugs detected, the method is useful in determining patterns of abuse which can lead to more effective and targeted programs. In addition, the cost of thin-layer chromatography testing is highly competitive and is usually the least expensive type of testing. However, the lowest priced TLC screens are often based on a single pH extraction and may lack sufficient sensitivity to detect recent use of certain drugs. Also, since TLC is a nondestructive form of analysis, the initially identified material in a sample can often be directly removed from the plate for further study.

**Limitations.** Thin-layer chromatography has a number of serious limitations that make it inappropriate for mass screening in many cases.

The detection limit of typical TLC systems is 1 microgram of drug per milliliter of urine. Although this corresponds to 1 part per million, it is not low enough to detect casual use a number of days after consumption. The exact values depend on the drug in question and the manner of use. Therefore, TLC may fail to detect drug use in some individuals due to a relatively high detection limit. False negatives will therefore be more common with TLC than with methods with lower detection limits. One study comparing immunological methods with TLC showed that while the TLC method used indicated a prevalence of 5.7% for the presence of drugs of abuse in the test population, a more sensitive immunological method detected a much higher level of drug usage (13.7%). The differences were clearly a result of the lower detection limit of the immunological procedure (a cutoff of 0.5 $\mu$g/mL for the immunoassay versus 1 to 2 $\mu$g/mL for the chromatographic procedure.) This drawback is not nearly as important when the method is used for medical reasons to detect overdose of drugs, since the urine levels of these compounds are usually far higher than the detection limit.

TLC testing is also more time consuming than other methods, since extraction is required and development requires a considerable amount of time. Although the direct hands-on labor time is relatively low, the procedures require that laboratory personnel be present. TLC analyses also consume far larger quantities of specimen than immunological procedures. A typical TLC assay requires 10 mL of urine for the extraction step versus low microliter quantities (10 to 50 $\mu$L) for typical immunoassays. Since extraction is required, not all of the available drug is removed from the urine and available for analysis. Optimal amounts of drug available range from 60% for TLC tests to 80% to 85% for immunological methods which are run on undiluted urine.[12] Availability varies considerably by drug and method of extraction (single pH or multiple; hydrolysis step).

The sensitivity of TLC systems is less than some other available methods. In addition, this method has a lack of specificity. Since multiple drugs can and do have similar migration patterns and interfering substances can appear in places where drugs would be expected, the specificity of the method is less than optimal. This lack of specificity combined with the general low prevalence of drug use in the screened population yields a low predictive value for TLC screening. TLC should, therefore, never be used as more than presumptive evidence of the use of drugs and must be confirmed by an alternate method in all cases.

The higher incidence of false-positive results will yield increased numbers of confirmation tests and, depending on the methods, may actually result in higher overall costs even though the actual screening test is less expensive. Also, a greater number of false negatives will be generated in comparison to more sensitive methods and this increased number of false negatives may actually yield a false sense of security to those interested in detecting users of drugs.

There are other, less obvious limitations to thin-layer chromatography when applied to mass screening programs when the actual prevalence of use is low. Proper interpretation requires skill and considerable experience, which may not always be available at the lowest price charged. In addition, there may be a financial incentive in reporting suspicious spots as negative if a laboratory's financial arrangement includes both screening and confirmatory tests. Conversely, a testing facility might have a bias toward describing suspicious spots as positive if that interpretation would result in an additional charge for a confirmation test.

The subjectivity of the test coupled with the various methods and procedures that can be used also make it difficult to standardize the tests not only between laboratories but within a single laboratory. This lack of standardization could result in multiple standards being applied to a company's employees depending on which laboratory and which technician performed the test in question. Such discrepancies could lead to legal challenges of the testing process.

Finally, there are certain problems inherent to the chromatographic procedure itself. The presence of certain compounds, such as the metabolites of phenothiazines can create background colorations which can either mask the presence of an unknown drug or, in some cases, be mistaken for a drug of abuse. In addition, certain compounds which are polar by nature, such as cocaine, chromatograph very poorly since the particles do not move far from the point of origin and are therefore difficult to detect. Also, since the developed plates are not permanent, physical evidence of the test results is not available if necessary. Photographs also often lack the resolution needed to distinguish the fine detail crucial to identification of the spots. The result is that in an arbitration or other judicial setting, the evidence used to determine the positive result would not be available. Under such circumstances, the memory of the individual who performed the test and records to document what the individual saw become important. However, the original determination is not subject to further examination, lessening the likelihood that the test results will be considered conclusive.

## High-Performance Thin-Layer Chromatography

High-performance thin-layer chromatography (HPTLC) is a newer method of separating compounds chromatographically. The major advantage of this method is that it is more rapid and more reproducible than traditional TLC. To achieve improved resolution of compounds, a much smaller particle size is selected for the stationary phase. These smaller particles are then placed on special plates in a much thinner film that is used in traditional methods. Finally, using specialized equipment, more precise flow rates of solvents can be achieved. The combination of a finer solid phase and a predictable solvent flow rate yields much greater resolution than is achievable with traditional methods. The distance required for separation of compounds is also less. The drug spreads over a smaller area of the plate and is more concentrated, which leads to easier detection and lower levels of sensitivity than are achieved with traditional TLC procedures. An intermediate approach is to use the special plates in a traditional development tank. This yields some improvement, but the lack of control of solvent behavior still persists and decreases precision. Even with improvements, HPTLC remains a presumptive screening method and is still subject to many of the problems associated with the classical technique.

The authors believe that thin-layer chromatography is of limited value in performing mass screening for drugs of abuse due to its lack of sensitivity, poor predictive value, and subjectivity. Although the method has great value in certain situations, namely when the prevalence of drug use in the tested population is low, other methods perform more satisfactorily.

## Immunological Systems

The most popular commercial methods for mass screening of urine for drugs use immunological techniques. They make up about 80% of the market share of reagents sold in kit form. However, most reagents for thin-layer chromatography are purchased in bulk as chemicals and the sales are, therefore, not traceable as drug screening kits. There are numerous variations of immunological procedures, including radioimmunoassay (RIA), enzyme immunoassay, and recently, fluorescent polarization techniques. There have also been other methods described in the literature, including immunological methods based on heme agglutination which are similar to pregnancy tests.[13] The two most popular immunological methods are EMIT, a product of the Syva Corporation of Palo Alto, California, and AbuScreen, manufactured by the Hoffman La Roche Corporation of Nutley, New Jersey. The most recent entry into the immunological market has been Abbott Laboratories' fluorescent polarization technique. This technique, however, has not been used as extensively as other methods because it is new.

Immunological techniques for the detection of drugs of abuse were first demonstrated by Spector and Parker in 1970.[14] These techniques have certain clear advantages over thin-layer screening methods but also have certain problems associated with their use in mass screening. The key factors to be considered, as with TLC, will be detection limits, specificity and sensitivity, range of compounds detected, and cost effectiveness when applied on a mass basis to unknown populations.

**Cross-Reactivity.** The first step in developing an immunochemical assay is to immunize an animal to produce antibodies to the given hapten, in this case, a drug. Since many animals will be immunized, the antibodies produced are not similar and may differ substantially in their reactivity to various analogues (compounds of similar structure) of the drug of interest. Although the antibodies produced by the various animals are pooled to minimize this effect, the resulting product detects compounds other than the drug of interest.

This lack of specificity for a single compound is called cross-reactivity and remains one of the major problems with immunoassays. Since the final product is not tested for cross-reactivity with all known analogues, the immunological test may give a positive reaction when a known (or unknown) analogue is in the urine even though the drug being tested for is not present. The use of monoclonal antibodies can diminish these problems but can never fully eliminate them. This problem has recently occurred with the EMIT product for cannabinoid when it was discovered that certain anti-inflammatory agents (ibuprofen, fenoprofen and naproxen) could give a false-positive result if present in the urine after therapeutic use. In addition, the drug fenoprofen was found to give false positive results for a number of other EMIT assays.[15] It is not unreasonable to assume that other cross-reactivity problems will continue to occur.

The scope of the problem of cross-reactivity was examined in a study of 162 commonly prescribed drugs. The parent drugs were added to urine in four exponential concentrations ranging from 1 $\mu$g/mL to 1,000 $\mu$g/mL and each concentration level was tested against seven EMIT procedures. None of the drugs gave false positives at the 1 $\mu$g/mL level and only 13 of the 1,134 individual tests were positive at the 100 $\mu$g/mL level. Nevertheless, the drugs, and not metabolites were added, and although most of the drugs would never appear in high concentrations, the study demonstrated that EMIT tests were subject to possible cross-reactivity when a relatively small number of drugs were tested.[16]

Cross-reactivity with other compounds remains the greatest problem with the immunological assay screening method, but the procedure is also necessary for detection of a fairly broad range of drugs. Since antibodies are relatively specific, it is possible that certain drugs will not be detected. A limited number of tests exist and they detect either individual drugs or certain classes of drugs. One of the advantages of cross-reactivity is its ability to detect drugs within a class since the antibody reacts with compounds of related structure. Compounds that are members of a class of drugs are detected to varying degrees depending upon their cross-reactivity with the original antibody manufactured for testing the class. Immunological screening programs run the risk of not detecting certain drugs of abuse (not part of the package) or underreporting others (lower cross-reactivity) because the antibodies used do not detect them as well. This is one of the major tradeoffs of using immunological methods for screening. Thin-layer methods can detect a broader range of compounds at higher concentrations, while immunological methods are limited to specific groups of compounds but are able to detect these compounds at far lower levels. For example, most immunological methods for opiates are directed to detect morphine. Nevertheless, the assays respond in varying degrees to other opiates, such as codeine and opioids (semi-synthetic opiates) like dihydrocodeine, allowing the assay to detect those compounds as well as the morphine that they are metabolized into. However, the assays do not detect synthetic opiates such as meperidine, or over-the-counter preparations containing dextromethorphan. Assays lacking any cross-reactivity would be of extremely limited value since most drugs would not be detected.

**Cutoff Values.**    Cutoff values for immunological systems vary depending on the test. As defined earlier, the cutoff value is the decision level that determines whether a sample result is termed positive or is reported as nondetected. The cutoff value is different from the limit of detection, which is the smallest amount of compound that can be detected by the system. Immunological tests have far lower detection limits than thin-layer methods, with some drugs detectable in the 5 ng/mL range. Cutoff values are often set at orders of magnitude greater than the detection limits. This improves the reproducibility of the assays since they are working well within their limits. Syva has selected cutoff values for its EMIT assay so that there is a 95% confidence that samples with more drug than the cutoff will test positively and those below the cutoff will be called negative.

The selection of a cutoff value has great effect on the performance of an assay when its predictive value is analyzed. One study of the EMIT assay for opiates showed sensitivity of 94.4% and specificity of 96% when a cutoff of 0.5 $\mu$g/mL was used. However, if the cutoff was raised to 1 $\mu$g/mL, the sensitivity fell to 93.6%, but the specificity rose to 98.4%.[17] The tradeoff in this situation is obvious if one considers a population with a drug use prevalence of 10%. The lower cutoff would have yielded a predictive value of 72%, while the higher cutoff would yield a predictive value for a positive result of 87%. Conversely, in the same situation, the predictive value for a negative result would have declined from 99.4% to 99.3%. Therefore, in the above situation with a 10% drug use prevalence, a very small percentage tradeoff is paid to decrease the number of false positives, while only an additional 1 in 1,000 true positives would be missed.

In some cases, cutoff values can be specified by the individual ordering the tests, but as will be discussed later, the determination of these values should be done in a rational and consistent manner. The existence of clearly defined and documented cutoff values is a major advantage of immunological systems. Since the tests are calibrated against a universal standard, tests performed in different laboratories should have similar performance characteristics. This is of particular benefit to multisite employers who wish to use different laboratories for convenience but want to maintain a similar, objective standard across locations.

The sensitivity and specificity of the various immunological assays vary because each tests has its own performance characteristics. The antibodies have different cross-reactivities (intended and unintended), and the actual performance of the test introduces a degree of variability. The manufacturer states that the cutoffs are set to have at least a 95% confidence level, which should correspond to a sensitivity greater than or equal to 95%. A study of the THC assay demonstrated a false-positive rate of 4% (specificity of 96%).[18] Other reports indicate similar values.[19] The data clearly indicate that the immunological tests have a higher sensitivity and specificity than do thin-layer chromatographic methods. However, the actual predictive value of a given assay will depend greatly on the population tested and the prevalence of use of the drug in the test group. Nevertheless, in general, there are far fewer false-positive results with immunological methods than with thin-layer methods. Also, because of the lower detection limits and lower cutoff values, false-negative results should not occur as frequently with immunological methods as with less sensitive methods. Nevertheless, immunoassays are screening tests and their results must be confirmed if definitive action is contemplated against an employee.

**Advantages.** Immunoassays lend themselves well to automation and this is one of the major reasons for their popularity in mass screening applications. They require small quantities of sample (microliter v milliliter) and because they use undiluted urine, no extraction step is necessary. In general, the antibody, the sample, and a tracer of some type (radioactive or enzymatic) are added in a prescribed order. After an appropriate incubation time, bound and free tracer are separated. EMIT tests do not require a separation step, which is of some advantage as compared to RIA. Similarly, the Abbott TDX system is a single-phase method and requires no separation step. Results are read out and compared to known calibrators that are run at the same time as the urine sample. Specimens that have results above the cutoff limit are considered positive, while those below the cutoff value are listed as nondetected. Since the results are compared to a known standard (a calibrator of given concentration), the tests have a greater degree of objectivity than do thin-layer methods. In addition, the instrument output from the analysis can be saved and serves as a permanent record of the testing of an individual sample. This is in marked distinction to thin-layer chromatography methods where the results of the tests can be viewed in only a subjective manner and are, in general, not permanent.

**Limitations.** Immunoassays are more costly on an individual test basis than thin-layer chromatography because the reagents themselves are relatively expensive and are subject to expiration. However, the labor costs involved in performing an individual assay are low because of the great potential for automation. In addition, the skills required are more commonly found in a clinical laboratory since they involve operation of a simple spectrophotometric system rather than interpretation of patterns on chromatographic plates. The average direct material cost of a ten-drug–panel-immunological screen is approximately $5.00,[20] which is far more than a TLC screen. Immunoassays become cost effective when confirmation testing is applied to all positive results. Since there are far fewer false positives, the number of confirmations required is lower.

In summary, there are two principle methods for screening large numbers of samples for drugs of abuse: immunological and chromatographic (TLC). When applied to situations of relatively low prevalence (10% to 15%) and where the quantity of drug is relatively small, immunoassays are preferred. They will yield fewer false-positive and false-negative results, they are objective, and the results are available for independent review. Thin-layer chromatography methods are more appropriate when the prevalence of drug use is high, or when the type of drug screened for is completely unknown, such as in a hospital emergency room setting. Regardless of the procedure, all urine screening methods should be considered presumptive and should be confirmed by an alternate method if any punitive action is planned by an employer.

## KDI Quik Test

A discussion of methods for screening drugs of abuse in urine would not be complete without mentioning a recently introduced test. The KDI Quik Test, marketed by Keystone Diagnostics, Inc, is an on-site test kit which uses chemically treated paper to simultaneously detect amphetamines, cocaine (including crack), morphine, and PCP at a cost of about $6.50 per test. A separate test for marijuana is also in development.

The main benefits of this method are that it can be performed quickly (in about 3 minutes), and it does not require instrumentation (as do the immunoassays) or experienced personnel (as does TLC). This may be important to clients who are waiting for test results before making hiring decisions. It may also reduce the anxiety for those undergoing testing as they will find out negative results immediately.

However, this method has the following significant limitations: 1) it does not detect marijuana; 2) it cannot distinguish among drugs, but can only determine that one or more may be present; 3) it is relatively insensitive; and 4) it may show false-positive results for individuals taking cold medicines. The latter limitation may cause so many false positives requiring confirmation that the test could no longer be cost effective. Because the sensitivity of the assay is in the microgram per milliliter range rather than the nanogram range, a large number of false-negative results may be expected. Though the detection limit of the assay would give positive results in people showing signs of intoxication, clinically normal subjects would probably test negative.

# ――― CONFIRMATION TESTING

Confirmation testing is the necessary second step following the detection of a positive result on a screening test. The purpose of confirmation is to eliminate any false-positive tests that may have resulted from the initial screening process. By that definition, we must use a test that is highly specific; there should be no false positives. In practice, most confirmation tests are not only more specific than screening tests but also far more sensitive. This high degree of sensitivity may, in fact, contribute to the high percentage of screening tests that are confirmed.

## Definition
There is no precise definition of what constitutes confirmation other than that it involves a second independent analysis. Confirmation is not the same as repeat testing. Use of the same assay a second time merely confirms the result of the first method of analysis and does not eliminate systematic error. Repeat testing does, however, eliminate the possibility of random error in the performance of an individual test. Examples of random error include mislabeled samples, instrument instability, or other events that affect isolated individual samples. Systematic error, on the other hand, involves errors which will affect all samples or members of a certain class of samples. In the case of an immunologic test, systematic error would include the presence of drug analogues that cross-react with the antibody used in the assay (for example phenylpropanolamine and the EMIT assay for amphetamines) or the presence of unrelated compounds that interfere with the performance of the assay. It would be expected that if the sample were rerun and the cause of the false positive was an analogue of the drug of interest, the repeat test would also be subject to the same source of error.

Confirmation testing as defined above also precludes the use of a test that is subject to the same type of error as the original screening test. For example, RIA should not be used to confirm EMIT testing because both tests are subject to many of the same possible sources of interference. Some sources of error will be removed by using different antibodies and a different tracer system. Nevertheless, both assays are immunological screening tests and subject to certain cross-reactivity problems. Therefore, a confirmation test should employ a different physical principal of separation and identification than the original test to insure that the same type of error does not occur twice.

Some laboratories will confirm thin-layer chromatography assays with either EMIT or RIA. This confirmation procedure does eliminate some sources of possible error since the two tests identify compounds using very different physical principles, namely differential solubility versus immunological reactivity. However, the results of such combinations should be considered presumptive because the confirmation test is not 100% specific and false positives can still occur. The reverse confirmation process (EMIT or RIA followed by TLC) will undoubtedly have a higher predictive value than an immunoassay by itself but will result in a large number of false-negative tests since the confirmation procedure lacks the sensitivity of the original screening procedure. Also, in the reverse confirmation process, since the second test is less specific than the screening test, additional false-positive tests are possible.

The combination of TLC followed by immunoassay does, however, have a valuable role in the confirmation process. The combination of the two methods will yield far fewer false positives than either method alone and will, therefore, decrease the number of samples that require a definitive confirmation technique because the prevalence of true positives receiving a second screening will be far greater than in the initial screened population. Since all tests are statistically more accurate when testing a population with a higher percentage of drug users, the reverse confirmation technique can actually decrease costs in some situations. As the number of false positives decrease, the predictive value of a positive result increases.

The remainder of this section will discuss the three most common "definitive" confirmation techniques. Each method will be described briefly and the applicability of each method in the medicolegal context of drug testing will be discussed. It should be noted that the scientific and legal requirements of testing laboratories differ. Although there is no specific legal right or wrong way to conduct testing, case law does provide some guidelines for the expected standard while scientific standards may differ depending on the situation. Confirmation testing is designed to confirm the presence of a compound previously identified as present by a screening test. Therefore, confirmation techniques are usually specific for a single compound and determine only if it is present or absent. Although confirmation tests frequently identify related compounds, that is not their primary role. The confirmation testing methods described below can, in some instances, be used to screen samples for unknown compounds. That is not how they are used, however, when testing for drugs of abuse.

The definitive confirmation techniques used to identify drugs of abuse all involve some form of column chromatography. The techniques are gas-liquid chromatography (GC), high performance liquid chromatography

(HPLC), and gas chromatography with mass spectrometry (GC/MS). These methods all offer high resolution, sensitivity to small quantities of the drugs of interest, and relatively rapid analysis time. Quantitation of compounds is also possible with each of the methods noted. Their usefulness in medicolegal screening depends upon the particular setting in which they are employed.

Samples for each of the three methods must be extracted from a urine sample because protein and other substances would interfere with the analysis and the polar nature of urine would affect the specific performance of the column. In addition, extraction provides a concentration step which allows smaller quantities of drugs to be detected.

## Gas-Liquid Chromatography

Gas-liquid chromatography involves the separation of a sample into its component parts while in a volatile state. The sample is moved over a stationary liquid phase by the movement of a mobile or gaseous phase. The sample is separated into its component parts by a number of factors, including an individual constituent's partition coefficient and the interaction of the sample constituent with the stationary phase.

The partition coefficient is a result of the vapor pressure of an individual component. Compounds with a high vapor pressure will usually remain in the gaseous phase and will, therefore, interact very little with the stationary phase. Such a compound is said to have a low partition coefficient. Conversely, compounds with a low vapor pressure will have a greater amount of solute present in the stationary phase and a smaller amount in the vapor phase. Therefore, a compound with a low partition coefficient will travel through a column in less time than a compound with a high partition coefficient.

Partition coefficients, however, are not only the result of differences in vapor pressure. Compounds can have interactions with the stationary phase based upon their unique chemical structure. Again, a compound that interacts with the stationary phase will be slower to pass through the column than one that does not have any interaction. This combination of vapor pressure and interaction factors leads to complex interactions during passage over a column and tends to further enhance the separation of materials.

Once separated, the compounds must then be detected. There are a variety of means of detecting the presence of compounds in the effluent of the column. These detectors generally will indicate both the retention time and quantity of material coming off the column at any given time. The compounds themselves are identified by the type of detector used, the specific column conditions, and the retention time relative to some standard. Most detectors in use do not actually identify a specific compound but rather identify the presence of a molecular type at a given time.

This is an important consideration in medicolegal contexts.

Gas-liquid chromatography requires that the sample pass through the column in vapor form. Samples are generally introduced in the form of liquids and are rapidly vaporized as they enter the analytic column. Therefore, the compound of interest must be 1) volatile at the column temperature in use, and 2) stable and not subject to pyrolyzation as it passes through the system. Compounds that do not meet either test can be derived and then analyzed. However, it is necessary to keep careful records of the procedure and documentation of its scientific acceptability since the compound being derived will no longer be the particular drug of abuse or its metabolite. Although scientifically this may seem completely appropriate, the laboratory must be prepared to defend its procedure in the adversarial and nonscientific arena of the courtroom.

Key factors in the use of gas-liquid chromatography are a consistent and uniform oven temperature, and the type of column used. Since the separation of compounds is based in part on their physical state, unplanned temperature differentials will interfere with this separation process. Cool spots may cause condensation of the solute while hot spots may damage the column packing material. Either of these occurrences would make the separation of compounds less than optimal. A change in temperature as small as 30 °C can result in a halving of the partition coefficient for some compounds, dramatically shortening the time of separation. In general, lower temperatures yield better separations, but the process takes longer. Therefore, it is very important to keep records of the instrument's performance over time and proof of its proper operation at the time of the analysis in question.

**Column Selection.** Column selection is equally important. The length and width of the column affect both its separation ability and the length of time that material takes to pass through it. Long columns enhance separation but are slower and have more mechanical problems (gas leaks, etc.). Wide columns are faster but often lack separation resolution, since the gas stream is not concentrated into a single front. The newest type of column is the capillary type which can be up to 500 feet long and as little as .25 mm in diameter. This type of column offers very high resolution of related complex materials but can not handle samples that contain large amounts of the compounds of interest.

**Detectors.** As noted above, there are a variety of detectors for identifying the presence of compounds in the gas effluent. None of them identify any specific compound but rather react to the presence of different molecular species in the gas effluent. The thermal-conductivity detector (TCD) has universal applicability and can detect the presence of any compounds in the gas stream. However, this detector has relatively low sensitivity ($1 \times 10^{-5}$) which limits its applicability. The thermal-conductivity method is nondestructive which means that the effluent can be collected for subsequent analysis.

The flame-ionization detector also has relatively broad applicability. It is much more sensitive than the TCD ($1 \times 10^{-12}$) but is limited to the detection of organic compounds, which is not a limitation in the field of drug testing. It is, however, a destructive technique and the effluent is not available for further analysis after completion of testing.

The electron capture (EC) and nitrogen-phosphorous (NP) detectors are more selective than the above systems. They are especially sensitive to electron-absorbing compounds and nitrogen- or phosphorous-containing compounds. Their sensitivity is in the range of $1 \times 10^{-12}$ for the specific molecular configurations with which they react best. EC is nondestructive while the NP is destructive and does not allow further analysis of the effluent.

**Internal Standards.** Gas chromatography can identify compounds by their retention times instead of by standard chemical identification procedures. In an effort to control fluctuations in oven temperatures, gas flow rates, and column condition, forensic analysis requires the use of an internal standard. An internal standard is a known compound which is added in a known amount to the sample prior to the extraction step. This compound will then appear at a characteristic position on the gas chromatograph and, more importantly, the compound of interest will appear at a fixed interval before or after this material. The ratio of the retention times of the internal standard to the compound of interest should be constant regardless of the instrument used or the operator performing the test.

Internal standards provide a number of advantages. First, they provide a clear reference point by which to identify the unknown compound. Second, they are necessary if quantitation of the unknown is desired. Since they are added in known quantities and go through the identical extraction and separation steps as the drug of interest, the ratio of the peak heights indicate the relative concentrations of each compound. Third, the appearance of the internal standard at the proper time provides evidence that the chromatographic procedure was properly performed. Finally, the appearance of the internal standard is evidence of the sensitivity of the assay; if a clear internal standard appears then one knows that concentrations equal to it should be easily detected.

**Advantages.** Gas-liquid chromatography has a number of advantages as a confirmation technique. It is a sensitive method and when appropriate detector and column combinations are used, it is able to detect drugs in quantities lower than the screening tests commonly used. Therefore, false negatives (or failure to confirm a true-positive screen) are not a problem for drugs present in low microgram or high nanogram concentrations (300 ng/mL or greater). Gas-liquid chromatography is also a fairly straightforward procedure, which although highly technical in nature, is readily reproducible. A wide variety of drugs can be confirmed using standard columns and detectors and the testing itself is quite rapid. In addition, the test results are objective, quantitative (if an appropriate internal standard has been run), and the records of the testing are permanent.

**Limitations.** The use of gas chromatography for confirmation is subject to a number of potential scientific and legal challenges. If an internal standard has not been run, the retention time determined from an individual run must be compared to the time from a previous run. This opens the laboratory to questions concerning the equivalence of the conditions of each analysis. Since temperature fluctuations, column conditions, and extraction procedures can all influence the result, retention time alone may not be sufficient to withstand legal challenge.

The presence of interfering substances is a well-known problem when using gas-liquid chromatography. Such substances may cause elevations of background levels or, more importantly, may chromatograph at approximately the same time as the drug of interest. Although steps can be taken to limit this phenomenon, the possibility of this type of interference can not be totally eliminated.

The major argument against gas chromatography alone as a confirmation technique is that it does not involve the physical identification of the compound(s) eluted from the column at a given time. Although the detectors are selective for different types of molecules, they do not discriminate between compounds. Rather, they indicate the amount of a solute dissolved in the carrier gas as it passes by the detection site. Identification depends on the comparison of retention time to either an internal standard or a previous run on the instrument. The lack of definitive physical identification means that gas chromatography is not 100% specific; it is possible that interfering substances or a co-eluting compound could cause a false-positive confirmation test. Although the likelihood of this is low, since a sample would first have to test positively on a screening test before being chromatographed, it is a possibility nonetheless.

## High-Performance Liquid Chromatography

High-performance liquid chromatography is another procedure which can be used to confirm the presence of drugs of abuse in urine samples. Its use is limited to a small number of drugs that cannot be easily identified by gas-chromatographic methods.

Liquid chromatography is a technique that involves the separation of a sample into its component parts while in a liquid state. The sample is moved over a stationary liquid phase by the movement of a mobile liquid phase. The actual separation of the sample into its component parts is caused by a number of factors including an individual constituent's partition coefficient and the presence of interaction of a constituent of the sample with the stationary phase. High performance liquid chromatography is an extension of this technique made possible by various technological advances.

In HPLC, the sample is first extracted from the urine using various organic solvents. This step removes protein and other potentially interfering substances. Since HPLC uses small diameter steel tubing, the sample must be free of all particulate matter. This may, in some cases, require the use of filtration devices. Once prepared, the sample is then dissolved in a small amount of the solvent that is used as the mobile phase in the system.

The specimen is injected into the flow of the mobile phase either manually or automatically. Then it is pumped over the column's stationary phase, which in the case of HPLC, is a liquid bonded to silica particles. As it passes over the solid phase, the compounds in the sample partition themselves between the mobile liquid phase and the stationary liquid phase. This interaction varies with even closely related compounds and is the basis for the separation observed with HPLC systems. The stationary phase can be either a polar compound or, in the case of reverse phase chromatography, a nonpolar compound. Reverse-phase chromatography is most commonly used for the identification of drugs.

HPLC columns can be operated either at room temperature or at elevated values in an oven. Since HPLC separates compounds dissolved in a liquid phase, drugs that decompose at the higher temperatures imposed by gas chromatography (such as benzodiazepines) can be efficiently detected.

**Detectors.** A variety of detectors are available to determine the presence and relative amounts of materials dissolved in the mobile phase. Ultraviolet and visible photometers detect the presence of compounds that absorb light while dissolved in the mobile phase solvent. Detectors operate either at a single wave length or are selective to specific wavelengths. Since compounds absorb light differently depending on their molecular structure, variable detectors permit the selection of the wavelength most appropriate for the compound of interest. A newer variant of this technique is the fixed-diode–array detector which can measure a series of wavelengths simultaneously and then reproduce the wavelength of interest for later analysis.

HPLC identification is based primarily on the retention time of the compound. Because of the importance placed on the time of elution, an internal standard should be used to control for variations between analyses. The use of an internal standard also permits quantitation which may be of value in selected circumstances.

Identification is also aided by the selection of specific wavelengths of light to be absorbed. Such selection enables the operator to demonstrate that the compound not only came from the column at the specified time for the drug of interest, but also that it absorbed light at the wavelength of interest. Fixed-diode arrays are most valuable for this type of identification since they permit comparison with absorption at different wavelengths of light.

None of the detectors described above, however, are specific for any single compound. In the case of the detectors routinely employed in gas chromatography, no specific physical identification of the elution material is made. Since the operator cannot entirely rule out the presence of an interfering substance that produces the same retention time and absorption pattern, the test is not 100% specific. Legal questions can be raised about the results of the analysis because of the possibility of unknown interferences.

**Advantages.** Advantages of the method include the fact that the compound does not have to be vaporized to be analyzed. This is of particular value in situations where the compounds decompose at the high temperatures required for gas-liquid chromatography. The instruments also allow the nondestructive analysis of compounds.

**Disadvantages.** Disadvantages include the presence of interfering substances in some cases and the fact that a true physical identification is not made.

## Gas Chromatography/Mass Spectrometry

The third and most widely accepted method is called gas chromatography with mass spectrometry (GC/MS). The instruments used for this method are a gas chromatograph, which separates the materials in the sample chromatographically, and a mass spectrometer, which is used as the detector. The difference between these instruments and the nonselective detectors previously described for gas chromatography is that the mass spectrometer can be used to identify the compounds as they pass through. It can determine the molecular weight of a compound to thousandths of an atomic mass unit (amu) and can characterize molecular fragments in a similar fashion. Mass spectrometry coupled with gas chromatography has become the method of choice for medicolegal drug identifications.

**Ionization.** GC/MS operates by ionizing molecules in a variety of methods. Once ionized, compounds break into characteristic fragments that can be identified by their mass (m) to charge (z) ratio (m/z). The relative abundance of the fragments is then compared to the most abundant fragment (called the base peak) which is normalized to 100% intensity. The base peak is usually an ion fragment, but in some cases may be the molecule itself.

Characteristic mass spectrums exist for each chemical compound. Stable isotopes of elements contained in a compound can also be readily separated from one another. This separation can be useful in quantitation steps (see below) and illustrates the resolving power of the instrument. Although different compounds may produce similar fragments when ionized, the fragments from different compounds will not appear in the same ratio. The mass spectrum has been referred to as a "chemical fingerprint" since it is unique for each compound. Most instruments are interfaced with a computer which can perform "off line" comparisons with known spectrums to aid in identification.

The mass spectrum produced for each compound varies somewhat with the mechanism used to produce the ion fragments. Electron impact is the most widely used method and subjects the sample coming from the gas chromatograph to a constant stream of high energy electrons. As the molecules are struck, they become ionized and consist of the molecular ion plus numerous fragments. The ions may hold a positive, negative, or neutral charge. Due to the design of the instrument's ionization chambers, the positively charged ions are directed towards the detector by an accelerating voltage. Of the various techniques, electron impact produces the most fragments.

Chemical ionization subjects the sample to an ionized reagent gas, which, when in contact with unionized reagent gas molecules, forms highly reactive intermediates that transfer a proton to the compounds in the ion chamber, creating positively charged ions. This technique produces great quantities of molecular ions and aids in the identification of unknown compounds. This method forms fewer fragments than the electron impact method.

The third method of ionization is called field desorption and is reserved for large molecular weight polar and nonvolatile compounds. The predominant ion produced by this method is the molecular ion, making the technique most useful for determining the molecular weight of different compounds.

Regardless of the means of ionization, the key to the instrument's operation is its ability to discriminate between ions of different molecular weight in a real-time environment. Electron impact produces the greatest number of ion fragments while field desorption produces the least. As noted above, the mass spectra produced by each method are unique for each compound. The detection of the ion fragments and the molecular ions requires the separation of these components into individual groups depending on their size (mass) and charge. A number of methods are frequently used in the clinical laboratory to separate the components, including quadrupole analyzers and ion trap detectors.

**Quadrupole System.**     A general discussion of the operating characteristics of the quadrupole system is outlined below. A specific discussion of this technique or others is beyond the scope of this section and readers should refer to more detailed texts for this information.

Quadrupole instruments direct the ion beam through the centers of four metal rods that form the quadrupole. These rods are oppositely charged by a direct current that directs the positively charged ions through their centers. At the end of the rods is the detector, which is an electron multiplier using dynodes of increasing negative charge. If the quadrupole merely directed all ions through it to the detector, the instrument would not be able to discriminate ions of different weights and charges. To detect these differences, the polarity of the charges on each of the metal rods of the quadrupole are rapidly changed by a radio frequency generator while the DC voltage on the rods is changed at the same time.

The rapidly changing polarity and voltages make the ions unable to travel directly through the oscillating field. At an optimum voltage and polarity, however, ions of a particular mass/charge (m/z) ratio can travel through the quadrupole and strike the detector. This full-spectrum tracing is accomplished by subjecting the metal rods to a very wide range of voltages and frequencies, allowing all the ions within a certain m/z range to strike the detector system.

The scanning of the quadrupole through the various voltages and frequencies takes a finite amount of time. Since sensitivity is a function of the number of ions that strike the detector per unit of time, the greatest sensitivity is obtained when only selected ion m/z ratios are scanned rather than the entire spectrum. This technique, selective ion monitoring SIM, is used extensively by laboratories to confirm the presence of a known compound with characteristic fragmentation products. Since the ion fragments of interest are known, the presence of other peaks is not crucial to the identification.

**Analysis.**     Analysis of compounds by gas chromatography/mass spectrometry requires careful attention to specimen preparation. Because of the need to ionize the specimen for analysis, all traces of water must be removed. Since a volatile sample is needed in most cases (direct probe injection does not require any chromatographic separation), the compound of interest must remain stable when heated to the column temperature. Samples containing drugs subject to pyrolyzation (eg, benzodiazepines) must either be analyzed at lower temperatures or detected from unique pyrolyzation residues.

Gas chromatography using mass spectrometry as a detector is often described as producing a compound's fingerprint. As with fingerprints, there are a number of elements that must be present to ensure the uniqueness of the mass spectra. Definitive identification is based on a strict set of guidelines, and the laboratory must adhere closely to the guidelines, or the validity of the analysis will be questioned.

The compound to be identified must elute from the column at the appropriate time to ensure that the chromatographic analysis has taken place and that the drug of interest has been separated properly from other compounds. The time of elution should be constant for similar instrument conditions. An internal standard can help guarantee the appropriate timing of the various constituents.

Once ionized and detected in the mass spectrometer, the compound should break into characteristic ion fragments. As noted, different methods of ionization will yield different spectra. Electron impact is most commonly used in drug analysis and produces the most complex spectra because of the severity of the ionization process. Most laboratories use the SIM technique, which focuses on several characteristic peaks in the identification process rather than on examining the entire spectrum. This technique provides a more sensitive analysis than full spectrum monitoring. If the sample contains the drug of interest, the analysis should produce sharp peaks at the characteristic peaks of the compound.

The peaks monitored must not only be present, but must also appear in a characteristic ratio. Ionization produces a characteristic fragmentation of the molecule as it enters the mass spectrograph unit. Therefore, the peaks monitored in a SIM analysis should appear in abundances that conform to those seen in a full-spectrum analysis. Typically, they are compared to the base peak, which is considered to have 100% abundance by convention (the base peak may be the molecular ion but usually is not when electron impact has been used for ionization). The appearance of the ions in the proper ratios is crucial to a SIM analysis since compounds can produce many of the same ions when they fragment. Their ratio to the base peak, however, should be characteristic for a single compound.

The combination of appropriate time of elution, appearance of the proper peaks on either SIM or total spectrum analysis, and appropriate relative abundance relationships between the peaks will yield a unique analysis for each particular compound. However, the analysis will not be a unique representation of a single compound if the three requirements are not met. Different compounds can have similar ion fragments, and interfering substances could potentially elute off the column at the same time as the compound of interest. Therefore, all of the tests should be met before a sample is considered positive for the drug of interest.

**Quantitation of Results.**    Quantitation of positive results of urine tests is sometimes requested. The reasons for quantitative results should be considered prior to establishing such procedures. Neither the presence of drugs in an individual's urine nor the level of the particular drug can be considered evidence of impairment because of many variables, including degree of hydration, time from the last dose, and pH of urine. Neverthe-less, quantitation may be requested for other reasons. For example, values can be used with some caution to observe the disappearance of THC metabolite from an individual's urine over time and to determine if the drug has been used since an earlier test.

Quantitation should be based on the result of a confirmation test and not a screening test. Values obtained from EMIT, RIA, or other immu-nological procedures are semiquantitative and, in most cases, are not in-dicative of the presence of a single compound. Proper quantitation requires the use of an internal standard run at the same time as the sample. The internal standard should be added at the beginning, before the extraction step, and go through the entire process of testing. Comparison of internal standard peak height to known drug standards can then be used to de-termine the amount of drug in a particular analysis. The internal standard peak height in the test analysis would be compared to the drug of interest, and this ratio would be compared to the ratios derived in the standard determinations.

The best internal standard is one that is very similar to the compound of interest in chemical reactivity, solvent solubility and chromatographic separation, but one that can be identified separately. The gas chromato-graph mass spectrometry method accurately distinguishes such com-pounds. Radioactively labeled compounds identical to the drug of interest can be added in known quantities prior to the extraction step. These labeled drugs will behave the same as the drug itself and can be extracted and analyzed with the same efficiency. They can be separated by the dif-ferences in the masses of their ion fragments rather than by their chro-matographic characteristics (which should be essentially identical). They must be labeled in a fashion that will prevent them from being confused with the nonlabeled drug during extraction, derivatization, or separation steps. For example, deuterium-labeled compounds will have certain frag-ments that differ in m/z ratio solely by the increased mass of deuterium as compared to hydrogen. The mass spectrograph can easily resolve these relatively large differences and can produce either full-spectrum traces of both simultaneously, or ideally, SIM patterns which include the charac-teristic ions of both compounds. This deuterated compound then acts as an internal standard for the time of elution and also allows direct quan-titation. The peak heights of the molecular ions can be compared directly and their ratio is in direct proportion to their concentration. In this man-ner the internal standard serves two purposes simultaneously.

Quantitation serves several purposes. It can be used to demonstrate the amount of a given drug present in a urine (or blood) sample. While the value of this information is limited, it does provide a basis of com-parison with previous tests and an avenue for speculation concerning re-cency or quantity of use. In addition, quantitation of a drug demonstrates the level of sensitivity of the assay in use and its ability to detect the compound. For these reasons, forensic analyses usually require quantitation.

**Advantages.**     Advantages of GC/MS include the high specificity and low detection limits of the method. The technique allows separation of compounds that are structurally closely related but have different pharmacological effects. The nature of the identification makes misidentification unlikely. The low detection limits allow compounds in nanogram quantities to be found.

**Disadvantages.**     The method, however, is time consuming and requires a high skill level for proper operation. Compounds must also be stable at the temperatures required for the preliminary gas chromatography step. In addition, derivation is necessary for identification.

# —— RESULT INTERPRETATION

The proper interpretation of the results of urine and blood tests is crucial to the implementation of a drug testing program. This section will review the meaning of the tests in terms of the methods that are used and the possible alternative explanations for both positive and negative values.

## Urine Tests
Immunoassays (RIA, EMIT, FPIA) have become the standard methods for screening individuals for drugs of abuse. One of the reasons is because they have greater sensitivity than alternative methods such as thin-layer chromatography. Immunoassays also offer greater specificity because of the nature of the antigen antibody reaction. Another obvious advantage is the relative ease with which they can be performed. However, the most important advantage of immunoassays is their relative reproducibility of positive and negative results because of the objective nature of the decision point.

The decision point in immunoassays is referred to as the cutoff value. Samples that contain the drug in a concentration below this value are considered negative, while specimens with greater activity are labeled positive. Therefore, a specimen that is reported as negative has less activity than the predetermined cutoff value although the drug may be present and could be detected by a lower cutoff or more sensitive method. For example, a specimen containing 80 ng of cannabinoid would be negative for marijuana at the 100-ng cutoff value but strongly positive if the alternative 20-ng cutoff were to be used. If RIA testing results on screening tests are compared to EMIT values, there may be discordance because of different cutoff values employed.

Positive and negative values on screening tests must therefore be judged by the cutoff level established for the method in use. Negative samples are not subject to further testing despite the fact that the drug may be present and detectable by alternative means. The cutoff level specified will affect the rate of positive results since lower cutoffs will by definition be more sensitive.

The results of screening tests alone must be considered only as presumptive evidence of the presence of the drug. There are numerous reasons for this. Immunoassays possess cross-reactivity with other compounds, which can cause a positive result even though the compound being tested for is not present. For example, amphetamine tests by EMIT are influenced by a large number of over-the-counter medications that contain legal amphetamine-like substances. Although the screening test may be positive, the actual drug is not present. Similarly, a number of nonsteroidal anti-inflammatory agents may interfere with the EMIT test for THC. Positive results may be false-positive when these compounds have been taken. The use of these drugs, however, does not mean that a positive result is by necessity a false-positive since the drug of interest may also be present at the same time.

The list of potential interfering substances that react with immunoassays is long enough to show that the results as stated above are merely presumptive. Thin-layer chromatography and other similar testing methods are subject to different, but nonetheless more serious, interferences that prevent their use alone. As noted above, however, negative results do not mean that the drug is not present but only that it has not been detected at the specified level.

Confirmation testing serves to eliminate false-positive results. The sensitivity and cutoff levels of confirmation methods are sufficiently low to ensure with reasonable certainty that true-positive screening results can be confirmed. However, the sensitivity and cutoff levels do not guarantee confirmation. An obvious example is THC, where the screening test is directed at multiple metabolites while the confirmation assay generally looks at one compound. This single compound may not be present in sufficient quantity to cross the threshold cutoff on the confirmation assay. Since only positive screening samples are tested, false-negative samples will not be detected. This is because negative results are presumed to be accurate.

Interpretation of negative screening tests should consider the following information. Samples that have been tampered with may contain the drug, but its presence may have been masked by the addition of extraneous compounds such as table salt. Or the urine may have been diluted either by in vitro action by the addition of water or by in vivo dilution caused by diuretics. This can be accomplished by a combination of large fluid intake and the use of simple agents such as tobacco or certain anti-hypertensive medications. Negative results can also mean that the particular drug an individual has used was not even subject to testing. For example, certain anti-anxiety drugs such as glutethemide are not routinely screened for, and other agents such as pentazocine (Talwin) do not react with immunoassays currently available. Negative results can also result from intermittent use of drugs with a period of abstinence prior to the collection of the sample. This period would, of course, vary with the drug ingested. Similarly, a single dose of a drug might not be detected, depending on the time prior to the test and the dose ingested.

Negative results mean that the drug was not detected under the assay conditions employed. Such results do not mean that the person never used drugs, is not a chronic user, or will never abuse drugs in the future. Careful sample collection is important to eliminate exogenous causes of false-negative results. It can not, however, account for a host of other factors mentioned, including dose, time from last dose, state of hydration, concentration of the urine, or the presence of a drug that is not part of the routine battery of tests.

Positive screening tests are followed by a second, more specific, confirmation test. Two possibilities exist. The initial positive screening result can be confirmed as positive at the specified cutoff value of the confirmation test, or it will be unconfirmed. Unconfirmed tests are considered negative for the purposes of test interpretation. Each possibility will be addressed separately.

Unconfirmed positive results mean that the drug or class of drugs identified on the initial screen could not be confirmed with the secondary method. A number of causes are possible. The initial positive value could have been the result of an interfering substance, as in the case of the amphetamines or THC described above. The drug was actually not present, and therefore the initial result was erroneous. Alternatively, the drug may have been present, but the confirmation test could not detect it. The failure to detect it could mean that the concentration was below the minimum value established by the secondary method. A good example would be a positive THC value at 20 ng of total cannabinoid in which the concentration of 11 or delta 9 tetrahydrocannabinol 9 carboxylic acid (9-carboxy-THC), the primary metabolite, is below the cutoff level of the mass spectrometry method used for confirmation. Or the gas chromatographic tracing produced does not meet all of the requirements established by the laboratory for an unequivocal positive result. In addition, it is possible that the wrong specimen was analyzed, the assay was incorrectly performed, or the specimen was tampered with between initial and confirmation procedures. Assuming that these last factors are eliminated or minimized, a negative confirmation following a positive screening test must be treated as if the initial screening test was negative. No action should be taken and it should not be inferred that the individual was not really negative but actually "a little bit positive." In an ideal situation, only negative and confirmed positive results should be reported. Neither preliminary results, such as positives pending confirmation nor partial reports indicating a number of drugs as negative and one or more pending, should be reported.

A positive result on a screening test followed by a positive result on the confirmation test is the final alternative possibility. Since this combination of results is the one likely to lead to some type of disciplinary or judicial action, a clear understanding of its implications must be present.

Positive confirmed results mean that the drug was found to be present above the specified cutoff value. Absolutely no inference of whether the individual was impaired can be made. A variety of factors contribute to this inability to clearly establish impairment.

Urine tests cannot establish the amount of drug ingested by the individual since the dose taken is not known, rarely volunteered, and impossible to establish because the purity of individual compounds varies. The time of ingestion cannot be determined either. The test results depend on the drug consumed (see individual sections). A large dose could have been taken many hours or days prior or a small dose could have been taken very recently. Similarly, the state of hydration of the individual directly affects the concentration of the urine and is a major determinant in concentration of drug measured. The pH of urine also affects the rate of excretion for many drugs and is another uncontrolled factor which affects concentration. Certain drugs, such as THC, are also affected by duration of use with long-term users excreting the metabolite long after the last use of the substance.

Impairment is determined by the amount of drug present in the blood, the individual's tolerance for the compound, and the time from ingestion to metabolism. Urine results cannot be readily correlated with blood results because of the numerous factors affecting concentration noted in the above sections. The consensus panel on impairment and driving noted that urine levels of drugs could not be used to determine impairment.[21]

Positive confirmed tests mean the drug is present. They do not prove impairment or absolutely guarantee that the individual consumed the drug. For example, passive inhalation of THC has been documented under specific research conditions. Marijuana can also be consumed orally without the knowledge of the individual and a positive result can ensue. Certain herbal teas are known to contain cocaine derived from the coca leaves from which the teas are made. Chronic ingestion can cause true positive confirmed cocaine drug screens. Poppy seeds consumed in moderate quantities can cause a true positive opiate screen with confirmation for morphine without the individual's active use of the drug or any impairment. Legally prescribed drugs containing codeine will result in a positive opiate screen and confirmed morphine result. Although codeine/morphine ratios can prove the ingestion of codeine, they cannot rule out the concomitant use of morphine. In fact, drug addicts in certain drug control programs obtain codeine prescriptions to "mask" their use of heroin or morphine.

The final interpretation of a positive confirmed result must, therefore, take into account the various possible legitimate or inadvertent reasons for the presence of the drug. Under no circumstances can impairment be inferred. In a similar manner, the duration of use, the number of times of use prior to testing, or the addiction status of the individual cannot be determined from a single urine test result. No prediction of future use can be made from the results of the test.

Multiple samples taken over time can be useful in determining duration of use and reuse of the drug. Individuals once positive subject to retesting following subsequent negative results can be inferred to have used the drug again assuming a sufficient time has passed from the negative result. This is because concentration factors can affect results over the short run, but, over time, individuals should repeatedly test negative if they are no longer using the drug. The one difficult exception is marijuana where the time course of clearance from the body is prolonged and relatively long periods of abstinence are required for chronic users to consistently test negative on screening tests. In all cases, the same cutoff on the screening test must be used. For example, an individual negative at the 100-ng cutoff value for THC should not be subject to retesting at a 20-ng level, since the results would not be comparable.

**Quantitation.** Certain laboratories offer quantitation of urine drug results. The value should be based on the value obtained from the mass spectrograph. The information provided is of limited value in most cases because elevated urine levels do not demonstrate impairment and cannot clearly determine how much of the drug was consumed.

## Blood Tests

Samples for blood analysis are usually used in the for cause setting following some type of incident. In usual practice, the urine screen is performed first. Only the drugs that are detected and confirmed in the urine are then subject to assay in the blood. The methods employed are different than the usual methods used in urine testing.

The test is usually gas chromatography/mass spectroscopy because plasma levels are generally far lower than levels found in the urine. For example, a single dose of cocaine has been predicted to yield a plasma level of 1 to 3 $\mu$g/mL[22] at the peak level shortly after ingestion. In contrast, typical urinary levels of cocaine and its primary metabolite must exceed 300 ng (3 $\mu$g) to be detected as positive by an EMIT test. Therefore, there is no simple way to screen a plasma sample for drugs at levels typically seen in the general user.

Blood levels can be important since they can indicate very recent use of a compound. For example, cocaine has a half life of approximately 1.5 hours meaning that in only 4.5 hours less than 25% of the peak level will be detected in the blood. Conversely, the urine may remain positive for 2 to 3 days after ingestion of a single dose of the drug.

Positive blood levels, however, are not proof that an individual is intoxicated at the time the sample was procured. A consensus panel of leading experts determined that except for alcohol, no easily defined drug levels in blood that would indicate impairment could be determined because of individual differences in metabolism of the drugs and the development of tolerance by certain individuals to the effects of these compounds.[23]

Positive blood tests do mean that a person has recently consumed drugs. This may be sufficient to corroborate other evidence available that the individual was impaired on the job. The drug levels themselves, however, cannot be used as the sole source of proof that the person was impaired. This is often difficult for employers to accept. However, the weight of scientific evidence demands that no absolute determinations be made based upon drug results alone.

## —— NOTES

1. R.S. GALEN, S.R. GAMBINO, BEYOND NORMALITY: THE PREDICTIVE VALUE AND EFFICIENCY OF MEDICAL DIAGNOSES. (John Wiley & Sons Inc., 1975).

2. P.F. Griner, R.J. Mayewski, A.I. Mushlin, et al., Selection and Interpretation of Diagnostic Tests and Procedures: Principles and Applications, 94 (pt. 2) ANN. INTERN. MED. 553–600 (1981).

3. J.R. Beck, E.K. Shultz, The Use of Relative Operating Characteristic (ROC) Curves in Test Performance Evaluation, 100 ARCH. PATHOL. LAB. MED. 13–20 (1986).

4. K. L. Radack, G. Rovan, J. Hedges, The Likelihood Ratio. An Improved Measure for Reporting and Evaluating Test Results, 110 ARCH. PATHOL. LAB. MED. 689–693 (1986).

5. H.J. Hansen, S.P. Caudill, D.J. Boone, Crisis in Drug Testing: Results of CDC Blind Study, 253 JAMA 2382–2387 (1985).

6. G.D. Lundberg, Mandatory Unindicated Urine Drug Screening: Still Chemical McCarthyism, 256 N. ENGL. J. MED. 3003–3005 (1986).

7. J.B. HENRY, ED. TODD SANFORD DAVIDSON'S CLINICAL DIAGNOSIS AND MANAGEMENT BY LABORATORY METHODS. (17th ed.) (W.B. Saunders Co., 1984).

8. B.L. Davidow, N. Petri, B. Quame, A Thin-Layer Chromatographic Screening Procedure for Detecting Drug Abuse, 50 AM. J. CLIN. PATHOL. 714–719 (1968).

9. J. E. Wallace, H. Hamilton, Analytic Principles. IN R.H. CRAVEY AND R.C. BASELT, EDS., INTRODUCTION TO FORENSIC TOXICOLOGY. (Biomedical Publishing Company, 1981).

10. N. Weissman, M.L. Lowe, J.M. Beattie, *Screening Methods for Detection of Drugs of Abuse in Human Urine*, 17 CLIN. CHEM. 873–881 (1971).

11. R.O. Bost, C.A. Sutheimer, I. Sunshine, *Relative Merits of Some Methods for Amphetamine Assay in Biological Fluids*, 22 CLIN. CHEM. 789–801 (1976).

12. *Id.*

13. G. Vanzetti, M. Cassani, D. Valente, *Detection of Morphine in the Urine by Heme Agglutination Inhibition with the Use of Lyophilized Reagent*, 29 CLIN. CHEM. 1367–1379 (1983).

14. S. Spector, C.W. Parker, *Morphine: Radioimmunoassay*, 168 SCIENCE 1347 (1970).

15. *Syva Customer Bulletin* (April, 1986).

16. L. V. Allen, M.L. Stiles, *Specificity of the EMIT Drug Abuse Urine Assay Methods*, 18 CLIN. TOXICOLOGY 1043–1065 (1981).

17. E. P. Van der Slooten, H.J. Van der Helm, *Comparison of the EMIT Opiate Assay and a Gas-Chromatographic-Mass Spectrometric Determination of Morphine and Codeine in Urine*, 22 CLIN. CHEM. 1110–1111 (1976).

18. H. J. Hansen, D.S. Lewis, D.J. Boone, *Marihuana Analysis: Results of a Recent Interlaboratory Survey*, 27 CLIN. CHEM. 1104 (1981).

19. Allen, *supra* at note 16.

20. DeCresce, personal data (1986).

21. R.V. Blanke, Y.H. Caplan, R.T. Chamberlain, *et al.*, *Consensus Report: Drug Concentrations and Driving Impairment*, 254 JAMA 2618–2621 (1985).

22. J. Ambre, *The Urinary Excretion of Cocaine and its Metabolites in Humans: A Kinetic Analysis of Published Data*, 9 J. ANAL. TOXICOL. 214–245 (1985).

23. Blanke, *supra* at note 21.

# —4—

# THE DRUGS OF ABUSE

Previous chapters have dealt with the principles of drug screening and the various available identification techniques. This section will discuss specific benefits and limitations of the various drug detection methods and the drugs of abuse with respect to their use and pharmacokinetics. Drugs of abuse can be categorized by their effects, as presented in Table 4–1.

Before embarking on a detailed discussion of the various drugs, one must consider the methods used to identify them. Urine screening for drugs of abuse is most frequently performed by immunoassay because the procedure is rapid, easy, requires little experience, and is more sensitive and specific, compared to most chromatographic techniques such as thin-layer chromatography. Immunoassays are also easily adapted to automation and can often be run on instruments already in the laboratory. For this reason, they are the methods of choice for most large commercial laboratories involved in screening programs. The most common immunoassay methods for detecting drugs of abuse are radioimmunoassay (RIA) (Roche Diagnostics Abuscreen), enzyme multiplied immunoassay test (EMIT) (Syva Company), and fluorescence polarization immunoassay (FPIA) (Abbott Diagnostics). There are two EMIT systems commercially available. The EMIT-dau (drugs of abuse, urine) can sometimes reveal substances at a lower concentration than the EMIT-test (single test); the latter is best suited for use in small laboratories and physicians' offices. The detection limits of the various assays are presented in Table 4–2. The detection limit is the concentration at which the drug can be detected with 95% proba-

**TABLE 4-1**

Classes of Drugs of Abuse

---

**Hallucinogens**

Phencyclidine (PCP)

Lysergic acid diethylamide (LSD)

Cannabis (marijuana)

**Stimulants**

Amphetamines

Phenylpropanolamine

Cocaine

**Depressants**

Alcohol

Sedatives and hypnotics

  Benzodiazepines

  Methaqualone

Opioids

Barbiturates

---

bility. Values above the detection limit are considered positive, and those below it are negative. By raising the detection limit, the specificity of the assay is enhanced (fewer false positives), and by lowering it, the sensitivity is increased (more false positives).

The urine excretion patterns of each drug determine the substance to be detected by a particular assay. For instance, if only trace amounts of the parent compound are found in urine, the assay will be directed at detecting a metabolite present in larger concentrations. The various compounds detected by assays are presented in Table 4–3. The excretion of drugs in urine varies during the course of the day and from day to day. Some drugs accumulate in fat in long-term users and are slowly released into the circulation; this phenomenon may give positive urine test results over a prolonged period. Many drug excretion patterns are affected by urine pH. Thus, under certain conditions, a subject may test positive subsequent to a negative test result. Table 4–4 addresses these variations in excretion patterns, and presents a general guide for the usual detection time associated with a drug dose.

**TABLE 4-2**
Detection Limits (mg/mL) of Immunoassays

| Drug | EMIT-dau | RIA | FPIA |
|------|----------|-----|------|
| Amphetamines | 300 | 1,000 | 300 |
| Barbiturates | 300 | 200 | 500 |
| Benzodiazepines | 300 | 200 | 200 |
| Cannabinoids | 20 | 100 | 25 |
| Cocaine | 300 | 300 | 300 |
| LSD | NA | 0.5 | NA |
| Methaqualone | 300 | 750 | NA |
| Methadone | 300 | NA | NA |
| Opioids | 300 | 300 | 200 |
| Phencyclidine | 75 | 25 | 25 |
| Propoxyphene | 300 | NA | NA |

Abbreviations: EMIT-dau = enzyme multiplied immunoassay test (drugs of abuse, urine); RIA = radioimmunoassay; FPIA = fluorescence polarization immunoassay; NA = not applicable.

# ── AMPHETAMINES

Amphetamines and metamphetamines are central nervous system stimulants that are easily absorbed after oral administration. There are few, if any, legitimate indications for their intravenous use. Amphetamines are useful in the treatment of hyperkinetic syndrome, a childhood disorder characterized by hyperactivity and inability to concentrate; they have a paradoxical calming effect in these children. Other therapeutic indications are for narcolepsy, since they prevent sleep attacks, and for obesity, since they cause weight reduction by drastically reducing appetite. However, because of their potential for abuse, amphetamines are no longer recommended for weight control. This has reduced the number of prescription abusers; unfortunately, street supplies are abundant.

**TABLE 4-3**

Substances Detected by Immunoassay

| Drugs | Assay | Major Substance Detected |
|---|---|---|
| Amphetamines | RIA | Amphetamine |
| | EMIT | Amphetamine, methamphetamine |
| | FPIA | Amphetamine, methamphetamine |
| Barbiturates | RIA | Secobarbital |
| | EMIT | Secobarbital |
| | FPIA | Secobarbital |
| Benzodiazepines | RIA | Nordiazepam |
| | EMIT | Oxazepam |
| | FPIA | Nordiazepam |
| Cannabinoids | RIA | COOH-THC |
| | EMIT | COOH-THC |
| | FPIA | COOH-THC |
| Cocaine | RIA | Benzoylecgonine |
| | EMIT | Benzoylecgonine |
| | FPIA | Benzoylecgonine |
| Methaqualone | RIA | Methaqualone |
| | EMIT | Methaqualone |
| | FPIA | Not available |
| Opioids | RIA | Morphine |
| | EMIT | Morphine |
| | FPIA | Morphine |
| Phencyclidine | RIA | Phencyclidine |
| | EMIT | Phencyclidine |
| | FPIA | Phencyclidine |
| LSD | RIA | LSD |
| | EMIT | Not available |
| | FPIA | Not available |

Abbreviations: RIA = radioimmunoassay; EMIT = enzyme multiplied immunoassay test; FPIA = fluorescence polarization immunoassay; THC = tetrahydrocannabinol; LSD = lysergic acid diethylamide.

**TABLE 4–4**

Approximate Detection Time Limits for Drugs of Abuse

| Drug | Approximate Dose and Administration Route | Detection Time |
|---|---|---|
| Amphetamines | 30 mg PO | 1–120 hr |
| | 15 mg PO | 1–72 hr |
| | 5 mg PO | 3.5–30.0 hr |
| Barbiturates | | |
| Short-acting | 100 mg PO | 4.5 days |
| Phenobarbital | 400 mg PO | 7 days |
| Benzodiazepines | 25 mg PO | 48 hr minimum |
| Diazepam | 10 mg PO | None detected |
| | 10 mg, 5 times daily | 3–7 days |
| Cocaine | 250 mg PO | 8–48 hr |
| Opioids | | |
| Heroin | 10 mg IV | 1–4 days |
| Meperidine | 100 mg PO | 4–24 hr |
| Methadone | 38 mg PO | 7.5–56.0 hr |
| Morphine | 10 mg IV | 84 hr minimum |
| Methaqualone | 150 mg PO | Up to 60 hr |
| | 250 mg PO | Up to 72 hr |
| | 300 mg PO | Up to 90 hr |
| Marijuana | 1 per week | 7–34 days |
| | Daily | 6–81 days |

Abbreviations: PO = *per os* (oral); IV = intravenous.

On the street, oral amphetamine preparations are known as "bennies," "dexies," "co-pilots," and "ups." Intravenous methamphetamine preparations are called "speed," or "crystal." In recent years, "look-alike" drugs have surfaced on the street; these physically resemble amphetamines with respect to color, shape, and capsule size and have been called "black beauties" and "white crosses."[1] Examples include phenylpropanolamine and pseudoephedrine.

Amphetamines are taken orally, as are other central nervous system stimulants such as methylphenidate and phenmetrazine. Occasional users generally take 5 to 15 mg, whereas addicts may require 100 to 2000 mg each day because of their developed tolerance. During the initial stage following oral intake, the user experiences euphoria, an elevation in mood, and increased alertness and energy. Students having to study for many hours at a time take amphetamines to stay awake during the night. Similarly, boring tasks such as long-distance driving become more tolerable. The drug also causes increased heart rate, elevated blood pressure, tremor, and anxiety. In chronic abusers, tolerance develops and larger doses are required. Increased dosages cause hyperirritability, restlessness, bizarre behavior, weight loss, and suspiciousness. Users no longer funnel their energies into useful activities. Still higher doses result in hallucinations and a psychosis similar to acute paranoid schizophrenia.

In contrast to amphetamines, methamphetamine is administered intravenously and produces a very intense euphoria lasting 2 to 3 hours. Seconds after the solution is injected, the user feels an intense pleasure and awareness, which is known as the "rush" or "flash." The drug may be injected continually for 1 to 3 days, during which time the user remains wide awake, does not eat, and may lose 10 to 20 pounds. This period is known as a "run." It is terminated by the "crash," a 24 to 36-hour period of sleep. After awakening with irritability and lethargy, the abuser may initiate another "run." Though amphetamines do not cause physical dependence, they do cause strong psychological dependence. Abusers feel a desire to continue taking the drug and to consume increasingly larger amounts to obtain greater euphoric effects.

Amphetamine and methamphetamine begin to be excreted in the urine within 20 minutes after administration. About 30% of an amphetamine dose is eliminated during the first day; methamphetamine is excreted as both unchanged drug (43%) and as the metabolite amphetamine (57%).[2] Urine pH has a marked effect on the excretion patterns of these drugs. Acid urine promotes excretion, whereas alkaline urine retards it. This fact is reflected in the plasma half-lives for these drugs; for example, a half-life range of 7 to 34 hours, would be short in acid conditions and long in alkaline conditions. Generally, urine concentrations in occasional users range from 0.5 to 4.0 mg/L and those in chronic intravenous abusers are higher, from 25 to 300 mg/L, for example. Consecutive urine samples from the same person may show great variability as urine pH fluctuates. RIA or EMIT immunoassay may give results which are initially positive, revert to negative, become positive again, and then finally stay negative 30 hours after administration. Since RIA can detect smaller amounts of drug than EMIT, it is conceivable that the above-mentioned consecutive samples would all test positive by RIA but would have fluctuating results with EMIT.

In contrast to EMIT, which detects both amphetamine and methamphetamine, RIA detects only amphetamine. Generally, these assays give positive results for 1 to 2 days after administration. However, with large doses, or if the urine has remained alkaline even with a smaller dose, positive results may persist for 7 to 10 days after ceasing drug intake. Though RIA cannot detect methamphetamine, if the drug is taken in a large enough dose, there may be sufficient amphetamine metabolite to cause a positive response.

Few compounds interfere with the RIA determination of amphetamines; p-methoxyamphetamine, a compound that does interfere, is a hallucinogenic, illicit drug that one would want to detect. However, p-hydroxyamphetamine is a compound used as an ophthalmic solution and a nasal decongestant, which, if detected, would represent a false-positive result.

The EMIT assay is broadly cross-reactive for many sympathomimetic amines, the most important of which are ephedrine and phenylpropanolamine. These decongestants are used in numerous over-the-counter cold, allergy, and diet preparations such as Nyquil, Primatene mist, Coricidin, Vicks Formula 44D, Robitussin, Sucrets, Dexatrim, Alka-Seltzer Plus, Allerest and Bayer children's capsules. False positive results could occur for about 12 hours after a dose if the urine is acidic; with an alkaline urine, positive results might persist for several hours longer. An optional EMIT *amphetamine confirmation kit* will usually eliminate interferences caused by ephedrine and phenylpropanolamine. Phenylephrine and pseudoephedrine may also cross-react in the EMIT assay, according to the manufacturer. They are present in products such as Sudafed, Robitussin PE, Chlor-Trimeton, and Dristan. In contrast, the FPIA assay for amphetamines shows little, if any, cross-reactivity with over-the-counter cold preparations containing phenylpropanolamine or ephedrine.

Phenethylamine, a product of urine decomposition, may accumulate in specimens after 1 or 2 days. In order to prevent this product from forming and falsely elevating results, urine should be refrigerated and preserved with 1% sodium fluoride if testing is delayed. Specimens can be stored in this manner for up to 1 year. Last, the presence of glucose in the urine may cause false-positive results with EMIT.[3]

# —— OPIOIDS

In a strict sense, the term "opiate" refers to narcotic analgesic drugs derived from the unripe seed capsules of *Papaver somniferum*, the opium poppy. These drugs are morphine and codeine. A good grade of opium contains 9% to 14% morphine. Semisynthetic derivatives of morphine and codeine, such as heroin and hydrocodone, are best classified as "opioids."

Fully synthetic opioids include meperidine, methadone, and propoxyphene. The effects of these drugs come and go quickly, usually within 3 to 6 hours. Methadone is an exception; it lasts 12 to 24 hours.

Heroin is the most abused opioid in the United States; it is used by about 90% of all narcotic addicts.[4] There are an estimated 800,000 daily heroin users.[5] Though it is an illicit drug in this country, it is still used for medical purposes in some countries, such as England. On the street, heroin is known as "dope," "smack," and "horse." Other abused opioids are morphine, codeine, and hydromorphone. Methadone and propoxyphene abuse have been gradually increasing.

In recent years a variety of "designer drugs" have surfaced. These drugs are synthesized in clandestine home laboratories and resemble available narcotics such as fentanyl and meperidine. Fentanyl is a very short-acting narcotic used as an anesthetic in more than 70% of all surgical procedures. At least six different analogues of this drug have shown up on the street, the most powerful of which is 3-methyl-fentanyl, known as "China white." It is 3,000 times more potent than morphine and has been *responsible for more than 100 overdose deaths in California.* As a group, these analogues are called "synthetic heroin." The principal meperidine analogue that has appeared is 1-methyl-4 phyenyl-4-propionoxy-piperidine (MPPP). This drug is about 25 times as potent as meperidine. When MPPP is improperly synthesized by the underground chemist, a different and very toxic product, 1-methyl-4-phenyl-1,2,5,6-tetrahydropyridine (MPTP), can be formed. MPTP causes severe Parkinson's disease by selectively destroying the substantia nigra, an area of the brain.[6] Abuse of MPPP and MPTP became conspicuous when young addicts developed Parkinson's disease.

Opiates are potent central nervous system depressants. After rapid intravenous injection of heroin, the user feels warm flushing of the skin and unique orgasmic sensations in the lower abdomen; this initial experience is known as the "rush." It is followed by a longer, dream-like euphoric state called the "nod," during which feelings of relaxation, contentment, apathy, and tranquility predominate.[7] Continued use rapidly leads to tolerance and, eventually, physical dependence. It has been estimated that 24 mg of heroin per day taken over several weeks is the minimum amount required to develop physical dependence. Users who are physically dependent begin to experience withdrawal symptoms as early as 8 to 12 hours after the last dose; these symptoms reach a peak intensity at 36 to 48 hours. Thus, the need for a constant supply of the drug to avoid withdrawal usually leads the abuser into a life of crime to finance the habit.

A typical addict requires about 100 mg of heroin each day, though some users with significant tolerance have administered up to 5 g daily. Before it is supplied on the street, pure heroin is "cut" or adulterated with substances such as milk sugar, mannose, and quinine. This increases the apparent volume of the drug as well as the profits reaped from it. In the end, a "bag" may contain 90 mg of material, of which only 3 mg is heroin. Most addicts take one large dose each day and prevent a "down" by administering several smaller doses.

Narcotic addiction may be treated by withdrawing the patient completely from the drug or by methadone maintenance. Withdrawal therapy is reserved for those patients who are highly motivated and use relatively small amounts of the drug. Therapy consists of substituting oral methadone for the abused drug in quantities sufficient to prevent abstinence symptoms. The methadone is gradually tapered and usually discontinued by the seventh to tenth day. In contrast, the goal of methadone maintenance is to stabilize the patient on a single daily dose of 50 to 100 mg rather than withdraw the patient altogether from the drug. Administering a large methadone dose can block the euphoric effects of heroin. Thus, the patient does not experience moods fluctuating between euphoria and abstinence. By relieving the necessity of obtaining heroin, the abuser can work or participate in a drug rehabilitation program. Also, since methadone has a long duration of action, the drug need be taken only once each day. Unfortunately, an illicit market has developed for methadone redistribution, and some people not previously addicted to heroin have become major abusers of methadone. Urine drug screening is useful in insuring that patients on methadone maintenance or narcotic withdrawal programs are not relapsing into their old habits of heroin abuse.

Narcotic analgesics are usually administered intravenously, though they may be taken orally or by nasal insufflation. They are retained in the plasma for only a short period, though urinary excretion may persist for 4 to 5 days, particularly with high doses ($\geq 200$ mg heroin). Excretion would be expected to be influenced by urinary pH. The most commonly abused narcotic analgesic, heroin, is injected intravenously. The drug is excreted in the urine predominantly as morphine (8%) and conjugated morphine (67%) over the course of several days, though the majority of the drug is eliminated during the first day.[8] Very little free, unaltered heroin is eliminated. Following an intravenous heroin injection, the urine concentration of morphine will peak at more than 100 mg/L at 5 to 9 hours; this level will drop to 1 to 2 mg/L after 24 hours.[9]

Because it is less potent than heroin, codeine is usually taken in much larger doses. It is usually taken orally by abusers in order to satisfy their addiction during periods of heroin shortage. Codeine is also used for masking heroin abuse prior to urine testing since both drugs cause morphine to be excreted. An addict can obtain a legal prescription for codeine and claim that the morphine identified in the urine is a result of the codeine rather than an illicit drug.

Following an oral dose, codeine is excreted in the urine in the form of free codeine (5% to 17%), conjugated codeine (32% to 46%), conjugated norcodeine (10% to 21%), and conjugated morphine (5% to 13%).[10] These substances vary in their excretion patterns. During the first hours following a dose of codeine, the urine concentrations of codeine and its metabolites exceed those of morphine. After 1 to 2 days, this ratio is reversed and morphine concentrations predominate until the drug is no longer detected. If a less sensitive technique, such as thin-layer chromatography, is used to screen urine on the third or fourth day after administration, it may appear that morphine is the only drug present.[11] Urine morphine/codeine ratios may be useful in identifying codeine use.[12]

Morphine is intravenously injected. It is excreted in the urine in the form of free morphine (10%) and morphine glucuronide (75%). Certain commercially available poppy seeds contain a significant amount of morphine. Consuming foods that are prepared with these seeds can result in false-positive results for morphine by immunoassay and chromatography. However, since urine drug levels are relatively low, they generally trigger a positive result for only several hours after ingestion.[13]

Urine screening for opioids is easily accomplished by using an immunoassay technique such as RIA, EMIT, or FPIA. The detection limit is 0.3 mg/L for RIA, 0.5 mg/L for EMIT, and 0.2 mg/L for FPIA. These figures mean that heroin addicts will test positive for 2 to 3 days after cessation of use, and possibly 4 to 5 days if large doses are taken. On the average, codeine metabolites can be detected with RIA for 2 days after use and morphine can be detected for 1 day, possibly 2 days if a low detection limit is used in the immunoassay.

Urine immunoassays are directed at morphine, since it is also a metabolite of heroin and codeine. The presence of codeine or morphine in the urine could indicate the use of heroin, morphine, or codeine. Fully synthetic opioids such as methadone, meperidine, diphenoxylate, and propoxyphene are poorly shown by these methods; however, separate EMIT assays are available for methadone and propoxyphene. FPIA can detect meperidine to a greater degree than the other assays. Various designer drugs, such as the fentanyl analogues, are not recognized at all with these assays, making them the perfect drugs for people to abuse when they are on parole or on probation.

Various related compounds cross-react with this assay. Ethylmorphine and pholcodine are used as cough remedies in Europe; both cross-react with EMIT and RIA and may give positive urine results for up to 40 days.[14] Dextromethorphan, a nonnarcotic, nonprescription cough suppressant, may also give false-positive results.

## ——— BARBITURATES

Barbiturates are central nervous system depressants. They are used therapeutically as sedatives, hypnotics, and anticonvulsants. Although the legal availability of these drugs has diminished, they are still frequently abused. In the parlance of the street culture, barbiturates are known as "goofballs" or "downs." The different types are referred to by their color; so that pentobarbital capsules are known as "yellow jackets," secobarbital as "red devils," phenobarbitol as "purple hearts," and amobarbital as "blue angels."

Barbiturates are almost always taken orally as capsules or tablets in doses of 50 to 250 mg. The effects resemble those of intoxication with alcohol. Low doses cause drowsiness, slurred speech, unsteady gait, and a general sluggishness. High doses can cause loss of consciousness, coma, and death. Chronic use of barbiturates, in particular ones whose effects are short-acting, leads to tolerance and physical dependence. It is estimated that the minimal dose of short-acting barbiturates required to produce a clinically significant degree of physical dependence is 400 mg/day taken for 2 to 3 months. Withdrawal symptoms experienced during periods of drug abstinence can be severe enough to cause death.

The most commonly abused drugs in this class are barbiturates with short durations of action, such as secobarbital, pentobarbital, and amobarbital. Secobarbital appears in the urine within 30 to 40 minutes of oral intake. Only a small portion (5%) of the drug is excreted unchanged; therefore, urinary concentrations of the drug are low (0.5 to 5.0 mg/L) during the first day. When large and potentially fatal overdoses are taken, secobarbital urine concentrations may reach 5 to 50 mg/L.[15] Barbiturates are stable in urine; preservatives are not necessary for testing done within 7 days of collection. Excretion patterns are not influenced by urinary pH.[16]

The RIA and EMIT methods detect primarily secobarbital; RIA is the more sensitive of the two techniques. EMIT testing can detect secobarbital and cyclobarbital (not available in the U.S.) during a 3 to 30-hour period after ingestion; however, amobarbital, butethal, and pentobarbital are not reliably identified. In contrast, with RIA one can detect all five of the above barbiturates for up to 72 hours.[17] Smaller drug doses (50 to 100 mg) are largely undetected with EMIT but test positive with RIA. Phenobarbital taken in a moderate dose (250 to 325 mg) can be detected in the urine by both methods for up to 9 days. Thus epileptic patients taking phenobarbital as an anticonvulsant would be expected to test positive with these assays.

The immunoassays exhibit no significant cross-reactivities with non-barbiturate analogues. Therefore, these assays primarily detect substances resulting from active drug use.

# ——— PHENCYCLIDINE

Phencyclidine (1-phenylcyclohexyl piperidine), also known as PCP, is a hallucinogen which was first marketed as a surgical anesthetic in the 1950s. It was removed from the market because patients receiving it became delirious and experienced hallucinations. It reappeared as a veterinary anesthetic in the late 1960s and soon thereafter was discovered as a drug of abuse. Its presence in the community has been difficult to control; according to some sources, up to one third of youths in drug treatment programs have tried the drug. One of the reasons for the wide availability of this drug is that it can be inexpensively and easily synthesized by amateur chemists in an underground laboratory.

Phencyclidine is used in powder, capsule, and tablet form. The powder is either snorted or smoked after mixing it with marijuana or vegetable matter such as parsley or oregano. Tablets and capsules are ingested. The powder form of phencyclidine is known as "angel dust"; the tablets or capsules are known as "peace pills," "hogs," and "elephant tranquilizers." Drug combined with organic matter is called "superjoint" and "rocket fuel." Like many other "street" drugs, the purity of phencyclidine varies. It is often misrepresented to the purchaser, usually as marijuana, cocaine, or LSD. A variety of PCP analogues, including cyclohexamine (PCE), phenylcyclopentylpiperidine (PCPP), phenylcyclohexylpyrrolidine (PCPy), and thienylcyclohexylpiperidine (TCP), cause a similar effect and are available on the street.[18]

Phencyclidine is most commonly administered by inhalation but can also be used intravenously, intranasally, and orally. Doses range from 1 to 3 mg for intranasal and intravenous use to 2 to 6 mg for oral use. The clinical effects of phencyclidine are dose related, but there are marked variations in response that are often bizarre and unpredictable in individual users. After low doses, the user thinks and acts swiftly and experiences mood swings from euphoria to depression. Visual hallucinations may occur. With larger doses, mood changes are totally unpredictable; a sense of unreality predominates, and irrational and violent actions may occur. Self-injurious behavior is one of the devastating effects of this drug; trauma is one of the leading causes of death from PCP intoxication.[19] In some patients, phencyclidine causes acute schizophrenic psychosis.

The plasma half-life of PCP varies significantly with dosage. Typically, it ranges between 7 and 16 hours, though it may last as long as 1 to 4 days in victims of overdosage. The drug accumulates in fat with repeated use, thus the plasma half-life may be longer in obese users. Though the excretion of PCP in the urine begins within 20 to 30 minutes after a dose, the rate of elimination depends upon the urine pH. Little drug is excreted under alkaline conditions, and test results may alternate between positive and negative as urine pH fluctuates.[20] Thus, it may be useful to assess urine pH before concluding that a negative result is valid. PCP is excreted in the urine as unchanged drug (4% to 19%) and conjugated metabolites (25% to 30%); up to 77% of a dose is found in urine and feces after 10 days.[21] Generally, the concentration of unchanged PCP in the urine is lower in ambulatory patients (0.04 to 3.4 mg/L) than it is in intoxicated ones (0.4 to 340.0 mg/L). Neither plasma nor urine PCP levels are useful in predicting the level of impairment caused by this drug.[22] PCP can usually be detected in the urine for 7 to 8 days after drug administration, though in chronic users levels may persist for 2 to 4 weeks. Because PCP is stable, chemical preservatives in specimens are not necessary.

Immunoassays are directed at detecting phencyclidine itself; their limit is 0.025 mg/L (RIA) to 0.15 mg/L (EMIT). The immunoassays are relatively specific for PCP and its metabolites, though cross-reactivity has been reported with thioridazine.[23] The pesticide parathion may cause a false-negative result with EMIT.[24] Gas chromatography has yielded false-positive results with diphenhydramine and doxylamine, antihistamines present in over-the-counter cold remedies.

## ⸻ BENZODIAZEPINES

The benzodiazepines are a group of structurally related central nervous system depressants used as sedative hypnotics. They include drugs that have ultrashort, short, intermediate, and long durations of action. The most popular of these are diazepam and flurazepam. Because benzodiazepines are among the most frequently prescribed drugs, there are many available for resale and abuse. Some of their popularity can be attributed to their wide margin of safety in dosing; pure benzodiazepine overdose is rarely, if ever, fatal.[25] However, if they are used in combination with alcohol (which promotes absorption) or other central nervous system (CNS) depressants, death can occur.

When taken in low doses, benzodiazepines cause sedation, drowsiness, blurred vision, fatigue, mental depression, and loss of coordination. In higher doses or with continued use, the drugs may cause confusion, somnolence, slurred speech, hypotension, and diminished reflexes. Chronic benzodiazepine use may produce physical dependence and a withdrawal syndrome in some patients which starts between 5 and 8 days after discontinuing use and lasts for weeks. This delayed onset is related to the long half-life of the drug (up to 90 hr) in some people. Withdrawal may range from minor symptoms such as insomnia and irritability to more severe manifestations such as delirium and convulsions.[26]

When taken for therapeutic purposes, benzodiazepines are administered orally or by intravenous or intramuscular routes. Abusers of the drug ingest only capsules or tablets. A typical dose may vary widely, from less than 1 mg to 200 mg, depending on the potency of the particular drug within this class.

Only trace amounts (less than 1%) of most benzodiazepines are excreted unaltered in the urine; most of the concentration in urine is conjugated drug.[27] The EMIT immunoassay is directed at detecting oxazepam, a urinary metabolite that is common to at least eight drugs in this class. It is believed that the EMIT antibody also reacts with oxazepam glucuronide, the conjugated form of this metabolite, since the level of free drug alone in urine would not be sufficient to cause a positive result. Unfortunately, the assay may not detect flurazepam, one of the more common drugs in this class. Flurazepam is excreted predominantly as conjugated hydroxyethylflurazepam (29% to 55%) and conjugated 3-hydroxydesalkylflurazepam (1% to 2%). The former compound is poorly detected with the assay; and the latter, though easily detected, may be in too low a concentration to give positive results.[28]

The EMIT assay is relatively specific for benzodiazepines, though it does cross-react with clidinium bromide. This may cause false-positive results in patients taking this anticholinergic drug to treat peptic ulcer, though this is unlikely given the low dose generally taken.[29]

EMIT has a detection limit of about 0.5 mg/L. This will generally give a negative result in individuals taking a single 10-mg dose of diazepam, a long-acting drug. However, when the same dose is taken for 5 consecutive days, positive results will most likely occur by day 3 or 4 and last for 5 to 7 days after the last dose.[30]

In contrast to EMIT, the RIA and FPIA for benzodiazepines is directed at nordiazepam. It has greater cross-reactivity for hydroxyethylflurazepam and, therefore, should be a more sensitive assay than EMIT for detecting flurazepam use.

Chlordiazepoxide, clonazepam, demoxepam, norchlordiazepoxide, and nordiazepam degrade rapidly when left at room temperature for several days. Diazepam, flurazepam, and desalkylflurazepam are stable. Specimens that cannot be analyzed immediately should be frozen or refrigerated; sodium fluoride alone may not adequately preserve specimens.[31]

# ——— METHAQUALONE

Methaqualone is a sedative hypnotic that was originally introduced as an alternative to the barbiturates. Its potential for abuse became quickly apparent. Though commercial sales were discontinued in 1983, the drug continues to be available through illicit channels. On the street, methaqualone is known as Quaalude (one of the former brand names), or just plain "ludes." One European preparation incorporating diphenhydramine is called Mandrax or "Mandrakes."

A typical methaqualone dose is 100 to 400 mg and is taken orally. The drug produces a loss of inhibitions, reduced awareness of one's actions, and a relatively long state of euphoria, drowsiness, and sedation. It is considered an aphrodisiac by some. When taken in combination with other sedatives or alcohol, methaqualone can cause respiratory arrest. Chronic users can develop physical dependence and a withdrawal syndrome which begins 12 to 24 hours after the last dose. Withdrawal may be very severe and may include seizures and hallucinations.[32]

The long-lived effect of methaqualone is due to its plasma half-life which averages about 35 hours and can be as long as 60 hours. Most of the drug is metabolized into pharmacologically inactive substances which are eliminated in urine as glucuronide conjugates. The drug may appear in the urine within 20 minutes of ingestion. The presence of the drug in the urine generally peaks within 8 hours and may continue for days. A typical dose is excreted in the urine as methaqualone (0.2%), methaqualone-N-oxide (6.6%), conjugated 4'-hydroxymethaqualone (10.3%), conjugated 2'-hydroxymethylmethaqualone (4.7%), conjugated 3'-hydroxymethaqualone (3.5%), conjugated 2-hydroxymethylmethaqualone (2.8%), and conjugated 6-hydroxymethaqualone (2.8%).[33] Urine concentrations of methaqualone usually do not exceed 0.2 mg/L; however, total concentrations of the metabolites range from 0.8 to 32.0 mg/L.

The EMIT and RIA assays are directed toward methaqualone; however, they will also detect the main metabolites. Since methaqualone is present in such small concentrations in the urine, it is probably the cross-reactivity with metabolites that is often responsible for positive results. Both assays can detect methaqualone at a concentration of 0.75 mg/L. When tested by RIA, urine drug concentrations reach a peak of 55 mg/L during the first hour and fall to a level of 1.6 mg/L over 4 to 5 days.[34] Urine can therefore test positive for up to 10 days after methaqualone use. Other psychoactive drugs have not demonstrated significant cross-reactivity with RIA and EMIT assays for methaqualone.

# —— LYSERGIC ACID DIETHYLAMIDE

Lysergic acid diethylamide (LSD) is a hallucinogen first prepared synthetically in 1938. Its psychological effects were discovered after accidental ingestion. Popularized in the late 1960s, it is being replaced on the street predominantly by PCP.

LSD or "acid" is administered by oral and nasal routes. It is ingested in the form of tablets, powder, sugar cubes, or "blotters" or postage stamps impregnated with liquid LSD. Clinical symptoms can occur with a dose as small as 30μg.

LSD is usually abused in order to have a unique experience; this is known as "tripping." Several weeks or months often separate the trips. "Flashbacks," spontaneous recurrences of the trip, may occur for months after LSD is taken. These usually diminish in frequency with time. LSD is not associated with physical or psychological dependence.

Symptoms usually begin 20 to 80 minutes after ingestion and usually last 6 to 8 hours. A variety of physiological changes, such as increased blood pressure and heart and breathing rate, occur. The most prominent effect is the change in sensory perception. Perceptions of size and distance are distorted, time sense is lost, and visual images and hallucinations appear to move kaleidoscopically. There may also be a sense of depersonalization and difficulty in distinguishing "self" from "nonself." Use of the drug contributes to fatalities and trauma, such as when the user jumps out of a window in order to "fly."

The plasma half-life of LSD is about 3 hours;[35] most of the drug is eliminated during the first day. It is extensively metabolized, and only a negligible amount of unchanged drug appears in urine. At present, RIA is the only immunoassay available for detecting LSD. It has a detection limit of 0.0005 mg/L. The assay can detect drug or its closely related metabolite(s) for several days after its use.[36] There is no significant cross-reactivity with other substances that might cause false-positive results.

# —— CANNABIS (MARIJUANA)

Marijuana is derived from the hemp plant, *Cannabis sativa*. All portions of the plant contain psychoactive substances called cannabinoids; however, the highest concentrations occur in the flowering tops and the lowest in the seeds. Various preparations are made from the plant. The term "marijuana" refers to the entire chopped and dried plant. The more potent "hashish" is the dried resinous exudate of the flowering tops. Marijuana is known by many names including "pot," "grass," "weed," "joint," "reefer," and "Mary Jane."

Marijuana is the most commonly used illegal substance in the United States. It is estimated that a minimum of 50 million people have tried it at least once, and 18 million are current users.[37] Surveys have shown that 8% to 20% of junior high school students and 40% of high school students have used marijuana, many of them regularly.[38] Thus, the majority of users are adolescents and young adults.

The predominant psychoactive substance in marijuana is delta-9-tetra-hydrocannabinol (THC). It is present in the plant from trace amounts to 10% by weight. A typical "joint" contains about 500 mg of marijuana, of which 1% is THC. About 50% of this (2.5 mg) is bioavailable. In contrast, the more potent hashish is 5% to 15% THC and cannabis oil is 11% to 28% THC.

Marijuana is usually abused by smoking or oral ingestion. It causes an experience that varies not only with dose but also with the personality of the user, the user's expectations from the drug, and various environmental and social factors. Low doses cause euphoria, passivity, relaxation, and increased auditory and visual perceptions. Moderate doses produce a more intense effect and may impair short-term memory, diminish learning ability, and cause thought disturbances and attention lapses. Large doses are associated with disorientation, depersonalization, paranoia, and even delirium or hallucinations. Physical changes include bloodshot eyes and increased heart rate; the latter may increase by 20 to 50 beats per minute after 1 or 2 "joints." When marijuana is taken in conjunction with alcohol, the effects of the drug are markedly amplified. Whether chronic marijuana use causes physical dependence is still controversial.[39]

Considerable interest has been generated about the long-term effects of marijuana. Current evidence suggests that continued marijuana use during adolescence may be associated with significant behavioral, social, and academic problems; this has been called the "amotivational syndrome." It is manifested by energy loss, diminished attentiveness at school, academic underachievement, and damaged relations with parents. The existence of this syndrome is a matter of controversy.[40] The high content of carcinogens in marijuana smoke and the long retention time after inhalation may contribute to the development of lung cancer.

When marijuana is inhaled, a clinical effect occurs within seconds or minutes, reaches a peak at 10 to 30 minutes and subsides by 2 to 6 hours. In contrast, when marijuana is ingested, the effects begin at 30 to 60 minutes, peak at 2 to 4 hours, and may persist for 8 to 12 hours.[41] After THC enters the blood, it is metabolized to 11-OH-delta-9-tetrahydrocannabinol (11-OH-THC); though this metabolite is also psychoactive, it is present in lower concentration than THC. When marijuana is inhaled, the low levels of 11-OH-THC may be undetectable. In contrast, when it is ingested, 11-OH-THC levels are much higher and may exceed those of the parent drug.

Another nonpsychoactive metabolite, nor-delta-9-tetrahydrocannabinol (THC-COOH), also rapidly appears in the blood, though its concentrations rise more slowly than those of delta-9-THC. After 20 to 30 minutes, the THC-COOH concentration exceeds that of the THC. Thus, an assay of THC-COOH in blood may be useful in determining whether marijuana has been recently smoked; if THC exceeds THC-COOH, marijuana has probably been smoked within the previous 30 minutes. The measurement of THC alone may also be useful in that plasma concentrations of 10 ng/mL, 20 ng/mL, and 50 ng/mL correlate with smoking within the preceding 2 hours, 1 hour, or 20 minutes, respectively. It has been suggested that an arbitrary cutoff of 10 ng/mL may be of value, since any functional impairment is likely to occur at a higher concentration.[42]

The major urinary metabolite detected after using marijuana is THC-COOH, which accounts for about 20% of a dose in a urine specimen taken 72 hours after use. In contrast, unchanged THC is present in only trace amounts, and 11-OH-THC (conjugated) accounts for only a small portion of the initial dose (and hence the amount excreted). The elimination half-life of THC-COOH in urine depends on the plasma THC half-life which averages 20 to 30 hours.

The most common urine screening techniques are RIA and EMIT. RIA can also be used to detect cannabinoids in blood. The detection limits for EMIT-st and RIA are 200 ng/mL and 100 ng/mL, respectively, while that for EMIT-dau is 20 ng/mL (though an optional 100 ng/mL cutoff is available which will eliminate positives due to passive inhalation). Both immunoassays are directed at detecting the major urinary metabolite THC-COOH. Because of cannabinoid cross-reactivity (there is no significant cross-reactivity with substances other than cannabinoids), the results obtained by immunoassay are greater than the actual concentration of THC-COOH. This cross-reactivity enhances the sensitivity of the method. In contrast, a confirmatory technique such as GC/MS is specific for THC, but less sensitive since it does not detect the metabolites. It gives consistently lower readings for a sample than when it is analyzed by immunoassay.[43] Therefore, positive results by EMIT may not be confirmed as such by GC/MS despite the actual presence of drug. The higher detection limit for RIA will yield fewer unconfirmed positives but more false negatives than the EMIT-dau assay using a 20 ng/mL cutoff.[44]

THC-COOH and metabolites can be detected in the urine at a concentration of greater than 20 ng/mL within 1 hour after smoking and somewhat longer after ingesting marijuana. Infrequent users usually have detectable levels for 2 to 5 days, and sometimes as long as 10 days after smoking.[45] However, this duration will vary according to the immunoassay that is used. For instance, in one study of six subjects who each smoked two marijuana cigarettes in a 2-hour period, all had urine concentrations of greater than 75 ng/mL during the first day. Though concentrations of greater than 20 ng/mL (EMIT-dau limit) continued to be present for several days, many of these subjects would not have tested positive by RIA or EMIT-st since these assays have higher detection limits.[46]

Heavy, chronic marijuana smokers may consistently test positive by EMIT for nearly 7 weeks (average about 4 weeks) after the last use, and it can take as long as 11 weeks before their test results drop below the cutoff to show negative results for 10 consecutive days. Users can also have one or more sequences of negative cannabinoid urine test results followed by a positive result.[47] This is because THC is lipophilic and is stored in the adipose tissue of chronic smokers.[48] It is gradually released back to the bloodstream where it is metabolized to compounds such as THC-COOH and eliminated in the urine.

Passive exposure to marijuana smoke can result in a positive urine test. However, the circumstances required are so extreme that this is highly improbable. Subjects exposed to smoke for 1 hour on each of 3 consecutive days do not generally have detectable levels (greater than 20 ng/mL) by EMIT-dau during the 24 hours after exposure, and are almost certain to have negative results if a method with a higher detection limit is used. With intense 2 hour passive exposure, urine levels reached as high as 60 to 70 ng/mL by EMIT and remained positive for 2 to 3 days.[49]

Though blood levels of cannabinoids are likely to correlate with a person's degree of exposure, urinary concentrations cannot be related to the level of impairment because of the many factors that affect metabolism of cannabinoids. A true positive test means only that the subject used marijuana at some time in the past, eg, hours, days, or weeks earlier. Potential interference between ibuprofen, naproxen, and fenoprofen and the EMIT cannabinoid assay using the enzyme malate dehydrogenase (MDH) has been reported. A reformulation has been developed to eliminate this problem.

Adulterants added to the urine specimen may cause false-negative EMIT results. These include acids such as lemon juice or vinegar, alkali such as chlorine bleach, or sodium chloride. A very dilute urine specimen will also cause a false-negative result, since the concentration of THC-COOH will be lower than the detectable limit. Dilution is often accomplished by adding water to a urine specimen or by drinking enormous volumes of liquid before testing. If an anticipated positive specimen does not test positive, the urine pH and specific gravity should be checked. Last, cannabinoids will degrade over time, even when stored frozen. They may lose up to 97% of their value over 3 months as determined by EMIT.[51]

# —— ALCOHOL

Perhaps the most common and most serious drug problem in the United States is due to the abuse of a legal substance, alcohol (ethyl alcohol). The costs associated with alcohol abuse are estimated at $30 to $40 billion annually when related accidents, crime, damage to health, and loss of productivity are considered. As many as 95 million people drink alcohol, and 9 million of these are classified as chronic abusers. Alcohol abuse has been involved in more than 50% of all fatalities caused by automobile accidents.[52]

Ethanol is contained in a variety of beverages: beer (4% to 6%), wine (4.5% to 12%), champagne (14% to 20%), and whiskey (40% to 55%).[53] Proof refers to twice the percent of ethanol content (ie, 80 proof whiskey is 40% ethanol). One ounce of whiskey contains about the same amount of ethanol as one bottle of beer or 4 oz. of wine.

The effects of alcohol are well known; it is a central nervous system depressant and anesthetic. Initially, the user loses inhibitions. This is followed by loss of judgment, personality change, memory impairment, and loss of coordination. Additional intake can lead to stupor and ultimately to coma and death.

The concentration of blood alcohol can be correlated with the amount ingested and its influence on the subject. Generally, a single shot of whiskey (1 oz) will yield a blood ethanol level of about 25 to 35 mg/dL. At 100 mg/dL, a driver is legally considered under the influence of alcohol, and at 150 mg/dL most people appear intoxicated. Blood levels of 250 to 400 mg/dL (achieved after drinking 10 to 15 oz of whiskey) can cause coma or death. These levels only apply to acutely ingested alcohol; chronic abusers can tolerate much higher concentrations since they can metabolize alcohol twice as quickly.

After ingestion, ethanol is absorbed in the stomach and reaches a peak concentration in 40 to 70 minutes. This is prolonged by 1 to 2 hours when eating precedes intake. Only 10% of ingested alcohol is excreted in urine, sweat, and breath. Most is metabolized in the liver, usually at a rate of 7 to 10 g of ethanol per hour (equivalent to 2/3 to 1 ounce of 90 proof liquor, 8 to 12 oz of beer, or 3 to 4 oz of wine) in a 70 kg person.

When an alcohol assay is performed for medicolegal purposes, a blood specimen is required because the blood drug level correlates well with the clinical effect of the drug. The puncture site must be cleaned with a nonalcoholic solution, in order to avoid an artifactual raised blood level. After collection, the specimen must be tightly stoppered to avoid loss of volatile constituents. There is a constant relationship between blood and urine alcohol; an average urine to blood ratio was found to be 1.35.[54] If the peak blood level has been passed and the subject has voided in the preceding 30 minutes, the urine concentration may be useful in predicting the blood level. In Europe, urine ethanol levels are sometimes accepted as legal evidence. Meaningful ethanol concentrations can also be obtained from saliva.

Serum ethanol is easily determined using a variety of clinical analyzers; however, gas chromatography is considered by many to be the preferred method. Breath analysis is a portable method used in some areas. The method may indicate falsely elevated levels when ingested alcohol remains in the mouth or when it is vomited. Some drug users may rinse their mouths with alcohol in an attempt to convince authorities that the cause of their intoxication is alcohol, thus avoiding more serious charges.

# —— COCAINE

Cocaine is one of the most frequently abused drugs in the United States. It is estimated that 30 million people have used it, and 5 million use it regularly.[55] By some accounts, 5,000 Americans each day try cocaine for the first time. Once considered a drug of the wealthy, the "champagne of drugs," cocaine is now used by all strata of society. The typical cocaine user is a young adult age 18 to 25 who earns a higher-than-average income and is often a professional.[56] The incidence of adolescent cocaine abuse has also increased at a rate faster than the abuse of any other drug, despite a stabilization in alcohol use and a drop in the use of marijuana.[57]

The increasing popularity of cocaine is probably due to a number of factors. It has an almost instantaneous onset of action, brief duration (very short half-life), and is believed to be a relatively benign, nonaddicting substance with few side effects. Relative to its frequency of use, there are fewer emergency room visits caused by use of cocaine than by other psychoactive drugs. Cocaine has a reputation for enhancing social interaction, can be used inconspicuously at gatherings, and is often an accepted form of drug use, as reflected by the open marketing of cocaine paraphernalia. In recent years, cocaine has become less expensive, and its availability and purity have increased.

Most of the cocaine entering the United States comes from either Colombia or Peru, where Indians have chewed coca leaves for centuries. Cocaine is an alkaloid extracted from the leaves of the *Erythroxylon coca* shrub. Cocaine hydrochloride is prepared by dissolving the alkaloid in hydrochloric acid to form a water soluble salt.[58] This fine-to-coarse white crystalline powder is known on the street as "coke," "snow," "blow," and "toot." It is slightly bitter and numbs the tongue and lips. In contrast, the cocaine alkaloid ("free base") is a colorless, odorless, transparent crystalline substance that is insoluble in water. Unlike cocaine hydrochloride, the alkaloid does not decompose when heated and can therefore be smoked. Many cocaine users prepare their own free base. The most common method uses baking soda dissolved in water, though a solvent extraction can also be performed.[59] Cocaine free base is called "crack" because of the popping sound made by the crystals when they are heated.[60] Crack has been gaining increasing popularity; it is smoked as a cigarette or heated in a water pipe and inhaled. It is almost pure cocaine. A variety of free base called "rock" has surfaced in California.[61] The widespread use of crack is probably due to increased availability and lower cocaine prices, which make it profitable to convert cocaine hydrochloride back to the original alkaloid.

Cocaine is usually sold in envelopes containing 250 mg of impure drug for about $25. The purity of street cocaine may vary from 25% to 90%, and may be as low as 5%. Substances used to adulterate cocaine are usually stimulants (amphetamines, PCP), anesthetics (lidocaine, benzocaine), or talc.[62] The first two compounds mimic the action of cocaine.

Cocaine is usually administered intranasally by "snorting," though it can also be smoked; injected subcutaneously or intravenously; or taken by oral, sublingual, vaginal, or rectal routes. Approximately 10% to 25% of users administer cocaine intravenously, often in combination with heroin (in which case it is called a "speedball"), morphine, or pentazocine. Most recreational users administer between 1 to 3 g of cocaine per week, with single doses ranging from 10 to 120 mg. A typical dose of 16 to 20 mg will cause central nervous system stimulation characterized by euphoria, overalertness, and a sense of overconfidence that encourages the user to take risks. The euphoric state lasts for about 20 minutes when cocaine is smoked, and for 1 to 1.5 hours after nasal administration. For this reason, additional doses must be taken frequently in order to maintain the euphoric state. Acute physical tolerance may develop after a second dose of cocaine and is manifested by a drug effect which diminishes more rapidly than would otherwise be expected, based upon the plasma drug level.[63] When taken in very large doses, cocaine can cause paranoid schizophrenic-like manifestations and convulsions; the latter may occur unexpectedly and lead to cardiac arrest. Sudden death has been reported in smugglers who place cocaine in a packet and swallow it. If the packet ruptures, a massive amount of the drug is absorbed into the gastrointestinal tract.[64] Another side effect found in chronic nasal users is a persistent "cold" secondary to the effects of cocaine on the nasal mucosa and septum.

Physical dependence has not been clearly demonstrated with cocaine. However, a psychological dependence does occur wherein users develop a compulsive need to acquire and administer the drug, even at the expense of all other activities.

Cocaine remains in the plasma for a very short period; its biologic half-life is estimated at 0.7 to 1.5 hours, with drug levels peaking within 15 to 30 minutes and persisting for 4 to 6 hours. Cocaine is excreted in the urine in the form of benzoylecgonine (35% to 54%), ecgonine methyl ester (32% to 49%), and ecgonine; all are considered pharmacologically inactive metabolites. Very little unchanged cocaine (1% to 9%) is excreted in urine; the extent to which it is eliminated is determined by urine pH.[65]

All three immunoassays used for cocaine detection are directed against the urinary metabolite benzoylecgonine. The EMIT-dau will give positive results for about 2 days after cocaine administration; the EMIT-st and RIA methods can give similar results for a slightly longer period (2.5 days). Specimens become positive at about 1 to 4 hours after use.[66]

False-positive results due to clinically significant concentrations of compounds structurally unrelated to benzoylecgonine are usually not encountered with any of the immunoassay methods. However, some herbal teas imported from South America may contain coca leaf in sufficient quantity to give positive results by immunoassay even though the tea drinkers do not become intoxicated.[67] This may be of particular interest to people in cocaine clinics who are under court order to stay off the drug. Screening techniques such as TLC require a higher concentration of the metabolite and therefore might give negative results under the same circumstance.

Last, 50% to 70% of urinary cocaine will degrade to benzoylecgonine over a 3-week period when the urine pH is 8, even if the sample is refrigerated and preserved with sodium fluoride.[68] Since the EMIT and FPIA methods detect predominantly benzoylecgonine and not cocaine, increasingly higher results would be expected when the sample is tested over time. This would not be expected with RIA, since the method identifies both cocaine and benzoylecgonine. The problem can be avoided by storing samples at pH 5.

## ——— NOTES

1. P.S. Jordan, *CNS Stimulants Sold as Amphetamines*, 38 AM. J. HOSP. PHARM. 29 (1981).

2. R.C. BASELT, DISPOSITION OF TOXIC DRUGS AND CHEMICALS IN MAN. (2nd ed.) (Biomedical Publications, 1982).

3. R.C. Baselt, *Urine Drug Screening by Immunoassay: Interpretation of Results.* In R.C. BASELT (ED.), ADVANCES IN ANALYTICAL TOXICOLOGY, Vol. 1, 81–123 (Biomedical Publications, 1984).

4. W.R. Martin, *Dependence on Narcotic Analgesics.* In S.N. PRADHAM AND S.N. DUTTA (EDS) DRUG ABUSE: CLINICAL AND BASIC ASPECTS, at 201 (C.V. Mosby, 1977).

5. E.J. Khantzian, G.J. McKenna, *Acute Toxicity and Withdrawal Reactions Associated with Drug Use and Abuse*, 90 ANN. INTERN. MED. 361–372 (1979).

6. J. Buchanan, *Opioids of Abuse-1985.* CLIN. TOXICOL. Update (from the San Francisco Bay Area Regional Poison Center), Vol. 7, (1985).

7. E.J. Simon, *Recent Developments in the Biology of Opiates: Possible Relevance to Addiction.* In J.H. LOWINSON AND P. RUIZ (EDS) SUBSTANCE ABUSE: CLINICAL PROBLEMS AND PERSPECTIVES, 44–56 (Williams and Wilkins, 1981).

8. S.Y. Yeh, C.W. Gorodetzky, R.L. McQuinn, *Urinary Excretion of Heroin and its Metabolites in Man*, 196 J. PHARMACOL. EXP. THER. 249–256 (1976).

9. H.W. Elliott, K.D. Parker, J.A. Wright, *et al., Actions and Metabolism of Heroin Administered by Continuous Intravenous Infusion to Man*, 12 CLIN. PHARMACOL. THER. 806–814 (1971).

10. BASELT, 1982, *supra* at note 2.

11. B.L. Posey, S.N. Kimble, *High Performance Liquid Chromatographic Study of Codeine, Norcodeine, and Morphine as Indicators of Codeine Ingestion*, 8 J. ANAL. TOXICOL. 68–74 (1984).

12. M.C. Dutt, D.S. Lo, D.L. Ng, S.O. Woo, *Gas Chromatographic Study of the Urinary Codeine-to-Morphine Ratios in Controlled Codeine Consumption and in Mass Screening for Opiate Drugs*, 267(1) J. CHROMATOGR. 117–124 (1983).

13. K. Bjerver, A. Jonsson, A. Nilsson, *et al., Morphine Intake from Poppy Seed Food*, 34 J. PHARM. PHARMACOL. 798–801 (1982).

14. G. Svenneby, E. Wedege, R.L. Karlsen, *Pholcodine Interference in Immunoassay for Opiates in Urine*, 21 FORENSIC SCI. INT. 223–226 (1983).

15. BASELT, 1982, *supra* at note 2.

16. L.O. Boreus, B. Jalling, N. Kallberg, *Phenobarbital Metabolism in Adults and in Newborn Infants*, 67 ACTA PAEDIATR. SCAND. 193–200 (1978).

17. B. Law, A.C. Moffat, *The Evaluation of an Homogeneous Enzyme Immunoassay (EMIT) and Radioimmunoassay for Barbiturates*, 21 J. FORENSIC SCI. SOC. 55–66 (1981).

18. BASELT, 1982, *supra* at note 2.

19. R.D. Budd, D.M. Lindstrom, *Characteristics of Victims of PCP-Related Deaths in Los Angeles County*, 19 J. TOXICOL. CLIN. TOXICOL. 997–1004 (1982–1983).

20. A.M. Khajawall, G.M. Simpson, *Peculiarities of Phencyclidine Urinary Excretion and Monitoring*, 19 J. TOXICOL. CLIN. TOXICOL. 835–842 (1983).

21. Baselt, 1984, *supra* at note 3.

22. BASELT, 1982, *supra* at note 2.

23. C.B. Walberg, R.C. Gupta, *Quantitation of Phencyclidine in Urine by Enzyme Immunoassay*, 6 J. ANAL. TOXICOL. 97–99 (1982).

24. V.R. Giblin, S.A. Hite, M.S. Samuels, F.A. Ragan, Jr., *p-Nitrophenol Interferes with EMIT Phencyclidine Urine Assay*, 7 J. ANAL. TOXICOL. 297 (1983).

25. D. J. Greenblatt, M.D. Allen, B.J. Noel, *et al.*, *Acute Overdosage with Benzodiazepine Derivatives*, 21 CLIN. PHARMACOL. THER. 497–514 (1977).

26. C.S. Mellor, V.K. Jain, *Diazepam Withdrawal Syndrome: Its Prolonged and Changing Nature*, 127 CAN. MED. ASSOC. J. 1093–1096 (1982).

27. U.R. Tjaden, M.T.H.A. Meeles, C.P. Thys, M. Van Der Kaay, *Determination of Some Benzodiazepines and Metabolites in Serum, Urine, and Saliva by High-Performance Liquid Chromatography*, 181 J. CHROMATOGR. 227–241 (1980).

28. Baselt, 184, *supra* at note 3.

29. *Id.*

30. K. Vereby, D. Jukofsky, S.J. Mule, *Confirmation of EMIT Benzodiazepine Assay with GLC/NPD*, 6 J. ANAL. TOXICOL. 305–308 (1982).

31. B. Levine, R.V. Blanke, J.C. Valentour, *Postmortem Stability of Benzodiazepines in Blood and Tissues*, 28 J. FORENSIC SCI. 102–115 (183).

32. D.R. Wesson, D.E. Smith, *Abuse of Sedative-Hypnotics*. In J.H. LOWINSON AND P. RUIZ (EDS) SUBSTANCE ABUSE: CLINICAL PROBLEMS AND PERSPECTIVES, 140–147 (Williams & Wilkins, 1981).

33. Baselt, 1984, *supra* at note 3.

34. R. Cleeland, M. Christenson, Usategui-Gomez, *et al.*, *Detection of Drugs of Abuse by Radioimmunoassay: A Summary of Published Data and Some New Information*, 22 CLIN. CHEM. 712–725 (1976).

35. G.K. Aghanjanian, D.H.L. Bing, *Persistence of Lysergic Acid Diethylamide in the Plasma of Human Subjects*, 5 CLIN. PHARMACOL. THER. 611–614 (1964).

36. H.W. Peel, A.L. Boynton, *Analysis of LSD in Urine Using Radioimmunoassay-Excretion and Storage Effects*, 13 CAN. SOC. FORENSIC SCI. 23 (1980).

37. National Institute on Drug Abuse, National Household Survey on Drug Abuse (1985).

38. Council on Scientific Affairs (AMA), *Marijuana: Its Health Hazards and Therapeutic Potentials*, 246 JAMA 1823–1827 (1981).

39. L.H. Hollister, *Health Aspects of Cannabis*, 38 PHARMACOL. REV. 1–20 (1986).

40. A. Kulberg, *Substance Abuse: Clinical Identification and Management*, 33(2) PEDIATRIC TOXICOLOGY, PEDIATR. CLIN. NORTH AM. 325–361 (1986).

41. Baselt, 1984, *supra* at note 3.

42. A.J. McBay, *Cannabinoid Testing: Forensic and Analytical Aspects*, LABORATORY MANAGEMENT (January 1985).

43. M.A. Peat, *The Analysis of Delta-9-Tetrahydrocannabinol and its Metabolites by Immunoassay*. In R.C. BASELT (ED) ADVANCES IN ANALYTICAL TOXICOLOGY, Vol. 1 (Biomedical Publications, 1984).

44. J. Irving, B. Leeb, R.L. Foltz, *et al.*, *Evaluation of Immunoassays for Cannabinoids in Urine*, 8 J. ANAL. TOXICOL. 192–196 (1984).

45. R.H. Schwartz, R.L. Hawks, *Laboratory Detection of Marijuana Use*, 254 JAMA 788–792 (1985).

46. Baselt, 1984, *supra* at note 3.

47. G.M. Ellis, Jr., M.A. Mann, B.A. Judson, *et al.*, *Excretion Patterns of Cannabinoid Metabolites After Last Use in a Group of Chronic Users*, 38 CLIN. PHARMACOL. THER. 572–578 (1985).

48. D.S. Kreuz, J. Axelrod, *Delta-9-Tetrahydrocannabinol Localization in Body Fat*, 179 SCIENCE 391–393 (1973).

49. G.A.W. Waterhouse, P.J.C. Pence, R.B. Forney, *Positive Urine Cannabinoid Levels Produced in Individuals Passively Exposed to Marijuana Smoke*. Abstract K27 (Toxicology Section). Abstracts of the 35th Annual Meeting of the American Academy of Forensic Sciences, Cincinnati (February 15–19 1983).

50. *Syva Customer Bulletin* (April 1986).

51. J.E. O'Connor, T.A. Rejent, *EMIT Cannabinoid Assay: Confirmation of RIA and GC/MS*, 5 J. ANAL. TOXICOL. 168–173 (1981).

52. J.C. Garriott, V.J.M. Di Maio, R.E. Zumwalt, *et al.*, *Incidence of Drugs and Alcohol in Fatally Injured Motor Vehicle Drivers*, 22 J. FORENSIC SCI. 383–389 (1977).

53. J.C. Garriott, *Forensic Aspects of Ethyl Alcohol*, FORENSIC PATHOLOGY, 3(2) CLIN. LAB. MED. 385–396 (1985).

54. F. Lundquist, *The Urinary Excretion of Ethanol by Man*. 18 ACTA PHARMACOL. Toxicol. 231 (1961).

55. H.I. Abelson, J.D. Miller, *A Decade of Trends in Cocaine Use in the Household Population*, 61 NATL. INST. DRUG ABUSE RES. MONOGR. SER. 35–49 (1985).

56. R.E. Mittleman, C.V. Wetli, *Death Caused by Recreational Cocaine Use: An Update*, 252 JAMA 1889–93 (1984).

57. A.M. Washton, M.S. Gold, A.C. Pottash, *et al.*, *Adolescent Cocaine Abusers*, (letter) 2 LANCET 746 (1984).

58. L. L. Cregler, H. Mark, *Special Report: Medical Complications of Cocaine Abuse*, 315(23) N. ENGL. J. MED. 1495–1500 (1986).

59. R.K. Siegel, *Cocaine Smoking*, 14 J. PSYCHOACTIVE DRUGS 271–343 (1982).

60. J.F. Jekel, D.F. Allen, H. Podlewski, *et al.*, *Epidemic Free-Base Cocaine Abuse: Case Study from the Bahamas*, 1 LANCET 459–62 (1986).

61. D.R. Wesson, D.E. Smith, *Cocaine: Treatment Perspectives*, 61 NATL. INST. DRUG. ABUSE RES. MONOGR. SER. 193–203 (1985).

62. Kulberg, 1986, *supra* at note 40.

63. M.J. Chow, J.J. Ambre, T.I. Ruo, *et al.*, *Kinetics of Cocaine Distribution, Elimination, and Chronotropic Effects*, 38(3) CLIN. PHARMACOL. 318–324 (1985).

64. M.M. McCarron, J.D. Wood, *The Cocaine "Body Packer" Syndrome: Diagnosis and Treatment*, 250 JAMA 1417–20 (1983).

65. Baselt, 1984, *supra* at note 3.

66. C. Van Dyke, R. Byck, P.G. Barash, *et al.*, *Urinary Excretion of Immunologically Reactive Metabolite(s) After Intranasal Administration of Cocaine, As Followed by Enzyme Immunoassay*, 23 CLIN. CHEM. 241–244 (1977).

67. R. K. Siegel, M.A. Elsohly, T. Plowman, *et al.*, *Cocaine in Herbal Tea* (letter) 255 JAMA 40 (1986).

68. R. C. Baselt, *Stability of Cocaine in Biological Fluids*, 268 J. CHROMATOGR. 502–505 (1983).

# —5—————————————

# THE EMPLOYER'S DECISION
# TO TEST

## ——— DECIDING WHEN TO TEST

The first issue every employer must address in formulating drug testing policy is: When should employees be required to submit to drug tests? Should the employer test all employees periodically in connection with physical examinations?[1] Should employers test on a purely random basis? Or should testing be confined to cases in which the employer has "cause" to believe an employee is impaired at work? If so, what kind of physical or behavioral evidence is needed?

Such questions are not easy to answer. Asked out of context and without some systematic approach, they can frustrate attempts to formulate a reasonable, efficient testing policy. The decision to test at random depends on the employer's evaluation of the scope of the drug problem at his plant in relationship to the type of operation he runs. Testing at random, once begun, may be fast and effective, but it has implications for workplace relations and legal expenses. On the other hand, testing for cause, which requires attention to the precise facts of a particular case, may have a better chance of surviving legal challenge, and may rid the employer of undesirable employees once and for all. Every option carries with it some obligation to follow procedural requirements. As litigation shows, each choice is loaded with practical and legal consequences, a fact that frustrated employers frequently miss when they hastily adopt someone else's "sample policy." Employers who blindly rely on a sample drug testing policy suggested by, or implemented at, another organization are likely to encounter legal problems and administrative headaches, even though the policy may have survived a legal challenge in the context of another operation. However, there can be a right answer to the questions of whether to test or not to test and how to do so for each employer taking a stand concerning substance abuse and its effect on the workplace.

## The Six Considerations

The question of "when to test" becomes meaningful and manageable when the employer addresses six considerations:

1. Whether the employer is a public entity;

2. Whether the employees to be tested are unionized;

3. Whether the responsibilities of the employees implicate public safety or raise other special considerations:

4. Whether a drug testing program may have an adverse impact on loyal and dedicated employees;

5. Whether there is evidence of an existing drug problem among employees to be tested; and

6. Whether there is any state or local legislation restricting drug testing in the employment context.

**Public versus Private Employees.**     The legal considerations for public and private employers in the drug testing arena are quite different. Because public employees possess important constitutional rights in the employment setting—the right to privacy and the right to be free of unreasonable search and seizure—public employers are faced with additional hurdles that private employers need not overcome. To varying degrees, arbitrators and courts have borrowed Fourth Amendment concepts and recognized that employees have some protectable privacy rights in the workplace.[2] Although the Fourth Amendment itself provides no protection to private employees, except in highly regulated industries (railroads, nuclear power plants, horse racing), unions regularly and insistently use federal Constitutional cases to raise the argument that private employees have privacy rights.[3] Still, while arbitrators have bandied about the "probable cause standard" for permitting searches in the industrial setting, they rarely require the kind of stringent proof required under the Constitution, where most of the precedents were established in the criminal context.[4] Thus, although the boundaries between public and private employees' protected rights may occasionally erode a bit, unionized private employers will likely enjoy more latitude in framing a drug-testing policy than public employers.

Nonunion private employers need not be concerned with Constitutional concepts even being loosely applied, unless they operate in those few states that have adopted an expansive view of the common law cause of action for invasion of privacy. Some state courts have lifted Constitutional privacy and Fourth Amendment doctrine "bag and baggage" from its Constitutional framework and plugged it into state law invasion of privacy law claims. In effect, they have created a remedy for private employees for unreasonable invasion of privacy and searches, which formerly only public employees enjoyed.[5] At this point, however, the common law applicable to drug testing remains in its infancy in most states.

In summary, then, constitutional guarantees give public employees a firmly established weapon with which to combat drug testing that private employees may invoke only by analogy. While private employers need not strictly abide by constitutional restrictions, if private employees' privacy rights are trampled, arbitrators and/or state courts may very well intervene.

**Union versus Nonunion Employees.**    In deciding when to test, unionized employers, whether in the public or private context, face another distinct set of legal hurdles not encountered by nonunion employers, which the collective bargaining agreement imposes upon them. Invariably, unionized employers will be required to establish that the formula for when employees are tested is "reasonable" under the law of the shop, unless they have agreed on a formula with the union in advance. In ruling on the reasonableness of the program, arbitrators will consider all of the surrounding circumstances, including the nature of the employer's operations, the responsibilities of employees to be tested, the safety risk posed by drug abusing employees, the scope of the drug problem among existing employees, fairness concerns, and the oddities of the language in the rules and programs to be applied. Because arbitrators, unlike judges, are not bound by the doctrine of *stare decisis* to follow precedent,[6] the results in the arbitral arena are less predictable than in the courts. While arbitrators are not free to substitute their own "brand of industrial justice" for "the law of the shop,"[7] their own personal views on the use of mind-altering drugs[8] and the volatile civil liberties issues drug testing raises will often creep into their analyses.[9] On the other hand, federal judges, irrespective of their personal views, are bound to set their personal views aside and adhere strictly to constitutional precedents of higher courts, in a drug testing case or any other case.[10]

Because arbitration is the preferred method of resolving disputes arising under a collective bargaining agreement, and the courts and National Labor Relations Board (NLRB) normally defer to arbitration in drug testing cases as they do in other cases, most of the action among unionized employers will take place in the arbitral forum, where there is always a "crap shoot" element. At the moment, the body of arbitral law governing drug testing policies is a tangled web of contradictory and inconsistent precedents, giving the results-oriented arbitrator substantial authority for any policy he wants.

Of course, federal courts may become involved in the drug testing fracas, even in the union context. Unions may seek injunctions in an attempt to block drug testing before it starts, or at least until an arbitrator rules on the subject. The union's burden in an injunction proceeding is far higher than in an arbitral challenge. Because of the strong national labor policy against injunctions in labor disputes, and the statutory restrictions in the Norris-LaGuardia Act, to obtain injunctive relief a union must show *inter alia* that the testing program will cause "irreparable injury" to its members, rendering the arbitral process a meaningless ritual. In other words, the union must show that the traditional relief arbitrators award, back pay and reinstatement, would not adequately remedy the injuries the drug testing program may visit on employees.[11] So far, in the private sector, the courts have generally reserved the extraordinary injunction remedy only for the more invasive forms of drug testing, such as discretionary random testing.[12] Thus, employers of a unionized workforce must look to arbitrators, not courts, to decide whether drug testing is properly undertaken.

Private sector nonunion employers may never be called upon to prove that their drug testing program is reasonable. Private sector nonunionized employees, who have neither the protections offered by a collective bargaining agreement or the U.S. Constitution, or, in some instances, state or municipal laws (*see* Chapter 2, text at notes 54–109) have been grasping at common law privacy doctrines with some success. As a practical matter, however, nonunionized employees in private industry have no legal weapon to oppose the implementation of drug testing, unless applicable state or local legislation restricts drug testing in the employment context. Once such employees are terminated on the basis of test results, however, some remedies are available.[13]

However, if a private employer stops short of terminating employees who fail the test and takes appropriate measures to minimize invasions of employees' privacy rights, its employees have few, if any, legal challenges to the testing per se. This is not to say that private nonunion employers *should* adopt agressive policies allowing drug testing at any time for any reason just because their employees have no ability to stop it. There are other important practical, if not legal, restraints that apply to all employers, such as the impact of a drug testing program on work force morale.

**Employee Morale.** Onerous drug testing programs often have a devastating impact on employee morale. All employees may find it humiliating and demeaning to be required to urinate into a bottle for their employer. They may also perceive a request for a drug test as an act of distrust: instead of assuming employees will come to work in a fit condition, the employer treats them like "sneaky children," requiring them to prove their innocence without evidence of guilt.

Moreover, because it is now well known that drug tests cannot detect impairment on the job, but can only show the presence of drugs in the system, drug tests may be perceived as a surveillance device for snooping into off-duty conduct and intruding into employees' private lives. Many employees feel it is none of the boss' business if they smoke marijuana on Saturday night in their own homes as long as it does not affect their jobs, and they would feel that their privacy had been grossly violated if their habits were disclosed to any other company personnel, even medical personnel. The threat that the employer may regulate what they can and cannot do on their own time may eventually convert loyal and dedicated employees to suspicious and antagonistic employees, or lead them to resign.[14]

**Employees' Job Responsibilities: Safety and Public Image.** The degree of safety risk posed by drug use on the job is clearly an important variable. Is a drug abusing employee a serious threat to himself or others, or is the greatest occupational hazard a possibility of stapling his finger? And whose safety is placed in jeopardy? Jobs implicating the safety of the general public, such as those in the medical professions, public transportation industries, and the military, present the most compelling case for drug testing.[15] Aggressive policies providing for random or periodic testing of employees without cause are most likely to pass muster in this context. Jobs where drug use could pose grave safety hazards to fellow employees, but not to the general public, present the second best case for drug testing. On the other hand, if a drug abusing employee is placing only his own safety in jeopardy, the case for testing without cause is weakened.

Apart from workplace safety, other relevant considerations may include whether drug use (even off-duty) by employees would undermine the public trust and public confidence in the organization. Using testing to detect and deter off-duty drug use may present problems for the employer who seeks to rely on test results to purge a workforce of substance abusers.[16] Particularly in the context of public employment, where the issue of public trust most frequently arises, there must be some balance between the public interest and private constitutional rights. Police officers are a good example of this category. They are charged with enforcing laws banning illegal drug use and may be expected to remain drug-free in compliance with the laws they enforce. Nevertheless, because police officers are public employees, and are therefore entitled to the Fourth Amendment's protection against unreasonable search and seizure, the courts have generally required at least a "reasonable suspicion" that a police officer is using illegal drugs before testing may be required as a condition of employment.[17] Unannounced random testing of police officers has been held unconstitutional.[18]

On the other hand, if drug use among employees would merely undermine the public's confidence in the company's products, an especially rigorous drug testing program would probably not be justified, unless the products are ultrahazardous to the public.[19]

There may be grounds to implement a testing program apart from public safety issues. A company's interest in running a profitable business is also justification for drug testing if there is some evidence that drug use is causing the company some loss. Employers have argued in this respect that drug testing is especially appropriate in employment settings presenting opportunities for the theft of drugs or other articles with "street value," as in health care institutions.[20] However, one arbitrator held that mere concern that liability insurance premiums will rise is insufficient justification for adopting a drug testing policy.

In deciding when to test, the responsibilities of the employees to be tested should be carefully analyzed. Any drug testing policy must be tailored not only to the employer's overall operation, but to the responsibilities in that operation of each category of employees. In most cases, the validity of the policy will hinge upon its reasonableness *as applied to the employees tested.* Thus, many employers in safety-sensitive industries have adopted hybrid policies, incorporating different approaches toward different groups of employees.[21] For example, such policies typically provide for periodic testing without cause for employees holding safety-sensitive positions, but testing only for "cause" with respect to other employees. If a periodic testing program is applied to all employees in a safety-sensitive industry without regard to their responsibilities, it may be successfully attacked as being overly broad. For example, there may be little reason to subject certain clerical employees to particularly onerous drug testing just because they happen to work at a nuclear power plant. The safety considerations applying to those employees may be no different from those applying in any other office setting.[22]

**Evaluating the Extent of the Workplace Drug Problem.**    Generally speaking, an employer thinking of subjecting employees to drug testing must be able to articulate a reason to do so. An honest evaluation of the extent of a drug problem at the workplace is a critical step in explaining why one tests, and why one tests as one does. Quite apart from legal concerns, the employer should be prepared to justify the cost of developing, implementing, and using a testing procedure in terms of the results it expects to obtain. The employer exercising its business judgement should certainly evaluate these costs: the expected frequency of tests (a periodic system-wide test of all employees is more expensive than isolated tests for cause); individual tests through and including GC/MS; litigation or arbitration if applicable; consultants' or supervisors' training; and lost job satisfaction and morale. Against these costs, the employer should weigh the costs of a decision not to test: the degree of lost productivity and/or inventory, health care costs, insurance costs, and associated costs it can reasonably attribute to substance abuse at the plant. If the employer has experienced no detectable problem attributable to drug use, or if the toll of alcoholism and drug use can be remedied without safety risks by resort to discipline and discharge for absenteeism or poor work performance, the employer has an important question to ask: Does my belief that illegal drugs are a social evil justify the costs of dealing with a nonexistent problem?

Legally speaking, employers are also well advised to avoid shooting at mice with elephant guns. Courts and arbitrators have scrutinized the evidence an employer presents, or the lack of it, to provide a rationale for testing. Showing the necessity for testing to a court deciding a case concerning public sector employees may allow the court to rule that the compelling state interest in eradicating existing substance abuse justifies searches and seizures conducted in a minimally intrusive way. In the private sector, demonstrating a need to test based on observed problems in the workplace may tip the "balance of harms" in the employer's favor where the union seeks an injunction to postpone implementation of a testing program pending arbitration. Arbitrators, too, will consider whether a testing program is in any sense "necessary" to determine if it is a reasonable procedure. Depending on their personal attitudes toward drugs and the "drug problem," arbitrators may be more willing to allow an employer to implement a testing program to prevent a drug problem where one does not already exist.[23]

A rampant, documented drug problem at a workplace will justify more aggressive and comprehensive action than an ungrounded fear for the future. Even so, other factors an employer must consider, particularly safety, will have a tremendous impact on just how far the employer should stretch its drug testing vigilance. We will compare below the possible employer approaches along a continuum of options.

**State or Local Legislation Regulating Drug Testing.**    State and municipal legislation regulating workplace drug testing is discussed in Chapter 2. In the context of determining whether and how to test, however, the possibility that new legislation will appear on the scene in a given jurisdiction is just as important as the nature of already-enacted laws. As of this writing, drug testing bills have been introduced and reintroduced in state legislatures nationwide. The careful employer must be prepared to make quick and repeated checks to determine whether any bill or ordinance is pending and might pass in its jurisdiction. To guard against liability, the employer should be prepared to revise an existing or proposed testing policy to provide for some standard similar to "reasonable suspicion" to test; procedural safeguards; GC/MS confirmatory testing; and protection of confidentiality of test results.

# What Are the Testing Options?

As the foregoing suggests, drug testing programs may be divided into two basic categories: (1) testing "for cause," where testing takes place only when the employer has cause to believe that the employee to be tested is impaired on the job, and (2) testing "without cause," where testing may be required on a random or periodic basis, even in the absence of evidence that employees tested use illegal drugs. Within these two broad categories there are many different policies, which have met varying degrees of court and arbitral approval when challenged.

In formulating a testing policy, it is helpful to view the various testing options as falling on a continuum from the most invasive form of testing, discretionary random testing, to the least offensive type, testing for "probable cause." A brief discussion of the various policies on the continuum follows.

### Testing without Cause

*Discretionary Random Testing.*    Under a discretionary random testing policy, management is vested with unfettered discretion to require employees to submit to a drug test at any time for good reason, bad reason, or no reason at all. Labor unions and civil rights organizations have reserved their most vocal and vitriolic criticism for such policies.[24] One federal district court described such testing as "draconian" and a "gross invasion of privacy . . . almost unheard of in a free society" in the course of issuing a temporary restraining order blocking the implementation of a random testing policy.[25]

Of particular concern to opponents of pure random testing is the potential for abuse inherent in such policies: they fear supervisors with an "axe to grind" against an employee may invoke random testing as a tool of harassment.[26] Most decisions rendered to date have indicated that pure random testing is unreasonable.[27]

*Systematic Random Testing.*    This form of random testing permits employers to test employees without "cause" and without notice. However, employees are randomly selected for testing pursuant to a predetermined formula. For example, one company established a policy whereby time cards of employees holding safety-sensitive positions were placed into a barrel at the end of each quarter. The cards of 10% of the employees were drawn in the presence of a designated union observer. Those employees whose cards were selected were required to report to the company's medical facility within one hour to provide urine samples. The advantage of such a program, of course, is the elimination of unbridled discretion in the hands of supervisors who may not otherwise apply the policy in a fair and evenhanded manner.

*Periodic Testing without Notice.*    Under these policies, employees are tested pursuant to a predetermined schedule. Typically, all employees are notified that they are subject to being tested at some undetermined point of time, but only the personnel department or medical department knows when. Here again, although employees may claim unfair surprise, the dangers associated with complete supervisory discretion are not present. Employers justify this type of testing as both an accommodation of employees' rights to know the conditions of employment, namely, that they are to remain free from drugs if they wish to work for the employer, and a program that allows the employer to pursue vigorously the employee who might otherwise remain undetected.

*Periodic Testing with Notice.* Periodic testing with notice usually occurs in connection with annual physical examinations,[28] physical examinations upon return from layoffs or extended illnesses, or at any other predetermined interval. Because such policies normally provide ample advance notice, not only that testing will take place, but when tests will be administered, this form of testing is more likely to be upheld, especially if the employer can demonstrate a pervasive drug problem unlikely to be otherwise detected in safety-sensitive positions.[29] Ample advance notice naturally undermines any later claim for invasion of privacy. The employee knows when he takes the job that a condition of employment is submission to tests. A disadvantage, of course, is that sufficient warning may also enable drug abusing employees to beat the system. Even a chronic cocaine abuser may avoid detection by the simple device of abstaining from cocaine for a few days before the test is administered.

*Testing after All Industrial Accidents.* A growing number of policies require drug testing after all industrial accidents.[30] Typically, both the perpetrator and the victim are required to submit to drug tests. Although accident testing is technically without cause, inasmuch as one cannot directly conclude from the mere occurrence of the accident that the employees involved were impaired by drugs at the time of the account, it is probably the most defensible form of testing without cause since, by definition, the accident has demonstrated that safety has already been threatened. Even courts deciding public sector cases are willing to recognize that the fact that an accident happens at all gives an employer reason to check to see if it happened because of drugs.[31] Indeed, in certain industries, government regulations specifically mandate drug testing after all accidents. If an employer, such as a bus company, is a common carrier that legally owes a high duty of care to the public it transports, the company also has a legal obligation to investigate whether the employee himself caused the accident. If he did, and the employer retains him, or if the employer never makes the effort to investigate, the employer may be negligent and subject to damages.

In the normal industrial context, however, blanket policies requiring drug testing after *all* accidents have been successfully challenged if they are not adequately related to triggering factors such as personal injury, accompanying evidence giving rise to suspicion of impairment, or property damage.[32] In one case, the arbitrator found that the policy reversed the normal principles of just cause by allowing a conclusion of probable impairment simply because the accident occurred. The arbitrator required some additional evidence to support the claim that there was reasonable cause to order a drug test.[33]

## Testing for Cause

*Testing after Accidents Involving Carelessness.*   Some employers, recognizing the pitfalls in testing after *all* accidents, have confined testing to accidents where some form of carelessness is involved. Other policies go further and require that the circumstances surrounding the accident support an inference that the carelessness is attributable to drug use. Inasmuch as such an approach is testing for "cause," it is likely to withstand the scrutiny of courts and arbitrators in most cases.

*Testing Based upon a Reasonable Suspicion of Impairment.*   Under this policy, testing is limited to employees whom the employer reasonably suspects are using drugs on the job, or reporting to work in an impaired condition. The so-called "reasonable suspicion" standard has been borrowed from the constitutional precedents pertaining to unlawful searches under the Fourth Amendment.[34] Although something less than "probable cause" is required to meet this standard, the employer must be able to articulate a reasonable basis for believing that an employee is using drugs or reporting to work under the influence of drugs before requiring a drug test. Moreover, the employer's suspicion must be "individualized" to the particular employees to be tested.[35] In other words, it is not enough for an employer to point to evidence that other employees in the same department are using drugs. The employer can point to evidence such as supervisors' observations of physical characteristics or behavior commonly attributable to alcohol or drug use,[36] poor performance,[37] unexplained unusual behavior,[38] or reports of on-the-job use or possession.

*"Probable Cause" Testing.*   Under a more conservative approach, testing is limited to situations where the employer has "probable cause" to believe that an employee is using drugs or is under the influence of drugs at work. This relatively strict standard has also been borrowed from cases arising under the Fourth Amendment. To meet this standard, the employer would need information just as reliable as that required by police to obtain a search warrant. This form of testing is the most conservative approach, and the most likely to withstand any and all challenges.

# IMPLEMENTING A DRUG TESTING PROGRAM

Once an employer has decided when drug testing will take place, the next issue is how to go about it. What form of drug tests should the company use? Who should perform the tests? Should the laboratory always confirm positive test results? How and where should management obtain urine specimens? Should management observers witness specimen collection? Who should receive the results? Should the employer require employees to sign consent forms? What if an employee refuses to sign? What action, if any, can an employer take against an employee who refuses to submit to a urine test? These practical considerations invariably come into play in implementing a testing program. Particularly when an employer contemplates disciplinary action based on the results of the test, they are loaded with legal significance. Indeed, in some circumstances, federal regulations and state laws regulate not only when testing may take place, but the mechanics of how it will be accomplished. Thus, to avoid legal headaches, employers wishing to implement a drug testing program are well advised to do their homework in advance and address each of these practical considerations prior to formulating a drug testing program.

## What Types of Tests Should Be Used?

All employers testing employees for drugs must first educate themselves about drug testing technology, its limitations, and costs. There is now an array of body fluid tests on the market, including tests for saliva, blood, and urine. In addition, tests have recently been developed that can identify illegal drug use based upon a noninvasive brain scan or on an analysis of a strand of hair. These tests offer varying degrees of specificity and accuracy. They also present a range of costs for which an employer must account; the list only begins with the actual price paid to the laboratory to perform the test. The initial expense of a test may not accurately reflect its ultimate cost to the employer. Just as it must review the circumstances and its goals when it decides whether to test at all, the employer must carefully evaluate the nature of its work force, the scope of the drug problem it must address, the safety and public image factors involved, and the total dollar amount (including litigation costs) it is willing to spend on the drug war, in order to make an informed decision about what test is appropriate for its work force.

The technological virtuosity of radioimmunoassay analysis on hair provides a good example of the pro-and-con juggling an employer must undertake before committing itself to a particular method of drug testing. Although few employers have used, or even have heard of, the use of radioimmunoassay on hair, it has some significant advantages over urinalysis. For instance, unlike urine tests, which can only determine cocaine use in the immediate past (36 to 72 hours), an analysis of a five-inch strand of hair can reportedly "give a month-by-month record of cocaine or other drug use reaching back nearly a year."[39] Furthermore, hair tests would enable employers to side-step all of the thorny privacy considerations that must be dealt with in securing urine specimens. Of course, if the employer's applicable work rule concerns only reporting under the influence, use, or possession on the property, hair testing is functionally useless to show a violation of those prohibitions, regardless of its low laboratory cost and sample collection simplicity. If, however, the employer outlaws all drug use including off-duty use, a hair test would seem to provide enough information to demonstrate a rule violation. But does it? "In a larger sense," notes one critic, "[RIA-H] hair testing could be more intrusive if a person really is carrying around months or even years of drug history on his or her head."[40] Whatever its utility, at this point, hair testing may not be sufficiently accepted in the scientific community to provide solid evidence in court or in an arbitration. An employer who adopts the RIA-H test as the test of choice to save on litigation over privacy issues may instead pay the price in seeing known drug users reinstated. Even if they cost more to confirm, other better-known and scientifically accepted tests may reduce costs overall. Among the alternatives, urine tests are simpler and less expensive than blood testing and far more reliable than saliva analysis or brain scans.

The choice among urine tests actually requires similar analysis. Each different form of urine test has its strengths and limitations. Urine tests fall into two basic categories: (a) screening tests, which are sensitive to varying degrees and relatively inexpensive, and (b) confirmatory tests, which are more expensive, but capable of identifying illegal drugs with more specificity and accuracy.

The principal characteristic of screening tests is the possibility of error. Thin-layer chromatography and liquid chromatography depend heavily on the lab technician's prowess at interpreting test results. Immunoassay identification of drugs and/or their metabolites by tests such as Syva's EMIT is renowned for the "false positive," that is, an ability to confuse some chemical compounds such as ibuprofen, an over-the-counter pain killer, for THC, the compound it is supposed to detect.[41] Screening tests also produce false negatives, depending on the cutoff levels the employer chooses, and the type of test.

In view of the possibility of error inherent in the various screening tests,[42] employers would be foolish to take any adverse action against an employee based solely upon a result reported from one of them. One federal court even held that the discharge of a school bus aide on the basis of one unconfirmed EMIT test was "arbitrary and capricious."[43] Arbitrators too have quickly reached a level of sophistication about drug testing technology that will cause them to require confirmation of screening tests if discipline is to be upheld.[44] Even the manufacturers of the various screening tests caution that positive test results should be confirmed by another testing method.[45] Where screening tests are concerned, a cheap price tag and speed do not justify the inconclusiveness of the unconfirmed results.

To provide convincing evidence of a rule violation, an employer should routinely arrange to have its testing laboratory run a confirming test on the screened sample which has tested positive. The most accurate and most frequently recommended confirmatory method is the gas chromatography/mass spectrometry (GC/MS) test. Although the GC/MS test is also the most expensive test, most sophisticated employers have decided to invest the money to secure the most accurate results available. While the medical community is in general agreement that a properly run GC/MS analysis is a very accurate medical and forensic procedure that will indicate the presence of a drug with a very high degree of certainty, opponents of drug testing continue to fear that drug testing is a generally unreliable and inaccurate procedure.[46] From the employer's standpoint, this simply makes it imperative for those who do test to go the extra mile and pay for the best available technology.

It may be appropriate for some employers in some circumstances to use screening tests to make employment decisions without confirmation. For instance, an employer may take the risk that other evidence (for instance, a supervisor's or a medical doctor's observation of an employee's behavior) will be sufficient to prove just cause to discharge the employee for being under the influence of a substance.[47] In one case, an arbitrator upheld a discharge for being "under the influence" where there were no test results at all. The arbitrator found that the company properly relied on reports from a medical consultant and an on-duty nurse who observed the employee's incoherent, unstable, and bizarre behavior. In such a case, if the nontest evidence is weak or botched, to test at all may be a waste of effort.

Where ability to meet initial job requirements is the issue, and not just cause to discharge, then employers may also risk challenges to reliance on unconfirmed screening test results. Significantly, the majority of drug testing in the employment context today involves job applicants, whose screening tests are more likely to be used without confirmation. While the majority of employers use confirmatory tests where current employees are concerned, many are unwilling to bear the extra expense to test mere applicants.[48] They contend that the additional cost and time required for qualified confirmatory tests is a burden outweighing the risk of screening out qualified applicants because of false test results. It is certainly more difficult for an applicant than a current employee to sue an employer for adverse action based on a drug test. However, notions of fairness and common sense militate strongly in favor of confirming *all* drug tests, in view of the unacceptable rate of false positives and otherwise inaccurate results screening tests generate.[49]

## Selecting a Laboratory

President Reagan's well-publicized war on drugs and the burgeoning interest in drug testing among employers have given birth to a cottage industry in drug testing. Some companies have been marketing inexpensive do-it-yourself kits. With such kits, the entire procedure can be accomplished "in-house" at a minimum of initial expense. The kits, however, are forms of what we have called "screening tests," and suffer from their limitations. At the same time, even when employers avoid these tests and contract with a laboratory, they face the hazard of fly-by-night laboratories which reportedly have sprung up throughout the country adversely affecting quality control.[50]

To combat growing quality control problems among laboratories engaged in drug testing, the College of American Pathologists has developed an accreditation program for such laboratories.[51] In view of the widespread, albeit false, notion that all drug tests are inaccurate, and possible quality control problems at some laboratories,[52] employers should retain only accredited, highly reputable laboratories to perform drug tests.

The drug testing business has also become a very competitive industry. Not only are rates negotiable depending upon estimates of the number and frequency of employees (and applicants) to be tested, but employers are invited to tour the facilities before retaining the laboratory's services. Sophisticated employers are availing themselves of this right to ensure that they have selected a reputable and reliable laboratory. Employers should also inquire as to whether the laboratory belongs to a major voluntary proficiency testing organization, such as the American Association of Clinical Laboratories or the College of American Pathologists, and, if so, what proficiency scores the laboratory has received.

In addition, employers are also well advised to submit "blind" samples to the laboratories under consideration as part of the selection process, and on a continuous basis thereafter. Employers should submit blank samples (specimens known to be free of drugs) and spiked samples (samples with known quantities of drugs) to verify the accuracy of the laboratory's procedures. This not only serves as a check on the laboratory, but it also enhances the credibility of the employer's overall procedures. It may be advisable to submit these samples as though they were procured from employees, without identifying them as a set of blind samples. Laboratories have been known to assign their best personnel, equipment, and efforts to samples identified as blind or test samples.[53]

It should also be emphasized that there is a difference between conducting tests for medical purposes and for legal purposes, where the procedures normally will be closely scrutinized in a court of law. Although virtually all laboratories are accustomed to performing tests for medical diagnoses, many have little or no experience in forensic toxicology. Accordingly, in selecting a laboratory, employers should also determine the laboratory's level of dedication to protocols carefully designed to ensure that tests are run properly, with clean, well-maintained equipment, competent technicians, and properly handled, stored, and treated samples. This is especially important the more the employer wishes to rely on the results of a sophisticated test such as GC/MS, without other evidence, to make employment decisions. GC/MS is sensitive and specific to such a degree that its operation has forensic consequences; however, a botched procedure ruins the validity of the results.[54] An employer concerned with the possibility of vigorous challenges to its testing program should inquire whether laboratory personnel are experienced in forensic toxicology and have previously provided testimony to support their findings. In short, with the background of sharp criticism levied against drug testing technology and the entire drug testing industry, employers must go to great lengths to ensure that they retain a competent, well-respected laboratory. Many employers are even hiring outside consultants for assistance in this difficult process.

## How to Collect Urine Specimens:
## Preserving the Individual's Dignity and Privacy

Many employers, in their zeal to establish a proper chain of custody of the urine specimen and ensure the integrity of the sample, require the presence of observers when urine samples are taken. In response, employees often refuse to submit to the test, even though they may contend they have no opposition to drug tests *per se*. They justify their refusal based upon the embarrassment and humiliation involved in performing this private bodily function in someone else's presence. When they have been disciplined or discharged as a result, arbitrators have generally been very receptive to such claims, with the result that they have unhesitatingly reversed management's actions. Moreover, in addition to providing a ready defense for employees refusing to submit to tests, requiring observers may also expose employers to employees' claims for invasion of privacy and intentional infliction of emotional distress.

On the other hand, without observers, some drug abusing employees are likely to beat the system. A black market for "clean" urine samples has developed in some metropolitan areas; all sorts of ingenious schemes have been developed for substituting drug-free urine samples for those of employees. A common ploy is to put clean urine into a balloon and smuggle it into the bathroom under an armpit, where it remains at body temperature. Indeed, there have been cases reported of employees who have used catheters or syringes to put someone else's urine in their bladders! Another problem is the potential for tampering with urine samples outside the presence of an observer. For example, applying salt to the sample or diluting the sample with water may be enough to avoid detection of some substances at some screening test cutoff levels.

Notwithstanding the potential for manipulation, however, many employers have shied away from requiring observers. Peter Bensinger, the former head of the Drug Enforcement Administration and a nationally recognized consultant on drug testing in the workplace, insists that: "Employees who cheat end up getting caught. They brag about it in the workplace, so observation is really a big red herring."[55] Regardless, absent some evidence that employees may tamper with the sample, invasion of privacy considerations associated with observers and the accompanying legal ramifications may outweigh the employer's interest in absolutely ensuring the integrity of the sample.

There are other precautions an employer can take to guard against sample tampering. Department of Health and Human Services guidelines, for example, recommend placing a bluing agent in the toilet water to avoid attempts to dilute the sample with water.[56] Some employers require that the sample be given in a totally empty room without a sink or toilet, but this procedure has its own hazards for dignity and employee morale. Other less drastic steps to avoid tampering include directing the laboratory to measure pH and specific gravity, and examining the color and volume of the specimen. To avoid substitution of samples, a medical technician or even a supervisor can take specimen temperatures to ensure freshness. Some employers also require that employees disrobe in a separate room and slip on hospital gowns. They are then taken to a totally empty room to provide the sample.

More and more companies are washing their hands of the messy problems involved in collecting samples by sending the employees or applicants to hospitals or medical departments and letting others handle the details. Having the sample taken in medical surroundings also tends to undermine invasion of privacy claims and other challenges since it is customary for people to submit to blood tests and urine tests in medical facilities. The downside is that relying on others to collect the samples will substantially increase the cost of drug testing, and it also presents logistical complications and possible delays. Nevertheless, employers who limit testing to circumstances where there is cause to believe an employee is impaired are well advised to bear the additional expense in dollars and time. However, while the employer may shift the responsibility for specimen collection to someone else, the employer is still obligated to establish the integrity of the sample collection procedure should test results be challenged. Accordingly, the employer should take steps to ensure that the facility selected has adequate procedural safeguards in place.

Employers large enough to have their own medical departments normally require that samples be collected there, under the direction of qualified medical personnel. From the employee's standpoint, it is presumably less invasive and embarrassing to provide a urine sample to a company nurse in a separate medical department than to a personnel manager, supervisor, or other nonmedical person outside a medical environment. Accordingly, to preserve the dignity of the individual, using in-house medical staff is the next best alternative to sending employees to outside medical facilities. Furthermore, in-house medical staff are presumably more familiar than lay personnel with medical testing procedures and the critical importance of chain of custody requirements.

Nevertheless, some employers have decided to remove their medical personnel from drug testing programs altogether. Certain medical directors have taken the position that it is inappropriate for a medical staff to provide diagnostic information about employees that will be the basis for personnel actions, because it violates doctor-patient confidentiality and undermines doctors' relationships with workers. Other corporate medical directors strongly disagree. They contend that substance abuse is essentially a medical problem and that it should be dealt with like any other medical problem.

In summary, to minimize invasion of privacy claims and morale problems, the dignity and privacy of the individual in the extremely delicate process of specimen collection must be preserved to the greatest extent possible. Insofar as there is a tension between protecting privacy rights and minimizing sample manipulation, the balance should be struck in favor of privacy. Otherwise, not only is the employer exposed to tort claims, but it may not be able to enforce its drug policy via the testing program.

## Consent Forms

Virtually all employers who test require employees to sign a consent form prior to submitting to a drug test. Generally, the form will recite words to the effect that the employee has voluntarily agreed to provide a urine specimen for the purpose of a drug test. It may also recite that the employee authorizes the release of the results of the test to appropriate company personnel. Some forms go one step further and require the employee to agree that the test results are not confidential information and may be used for whatever purpose the employer deems appropriate.

Employers attempt to invoke the written consent form as a shield against invasion of privacy claims, defamation or other tort claims, and certain arbitral challenges to the reasonableness of relying on test results (usually involving a defense of coercion or lack of reason to test). Employers argue that by signing a consent form, the employee has voluntarily agreed to the tests and has agreed to disclosure of the results. Accordingly, the employee has thereby waived any privacy rights that he may otherwise have had in the substances contained in his urine. After all, an employee is certainly placed in an awkward position to assert an expectation of privacy in his urine after he consents in writing to have it tested.

However, the employee will invariably counter that he signed the consent form under "duress" because he feared losing his job. A number of arbitrators and other decision-makers have been very receptive to the duress defense when the employee legitimately felt that his job was in jeopardy. Another line of arbitrators has strictly enforced signed consent forms and held that employees have thereby forfeited their right to challenge the decision to test.

An employer should not take great comfort in its ability to hide behind a consent form to avoid the morass of legal problems associated with drug testing. On the other hand, there is little, if any, risk from the employer's perspective in requesting that employees sign consent forms. Whether or not they provide a complete defense to later legal challenges, they will certainly provide some ammunition for the employer's defense.

The next question is what, if any, action can the employer take if the employee refuses to sign the form? At least one arbitrator has held that the employer may properly discharge an employee for insubordination for violating a management directive to sign a consent form. That arbitrator reasoned that, even if the drug test was unreasonably requested, the employee should have adhered to the well-established maxim: "Obey now, grieve later." It would appear, however, that most decision-makers will not uphold independent disciplinary action based solely upon an employee's refusal to sign a consent form. For example, in one dispute an arbitrator found that a transit worker was improperly terminated for refusing to sign a consent form prepared by investigators, even though a company rule stated that "refusal [of an employee suspected of drug use] to submit immediately to this test will constitute acknowledgment by him of his guilt." The arbitrator found that the employee balked at signing the consent form not because he was unwilling to submit to the test, but because he could not understand the form. According to the arbitrator: "It . . . appears that the grievant was not offered the urine bottle for the obtaining of his urinalysis until he would sign the consent form. The issue then became one of signing the consent form and not the furnishing of urine."[57] Thus, even though an employee refuses to sign a consent form, a factual question may remain as to whether he refused to submit to the test.

## Refusal to Take a Test

Normally, a refusal to sign a consent form goes hand in hand with a refusal to take the test. The more significant question is what, if any, action can be taken against the employee who refuses to take the test? Is the refusal to submit to a drug test just cause for discharge? If the test is requested "without cause" as part of a random or periodic testing program, and there is no independent evidence that the employee is using drugs or reporting to work "under the influence," and the employee had no notice of the consequences of his refusal to submit to the test, a refusal will probably not amount to just cause for discharge under traditional notions of industrial justice.[58] Likewise, even if there is cause to test, but the employer's demand requires a particularly intrusive invasion of an employee's privacy, the employee may be justified in refusing to submit to the test. In one case, an employee who would have been forced to disrobe entirely in the presence of an observer to give the sample was reinstated after refusing to take the test.[59]

On the other hand, if a collective bargaining agreement specifically provides that a refusal to take a test amounts to grounds for discharge, an arbitrator may be precluded from second-guessing the parties' agreement that discharge is an appropriate disciplinary measure, based upon the general principle that an arbitrator has no authority to alter or amend the parties' agreement.

Absent a contract provision, however, even when the employer implements a rule under its management right to do so, it is unlikely that an employer can justify a discharge based solely upon a refusal to take a test. A rule creating an absolute presumption of guilt for refusal to submit to a test has been held to be unreasonable and void.[60]

If an employer has other evidence that an employee has used drugs on the job or reported to work under the influence, arbitrators may be willing to draw an adverse inference that the employee was under the influence based upon the employee's refusal to submit to the test. After all, the employee has, in effect, declined an opportunity to establish that he was drug-free. It may be argued that to draw an adverse inference would violate the employee's right to be free of self-incrimination or to be protected by the "just cause" requirement in a contract. Frequently, unions and civil libertarians have taken the position that drug tests should not even be admissible, because they compel the employee to incriminate himself when he submits to the search.[61]

However, analogies to the criminal justice system may not be appropriate, particularly in the private sector.[62] Most arbitrators agree that an employee has no right to be free of self-incrimination vis-a-vis the employer. In other words, although an employee's exercise of his right to remain silent may not be held against him in any subsequent criminal proceeding, the employee is not immune from employer discipline based on his failure to cooperate in the employer's investigation.[63]

Thus, while an employee's refusal to take a test may not supply just cause for discipline in and of itself, it may be considered as evidence that the employee is guilty of the underlying offense. However, if there is no independent evidence of drug use or impairment leading up to the test, evidence of refusal to take a test would almost certainly not provide sufficient evidence of drug use or impairment.[64]

## Presumptions of Influence of Drugs Based upon Refusals

Anticipating that some employees will refuse to submit to tests, some employers have incorporated presumptions into their rules or policies. For example, some rules provide that a refusal to test amounts to prima facie evidence that the employee is intoxicated or under the influence; or that a refusal amounts to acknowledgment of guilt. Those arbitrators who have considered such presumptions have found that an employer cannot rely on what it considers to be an "admission" where a refusal to take a test is involved. According to one arbitrator, such a result would reverse the normal just cause principles which mandate that the employer prove just cause to discharge the employee. The arbitrator wrote:

> "This is a palpable reversal of normal 'just cause' principles. Submission of blood tests can be resisted for a variety of reasons other than a sense of guilt. There is no necessary proximate relationship between obduracy and intoxication. An employer has the usual burden of establishing grounds for discharge, independently of the employee's compelled self-incriminatory statement or cooperation."[65]

## Dealing with Prescription Drugs

Employers who engage in drug testing must devise a method to deal with a seemingly innocuous aspect of off-duty conduct which may still affect on-duty performance, and the validity of test results as well: the American trust in and reliance on over-the-counter and prescription drugs to solve every conceivable kind of health problem. Prescription drugs present a balancing problem. Employers must comprehend and address the dual nature of prescription drugs, implied in their name. They are both a medical *prescription* to solve a health problem, and they are undoubtedly *drugs*, with varying pharmacological effects on behavior and performance.

Prescription drugs may be harmful to the user, other employees, and the public, if they become drugs of abuse. Just because the drug an employee uses is a prescription drug, as opposed to a "street" drug such as marijuana, there is no guarantee that it will not affect his job performance even when he takes it as prescribed. Pain killers, antihistamines, and even some antibiotics are routinely dispensed with labels warning that they may cause drowsiness and should not be used while driving or operating machinery. An employee's abuse of a prescription drug may lead to disastrous consequences just as drunkenness may. Employers have argued that because even lawfully obtained prescription drugs can cause job hazards, it is their right—and perhaps even obligation—to know about all foreign substances employees ingest that may affect their "fitness" to perform their duties. Toward that end, many employers have incorporated into their general substance abuse policies various reporting requirements, obligating employees, on a continuous basis, to apprise their superiors of all legally prescribed, as well as over-the-counter, medications they are taking which could possibly affect their fitness to perform the job. Although such policies are becoming more and more common, few decision-makers have addressed their validity.

Prescription drugs also present legal problems for employers if employees use the drugs properly and the drug testing procedure does not account for that possibility. Questions of effect on performance aside, the lawful ingestion of lawfully prescribed prescription drugs may influence test results. When an employer's disciplinary or hiring policy penalizes or rejects employees based solely on the results of an unconfirmed screening test, the employer risks the range of adverse legal and practical consequences we have discussed elsewhere, due to the significant occurrence of cross-reaction and "false positive" results prescription drugs may cause.[66] Even if the employer confirms test results but prohibits "drugs" across the board without regard for where they come from or whether they are legal as taken, disciplining an employee for a positive test result for something such as "barbiturates" may be unjust and unenforceable without knowledge of why the substance is present. The employee taking the drug identified as a "barbiturate" may be able to show, if asked, that he has taken it for years as part of a supervised regimen to prevent epileptic seizures, and that it helps him to be fit for his job.

Zeal for comprehensive coverage in work rules regarding substance abuse has gotten at least one employer into trouble regarding prescription drugs. An arbitrator reviewing a newly drafted substance abuse policy found unreasonable a rule which prohibited "controlled substances" as they were defined under state law. The rule reached too far, the arbitrator found, and was therefore not reasonably related to the employer's legitimate concerns about "the employee's ability to function properly and lawfully on Company premises" and to do so safely.[67] What the rule's blanket prohibition failed to account for was prescription drugs' usefulness—even necessity—in improving an employee's performance under some circumstances.[68]

For the employer, obtaining knowledge sufficient to make a decision about whether the substance in question is helpful or harmful is the fulcrum of the prescription drug balance. Disclosure is the obvious way to effectuate the balance between "good" and "bad" prescription drug use. There are several practical methods available to obtain the necessary information about prescription drug use which would affect job performance. Each of these methods could be adopted to fit the needs of a particular drug testing policy:

1. Incorporate in the testing consent form a space for employees to list all prescription drugs they are currently taking and have taken in some specified time period.

2. Provide a separate form for employees to complete whenever they are asked to submit to a physical, which may include a drug screen.

3. Promulgate and post a rule requiring employees to present return-to-work slips upon returning from an illness which indicate whether the employee has been given a prescription, and if so, what it is.

4. Promulgate and post a rule requiring employees to inform a supervisor any time they take a prescription or over-the-counter drug, and provide that management will determine whether the employee is fit to perform his duties while taking the drug.

5. Require employees returning from illness or layoff to submit to a physical to determine fitness for duty. Provide that failure to disclose prescription drugs to medical personnel is falsification of records and could subject the employee to discipline.

In some form, this information must be secured by employers testing their employees' urine samples. Otherwise, employees testing positive for illegal drugs will inevitably claim that the positive results were due to undisclosed prescription drugs. GC/MS testing will eliminate the possibility that false positives due to cross-reactivity have occurred, but it will not distinguish between legal and illegal use of a compound which is a controlled substance.

Some employees may contend that requiring them to disclose what prescription drugs they take is in and of itself an unjustified invasion of privacy. They feel, for example, that it is none of the boss's business if they are taking prescription drugs such as birth control pills, or Valium. Where privacy is an issue, but safety is one as well, the employer who insists on full disclosure may still provide that *for purposes of a drug policy*, employees need not disclose use of certain substances, such as birth control pills. For other reasons, however, where employees' health is of concern for productivity and safety, an employer may still need to know about the use of drugs such as medication for hypertension. The best way to handle touchy cases is to provide tight security on any information the employee submits, and to make every effort to "sell" the disclosure requirement as a necessity, not an onerous burden. Employers should make it clear, when necessary, that disclosure is a condition of continued employment.

## Providing Employees with Their Own Urine Samples
Because of the widespread concern over the accuracy of the methods drug testing laboratories use, some suspicious employees have begun demanding that they be provided with their own samples so that they can have their

own drug test performed at a laboratory of their own choice. Occasionally unions have negotiated this type of option. Indeed, some of the new or pending state drug testing statutes require that employees be provided with their own sample.[69] From the employer's perspective, this will open the door to conflicting medical test results. The difficulty is that the employer may have no control over where the employee's sample is tested. With the advent of fly-by-night testing laboratories, and the consequent quality control problems, the chorus of conflicting test results is no mere academic concern. If the employer bases any adverse employment action on the test results and the action is later challenged, the resolution may hinge upon a "battle of the experts," which is always expensive, and often risky. Thus, providing employees with their own urine samples may create additional headaches.

On the other hand, refusing to provide samples upon request may well smack of unfairness and undermine the entire drug testing program's credibility. Employees will argue that because of the widely reported abuses and quality control problems of drug testing laboratories, their future should not hinge upon the employer's choice of laboratories.

If employers do provide samples, they may also consider imposing a requirement that the employee have the sample tested at an accredited laboratory.[70] Significantly, many employers, anticipating later challenges of test results, require that laboratories maintain and freeze part of an original sample so that further testing may be performed if the employee challenges the results later.

## Establishing a Written Testing Policy

Some of the recently passed state statutes mandate that employers establish a written policy delineating when and how drug testing will take place, and how sample security and employees' privacy will be protected, before they engage in any drug testing of employees.[71] Failure to provide a written policy under such a statute may mean that testing is invalid, that employment decisions made on the basis of a test result may be reversed by a court injunction, that the employer is subject to civil damages, and occasionally, criminal misdemeanor penalties.[72] Whether or not a statute exists which mandates a written policy, a unionized employer is certainly well advised to establish one and to take appropriate steps to ensure that employees are aware of its terms.

A written policy should reflect due consideration of the factors justifying (and calling into question) the decision to test. It must relate to the terms of the basic work rule prohibiting drugs, to the realities of testing, and to the goals management states as its rationale for imposing testing in the first place. Otherwise, the union may challenge the policy as unreasonable.[73] When a statute mandates a full range of procedural protections, the policy must include these.[74] The policy cannot be too specific, or contain employee protections the employer is not willing to observe. If supervisory personnel do not follow the policy's provision, unionized employees can challenge the policy's application to particular cases on grounds of procedural omissions.[75]

Non-unionized employees as well have an increasing chance at success in combating discipline based on poorly implemented written policies, in the form of lawsuits for a breach of the policy's terms. A non-unionized employee would sue under a theory that the policy's terms create an implied employment contract binding on the employer. The employee would argue that explicit statements that a test will be confirmed with GC/MS, that testing will be done only upon reasonable suspicion, that the company will offer rehabilitation before discharge, or that the company will offer progressive discipline can become a contract binding on the employer when the employee continues to work after being notified of them.[76] Employers with non-unionized employees thus should carefully consider whether a written policy is desirable if no statute requires one. Where a written policy is desirable for any reason, and it is given to employees, non-unionized employers should carefully and clearly inform employees that the policy they receive is not intended to be a legally binding contract, and that the employer reserves the right to change the policy or decide not to apply it.[77] The disclaimer of legal effect should be conspicuous to the point of being unmistakable, perhaps set out in large bold type inside a box right at the beginning of the testing policy or personnel manual containing the testing policy.[78] Finally, the legal effect of a written policy and a disclaimer depends on the state in which the employer operates, and employers contemplating writing a policy should consider consulting legal counsel.

Despite its potentially restrictive character as far as the employer's ability to react to workplace drug abuse is concerned, a written policy may be the only proof that employees were notified of the possibility that drug tests may be required. Particularly in the union context, proof of advance notice may be a key ingredient to successfully defending a subsequent legal challenge. It may be true, generally speaking, that employers do not need a written rule or policy to discipline or discharge employees for conduct such as theft or selling illegal drugs; that is so universally understood to be bad that anyone would know not to do it.[79] As far as arbitrators are concerned, it is not the case now, if it ever was, that employees can be expected to understand, without a warning, that drug and alcohol use, which is an undeniable part of American culture, has no place on the job.[80] Oddly enough, the employer with a pervasive drug problem in the workplace may face the most difficulties, particularly if the problem is long-standing and an unwritten testing policy is implemented—and if it is implemented with no announcement. In cases involving possession and use of drugs on the employer's property, arbitrators have overturned discipline where the union successfully demonstrated that management was understood to look the other way regarding drug use.[81] However, when a company-wide or individual situation develops which presents serious and immediate risks, an employer's decision to test without a written policy may survive, particularly if the employer has a contractually reserved right to require employees to submit to physical exams to determine fitness for employment.[82]

## —— NOTES

1. Physical examinations are widely acknowledged to be appropriate, effective tools to determine whether new employees, or employees returning from illness or layoff, are fit to perform their jobs. See Wrightsell v. Chicago 678 F. Supp. 727, 2 IER Cases 1619 (N.D. Ill. 1988) (dismissing claim that testing police officers for drugs, via urinalysis as part of regular return-to-work exam, is unconstitutional); Williams Pipeline Co., 78 LA 617 (Moore, 1982); American Standard, WABCO Div., 77 LA 1085 (Katz, 1981). See, generally, ELKOURI & ELKOURI, HOW ARBITRATION WORKS, 4th ed. 580-81 (BNA Books 1985). There are arguments that they are not excuses for performing the type of testing which detects off-duty drug use, on the grounds that there is no proof that off-duty use will have an impact on fitness to perform upon returning to work. See, e.g., Alcan Aluminum Co., 88 LA 386, 389–390 (Kindig, 1986). But, cf., Chicago Transit Authority (Larney, June 2, 1986) (unreported) (discounting union challenge to use of positive drug test obtained in return-to-work physical after layoff). See also Transport Workers' Union of Philadelphia, Local 234 v. Southeastern Pennsylvania Transportation Authority, 678 F. Supp. 543, 127 LRRM 2835 (E.D. Pa. 1988) (return-to-work testing of public employees is an indiscriminate invasion of rights).

2. See, e.g., Union Plaza Hotel, 87-1 ARB ¶8072 (McKay, 1987).

3. They occasionally prevail, even in suits for injunctive relief. See Graphic Communications Union Local 17(m) v. Stone Container Corp., ___ F. Supp. ___, 3 IER Cases 261 (S.D. Ind. 1988) (court granted preliminary injunction to union, finding that drug testing policy invaded employees' "privacy rights") (appeal filed).

4. It should be noted, however, that the vast majority of courts have applied a "reasonable suspicion" standard rather than a probable cause standard in the drug testing context. National Federation of Federal Employees v. Weinberger, 818 F.2d 935, 2 IER Cases 145 (D.C. Cir. 1987); American Federation of Government Employees v. Weinberger, 651 F. Supp. 726, 1 IER Cases 1137 (S.D. Ga. 1986); Penny v. Kennedy, 648 F. Supp. 815, 1 IER Cases 1047 (E.D. Tenn. 1986); Lovvorn v. City of Chattanooga, 647 F. Supp 875, 1 IER Cases 1041 (E.D. Tenn. 1986); Capua v. City of Plainfield, 643 F. Supp. 1507, 1 IER Cases 625 (D. N.J. 1986); Jones v. McKenzie, 628 F. Supp. 1500, IER Cases 1076 (D.D.C. 1986); Caruso v. Ward, 133 Misc. 2d 544, 506 N.Y.S.2d 789, 2 IER Cases 238 (N.Y. Sup. Ct. 1986); Patchogue-Medford Congress of Teachers v. Board of Education of

the *Patchogue-Medford Union Free School District,* 510 N.E.2d 325, 2 IER Cases 198 (N.Y. App. Div. 1987); *Fraternal Order of Police, Newark Lodge 12 v. City of Newark,* 216 N.J. Super. 461, 524 A.2d 430, 2 IER Cases 437 (1987); *King v. McMickens,* 120 A.D. 2d 351, 501 N.Y.S. 2d 679 (N.Y. App. Div. 1986); *City of Palm Bay v. Bauman,* 475 So. 2d 1322 (Fla. App. 1985). Thus, in the majority of cases, a public employer need only articulate a reasonable basis for believing an employee is violating a drug prohibition, without the need to demonstrate facts giving rise to "probable cause," to justify the "search and seizure" of an employee's urine.

5. In most states, however, the common law tort of invasion of privacy has not been interpreted to restrict employers to the extent of the constitutional protections. Thus, the employee might have to prove that the employer had a bad motive. The tort generally applies only to certain types of invasions, such as disclosure of private facts to the public. *See, Payton v. City of Santa Clara,* 132 Cal. App. 3d 152, 183 Cal. Rptr. 17 (1982).

Some states have created a statutory or constitutional right of privacy apart from the right protected in the federal constitution. In recent years, a plethora of common law invasion of privacy cases have been filed, and the explosion of new precedents is only beginning. Recently, however, the Ninth Circuit Court of Appeals held that federal law preempted a unionized employee's anti-drug testing claim resting on privacy rights and the right to be free from unreasonable search and seizure arising from the California Constitution. *Utility Workers Local No. 246 v. Southern California Edison Co.,* ____F. 2d ____, 128 LRRM 2317, (9th Cir. 1988).

6. Awards may have great value in clarifying reasoning and providing a guide, but in the interest of resolving particular industry-related problems, arbitrators may exercise discretion regarding earlier awards. American Arbitration Association Code of Professional Responsibility §II(G), *quoted in* ELKOURI & ELKOURI, HOW ARBITRATION WORKS, 4th ed. 418 n.22 (BNA 1985).

7. *Steelworkers v. Enterprise Wheel & Car Corp.,* 363 U.S. 593, 597 (1960); *Steelworkers v. Warrior & Gulf Navigation Co.,* 363 U.S. 574, 581–82 (1960).

8. One analysis placed arbitrators in three categories according to their views on the proper approach to drug use issues in the workplace: the physical view, the psychological view, and the therapeutic view. According to the authors, arbitrators who hold "the physical view" believe that alcoholics possess an innate physical vulnerability to alcohol, develop a need, and progress to obsession and addiction. Those arbitrators who follow "the psychological view" believe addiction results from disturbing emotional experiences resulting in a need for relief, gratification, and self-esteem. Others will not consider alcohol to be an illness: they take the "strict responsibility" view that employees, including alcoholics, have the responsibility to exercise self-discipline. DENNENBERG & DENNENBERG, ALCOHOL AND DRUG ISSUES IN THE WORKPLACE, 1–17 (BNA Books, 1983).

9. *See, e.g., Union Plaza Hotel,* 87-1 ARB ¶8072 (McKay, 1987) (arbitrator reviews federal cases on civil liberties aspects of privacy issue where grievant refused to submit to testing where observation was required).

10. It may also be fair to assume that federal judges as a group, because of their legal background and their duty to enforce the criminal laws banning illegal drug use, may be less tolerant of drug use than private arbitrators.

11. *Boys Markets, Inc. v. Retail Clerks Local 770*, 398 U.S. 235, 74 LRRM 2257 (1970); *Local Lodge No. 1266 v. Panoramic Corp.*, 668 F.2d 276, 109 LRRM 2169 (7th Cir. 1981); *Oil, Chemical and Atomic Workers Local 6-10 v. Amoco*, 653 F. Supp. 300, 123 LRRM 2934, 2936 (D.N.D. 1987) (discharge for violation of testing program's rules or procedures may be remedied by an arbitral award and does not constitute irreparable injury); *Oil, Chemical and Atomic Workers Local 2-124 v. Amoco*, 651 F. Supp. 1, 123 LRRM 3104, 3108 (D. Wyo. 1986) (same); *IBEW, Local 1900 v. PEPCO*, 634 F. Supp. 642, 644, 121 LRRM 3287, 3288 (D.D.C. 1986) (same); *IBEW, System Council U-9 v. Metropolitan Edison Co.*, No. 86-4426, slip op. (E.D. Pa. Aug. 14, 1986) (union agreed damages would remedy injury from discharge).

12. *IBEW, Local 1900 v. PEPCO, supra*, note 10 (Court denied injunction on employer's agreement not to implement random testing pending arbitration); *IBEW, System Council U-9 v. Metropolitan Edison Co., supra*, note 10; *Murray v. Brooklyn Union Gas Co.*, 122 LRRM 2025 (N.Y. Sup. Ct. 1986) (oral proceedings).

13. For example, if the employer were contractually bound to terminate employees only for just cause because of a handbook, or oral or written promises, or to provide warnings and/or a chance to improve, the employee could bring a breach of contract suit in state court. *See, e.g., Duldulao v. St. Mary of Nazareth Hospital Center*, 136 Ill. App. 3d 763, 91 Ill. Dec. 470, 483 N.E. 2d 956 (1985).

In some states, the employee may also bring a claim for breach of an implied covenant of good faith and fair dealing. A handicap discrimination case or other discrimination case is another possibility.

14. *Cf., Texas Utilities Generating Co.*, 82 LA 6 (Edes, 1983) (employer improperly required employee to take test, but employee's resignation, in belief failure to take test would equal admission of guilt, was voluntary; employer not obligated to rehire him).

15. *Deaconess Medical Center*, 88 LA 44 (Robinson, 1986); *Division 241, Amalgamated Transit Union v. Sucsy*, 538 F. 2d 1264 (7th Cir.), *cert. denied*, 429 U.S. 1029 (1976); *Chicago Transit Authority* (Larney, June 2, 1986) (unreported); *Chicago Transit Authority* (Goldberg, November 21, 1985) (unreported); *U.S. Air Force Logistics Command*, 78 LA 1092, 1103 (Feldman, 1982). *But see, Capital Area Transit Authority*, 69 LA 811 (Ellmann, 1977) (regardless of public interest, basic procedural requirements must be met); *Bay Area Rapid Transit Authority*, 87-1 ARB ¶8084 (Concepcion, 1986) (policy is unreasonable to the extent it intrudes beyond necessities imposed by safety and public contact).

16. Detecting off-duty drug use and imposing a penalty for it may have implications as well for nonunion employees, for instance, when these employees claim an invasion of privacy or an employer's failure to reasonably accommodate a handicapping condition of addiction.

17. *See, e.g., American Federation of Government Employees v. Weinberger*, 651 F. Supp. 726, 1 IER Cases 1137 (S.D. Ga. 1986); *Penny v. Kennedy*, 648 F. Supp. 815,

817, 1 IER Cases 1047 (E. D. Tenn. 1986); *City of Palm Bay v. Bauman,* 475 So.2d 1322, 1324 (Fla. App. 1985); *Caruso v. Ward,* 133 Misc. 544, 506 N.Y.S. 2d 789, 792, 2 IER Cases 238 (Sup. Ct. 1986).

18. *See, Capua v. City of Plainfield,* 643 F. Supp. 1507, 1 IER Cases 625 (D.N.J. 1986); *Fraternal Order of Police, Newark Lodge 12 v. City of Newark,* 216 N.J. Super. 461, 524 A.2d 430, 2 IER Cases 437 (1987).

19. *See, Rushton v. Nebraska Public Power Dist.,* 653 F. Supp. 1510 (D. Neb. 1987); *Bath Iron Works Corp.* (Schmertz, June 30, 1986) (unreported) (production of ships for Navy, using skilled workers, justifies drug testing to ensure quality control). *Cf., Oil, Chemical & Atomic Workers Local 2-124 v. Amoco,* 651 F. Supp. 1, 123 LRRM 3104 (D. Wyo. 1986); *Arco-Polymers, Inc.,* 69 LA 379 (Milentz, 1977) (discharge for off-duty conviction for heroin sale justified to prevent drug problem where explosive chemical products produced).

20. *See, e.g., National Treasury Employees Union v. Von Raab,* 816 F.2d 170, 2 IER Cases 15 (5th Cir. 1987), *cert. granted,* ___ U.S. ___ (March 1, 1988).

21. *See, e.g.,* the policies discussed in *International Chemical Workers Union and Local 4 v. Olin Corp.,* Case No. 87 C 5745 (N.D. Ill. June 15, 1987) (Mem. order) (Kocoras, J.); Executive Order 12564, 51 Fed. Reg. 32889, 32892 (1986). *See, also, McDonnell v. Hunter,* 809 F.2d 1302, 1 IER Cases 1297 (8th Cir. 1987) (prison may test by uniform or systematic random means those employees with regular contact with prisoners; other employees may be tested only upon reasonable suspicion).

22. *See, Bay Area Rapid Transit Authority, supra,* note 14.

23. *See, e.g., Arco-Polymers, Inc.,* 69 LA 386 (Milentz, 1977); *Wheaton Industries, Inc.,* 64 LA 826 (Kerrison, 1975).

24. Among many examples, *see, e.g., Union Fights Drug Tests,* Jackson (MS) Citizen-Patriot, March 13, 1986; 212 DAILY LAB. REP. A-3 (BNA, November 3, 1986) (Teamsters for a Democratic Union criticize trucking industry drug testing practices); 225 DAILY LAB. REP. A-5 (BNA, November 21, 1986) (R. Lieberwitz, Cornell Univ. N.Y. State School of Industrial Relations); 72 DAILY LAB. REP. A-9 (BNA, April 16, 1987) (building trades oppose employer-imposed substance testing).

25. *IBEW, Local 1900 v. PEPCO,* ___ F. Supp. ___, 121 LRRM 3071 (D.D.C. 1986). The same court lifted the injunction, but only after the employer had agreed to refrain from random testing, except under certain pressing circumstances, until an arbitrator could hear the merits of the union's challenge. *IBEW, Local 1900 v. PEPCO,* 634 F. Supp. 642, 121 LRRM 3287 (D.D.C. 1986).

26. *See, e.g.,* 213 DAILY LAB. REP. A-4 (BNA, November 4, 1986) (remarks by G. Upshaw *re* NFL abuse of drug tests).

27. *See, Metropolitan Edison Co.,* AAA Case No. 14 300 093886 (Aarons, Oct. 9, 1986), reported at 191 DAILY LAB. REP. A-6 (BNA, October 15, 1986); *Amalgamated Transit Union, Local 1277 v. Sunline Transit Agency,* 663 F. Supp. 1560, 125 LRRM 3154 (C.D. Cal. 1987). *But see Deaconess Medical Center,* 88 LA 44 (Robinson, 1986) (hospital may require nurse with known substance abuse

problem to submit to random testing as condition of continued employment after her initial failure to complete rehabilitation); *McDonnell v. Hunter, supra* n. 20; *Transport Workers' Union of Philadelphia, Local 234 v. Southeastern Pennsylvania Transportation Authority*, 678 F. Supp. 543, 127 LRRM 2835 (E.D. Pa. 1988).

28. *Chemical Workers Local 6-10 v. Amoco Oil Co.*, 635 F. Supp. 300 (D. N.D. 1986); *Oil, Chemical and Atomic Workers Local 2-124 v. Amoco Oil Co.*, 651 F. Supp. 1 (D. Wyo. 1986).

29. Upholding testing as part of return-to-work physicals: *Wrightsell v. Chicago*, 678 F. Supp. 727, 2 IER Cases 1619 (N.D. Ill. 1988); *Jones v. McKenzie*, 628 F. Supp. 1500, 1 IER Cases 1076, *rev'd on other grounds*, 833 F.2d 335, 2 IER Cases 1121 (D.C. Cir. 1987) (school bus drivers); *Harris v. Washington*, No. 84 C 8812 slip op. at 6–8 (N.D. Ill. Feb. 6, 1985) (police). *But see Transport Workers Union of Philadelphia, Local 234 v. Southeastern Pennsylvania Transportation Authority*, 678 F. Supp. 543, 127 LRRM 2835 (E.D. Pa. 1988) (public transit employees).

30. *See, e.g.,, Boise Cascade Corp.*, (Kagel, Jan. 8, 1987) (unreported).

31. *Division 241, Amalgamated Transit Union v. Sucsy*, 538 F.2d 1264 (7th Cir.), *cert. denied*, 429 U.S. 1029 (1976); *Taylor v. O'Grady*, 669 F. Supp. 1422 (N.D. Ill. 1987); *International Chemical Workers Union and its Local 4 v. Olin Corp.*, No. 87 C 5745 (N.D. Ill. July 16, 1987). *But see Railway Labor Executives' Ass'n. v. Burnley*, 839 F.2d 575, 2 IER Cases 1601 (9th Cir. 1988).

32. *Boise Cascade, supra* note 28.

33. *Id.*

34. One of the first cases to address the invasiveness of a drug test search held that the search was not unduly invasive if it was based on "reasonable suspicion." *Division 241, Amalgamated Transit Union v. Sucsy, supra* note 31.

35. *Feliciano v. City of Cleveland*, 661 F. Supp. 578, 2 IER Cases 419 (N.D. Ohio 1987).

36. *American Standard, WABCO Div.*, 77 LA 1085 (Katz, 1981) (discharge proper for refusal to submit to reasonably justified test: employee observed to be unsteady, glassy-eyed, slurred in speech, staggering, swaying, disoriented); *Pacific Motor Trucking*, 86 LA 497 (D'Spain, 1986) (odor of alcohol); *Roadway Express*, 87 LA 224 (Cooper, 1986) (supervisor reported disoriented, confused behavior).

37. *Crown Zellerbach Corp.*, 87 LA 1145 (Cohen, 1986) (aberrant behavior, inability to perform job, failure to provide explanation).

38. *United States Steel Corp.*, 77 LA 854 (Hales, 1981) (employee properly tested: observed speeding past stop sign); *Georgia Power Co.*, 87 LA 800 (Byars, 1986) (deliberate, unexplained violation of safety procedure, abusive language to foreman, absence without notice). *But see General Felt Industries, Inc.*, 74 LA 972 (Carnes, 1979) (behavior more boisterous than usual, insufficient to warrant test).

39. National Law Journal, Monday, July 27, 1987, p. 3.

40. Allen Ader, legislative counsel for the American Civil Liberties Union, *quoted in* National Law Journal, *supra* note 39, at 8.

41. *See also,* Syva Customer Bulletin, April, 1986; Zeese, *Marijuana Urinalysis Tests,* 1 DRUG L. REP. 25, 26 (1983).

42. Center for Disease Study, *Crisis in Drug Testing,* 253 JAMA 2382–87; *Mandatory Drug Testing in the Workplace,* ABA J. 34 (August 1, 1986).

43. *Jones v. McKenzie,* 628 F. Supp. 1500, 1 IER Cases 1076 (D.C. Cir. 1986), *rev'd on other grounds,* 833 F.2d 335, 2 IER Cases 1121 (D.C. Cir. 1987). *See also Storms v. Coughlin,* 600 F. Supp. 1214, 1221 (S.D.N.Y. 1984) (unconfirmed EMIT results are not generally accepted in the scientific community as reliable concerning positive results).

44. In a case involving suspected alcohol intoxication, one arbitrator rejected the company's effort to rely solely on supervisors' observations, without any test results. He wrote, "to discharge a person for suspected but unconfirmed intoxication is to discharge unjustly." *Durion Co.,* 85 LA 1129 (Platen, 1985). *See also Alcan Aluminum Co.,* 88 LA 386 (Kindig, 1986) (arbitrator will not fault testing procedure which included confirmation of positive result, and allows company to rely on positive test result); *Roadway Express, Inc.,* 87 LA 224 (Cooper, 1986) (arbitrator upholds reliance on a positive immunoassay screen confirmed by GC/MS; "no one has suggested that those tests are inferior to any tests used today").

45. *See, e.g., Drug Testing in the Workplace: The Legal Dilemma,* ABAJ 52 (November 1, 1986).

46. A study of 1,090 companies conducted by the American Management Association revealed that, as of January, 1987, only slightly over 20 percent of the companies surveyed did drug testing. Of those who did not test, 8.6 percent had rejected the idea of testing. About two thirds of these 94 firms doubted the accuracy of test results. AMERICAN MANAGEMENT ASSOCIATION, DRUG ABUSE: THE WORKPLACE ISSUES 13 (1987). More and more frequently, the attack focuses on testing's inability to isolate the "when" and "why" of drug use, and its inability to quantify impairment.

47. *Hussman Corp., Food Store Div.,* 87-2 ARB ¶8326 (Maniscalco, 1987).

48. Siegel, L., *Workplace Drug Testing—The Legal Issues,* in AMERICAN MANAGEMENT ASSOCIATION, DRUG ABUSE: THE WORKPLACE ISSUES 47 (1987).

49. J. Morgan, *Problems of Mass Urine Screening for Misused Drugs,* 16 J. PSYCHOACTIVE DRUGS 305 (Oct.–Dec. 1984).

50. Morgan, *supra* note 49.

51. The program is an entirely voluntary one for member laboratories and involves a fee. *Employment Testing* 2-3.2 p. D:10 (1987).

52. San Diego Gas and Electric Company sued a testing laboratory recently for compensatory and punitive damages in excess of $500,000. The company alleged that the laboratory's negligence, fraud, and deceit in undertaking urine screens led to the company's settlement of a grievance over a termination for a test positive for marijuana. *San Diego Gas and Electric Co. v. National Health*

*Laboratories, Inc.*, Case No. 4380, San Diego Supreme Ct., filed April 23, 1987, *reported in* 90 DAILY LAB. REP. A-3 (BNA, May 12, 1987).

53. Remarks of Dr. John P. Morgan, ABA Satellite Seminar, "Drug Testing in the Workplace," June 25, 1987. *See also* Hansen, Caudill, & Boone, *Crisis in Drug Testing: Results of CDC Blind Study*, 253 JAMA 23 (April 26, 1985). Hansen, Caudill, and Boone evaluated the urine screens performed at 13 laboratories serving methadone treatment facilities. They submitted blind samples and found that the laboratories took greater care with known evaluation samples than with routine samples. *Id.*

54. *See, e.g.*, J. Morgan, *Problems of Mass Urine Screening for Misused Drugs, supra* note 49; Hansen, Caudill, Boone, *supra* note 53.

55. *Companies Find They're in Clear on Drug Testing*, Chicago Tribune, June 13, 1987, at sec. D p. 1.

56. Department of Health and Human Services, Alcohol, Drug Abuse and Mental Health Administration, *Scientific and Technical Guidelines for Drug Testing Programs*, February 13, 1987, *reprinted in* IERM 595:571 *et seq.* (BNA).

57. *Southern California Rapid Transit District*, 76 LA 144, 151 (Sabo, 1979).

58. *See, e.g.*, *Gem City Chemicals, Inc.*, 86 LA 1023 (Warns, 1986) (testing unreasonable and intrusive on privacy rights; employee improperly discharged for refusal to take test as part of industrial physical); *Foote & Davies, Inc.*, 88 LA 125 (Wahl, 1986) (discharge for refusal to submit to test improper; company had no enforced rule or policy on tests).

59. *Union Plaza Hotel*, 87-1 ARB ¶8072 (McKay, 1987).

60. *Faygo Beverages, Inc.*, 86 LA 1174 (Ellmann, 1986).

61. *See, e.g.*, *National Treasury Employees Union v. Von Raab*, 816 F.2d 170, 2 IER Cases 15 (5th Cir. 1987), *cert. granted*, ___ U.S.___ (March 1, 1988). The court in that case rejected the union's claim on the ground that urine and blood samples reveal "physical characteristics" only, and not knowledge the tested person might have to which he could testify in a legal proceeding. Where a testing policy also involves questions about medications taken or drugs used, the Fifth Amendment (applicable in the public employment context) protects employees only from "compelled disclosure of incriminating information, not information that is merely private."

62. *See, e.g.*, *Consumer Plastics Corp.*, 88 LA 208, 212 (Garnholz, 1987), where the arbitrator rejected the union's attempt to defend the grievant by claiming an undercover agent entrapped him into possessing drugs at work. The arbitrator wrote:

> "This is not a criminal matter. Entrapment [a defense to government action in a criminal case, rooted in 4th Amendment protections against illegal searches and seizures and the 5th Amendment privilege against self-incrimination] is not a defense in a civil matter. . . . As was stated by Arbitrator James P. Whyte: '. . . The job of the arbitrator, in contrast to the function of a judge or jury, is to interpret and apply the collective bargaining agreement.' *Rust Engineering Co.*, 85 LA 407, 409 (1985)."

See also *Georgia Pacific*, 85 LA 542 (King, 1985) (a discharge for drug use can be based on uncorroborated testimony of an undercover agent; the amount of proof necessary is less than that required in the criminal law).

63. *Shell Oil Co.*, 81 LA 1205 (Brisco, 1983) (employee properly discharged for refusal to open lunch box in unannounced search; employer had reason to believe box contained gun and drug; employee knew he would be disciplined for refusal); *Kraft, Inc.*, 82 LA 360 (Denson, 1984) (employees properly disciplined for refusal to submit to search when they were discovered sneaking into area where marijuana smoke was smelled); *Shell Oil Co., Deer Park*, 84 LA 562 (Milentz, 1985) (discharge proper when employee refused to open car to permit search after marijuana was seen on dashboard); *Prestige Stamping Co.*, 74 LA 163 (Keefe, 1980) (employee insubordinately refused to obey orders to produce newspaper hiding bag suspected of containing drugs); *Michigan Consolidated Gas Co.*, 80 LA 693 (Keefe, 1983) (employee, who disobeyed order not to flush toilet in course of investigation of charges that he sold white packets, properly discharged). *But see Houston Lighting and Power Co.*, 87 LA 478 (Howell, 1986) (discharge of employee for "failure to cooperate" in investigation of drug use, by reason of deception, improper; employee submitted to tests).

64. *American Standard, WABCO Div.*, 77 LA 1085 (1981), demonstrates how evidence of insubordination is linked to, but is not the same as, evidence of use or impairment. Arbitrator Katz upheld the discharge of an employee observed to be unsteady, glassy-eyed, and slurred of speech, who repeatedly refused to take a drug test. The test was reasonably ordered, based on the observations, the arbitrator ruled, and discharge was appropriate due to the combination of the observations of impairment and the refusal to submit to the test.

65. *Faygo Beverages*, 86 LA 1174 (Ellmann, 1986).

66. An example of a cross-reactivity problem is the EMIT immunoassay's tendency to produce false positive results for "amphetamine"—whether legally or illegally taken—from ephedrine and phenylpropanolamine, compounds used as decongestants in many over-the-counter cold, allergy, and diet preparations. The Amphetamine Confirmation Kit for use with EMIT tests is optional. Glucose in urine, and a product of urine decomposition in improperly stored samples may also cause false positives for amphetamines in EMIT tests.

67. *Hoover Co.*, 77 LA 1287, 1290 (Strasshofer, Jr., 1982).

68. *Id.*

69. Minn. Stat. §181.953(9) (second test at employee's expense); Montana Rev. Code Ann. § 39-2-304(3); Rhode Island Ga. Laws §28-6.5-1(F), as amended by Ch. 540, L.1987; Vt. Stat. Ann. ___ 21, §514(6)(B) (employee may request blood sample be taken). *See also*, pending amendment to Illinois House bill 937, §(2)(C)(i) and (iii).

70. *See* discussion in text following note 49, *supra*.

71. *See* Utah Code Ann. §§34-38-7, 6; Minn. Stat. §181.952; Vt. Stat. Ann. §514(2); Mont. Rev. Code Ann. §39-2-304(5) (misdemeanor); Vt. Stat. Ann. §519 (civil

action for damages and injunctive relief; state action for civil penalty; criminal misdemeanor penalty).

72. Minn. Stat. §181.956 (civil action for damages, injunctive relief); Mont. Rev. Code Ann. §39-2-304(5) (misdemeanor); Vt. Stat. Ann. §519 (civil action for damages and injunctive relief; state action for civil penalty; criminal misdemeanor penalty).

73. See discussion in Chapter 6.

74. In addition to the statutes cited in notes 69, 71, 72, supra, the following state laws provide a starting remedy for violation of procedural protections which must be included in a drug testing program: R.I. Gen. Laws §28-6.5-1(F) (civil action including injunctive relief; punitive damages; misdemeanor); Iowa Code §730.5.11; Ct. Gen. Stats. ch. ___ sec. ___ (civil action for damages, injunctive relief).

75. See discussion in Chapter 6 in text at notes 202–217.

76. One federal court applying state law rejected a theory that a comprehensive drug testing policy constituted a contract changing an at-will employee to an employee who could be terminated only for cause. See Greco v. Halliburton Co., 674 F. Supp. 1447, 2 IER Cases 1281 (D. Wyo. 1987). Several states have upheld suits based on this type of theory. See e.g., Duldulao v. St. Mary of Nazareth Hospital, 505 N.E. 2d 314, 1 IER Cases 1428 (1987); Vinyard v. King, 728 F.2d 428, 115 LRRM 3563 (10th Cir. 1984) (applying Oklahoma law); Lincoln v. Sterling Drug, Inc., 622 F. Supp. 66 (D. Conn. 1985) (Connecticut law); Barger v. General Electric Co., 599 F. Supp. 1154, 121 LRRM 2058 (W.D. Va. 1984) (Virginia law); Smith v. Teledyne Industries, Inc., 578 F. Supp. 353, 115 LRRM 2901 (E.D. Mich. 1984) (Ohio law); Brooks v. Trans World Airlines, Inc., 574 F. Supp. 805, 114 LRRM 3136 (D. Colo. 1983) (Colorado law); Leikvold v. Valley View Community Hospital, 141 Ariz. 544, 688 P.2d 170, 116 LRRM 2193 (1984); Pugh v. See's Candies, Inc., 116 Cal. App. 3d 311, 171 Cal. Rptr. 917, 115 LRRM 4002 (1981); Salimi v. Farmers Insurance Group, 684 P.2d 264, 1 IER Cases 1403 (Colo. App. 1984); Finley v. Aetna Life & Casualty Co., 5 Conn. App. 394, 499 A.2d 64, 120 LRRM 3519 (1985); Jackson v. Minidoka Irrigation District, 98 Idaho 330, 563 P.2d 54, 115 LRRM 5040 (1977); Wyman v. Osteopathic Hospital of Maine, Inc., 493 A.2d 330, 119 LRRM 3438 (Me. 1985); Staggs v. Blue Cross of Maryland, Inc., 61 Md. App. 381, 486 A.2d 798 (1985); Toussaint v. Blue Cross & Blue Shield, 408 Mich. 579, 292 N.W.2d 880, 115 LRRM 4708 (1980); Pine River State Bank v. Mettille, 333 N.W.2d 633, 115 LRRM 4493 (Minn. 1983); Enyeart v. Shelter Mutual Insurance Co., 693 S.W.2d 120, 119 LRRM 3319 (Mo. App. 1985); Morris v. Lutheran Medical Center, 215 Neb. 677, 340 N.W.2d 388, 115 LRRM 4966 (1983); Southwest Gas Corp. v. Ahmad, 99 Nev. 594, 668 P.2d 261, 114 LRRM 2633 (1983); Woolley v. Hoffman-LaRoche, Inc., 99 N.J. 284, 491 A.2d 1257, 1 IER Cases 995 (1985); Forrester v. Parker, 93 N.M. 781, 606 P.2d 191 (1980); Bolling v. Clevepak Corp., 20 Ohio App. 3d 113, 484 N.E.2d 1367 (1984); Langdon v. Saga Corp., 569 P.2d 524, 115 LRRM 4975 (Okla. Ct. App. 1976); Yartzoff v. Democrat-Herald Publishing Co., 281 Or. 651, 576 P.2d 356, 115 LRRM 5061 (1978); Osterkamp v. Alkota Mfg., Inc., 332 N.W.2d 275, 115 LRRM 2824 (S.D. 1983); Hamby v.

*Genesco, Inc.*, 627 S.W.2d 373 (Tenn. App. 1981); *Piacitelli v. Southern Utah State College*, 636 P.2d 1063 (Utah 1981); *Thompson v. St. Regis Paper Co.*, 102 Wash. 2d 219, 685 P.2d 1081, 1 IER Cases 392 (1984); *Mobil Coal Producing, Inc. v. Parks*, 704 P.2d 702, 1 IER Cases 1341 (Wyo. 1985).

77. *Belfatto v. Robert Bosch Corp.*, No. 86 C 6632, slip op. (N.D. Ill. April 14, 1987); *Bailey v. Perkins Restaurants, Inc.*, 398 N.W.2d 120, 122 (N.D. 1986); *Leikvold v. Valley View Community Hospital*, 141 Ariz. 544, 688 P.2d 170, 116 LRRM 2193 (1984); *Woolley v. Hoffman-LaRoche, Inc.*, 99 N.J. 284, 491 A.2d 1257, 1 IER Cases 995 (1985).

78. *See, e.g.*, cases cited *supra* note 77.

79. *See, e.g.*, *Philco Corp.*, 45 LA 437, 441 (Keeler, 1965) ("Company does not have to establish that it had, or that it had communicated specific rules for certain well-recognized proven offenses such as drunkenness, theft or insubordination.")

80. *Foote & Davies, Inc.*, 88 LA 125 (Wahl, 1986) (despite alleged past practice of requiring submission to tests, company could not penalize employee for refusal to take blood test when it had no written policy regarding tests); *Union Oil Co. of California*, 88 LA 91 (Weiss, 1986) (suspensions improper where company had no written rule prohibiting mere presence of illegal drugs in employees' systems, and no written policy announcing that employees would be submitted to screening tests without notice); *Bamberger's New Jersey*, 60 LA 960 (Trotta, 1973) (no written notice that employees must submit to urine tests and that failure to take test will result in discipline, means discipline is invalid); *Capital Area Transit Authority*, 69 LA 811 (Ellmann, 1977) (work rule's prohibitions against drugs are reasonable, but testing requirement, not circulated to employees or union, was invalid because it was not posted); *CFS Continental, Inc.*, 86-1 ARB ¶8070 (Lumbley, 1985) (agreement was silent *re* testing; decision to conduct a surprise test with 24 hours advance notice to union was inappropriate and unreasonable, as company had not previously posted a testing policy).

81. *See e.g.*, *Watauga Industries, Inc.*, 78 LA 697 (Galambos, 1982) (discharge too severe when employer took no action to "pass the word" that rampant marijuana smoking would no longer be tolerated); *Union Oil Co. of California*, 88 LA 91 (Weiss, 1977) (discharge improper where employer relying on positive tests could not distinguish on-duty from off-duty uses; employer had no published rule; and employer had given no notice that employees would be discharged on the basis of positive test results).

82. *See, e.g.*, *Deaconess Medical Center*, 88 LA 44 (Robinson, 1986) (the arbitrator found that the employer could require a nurse to submit to periodic random testing as a condition of continued employment, even though the contract and work rules were silent regarding drug testing); *American Standard, WABCO Division*, 77 LA 1085 (Katz, 1981) ("witness for employment" physical exams may include drug screens where there is reasonable cause to suspect unfitness,

even though company has no posted testing policy). *Cf. Arco-Polymers, Inc.*, 69 LA 379 (Milentz, 1977) (upholding discharge of an employee arrested for dealing heroin off-duty; despite absence of violation of workplace rule, arbitrator finds sufficient adverse effect on plant, and sufficient interest in preventing a drug problem before it starts, to uphold discharge).

# —6——

# UNION CHALLENGES TO TESTING

## ——— THE UNION'S PERSPECTIVE

A president of a union local picks up a magazine and reads an article discussing the existence of a serious national drug problem, and at the same time the article notes that the problem has leveled off.[1] Union representatives and stewards tell him horror stories of two kinds: about employees who claim to have been wronged by drug testing, and about the wrongs drug-using employees have done to company property, the public, and other employees.

He knows that the union must process all members' grievances which raise critical fairness issues. Some grievances, however, if upheld, may cause serious problems for other union members or the public. Winning a grievance that reinstates an alleged thief for procedural defects of notice or in the investigation of the case is one thing; only the profit margin suffers. Winning the reinstatement of an admitted drug user because the company botched procedures involved in discharging him for a major accident increases safety risks for the public or other employees when that employee returns to work.

Successfully negotiating for a rehabilitation program (or forcing a more consistent use of an existing program in arbitration) has its own contradictions as well, and presents its own job satisfaction problems. A discharged employee submits to counseling to get his job back, and then an accident occurs. Employees hear the rumor "it was drugs" and wonder

165

what the safety committee is doing about getting substance abusers off the road or away from machinery. Not one of these worried employees, however, wants to be bumped out of a noncritical job for the benefit of a more senior employee who decides to seek help, change to a less safety-critical job, and enter an employee assistance program *before* he causes an accident.

There are other sad experiences that may damage both individual employees and the bargaining unit as a whole. For example, fear of needles costs a senior employee his job after he is involved in an accident and refuses to allow the company's doctor to draw blood, pursuant to company policy. He offers to submit a urine sample instead, and the company refuses and terminates him because the drug testing program requires adherence to its procedures without deviation. Employees complain bitterly that they are unexpectedly asked to urinate in a bottle in front of a supervisor; they blame the union for the indignity. Supervisors who for years have accommodated long-term employees' alcohol, health, and personal problems with understanding now must fire those who are reported to test positive for metabolites of marijuana, ingested who knows how long ago. An employee with no work problems who tests positive for marijuana or cocaine metabolites swears up and down that he has "never used." The union president believes these employees and understands the limits of testing procedures, but he also knows that some employees have their limits. He knows there is a market for "pure" human urine, and that some employees buy it to be prepared in case of testing. Then there is the employee who uses pot off-duty but has no problems at work. The union president also knows that the supervisor who fires the pot-smoker when he tests positive, suspends him without pay, or insists he attend a drug-abuse program drinks off duty. Where is the balance?

The union president in these hypothetical examples must be fair. The union must offer the same procedures and services to all members whether they are substance abusers or not. It must offer fair access to the services it administers under a contract with an employer (eg, safety programs, safety vigilance, and the grievance/arbitration process) consistent with its duties as exclusive bargaining agent for all members.[2] It must offer internal union procedures to every member on an equal basis to avoid liability, for instance, for federally prohibited discrimination,[3] commission of unfair labor practices,[4] state-prohibited discrimination on the basis of handicap,[5] and violation of the employees' "Bill of Rights" as union members under the Labor-Management Reporting and Disclosure Act.[6] Meanwhile, it must consolidate its power among members by obtaining the best benefits possible and by spending resources—particularly union dues—in the most efficient way. It must decide whether to negotiate, arbitrate, or capitulate. The union must, therefore, continually weigh the costs of each possible approach to employers' decisions to fight the drug war. Should the union become an ally, and if so, with whom?

Most labor unions have decided that drug and alcohol testing is first and foremost a threat to members' rights, and, therefore, a threat to the union's security as the employees' exclusive bargaining representative. Especially when bargaining on economic issues results in little or no gain, or in concessions, unions may fear that their inability to prevent intrusions into members' rights will erode members' support for the union's continued existence.[7] The employer's decision to impose drug testing and to discipline or discharge employees may appear to unions to be a campaign to purge the bargaining unit of troublemakers, or to discredit the union.[8]

Few unions, however, have followed advice circulating among labor law academics to fight drug testing policies tooth and nail.[9] Instead, many increasingly acknowledge that the employer's and the individual employees' concerns about a safe work environment deserve consideration. Some unions, representing employees who drive, provide public transportation, or work in safety-sensitive jobs, have accepted or even bargained on their own initiative for programs that link a reliable testing program to reasonable disciplinary presumptions, opportunities for rehabilitation for employees with alcohol or substance abuse problems, and procedural safeguards. This type of integrated, bargained-for program more and more frequently includes the following types of provisions:

1. Employee Assistance Programs (EAPs): Unions look for programs providing substance abuse counseling to all employees, not just those who volunteer. Volunteers are not to be disciplined for volunteering, but they may be removed from driving, equipment operating, or safety-sensitive jobs. These programs provide counseling as a first alternative to suspension or discharge, or after a mandatory referral by a supervisor for poor job performance. Agreements frequently provide a mandatory period of initial participation in an EAP. A broad EAP provision may make it politically feasible for a union to agree to regulation of off-duty drug use, or to presumptions of intoxication or other cutoff levels.

2. Testing Programs: Unions insist on highly accurate confirming tests and pristine scientific procedures. An enzyme-multiplied immunoassay technique (EMIT) is generally accepted as an initial urine screen, provided that a positive result will be confirmed by gas chromatography/mass spectrometry (GC/MS). Agreements may provide that the confirming test be supplemented with a GC/MS test of the employee's blood sample. The Teamsters' National Master Freight (NMF) agreement and the Washington Metropolitan Area Transit Authority (WMATA) testing agreement, following the testing program used in the U.S. military, provide that the employee is presumed intoxicated or under the influence if certain minimum levels of alcohol or drugs

are detected in a blood or urine sample. For alcohol, the level is .05%, or on a sliding scale, depending on elapsed time from the beginning of the work day. For drugs or their metabolites, the levels are 80 ng/mL THC (U.S. military program); 30 ng/mL THC (NMF agreement); 5 ng/mL THC in blood, 10 ng/mL in blood plasma (WMATA agreement).

3. Obtaining samples: Unions insist that the employer may test for drugs only upon reasonable cause. Occasionally, they will agree that reasonable cause may be presumed in the case of a serious accident or injury. Failure to submit to the test may be grounds for discharge. Less frequently, employees may be required to allow supervisors of the same sex to accompany them—but not to watch—when samples are taken. Employees may be allowed to give second samples that will be preserved for tests by the union's laboratory.

4. Procedural provisions: Unions will wish to establish procedures for documenting and corroborating observations of employees and for the preservation of verifiable samples through the "chain of custody." Union agreements on drug testing may provide that a supervisor must complete a report on his observations of the employee at the time it was determined the employee should be tested. Agreements may provide that the chain of custody of the sample be documented. Unions will seek an agreement that violation of these procedures invalidates disciplinary actions.

Union challenges to a testing program will be reduced if an employer (1) emphasizes the seriousness of the need to combat the drug problem in the workplace (accompanied by evidence to show there is a problem) and the importance of safety and performance for everyone involved; (2) promulgates a policy that accounts for the scientific limits of testing; and (3) develops procedures that provide greater certainty and fewer arbitrable questions.

At present, however, if employers institute severe measures in the "war on drugs," they may provoke an equally severe response from labor unions. Union challenges to drug testing—to invalidate drug and alcohol testing policies as a whole, and to remedy the effects of particular procedural practices and discipline in individual cases—take several forms. The union's principal weapon in court is the injunction to suspend the operation of a testing program either pending arbitration under a collective bargaining agreement, or indefinitely, for violations of constitutional rights. Unions representing employees covered under state or federal labor relations acts may attempt to prevent an incursion into their power by filing unfair labor practice charges on grounds that the employer implemented its testing policy without first bargaining with the union. A union may also seek to arbitrate the dispute, claiming that a testing policy or particular discipline violates the collective bargaining agreement.

# ——— INJUNCTIONS

Various statistics show that employers increasingly feel a pressing need to implement drug and alcohol testing programs immediately to solve workplace drug problems or to answer the public perception that problems exist.[10] No comprehensive study analyzes the correspondence between perceptions of a drug abuse problem and an actual problem. There is evidence, however, that employers are developing and imposing testing programs based on speculation, rather than knowledge about workplace substance abuse.[11] As employers transform fear to suspicion and suspicion to concrete work rules, labor unions quickly meet the challenge with suits to enjoin the use of a new or changed testing program.

In the public sector, the union files suit both to enjoin the use of the program and, at the same time, to have the program declared unlawful as a violation of employees' constitutional rights. In the private sector, the union's goal is to preserve the status quo until the appropriate arbitrator or tribunal decides whether the drug testing program is reasonable under the existing contract, or whether the employer imposed it in derogation of federal and state law concerning the obligation to bargain. The issue for the union in a suit for injunction generally concerns the integrity of the arbitration process and bargaining obligations more than it concerns the actual testing program. A union that might accept a reasonable program based on reasonable work rules would resent an employer's decision to impose a testing program implemented without discussion, notice, or a mutual understanding. This is particularly the case when a new program includes provisions that are anathema to unions: random testing, a prohibition of all use of drugs, even off-duty use, and severe discipline with no option for rehabilitation.

When the employer and the union have a contract including an agreement to arbitrate, the union will generally seek an injunction requiring the employer to postpone the program until an arbitrator can rule upon its propriety under the contract. If the employer refuses to arbitrate at all, unions can protect contractual arbitration provisions by filing suit under Section 301 of the National Labor Relations Act (NLRA) and similar state law provisions applicable in the public sector to force the employer to perform its agreement to arbitrate disputes over the new or changed drug testing program.[12] In some cases, the appropriate labor relations agency will also seek to stay the start of the program pending the resolution of unfair labor charges based upon the employer's failure to bargain before the program was implemented.[13]

## Union Injunctions in the Private Sector

To the extent that a union's suit for injunction in the private sector involves a "labor dispute," and does not raise critical issues involving the grievance-arbitration process, the suit is prohibited in the federal courts under §4 of the Norris-LaGuardia Act.[14] That act forbids federal courts to exercise jurisdiction to enjoin certain broadly defined conduct in connection with labor disputes. It is clear that the act does not prevent suits to enjoin a wide variety of conduct—union or employer—that involves a breach of a collective bargaining agreement, when the agreement contains a mandatory grievance-arbitration procedure encompassing the parties' dispute over the breach.[15] Courts[16] may therefore hear unions' suits for injunctions to halt employer conduct such as the implementing of new rules, in order to preserve the status quo pending arbitration.[17]

Generally speaking, a union will survive a jurisdictional challenge to its suit for injunction by alleging only a few significant facts. The union must meet the following basic requirements to avoid dismissal under the Norris-LaGuardia Act. First, the union must allege facts to show that the employer breached the parties' collective bargaining agreement when it implemented the drug testing program.[18] It must show that the agreement contained a mandatory arbitration clause encompassing the imposition of a testing program, or evidence of an agreement requiring the employer to arbitrate the testing program issues as a quid pro quo for the union's agreement not to strike.[19]

In order to obtain the injunction after it has established the court's jurisdiction, the union must show a court that the injunction it seeks is the only means of preserving the integrity of the arbitration process itself, or the meaning of an arbitration award.[20] This final requirement concerns whether "it is necessary to prevent conduct by the party enjoined from rendering the arbitral process a hollow formality in those instances where . . . the arbitral award when rendered could not return the parties substantially to the *status quo ante*."[21] The union must also allege facts to show the presence of the common law's basic equitable underpinnings for injunctive relief: irreparable harm to union members if the testing program is not enjoined;[22] a balance of harms showing that possible harm to employees in the absence of an injunction is clearly greater than the possible harm to the employer if the program is enjoined; and a reasonable likelihood of success on the merits. The last factor involves little more than stating some nonfrivolous argument the union intends to raise before the arbitrator.[23]

Recent decisions in the drug testing area indicate that the "irreparable harm," "balance of equities," and "integrity of the arbitral process" factors are potentially difficult to apply. They overlap in several respects, so the critical question in a suit for injunction really is: Assuming that the harm the union alleges from the immediate imposition of the testing program is genuine, will the regular grievance-arbitration procedure substantially remedy the harm? If it will, no injunction is necessary, because no real harm threatens the union or the arbitration process. Recent decisions indicate that obtaining injunctive relief seems to depend on the union's ability to paint a careful picture of a new testing policy's likely tendencies to harm employees in ways an arbitrator cannot remedy.

Allegations of harm that do not go beyond a claim that employees will suffer more severe discipline or swifter discharge are unlikely to win an injunction. Courts have reviewed allegations of this type and rejected claims for injunctive relief, relying upon the arbitrator's ability to reinstate employees and award them back pay. One court reasoned that if the arbitrator invalidated changes that increased the swiftness and severity of penalties under an existing policy, he could do away with any threat to the integrity of the bargaining process by making disciplined employees whole through reinstatement and back pay.[24] Likewise, widening the scope of existing drug rules to include testing upon suspicion of drug use, where the prior system allowed discipline based on supervisors' evaluations alone, has been upheld on grounds that the testing caused no irreparable harm. One court refused to issue an injunction in such a case because the changes that the company implemented actually improved the presentation of evidence in the existing process. The court found that any discipline resulting from the new disciplinary scheme could be halted or reversed, and affected employees could be made whole after the company implemented the plan and the arbitrator decided the contractual issues.[25]

Stigma resulting from the imposition of a testing program is probably insufficient to warrant an injunction. When humiliation exists as a result of an earlier drug testing policy and the new, more severe policy merely increases it by imposing stricter penalties, humiliation is no source of harm to the integrity of the arbitration process, and is, therefore, insufficient as a ground for injunctive relief.[26] However, a showing of humiliation stemming from the invasiveness of random testing combined with damage to the employee's reputation led one court to grant an injunction forbidding the employer from implementing its testing program pending arbitration.[27] One private sector union successfully argued that the employer's changes in its existing testing program harmed employees by invading their privacy and damaging their reputations. In addition to requiring employees to submit to tests when reasonable grounds existed to believe they were working under the influence, or suspected of using drugs at work, the company required testing, including random testing, as part of its mandatory routine physical and as a follow-up to drug or alcohol rehabilitation. The court found that the union did not demonstrate irreparable harm based on the increased possibility of discharge, but the allegation of invasion of privacy nonetheless warranted an injunction.[28]

Another, somewhat less well-defined argument unions put forward is that employees will be irreparably harmed because of deprivations of privacy rights drug testing programs may cause. The argument involves a type of speculation, one court held, that does not justify concluding that employees will be irreparably harmed, given the limited right of privacy involved in private sector cases. The court stated:

> "It should be noted that the matter of confidentiality is expressly written into [the] plan and there is not reasonable basis to conclude that otherwise private information will become public. Additionally, the notion that inappropriate treatment will be mandated is highly speculative and also does not afford a present basis upon which to base a judicial decision of injunctive relief. The right of privacy of an employee of a private company to be free from drug testing programs is not absolute. There is no evidence which compels the conclusion that the employees' rights of privacy, whatever the breadth of those rights, will be violated in these circumstances. More significantly, there is no reason to conclude that any damage that may be incurred is irreparable in nature and not within the power of the arbitrator to recompense or otherwise vindicate."[29]

Unions continue to make this challenge, however. In light of the first wave of decisions allowing testing based on reasonable suspicion until an arbitrator decides the contractual questions, unions have begun to focus on drug testing policies' alleged intrusions into privacy. They rely on cases involving state and federal employees, or employees in industries where state action is involved, to argue that private sector employees have an amorphous "right to privacy" that should somehow be protected. In isolated cases unions have successfully convinced courts to protect "privacy," and they have done so without defining the source of the right.[30]

Practical concerns for safety may shift the balance of harms in the union's favor. In one recent case a company with an existing testing policy introduced more severe measures. The court[31] held that the existing policy adequately protected public safety and allowed the arbitrator to address the newer, more stringent measures. The court found that the existing policy tipped the equitable test for balance of hardships to the union: the existing policy meant that the employer would not suffer if the changes were not implemented during the 40 days or so it took to resolve the arbitration.[32] Thus, an existing policy may indicate that the workplace drug problem is sufficiently under control to warrant maintaining the status quo until an arbitrator can review the new, more stringent measures. Significantly, one court has indicated that the union need not show that the status quo temporarily meets safety concerns *unless* the employer can first justify the need for more draconian measures, or for any policy at all. The court granted an injunction where the company presented no evidence that there was any drug abuse problem at its facility, stating that "to arbitrarily test without any reason whatsoever is an infringement on the rights of the individuals."[33]

Litigation to enjoin drug testing balances on the question of harm and does not suggest any easy answers for the union and employer squaring off on the drug testing issue. Cases do suggest that lawsuits for injunctions to preserve the status quo are fairly inevitable if an employer unilaterally imposes a strict testing policy without bargaining with the union, or even if the parties agree to disagree about the policy and the employer wishes to implement it before arbitration. An injunction in the private sector is more likely to issue when the drug testing program involves some form of random testing imposed without objective evidence of a workplace drug problem.

Although the union seeks the injunction, it is the employer who must first evaluate whether the workplace situation warrants particularly severe and immediate procedures. The decision may come down to whether the cost of litigation to delay implementation by means of injunctive relief is worth the extra few months of coverage under the new testing policy. In any private sector situation where a mandatory arbitration clause is not part of a quid pro quo arrangement for a no-strike clause, or where the clause is somehow limited so that it does not cover the dispute over testing, the employer must also consider the possibility of a strike in response to the company's refusal to bargain.

## Union Injunctions in the Public Sector

Recent decisions indicate that courts are willing to grant injunctions to public employee unions seeking to prevent the imposition of a drug testing program that invades employees' constitutional rights.[34] In these cases, the issues of irreparable harm and likelihood of success on the merits are subsumed as part of a larger issue, whether the proposed testing program violates constitutional rights.[35] A public employee union is more likely to win a permanent injunction when the plan it challenges is both highly invasive of employees' constitutional rights and without protective procedural standards to regulate the abuses which testing may impose on constitutional rights.

# —— UNFAIR LABOR PRACTICE CHARGES

No union is likely to allow the shadow of workplace drug abuse problems to obscure the employer's obligation to bargain over drug testing programs; that obligation is the source of the union's reason for existence. Generally speaking, the private sector employer's duty under the National

Labor Relations Act (NLRA) to bargain with the union representing its employees extends to all proposed management actions regarding "wages, hours, and other terms and conditions of employment"—the "mandatory" subjects of bargaining.[36] The Railway Labor Act, the federal labor statute which regulates rail and air carriers, imposes a similar duty to bargain over "working conditions" which are mandatory subjects.[37]

A mandatory subject of bargaining is anything "germane to the 'working environment' " which "is not among those 'managerial decisions' . . . which lie at the core of entrepreneurial control."[38] Failing to bargain over mandatory subjects is an unfair labor practice under sections 8(a)(5) and (1) of the NLRA.[39] With some exceptions,[40] the duty to bargain prohibits an employer from unilaterally changing its employees' wages, hours and terms, and conditions of employment. Thus, unilateral change in a mandatory subject of bargaining, before the expiration of an existing agreement or while negotiations for a new or successor agreement are under way, is usually a per se violation of the NLRA, absent the union's waiver or acquiescence.[41] To avoid liability under §8(a)(5), the change imposing a drug testing program must generally occur only after the parties reach impasse in negotiations for an agreement, and it must be reasonably related to the employer's last proposals prior to impasse.[42] The statutory definition of the duty to bargain thus presents the National Labor Relations Board (NLRB) with two questions: 1. Is drug testing a mandatory subject of bargaining either in and of itself or because it is a substantial change in working conditions, and 2. In any particular case, do any of the defenses to liability apply?

## Mandatory Subjects of Bargaining

Neither the NLRB nor the courts have yet ruled on whether a drug testing program is a mandatory subject of bargaining whose implementation in all cases constitutes a change in working conditions and requires an employer to bargain. The NLRB's General Counsel, however, has issued a guideline memorandum concerning drug or alcohol testing.[43] It is the General Counsel's position that drug testing of job applicants and current employees is a mandatory subject of bargaining. The General Counsel has therefore directed the regional offices to issue complaints unless a union clearly and unmistakably waived its bargaining rights by language in a contract, inaction, or past practice. The NLRB will also continue to refrain from issuing a complaint when a case presents questions, arising under a collective bargaining agreement, which are deferred to arbitration.

The Board has received instructions that it is to seek reinstatement and back pay for employees terminated as a result of unilaterally implemented policies. Employers may, however, show that this remedy is inappropriate, by proving that the employee is in fact a drug user, and that his position is incompatible with drug use, based on the type and amount of drug detected.[44]

The General Counsel's position is largely based on existing NLRB case law regarding the duty to bargain. For instance, it has been clear for some time that if new or more severe discipline is involved for current employees, an employer must notify a union of the new disciplinary program and bargain before putting the program into effect. New work rules which result in discipline or increased penalties in contexts other than the drug testing area are regularly held to trigger the obligation to bargain.[45] Even if the employer touts a drug testing program as a measure addressing solely safety or rehabilitation, a union is likely to insist that the employer bargain over its implementation. Both physical examinations[46] and changes in plant safety rules[47] have been held to be mandatory subjects of bargaining that require notice and an opportunity to bargain before being implemented. In a case involving the employer's decision to implement a pulmonary function and audiometric medical screening program, the NLRB found a violation of Sections 8(a)(5) and (1) of the NLRA because the employer used the screening tests to deny employment to applicants and to terminate new employees without bargaining over this use of the test results.[48] The use of the tests to establish safety data for Occupational Safety and Health Administration (OSHA) purposes and to assign employees to jobs was permissible, the Board found, because the union had been informed of these uses and acquiesced in them.[49]

In the General Counsel's view, the obligation to bargain over the "substantial change" drug testing has upon working conditions extends to the particulars of how the testing will be conducted, how the test results will be used, and what impact the test results or refusal to submit to a test will have on employment. This result stems from the Board's prior decisions concerning polygraph tests and physicals. With respect to polygraph tests, the Board had held that required bargaining includes the "validity and integrity of the testing procedure," the breadth of the test, and the qualifications of persons who devise and administer the test, as well as the impact the test results will have.[50]

The General Counsel's position regarding preemployment testing of applicants as a mandatory subject of bargaining presents the NLRB and the courts with previously undecided issues. Job applicants are not members of the bargaining unit, but any employer proposal relating to them which "vitally affects the 'terms and conditions' of . . . employment" of employees who are in the bargaining unit may be a mandatory subject of bargaining.[51] The General Counsel's position is that screening out potential employees who have used drugs necessarily interests current employees who use drugs and may be concerned with invasive penalties for off-duty drug use. The NLRB's prior cases held that conditions of becoming employed, where agreements to use hiring halls are concerned, are mandatory subjects of bargaining.[52]

## Waiver and Deferral

The union must take its contract into account before deciding whether to file an unfair labor practice charge over a new drug testing program. In some circumstances, the union may have agreed to contractual language that waives its right to bargain about drug testing. Thus, under existing case law, the employer's decision to implement a drug testing program unilaterally during the term of an existing agreement may not be a breach of its duty to bargain under Section 8(a)(5) if the contract contains a management rights clause that expressly permits the employer to change work rules or safety policies.[53] The NLRB will soon test whether the management rights clause must specifically refer to drug testing, or whether freedom to change "work rules," "safety policies," or "physicals" is sufficient. The General Counsel has reasoned that drug testing is analogous to physical examinations and polygraph tests, matters the NLRB has previously determined to be mandatory subjects of bargaining. These matters do not constitute new "rules," which many employers have discretion to impose under management rights clauses preserving the right to impose new work rules unilaterally. Instead, they are special means of enforcing rules, the General Counsel argues, and represent a substantial change in working conditions necessitating bargaining, notwithstanding the usual type of management rights clause.

The union must also consider whether it has given up its right to insist on bargaining by failure to act. A union may waive its right to bargain if it has "consciously" allowed similar unilateral changes to go unchallenged in the past.[54] It may likewise waive a right to bargain if it fails to respond to the employer's "clear and unequivocal" notice of a proposed change with a request for bargaining.[55] A union's unfair labor practice charge after the new testing program is a *fait accompli* sufficient to invoke bargaining obligations without a prior formal request for bargaining.[56]

There is no waiver, however, when the union fails to discuss a new program the employer wishes to implement during the term of an existing contract. Section 8(d) of the Act provides that the duty to bargain "shall not be construed as requiring either party to discuss or agree to any modification of the terms and conditions contained in a contract for a fixed period, if such modification is to become effective before such terms and conditions can be reopened under the terms of the contract." The union's failure to discuss a unilateral modification of an existing agreement is no defense for the employer charged with unlawfully making a unilateral change of a contract term in violation of Section 8(a)(5).[57]

When the employer does seek to implement a change during the term of an existing agreement, if there is a bargaining demand, the parties must discuss any bargainable issues that are not treated in the contract and that the parties have never discussed.[58] The NLRB will narrowly construe "zipper" or "wrap-up" clauses,[59] which normally operate as a waiver of a right to bargain over any subject not "zippered" into the contract, and will look to bargaining history and other factors for a conscious waiver.[60]

The NLRB will dismiss a complaint alleging a §8(a)(5) violation when the employer relies on existing work rules and contractual authority to implement a testing program, if this reliance does not mask bad faith, an attempt to undermine the union, or anti-union animus.[61] Where the charge involves the union's and the employer's conflicting interpretations of whether the agreement requires bargaining, the NLRB will recommend arbitration.[62] If an arbitrator has already determined that a change was permissible under the contract, the NLRB will not find that there was any modification of the contract at all, let alone one that could be called unlawful.[63] Such a finding means that the employer need not show an "unequivocal" waiver to have the charge dismissed because the arbitrator's finding, relying upon contract language, presumes that the parties bargained over the change and it was covered by contract language.[64]

## Bargaining in Good Faith

Assuming the union clears all the hurdles concerning waiver and its acquiescence to the employer's conduct, and that the parties do meet before a unilateral change is imposed, the union will expect the employer to "meet at reasonable times and confer in good faith with respect to . . . the negotiation of an agreement. . . ."[65] The "good faith" standard has fathered more litigation and frustration than certainty,[66] because the success of an 8(a)(5) charge alleging refusal to bargain in good faith requires a review of the "totality of conduct."[67] In general terms, good faith requires both sides to participate in negotiations with an intent to find a basis for agreement.[68] It does not require that an agreement be reached.[69] Similarly, it does not require either side to make concessions or back down from a "firm, fair" offer.[70]

Various factors, in varying combinations, tend to support a refusal to bargain charge.[71] A best-case scenario for a union that has filed a refusal to bargain charge can be sketched out. For instance, a union's case is best if an employer:

1. Proposes a draconian drug testing policy, including predictably unacceptable features like random testing, supervised sample production, immediate discharge for an off-duty drug user, discharge for unconfirmed positive test results, and curtailed employee assistance programs (if they existed before for other reasons). The NLRB has held that initial proposals which are outrageous or unjustified on their face are evidence of bad faith bargaining.[72]

2. Refuses to meet or obstructs meetings by causing delay, scheduling meetings arbitrarily, cancelling meetings, insisting on inconvenient times or locations, or putting arbitrary time deadlines on discussions at meetings. The NLRB has held that this type of conduct is evidence of a bad faith attempt to frustrate discussion of proposals.[73]

3. Refuses to consider union counterproposals. While the NLRA does *not* require either side at the bargaining table to back down from a position in order to reach agreement, it does require the parties to demonstrate some willingness to review and consider the other side's proposals. An employer thus may not announce to the union that it has considered all the angles, knows what is best for employees, and has come up with the only possible acceptable solution to the workplace drug problem. This kind of an initial statement, the NLRB has held, is strong enough evidence of bad faith to discourage any bargaining at all.[74] Because the duty to bargain extends to the terms of a drug testing program as well as whether one will be implemented at all, the employer must at least listen to counterproposals concerning all details of the program.

4. Hinges the entire agreement on obtaining agreement on nonmandatory or impermissible subjects of bargaining.[75]

5. Refuses to provide information, either specific information about proposals with economic impact (where economic reasons are the justification for the proposal) or reasonable justifications for proposals.[76]

6. Frustrates a final agreement by providing negotiators with no authority to agree, withdrawing proposals already agreed upon, introducing new proposals, or otherwise complicating bargaining to create insoluble problems.[77]

7. Refuses to finalize an agreement, either by delaying meetings, refusing to seek approval of the agreement, or refusing to sign the drafted agreement.[78]

## ——— ARBITRATION

A union is most likely to use arbitration to challenge a drug testing procedure. Academics and legal theorists say that arbitration satisfies internal union political constraints, keeps members happy, and fosters peaceful labor relations.[79] Where drug testing is concerned, arbitration may also cost the union; expensive expert witnesses on toxicology and pharmacology are often indispensable.[80] Despite the cost, arbitration often accomplishes all of a union's goals. It settles disturbing questions about the limits of employee privacy and management rights. Unions appear to be using unfair labor practice charges infrequently, in part because a midterm unilateral change in work rules raises issues that a union can more frequently win in arbitration than in an NLRB hearing. Many of the lawsuits unions file seek injunctions to prevent implementation of new programs before the issues they raise can be arbitrated. Although the arbitration clause in the parties' contract may limit the scope of an arbitration, the range of possible cases for an arbitrator is wide and can include questions concerning the propriety of imposing the testing system as a whole during an existing contract, the reasonableness of particular new rules or procedures, and whether there is just cause for a particular instance of discipline for discharge. Issues that may prompt a grievance and result in arbitration arise from the moment an employer announces, implements, or strengthens a drug testing program without first bargaining over its terms, and they subside only after the program is finally implemented and has settled into patterns of use.

## Arbitrability

A grievance, and eventually a request for arbitration, will likely emerge soon after an employer takes any sort of action to implement a new drug testing program or change an existing one. A union generally need not wait to attack the program until an employee is actually asked to take a test, disciplined for refusing to take a test, or disciplined or discharged based on the results of the test.[81] It may challenge the propriety of unilateral implementation, or the reasonableness of the testing program or any part of it, as soon as the program is implemented.[82] In fact, if it does not make its challenge within the appropriate time period for filing a grievance under the collective bargaining agreement, it may have given the employer a timeliness defense against arbitration of the merits of the dispute over the testing program.[83]

Procedural reasons for refusing to arbitrate (untimeliness or failure to follow contractually required procedures, such as submission to steps of the grievance process) are normally questions for an arbitrator to decide, based on the contract. The employer's refusal to arbitrate at all, whether for substantive reasons that support an argument of non-arbitrability or because procedural prerequisites to arbitration were not met, may involve litigation under §301 of the NLRA, alleging a breach of an agreement, or seeking a stay of arbitration or injunction to compel arbitration.

Section 301(a) of the NLRA provides that a party to a labor agreement may sue in federal court for relief for a breach of the agreement.[84] The Supreme Court has declared that this section expresses a federal policy that federal courts should enforce agreements to arbitrate to preserve industrial peace.[85] Whether a particular contract at issue requires submission of a dispute to arbitration is decided by the courts, not arbitrators or the NLRB.[86] The courts must apply the federal common law which the Supreme Court has directed them to derive from national labor law policy.[87]

This federal common law favors industrial peace, which the Supreme Court has found to depend on arbitration and the uniformity of federal law, as opposed to diverse state common law solutions to labor problems.[88] Federal common law in the labor field thus preempts law suits grounded in state legislation or state common law whenever such law suits concern issues which amount to a breach of contract under §301(a). Thus, many state court law suits for remedy for a state common law breach of contract or tortious conduct in the employment setting involve litigation over the arbitrability of the underlying dispute to determine if the suit is preempted and should be dismissed.[89]

Under some circumstances, an employer that refuses to arbitrate can prevail in court on the ground that the grievance is not subject to arbitration as a matter of contract. One court of appeals affirmed a district court's judgment that an attendance control plan was not subject to arbitration. The contract in that case excluded from the definition of arbitrable grievances any disputes that did not concern the provisions of the collective bargaining agreement. The employer argued, and the court agreed, that the attendance policy was just that—a policy—and not a term of the agreement, even though it could lead to discipline, which was properly an arbitrable matter under the agreement. Speculative problems of application, the court found, did not warrant granting an arbitrator jurisdiction to evaluate the policy.[90]

When an employer allows a grievance to reach an arbitrator directly without litigation, the employer may still argue that the grievance is not appropriate for arbitration, that is that the grievance is not ripe for adjudication. If the rules making up a plan are clear enough to provide the arbitrator with some idea how the plan will be applied in specific cases, arbitrators will entertain challenges to management's right to impose them.[91] Some arbitrators, however, have found it difficult to review detailed plans, such as drug testing plans, in the abstract. They reason that it is impossible to determine whether any given provision is reasonable without some actual knowledge of how it will be applied in the day-to-day operations of the plant.[92] Arbitrators taking this position are likely to let a plan operate until specific cases of applications of its provisions arise. Like judges who deny requests for injunctive relief, these arbitrators will rely on future arbitrations to make whole those employees involved in disciplinary "test" cases.[93]

Assuming they survive the employer's jurisdictional arguments and reach a hearing on the merits, the union's challenges to a drug testing program take three forms. They attack (1) the propriety of unilateral implementation, (2) the "reasonableness" or content of the program or its parts, and (3) the "fairness," "arbitrariness," or "reasonableness" of the employer's application of the program's requirements and penalties to particular cases.

## Unilateral Implementation

Perhaps the most difficult (and therefore infrequent) union challenge to drug testing in the arbitration context arises when the union attempts to invalidate the entire unilaterally implemented policy because the policy is some sort of one-sided interference with a bargained-for relationship. This type of challenge makes an implied or explicit claim that the testing program breaches the agreement because it was improperly implemented. It may mean that the drug testing program is not within the scope of management rights; that is, depending on the contract, that no rules, or no rules concerning drug testing, can be imposed unilaterally. It may mean that management went about the procedure incorrectly. The claim is normally the easiest one for management to defeat in the arbitration setting, as long as the collective bargaining agreement fits the normal pattern and reserves to management broad authority to make work rules.

## Contract Language

The arbitrator's task is to interpret the parties' collective bargaining agreement and to apply its terms, not his own judgment or other law, to the question before him.[94] Under this principle, whether an arbitrator ultimately finds a duty to bargain necessarily depends on the collective bargaining agreement's provisions, particularly the scope of its management rights clause. Language in an agreement frequently reflects the peculiarities of particular bargaining situations, but general principles apply. Management retains the most latitude to impose a testing policy when a collective bargaining agreement reserves to the employer, without exception, the right to make all reasonable work rules necessary for the conduct of business.

Provisions of the agreement other than the management rights clause, however, may limit the freedom to implement policies. Even when an agreement does not explicitly provide that the right to adopt rules is limited to rules "not inconsistent with the terms" of the agreement, arbitrators have implied this limitation. Thus, management's decision to impose a drug testing policy that required a presumption of intoxication when an employee refused a test was deemed improper in one case, because the presumption reversed the normal principles of the just cause requirement contained elsewhere in the agreement.[95] However, in an agreement that otherwise allows management to adopt rules unilaterally, language requiring the company to "discuss" the rules means just that. It does not limit the scope of management rights. Arbitrators usually find only that the company must talk over the rules with the union before they go into effect, not that it must bargain as a matter of contract.[96] On the other hand, a clause separate from the management rights clause that requires the company to meet and confer with a labor-management safety committee has been held to limit management's right to impose work rules and plans concerning drug testing.[97]

Language incorporating existing rules into an agreement will invalidate a unilaterally imposed drug testing program containing new or more severe anti-drug provisions that conflict with existing anti-drug rules,[98] unless the agreement allows management to post "additional" rules.[99] A "zipper" clause also may prevent implementation of a drug testing program. Zipper clauses typically provide that the agreement as written constitutes the parties' entire agreement, that there is no agreement with respect to any matters not contained in the agreement, and that the agreement may not be modified except by express mutual consent. A zipper clause might read:

> "It is understood and agreed that this Contract contains all the agreements of the parties and that the same may be amended or altered only by agreement in writing signed by the parties.
>
> The Company and the Union agree that all matters desired by either party have been presented, discussed and incorporated herein or rejected. Accordingly, except to the extent expressly stated to the contrary above, it is agreed that for the life of this Agreement each party voluntarily and unqualifiedly waives the right and each agrees that the other shall not be obligated to bargain collectively with respect to any subject or matter, whether or not referred to in this Agreement."[100]

A "zippered" agreement that contains agreements about drug testing may preclude management from altering those provisions. In contrast, in a zippered agreement that is silent on the subject of drug testing, management may have the right to implement a testing program as a work rule without committing a breach of contract.[101]

## Past Practice

If an unzippered contract is silent on the drug testing issue, management's practice in the past regarding drug use and abuse on the job may affect its present ability to implement a new drug testing policy. The essence of a past practice argument is that management is prevented from changing the terms or conditions of employment, such as a work rule or shop procedure, because the practice has been around so long that it is not only relied upon, it is an implied part of the contract. A union may claim that new, stricter drug rules and a new drug testing program unreasonably conflict with preexisting workplace discipline, by increasing penalties or penalizing off-duty conduct or other conduct that had long been tolerated. Providing arbitrators with sufficient evidence concerning past practice may be burdensome. A union claiming that a new program breaches a term made part of the contract by means of past practice will have to establish by strong evidence some version of three elements: (1) the practice is clear, well understood, and easily identifiable; (2) it has endured over a reasonable period of time; and (3) it is something both parties agreed to by their acceptance of it, as the practice continued unchanged over time.[102]

Past practice arguments may see some success in cases where the union is up in arms over revisions to disciplinary policies. A few arbitrators have invalidated changes in the severity of penalties applicable to drug-related offenses.[103] Others, however, look to management's reasons for stiffening penalties or changing the mechanics of the disciplinary process and find that management has not waived any of its rights to manage the work force and run its operation merely because it failed to address a problem that never existed previously.[104]

## Reasonableness of Rules, Program, Policy Generally

An employer may have the right under the contract to impose new rules and policies, including a drug testing policy. That does not mean that a union may not challenge the policy's reasonableness. A challenge to a testing program's reasonableness argues that the policy somehow interferes with employee rights that the union considers protected by contract. The widely accepted test of the reasonableness of a plant rule or policy is: " 'whether or not the rule is reasonably related to a legitimate objective of management.' "[105]

The outcome of the arbitral test of a work rule's reasonableness depends ultimately on the union's skill at painting a black picture of the policy's arbitrariness, unworkability, and intrusiveness. As general knowledge about both the drug problem and drug testing increases, that task may become increasingly difficult for the union, but not impossible. Almost any management objective can be dressed up as a legitimate objective related to efficiency, safety, or public image, but unions have found ways to punch holes in testing programs by focusing the inquiry on programs' failures to meet their objectives.

**Management's Legitimate Objective.** In order to establish that a plan is unreasonable, a union must either demonstrate that the plan's stated objective is not legitimate, or that the plan as it is written cannot meet the objective and instead serves either some invidious purpose or no purpose other than infringing employees' rights. Without fail, arbitrators acknowledge the legitimacy of goals such as workplace safety, productivity and efficiency, good public image, and public safety.[106] In part because it is easy to design a testing plan that fosters safety, there are few published awards involving all-out challenges to the reasonableness of entire testing policies, despite the apparent furor over drug testing programs. It is increasingly clear that unions do not react to a prohibiton of drugs in the workplace, but rather to the mechanics of the prohibition.

For instance, unions rarely make frontal attacks on the reasonableness of the usually prohibitory work rule, which underlies the testing policy, forbidding both the use or possession of drugs or alcohol on the property and reporting for work "under the influence." A typical rule of this type provides:

> "Employees shall not report for work under the influence of intoxicants or illegal drugs and shall not bring, consume or have in their possession any intoxicants or illegal drugs of any type on company premises."[107]

Arbitrators have universally declared these rules to be unquestionably reasonable as a proper exercise of management's legitimate right to run its business free of the adverse effects of drug and alcohol use.[108]

**The Off-Duty Conduct Issue.**     Unions may, however, attack rules that attempt to regulate off-duty conduct. The most critical "reasonableness" problems involve employer attempts to regulate all off-duty conduct, without regard to its actual (or reasonably likely) effect on job performance and safety, and to directly prohibit off-duty drug use. This approach involves the presumption that some off-duty drug-related conduct may sometimes have some impact on the workplace. One federal appellate court, with regard to this sort of presumption, held that "off-duty/off-premises conduct involving the illegal use and sales of drugs is not per se justification for a worker's discharge."[109] The same court also stated, however, that:

> "The public policy which favors arbitration does not mandate that an arbitrator ignore the potential safety hazards which addictive drug use and dealing can present in the . . . work environment in favor of the narrow view that off-duty conduct can never affect an employee's work status."[110]

Determining where to draw the line is a source of confusion and dispute. Management frequently relies on various presumptions that automatically link off-duty conduct to intoxication and work "under the influence." Unions repeatedly point out that, practically speaking, presumptions that all drug use has bad effects are inherently tainted with unexamined prejudices about drugs. In the first place, they beg the question of whether off-duty conduct is properly within management's reach. Unions explain that an employer would not consider prohibiting all use of alcohol, or refuse ipso facto to hire an alcoholic.[111]

This is understandable; alcoholism is a controllable, if chronic, disease, and the social use of alcohol (even tending toward abuse) is widely accepted. Medical science also understands alcohol's pharmacological and behavioral effects in enough detail to make predictions about how alcohol consumption will affect performance, so much so that state legislatures have established presumptions of levels of intoxication based on blood alcohol content. Employers have used these legislative presumptions for years with respect to alcohol to define "intoxication," "impairment," and "under the influence."[112] Off-duty conduct problems arise where drugs are concerned because such easy presumptions about levels of impairment and effects on job performance cannot be based on available information about abusable over-the-counter, prescription, and illegal drugs for which one can test. Unions know as well as anyone that metabolites of abused substances may remain in the body for long periods (for instance, up to seven weeks for Delta 9-THC). They know that the various screens and GC/MS analysis can detect metabolites and establish use, but currently cannot link metabolite levels to conclusions about the time of ingestion, the amount ingested, and the level of impairment, if any.[113]

For a union, drug testing is inherently intrusive; it inherently examines only off-duty conduct, simply because it cannot pinpoint the time of ingestion or effect on the workplace. It cannot meet the typical standards in most work rules: "use" on the job or work "under the influence." Drug testing is therefore an insidious means of subverting the normal requirement that an employer have just cause to discipline or discharge. The AFL-CIO has taken the position that off-duty conduct which cannot be shown to affect job performance is not management's concern, and never just cause for a job action.[114]

**Reasonableness of Policies Reaching Off-Duty Conduct.** The most fertile ground for dispute about a testing program's ability to meet management's objectives is the issue of precisely what employee conduct the prohibitory work rule and program affect. Some basic principles apply. The company can prohibit almost any type of conduct on or affecting the job, even if it stems from off-duty causes, as long as the prohibition is not discriminatory or does not violate some law or public policy. An employer can normally discipline an employee for off-duty conduct if that conduct has some demonstrable bad effect on the company's reputation or product, if the conduct makes the employee unable to work, or if other employees cannot or do not want to work with the employee.[115] Thus, as one might expect, an employer may establish penalties for all absenteeism, including absenteeism resulting from an off-duty drinking or drug binge. It cannot, however, fire someone summarily for being an alcoholic where alcoholics are protected from discrimination on the basis of the handicapping condition of alcoholism and where the employee's performance is not affected or the condition could be accommodated.[116] Union eyebrows rise when employers attempt to impose a definition of prohibited conduct that is contradictory, confusing, or unrelated to scientific principles or workplace facts.

Unreasonable rules may be the result of drafting problems. For instance, a work rule may be unreasonable because it is overbroad and prohibits use of drugs properly prescribed to treat a condition not otherwise affecting the job. Thus, a work rule prohibiting use or being under the influence of "controlled substances," in addition to narcotics and alcohol at work, was deemed to be unreasonable because it was not related to the company's legitimate concern that employees function "properly and lawfully" on company premises and perform their jobs satisfactorily and safely. One arbitrator reviewing such a rule noted that prescription drugs, which the rule covered, might actually improve the employee's chances of fulfilling safety and performance objectives, and that a "blanket proscription" of all controlled substances unreasonably failed to take this into account.[117] Many employers prevent the invalidation of such a rule by requiring employees to report what prescription drugs they take, so that the company is on notice and may determine whether the employee is fit to work while taking the prescription drug.[118]

Other reasonableness challenges may have to do with the policy's scope. If the company's stated objective is safety, a union may claim that a comprehensive testing program that applies to too many or to too few employees is unreasonable. In one recent decision, an arbitrator declared an entire policy unreasonable because the only conceivable standard for application he could discern was bargaining unit affiliation. The policy applied to every member of the bargaining unit, rapid transit workers and clericals alike, and to no employees outside the bargaining unit.[119]

Employers have attempted to make drug testing more acceptable and have avoided full-scale rules prohibiting all off-duty use by making testing independent of the tested employee's ability to perform his job. They may try to supplement the standard "impairment" or "under the influence" work rules by creating parallel presumptions about use of drugs and alcohol. This approach appears to preserve the usual work rules prohibiting working "impaired" or "under the influence," which are directed to on-the-job drug use and are therefore less objectionable to a union. A union might still successfully challenge the reasonableness of any testing or enforcement procedures that effectively extend management's anti-drug vigilance beyond the scope of narrow rules into the realm of private conduct.[120]

For instance, employers may lose challenges to their policy decisions to presume intoxication or "under the influence" when an employee refuses to submit to a drug test.[121] One arbitrator found that the employer cannot rely on what it construes to be an "admission" where a refusal to test is involved; it must still prove that there was just cause to discharge the employee for violation of the rule prohibiting "impairment." To allow an employer to adopt a policy including such a presumption of intoxication, the arbitrator held, would reverse the normal just cause principles.[122] In most cases, to discipline for refusal to take the test, the employer need only call the refusal an insubordination. Where the employee who refuses to submit has had adequate notice of the testing procedure and there were sufficient grounds to order the test, the charge will stand.[123]

Evidence of the presence of drugs in the system, without evidence linking concentrations of the substance to some level of impairment, may not be enough to establish a violation of the standard "under the influence" rule.[124] This issue most frequently arises when an arbitrator must decide whether management had "just cause" to discharge an individual; it is dealt with more fully below in that context. It can arise in the context of a reasonableness challenge to an entire policy as well. A rule that presumes that the mere presence of the drug constitutes impairment is probably unreasonable, given the state of scientific knowledge.[125] On the other hand, a rule which makes no claim that a violation depends on proof of "impairment" may avoid this problem. Such a rule establishes a cutoff point: a confirmed test showing the presence of a substance at a level higher than the cutoff is deemed grounds for discipline or other action without reference to impairment. To date few arbitrators have ruled on a "cutoff" arrangement, but most of those who have done so found such a rule to be reasonable, or indicated approval of that type of rule.[126]

Regardless of the nature of the prohibitory rule, an arbitrator may be less likely to tinker with decisions to control off-duty drug use when the prohibition is clearly related to the employer's safety needs. Arbitrators have recognized that employees in safety-sensitive jobs (particularly public sector jobs with high exposure to the public) have a lesser expectation of privacy than those in noncritical jobs.[127] These employees may even be subjected to compulsory testing if reasonable grounds exist to believe it is necessary.[128] In one instance, an arbitrator went so far as to put the burden of demonstrating no job impairment due to off-duty conduct on the employee. The employee was allowed to return to work on the condition that he would discontinue his use of marijuana. He was tested when he returned, and the test results were positive for marijuana, in violation of the condition. The arbitrator upheld the decision of the public utility company-employer to discharge the employee, whose actions "were under careful scrutiny by the public," because the employee "failed to challenge the nexus between the presence and inability to perform."[129]

When an employer can establish an observable connection between its employees and service to the public or public safety, a union will have a more difficult time winning an arbitration in which reasonableness of a prohibiton of off-duty use of drugs is an issue. The employer is most likely to win if the rule prohibits off-duty drug use by public employees "to the extent that such employee conduct adversely affects the company's business interests."[130] This type of rule acknowledges the need to balance the employee's interests and the company's interests, and expressly acknowledges the arbitrability of the "adversely effects" standard. Where an employer uses such a rule, it must expect to prove the adverse effect of drug use at an arbitration hearing just as it proves "just cause" to discharge. If it does not, it may lose its discharge case.[131]

Even where prohibitory rules clearly reach the off-duty conduct of employees with less safety-sensitive or publicly visible jobs, arbitrators will find some limited types of regulation of off-duty conduct reasonable. Employers may prohibit any off-duty conduct that intrudes on the workplace. There is no doubt that an employer may prohibit drug use that is technically off-duty, in that the employee is off the clock, if the employee is on the plant grounds or in route to another job.[132] Likewise, the employer may prohibit even chronic off-duty substance use if it affects job performance.[133]

Arbitrators will also uphold regulations of off-duty conduct that reach a possibility of harm, if the link between the off-duty conduct and potential harm to the employer or the public is clear. One link arbitrators recognize is time—the proximity of drug use to work time. There is little question that when safety or public image is involved, employers may reasonably prohibit all alcohol and drug use in some appropriate period prior to the start of the employee's shift. As the period of time the employer regulates lengthens, however, arbitrators may be less likely to allow a restriction of off-duty conduct. An employee who uses a drug at lunch may be considered to be under his own and not the employer's control for purposes of pay calculation under federal wage and hour laws, but arbitrators recognize the possibility that the drug he uses on his 40-minute lunch break may affect his performance when he returns to work. Arbitrators have upheld rules prohibiting drinking during employees' lunch breaks, even if the breaks are taken off the premises.[134]

Likewise, employers may reasonably prohibit drinking during a longer period, such as a four-hour "swing" between split shifts.[135] Arbitrators have also upheld discipline for violation of rules prohibiting drinking within 12 or 24 hours of the start of the shift for safety-sensitive jobs.[136] Even though arbitrators applied the rules in these cases, they refused to apply them strictly, choosing to review circumstances and reduce penalties based on the supposition of insignificance, in terms of actual impairment, of the drinking that violated the rule.

Prohibiting off-duty conduct such as the sale or use of illegal drugs has been held to be reasonable as well. As one arbitrator put it, "the seriousness of the drug problem generally and the valid interest of an employer in preventing drug abuse among its employees, warranted a finding that a Company has a right to act immediately to protect its own interest and the interest of the employees."[137] Cases involving discharge for convictions, like other cases, will turn on the degree of harm the conviction may cause to the employer, measured on the sliding scales of whether public image and safety are justifiably important management concerns.[138] Some arbitrators refuse to allow the employer merely to presume a bad effect on the workplace resulting from an off-duty conviction and require proof.[139]

**Reasonableness of Policy in Light of Notice.**    A union may focus also on more pedestrian matters than the scope of the employee conduct regulated. It may take issue with the reasonableness of the company's method of providing notice of the procedure and putting it into effect. Arbitrators generally find that proper notice is part of the basic "industrial due process" right of employees who must live with a company's rules and procedures.[140] Proper notice is more a matter of "how much" than of "how." Management usually retains the right to determine how to give employees notice of rules and policies affecting their working conditions, absent contract language requiring a certain form of notice or a well-established practice of providing notice in a particular way. It can decide whether to post the document establishing a testing procedure in full, to summarize salient points in a letter or leaflet, or to communicate verbally the points of a testing program. If a company's notice does not convey the terms of prohibitory rules and the mechanics of the testing procedure in a clear and understandable manner, arbitrators find testing programs or parts of them to be unreasonable.[141] Issues usually arise with respect to the propriety of ordering a test under a policy in the first place,[142] or the propriety of policies concerning refusing the test.[143] Arbitrators reason that as a basic matter of fairness, an employee should be aware of any requirement that may involve her in an insubordination if she refuses to comply.[144]

The key element in the reasonableness test of notice seems to be whether management relies on the program without deviation, but leaves employees in the dark about the fixed system of requirements and penalties it applies. Where there is no established program but employees know drug use is prohibited in some way, management may be able to test on a case-by-case basis.[145] This is particularly the case where the employer must deal with an employee who has a known substance abuse problem. Thus arbitrators have allowed employers to require employees to submit to testing—even random testing—as a condition of keeping a job already endangered by poor performance or violation of prohibitory rules regarding drugs.[146] In an emergency situation, management may be able to test without prior notice to employees.[147] Particular actions such as these, however, are subject to the same sort of "reasonableness" test arbitrators apply to comprehensive programs. A union may be able to invalidate the results of discrete actions if there is no evidence of a problem or that the measures actually taken were necessary to remedy the problem. In such cases the employer must establish a rationale for the test equivalent to proof of the "reasonable suspicion" that is a part of formalized drug testing programs.

In general, however, very little evidence will establish that a workplace drug problem exists and must be remedied with a comprehensive testing program. In fact, to impose a policy, as far as some arbitrators are concerned, there need be only some evidence that there might be a problem.

Arbitrators have taken the position that "neither inability to document a drug problem among employees, nor a lack of specific proof of such a problem, precludes an employer from seeking to avoid the development of a drug problem."[148]

**Reasonableness of the Policy's Severity.**    In the same light, a testing procedure and its underlying rules need not be kind to be reasonable. Arbitrators presume that an employer that has decided to address a (perceived) drug problem may meet it head on, with severe penalties, including immediate discharge for infractions.[149] These penalties may not conflict with a contractually established preexisting progressive discipline system or employee assistance program, however; if they do, they violate the collective bargaining agreement.[150]

With so many hurdles to leap, a union is not likely to launch an all-out arbitral offensive against a drug testing policy if the policy meets a few minimal requirements. The parallels to policies that unions (eg, the Teamsters) have actively bargained for are unmistakable. The policy built on basic, comprehensive, comprehensible work rules that are anchored in scientific and workplace facts will probably avoid litigation and arbitration. It will be indisputably announced (and, if the union has its way, offered for bargaining or comments prior to implementation). Its prohibitions will be only as strict as they must be when they may impinge directly or indirectly on off-duty conduct.

## Application of the Testing Policy

A policy that survives a "reasonableness" test must still accommodate human frailty. Problems with the actual, day-to-day implementation of a program arise from sources as diverse as the disgruntled employee first asked to submit to a test, the supervisor who jumps the gun and orders a test without the grounds required in the policy, the union representative who advises an employee to grieve for political reasons, and the testing laboratory which might do well to test its own technicians.[151] Each of these problems subjects management decisions about discipline or work orders to a grievance and arbitration over whether the policy is reasonable as applied in particular cases.

The term "reasonable application" encompasses issues such as the propriety of ordering a test in the first place for an individual employee, the employee's refusal to take the test, and problems associated with intrusions on the employee's privacy as the sample is taken. It concerns what happens to the sample: how it is handled in the "chain of custody," the correctness of the test performed on it, and the strengths and weaknesses of the testing method in general. It also involves what management does with the results of the test: issues of investigation, determinations of just cause to discipline, and decisions about rehabilitation versus penalty. Issues concerning attention to procedure percolate around every other issue.

Challenges to particular applications of a drug testing policy by unionized employees almost always arise as the result of a grievance over discipline.[152] Particular questions of "reasonable application" in the arbitration context are therefore part of the general issue at the heart of all arbitrations over discipline: "Was there just cause to discipline/discharge grievant, and if not, what is the remedy?" With this larger issue in mind, the various issues of reasonable application will be viewed from three perspectives: (1) the mechanics of the testing procedure itself—the reasonable application of rules and procedures requiring the test and setting out technical requirements for the testing process and handling the sample; (2) reliance on results—the reasonable application of prohibitory work rules and presumptions to particular cases, including a look at the problems of relying on test results as proof of "impairment" and a discussion of the effects of employee assistance programs and other accommodations to employee's problems; and (3) the general procedural issues a union may raise in the arbitration setting.

## The Mechanics of the Testing Procedure

**Reasonable Cause.** Frequently, testing programs may require an employee to submit to drug testing under specified conditions. The conditions range from the quantity of evidence of a rule violation a supervisor must have to order a test, to a listing of particular behavior or events, such as accidents, which trigger a test requirement. More and more, testing programs do not allow testing until the appearance of a "reasonable cause" or "reasonable suspicion" of use, possession, or working under the influence. Unions occasionally argue that this sort of requirement stems from employees' constitutional rights to be free from unreasonable search and seizure, and that discipline following a decision to order a test that cannot be shown to be based on reasonable cause is invalid. Where unions represent public sector employees, the argument is proper. With two exceptions, however, any requirement that a decision to test be based on "reasonable cause" in the private sector (where employer action does not equal the governmental action the constitution restricts) must come from the testing policy itself or from the contract.

One exception stems from state statutes regulating the testing of state and private employees for drugs. Nine states have enacted such statutes, and bills are pending in many other states and municipalities. These statutes require an employer to have reasonable suspicion—or in two states, probable cause, a higher standard[153]—before it can test for drugs. In cases where they apply, such statutes[154] may lead some arbitrators to consider the statute's standards to be an implied part of the collective bargaining agreement.[155]

The other exception arises if a state constitution provides for specific citizens' privacy rights which the courts apply to the private sector, as they do in California.[156] To date, no state court has decided whether these types of constitutional provisions prohibit the intrusions unions point to when challenging drug testing programs. Unions have attempted to make the state constitutional privacy protections part of their arsenal, however, even in arbitration cases.[157]

Regardless of the applicability of federal and state prohibitions against invasion of privacy, arbitrators may find some source for a privacy right and a "reasonable cause" requirement if the testing program does not explicitly contain one.[158] One source is the contract provision requiring management to have just cause to discipline and discharge. The "just cause" provision is the employees' safeguard against arbitrariness; it requires management to prove its grounds for taking adverse action against employees. One arbitrator concluded that a unilaterally promulgated testing policy was unreasonable because it allowed testing upon mere suspicion of substance misuse and further allowed a presumption of intoxication if the employee, reacting to the order to test based on a mere suspicion, refused to submit. The arbitrator wrote, "mere suspicion may quicken investigation, but it is not the same as proof."[159]

Just what constitutes "reasonable cause" is the arbitrable issue on which the validity of a decision to discipline frequently rests. A "reasonable cause" or "reasonable suspicion" requirement normally demands that the supervisor ordering a test have some basis in fact for his decision.[160] He may rely on observation of the employee's behavior (gait, attitude, speech, odor, judgment, performance, balance). If he does so, published awards indicate that his decision to order an employee to submit to a test is more likely to be upheld when the observations can somehow be linked to a likelihood that the employee is not capable of performing his job. Thus, an observation that employees were simply more boisterous than usual was held to be insufficient grounds to justify a test.[161] Noticing a cigarette in an employee's car that is presumed but not proven to be marijuana has likewise been held to be an inadequate reason to require an employee to submit to a test.[162] On the other hand, arbitrators in several cases have held that there was reasonable cause to test where an employee was involved in unusual, unexplained behavior and exhibited signs of some sort of intoxication.[163] One arbitrator acknowledged the propriety of a test ordered because the employee's regular return-to-work physical revealed a high blood enzyme level indicative of continual high levels of THC—and therefore of marijuana use.[164]

A supervisor's judgment is only as good as his observations, a union will argue. The quality of those observations is subject to a wide range of union challenges. The union may attempt to build a case that the observations are the creations of a discriminatory motive.[165] It may make an attack on cross-examination, or with other witnesses, to claim they are tainted with subjectivity or perceptual limitations.[166] It may produce an expert who will testify that they are not based on adequate knowledge of the behavioral indications of alcohol or drug use.[167]

To limit these types of challenges, employers may adopt testing programs that notify employees of a nonexclusive list of types of behavior that will warrant submission to testing.[168] This approach does not prevent the union from attempting to convince an arbitrator that the observations were wrong, but it does reduce the likelihood that the union will be able to prevail on a defense that the type of conduct observed did not justify a test. However, detailed policies designed to build the best prehearing case for the employer may have drawbacks. If a supervisor does not properly document his observations under such a policy, or obtain another supervisor's observations if that is necessary, or otherwise fails to follow procedures, the union's opportunity to demonstrate that he ordered testing without reasonable cause is not limited to the normal attack on credibility through cross-examination. The union may argue further that the decision to test is void because it deprived the employee of the testing program's procedural guarantees.[169]

**Tests Mandatory after Accidents.** Employers may in addition adopt policies that require testing, without any supervisory discretion or subjective judgment, upon the occurrence of specific behavior or events. For instance, employers may provide that testing is mandatory when an accident occurs.[170] Such provisions won approval in the public sector in the 1970s when transit employees challenged a metropolitan bus company's policy of testing "operating employees directly involved in any serious accident such as a collision of trains, collision of buses, derailment, bus and person [sic] or *serious* collision with vehicle or fixed object."[171] Policies such as these may irk a union because they are, practically speaking, a presumption of "reasonable suspicion" that allows management to test without reference to the facts surrounding the accident and the employee's conduct before and after it. Occasionally an arbitrator will agree that the presumption is inappropriate, especially where the plant rule involved is the type that prohibits working "under the influence." As one arbitrator put it, "accidents can occur for many reasons such as carelessness of co-workers or faulty equipment which have nothing to do with the injured worker."[172] The presumption that there is cause to test is stronger when the test is mandatory only in instances where there is evidence of carelessness, or some independent evidence of unusual behavior indicating drugs might be a factor in the accident.[173]

Generally speaking, a presumption that an accident justifies a test is more likely to succeed if the employer's operation involves demonstrable safety risks to employees or the public.[174] Even if an arbitrator allows the presumption of reasonable suspicion to stand, unless the parties or an arbitrator define what constitutes a serious accident, the union may still challenge any particular decision to test after an accident on the grounds that the accident was not the type that gives rise to a need to test or a reasonable suspicion that an intoxicant of some sort was involved. In other words, the union may challenge the company's judgment that an accident was serious, or if the work rule requires it, that carelessness or independent evidence of drug use was present, with the same tactics it employs to discredit a supervisor's observations leading to a decision that reasonable suspicion exists to test.

**Tests Mandatory after Absence from Work.**     Arbitrators have approved mandatory testing upon return from layoff or illness as well as after accidents.[175] One emerging issue is the reasonableness of the application of rules prohibiting drug use or "impairment" on the job to mandate drug testing as a part of preemployment or recall physicals. Management's basic right to require physicals like these is difficult to dispute: management has the right to determine whether employees are fit to work.[176] When the physicals include a drug screen, it is widely acknowledged that part of the "fitness" determination includes finding out if employees use drugs or are "under the influence" of drugs or alcohol.[177] An employee who has been on indefinite layoff may test positive for a substance prohibited under the contract. While on layoff this employee was not under the employer's control, and maintained no connection to the plant other than through his seniority rights. The application of a workplace drug prohibition to a returning employee will probably be deemed reasonable if the company emphasizes that safety considerations are the basis for the testing program. The union has a chance of success if the company effectively ignores the presumption of unfitness that is involved in a decision to refuse to rehire a drug user. One arbitrator reinstated employees terminated after a recall physical in part because the employer, without apparent concern for safety, let them work for four weeks from the time they were tested to the time test results came back positive.[178]

**Refusal to Take the Test.**     The validity of a decision to subject an employee to a drug test is important for reasons other than the ultimate use of test results to mete out discipline. Employees may well refuse to submit to the test, whether from fear of exposure, anger at the intrusion, or reliance on advice from the union. It is a basic principle of industrial relations that an employee must "obey now, grieve later;" he has few justifications to refuse an order.[179] He is insubordinate if he refuses to comply with a legitimate work order that does not raise a bona fide fear for his safety or a bona fide belief that his contractual rights will be violated if he obeys the order.[180] Under the latter exception, where no rule or policy provides for drug testing, or employees have not been notified of the policy or that they will be fired for refusing to take the test, arbitrators will reinstate employees discharged for refusing to take the test.[181] If the policy is clearly in place and employees are notified of the consequences of refusal to submit to drug tests, some evidence that the order to submit was based on a desire to harass, or other arbitrary or capricious conduct, may mitigate the consequences of an insubordinate refusal to submit.[182] Many arbitrators, however, will find that insubordination is inexcusable where employees know of a rule, and that the employee's proper course of action is to give a sample and grieve afterward for a remedy.[183]

**Reliance on Test Results.** Many arbitration decisions since the early 1970s turn on management's ability to rely on test results alone to establish "just cause" to discharge employees. A surprising number of decisions reinstated employees on the grounds that management had somehow failed to demonstrate a link between the basic facts the test established and a fair reason to discharge the employee involved. These cases uniformly involve the collision between the contents of what we have called the "standard" work rules and the scientific limits of the testing procedure. The "standard" work rule prohibits use or possession of drugs or alcohol, and reporting to work "under the influence of" or "impaired by" these substances. The scientific limits of the testing procedure center around its sensitivity. Urine screening confirmed by GC/MS involves two contradictory aspects of the testing procedure's sensitivity that an arbitrator must account for as he attempts to determine whether the employee conduct detected gives management any cause to terminate the employee's services.

First, the GC/MS is *so specific* that when it is properly performed on a properly protected and identified sample, it provides close to 100% certainty that one of the tested-for substances has been ingested at some point. Thus, an employer who receives a report of a positive GC/MS test from a respected laboratory knows almost certainly that he employs someone who has used drugs. But the second aspect makes this knowledge fiendish from the union's (and some scientists') perspectives. GC/MS testing is *not specific enough* to indicate anything other than a *past* event. It will not tell anyone—lab technician, physician, or supervisor—what the test subject's current behavior is. As a recording technique, it provides no additional information about the past upon which it reports. It will not allow anyone to decide conclusively that at the moment of an accident, lapse in judgment, mistake, stumble, or slur, the employee was affected, positively or negatively, by a substance prohibited under the applicable rule.[184] However, the presence of a substance in an employee's system must raise in a supervisor's and an arbitrator's mind a question concerning the employee's performance and safety.

Given this technological context, the wording of the work rule an employee's substance abuse has violated can be critical if management relies on positive test results as a just cause to discipline or discharge. Arbitrators have found, under varying circumstances, that an "under the influence" or "impairment" rule limits the employer's ability to discharge an employee based solely on test results.[185] Thus, one arbitrator reinstated an employee even though a blood alcohol test showed a "substantial amount" of alcohol in the blood, on the grounds that there was no proof that the amount found made the grievant unable to work.[186] Similarly, an arbitrator reinstated an employee found to have 280 ng/ml of cannabinoids in his urine sample, because the employer offered no proof that this amount was sufficient to impair the employee.[187]

In a series of decisions affecting the transit industry, arbitrators have reinstated employees discharged on the basis of positive urine test results on the grounds that the test results did not establish that the employees were "under the influence" when the event triggering the decision to test occurred. These arbitrators strictly construed written work rules and rejected the claim that a work rule stating that "use of illegal drugs is forbidden," prohibited all use of drugs at any time, including off-duty time. They then gave weight to expert testimony that even GC/MS tests will not "prove" impairment.[188] The inability of the testing process to distinguish between on-duty and off-duty use for drugs other than alcohol has led another arbitrator to reinstate employees testing positive for cannabinoids on grounds that there was no way to distinguish whether they violated a rule prohibiting only on-duty drug use, possession, or impairment.[189]

Arbitrators who do give weight to test results on the issue of impairment increasingly require a company relying on test results to use the best test available for the purpose. Where alcohol is concerned, a union has successfully challenged a discharge based on analysis of a urine sample, since blood tests provide more accurate information. Although a urine sample will reveal the presence of alcohol, the arbitrator in this case reinstated the tested employee on the grounds that the employer had not proved he violated a rule prohibiting reporting "under the influence" of alcohol. Without a measurement of blood alcohol content, the arbitrator found, the employer could not establish whether the level of alcohol present when the employee was tested reached the level of "influence."[190] In another case, an arbitrator decided that a blood test is the equivalent of "documentation" of intoxication from alcohol. The arbitrator reinstated an employee discharged solely on the basis of supervisors' observations and found that documentation was necessary for proof of just cause.[191] Similarly, where testing results indicate the presence of substances other than alcohol, arbitrators are now wary of upholding discipline or discharges based on unconfirmed tests.[192]

Increasingly, arbitrators have become comfortable with the limits of the available testing procedures and will acknowledge that the employer may rely on test results as one factor demonstrating just cause for discipline or discharge under certain circumstances. Some will go so far as to conclude that test results indicating a high level of a prohibited substance in the employee's system is sufficient to warrant a conclusion that the employee is "under the influence."[193] Arbitrators frequently seem to do their own research on drug-related issues.[194] Properly presented expert testimony will go a long way toward justifying reliance on test results to the extent the underlying work rule allows.[195] Some objective evidence of unusual or unsafe behavior, or a competent clinical evaluation by a medically trained observer, will often bridge the gap between the positive test result and the conclusion that an employee was impaired.[196] This is especially true if the job involved is a safety-sensitive job or involves a safety factor—in this sort of case, management may only have to prove "impairment," and thus just cause to discipline, by a preponderance of the evidence.[197] Where no risk of harm can be demonstrated, however, to link evidence of the ingestion of a substance to a performance problem, discharge may be an excessive penalty.[198] The employer's ability to prove that the sample is properly protected in the chain of custody,[199] and that required testing procedures are properly followed,[200] makes it more difficult for a union to convince a knowledgeable arbitrator to ignore test results and force an employer to ignore them as well. In addition, evidence other than test results is frequently sufficient to prove that a subject is impaired or "under the influence." Thus, stronger evidence of the same type an employer presents to justify reasonable suspicion may be sufficient to demonstrate just cause to discharge for impairment or being "under the influence," even without test results.[201]

## Employers' Procedural Violations in Drug Testing Cases

In cases involving drug testing, unions may raise a plethora of procedural issues as reasons to set aside discipline or discharge.[202] Arbitral "law" has long recognized that the collective bargaining relationship that requires an employer to have just cause to discipline or discharge carries with it some basic notions of fundamental fairness, some idea that there are rules to the game. The need to follow established rules until notice is given that the rules are to change is sometimes called "industrial due process": employees may be subjected to tests under the rules, or fired under the contract, but in the process they are entitled to the procedures that ensure they are tested or fired fairly. The essential question for an arbitrator is not whether a disciplinary action was totally free from procedural error, but whether the process was fundamentally fair. In order to overturn the employer's action on procedural grounds, he must find that there was at least a possibility, however remote, that the procedural error may have deprived the grievant of a fair consideration of his case.[203] In the past ten years, arbitrators have sustained, in whole or in part, approximately half of the reported challenges to drug-related discipline or discharge that allege procedural violations.[204]

Unions can and do pounce on several types of procedural omissions that may deprive an employee of fair treatment or fair and accurate test results. If employees are charged wih using illegal substances—implying some moral turpitude—some general fairness concerns become especially sensitive to employees and unions. From another perspective, when the employer becomes strict about a drug-free workplace, unions that must try arbitration cases over the resulting grievances look for every possible way out from under the seemingly overwhelming presumptions and penalties. They raise issues which might sound more appropriate to the public defender's office, but some arbitrators have recognized the employee rights that unions champion in these cases. They have reinstated employees who had no warning of the consequences of their use of a particular substance,[205] employees punished twice for the same offense,[206] and employees summarily suspended without having been interviewed or investigated.[207] One arbitrator gave weight to union arguments that discipline is improper when employees experience a delay in learning of test results.[208] In a similar vein, one arbitrator reinstated a discharged employee because neither the employee nor the union was present at the termination meeting. The arbitrator stated, "In the conduct of discipline it is as important to maintain the integrity of the process as it is to discipline (an employee) for just cause."[209] In other cases, unions argued that the employer unfairly denied employees the right to have union representation at investigatory interviews that might lead to discipline.[210] One arbitrator agreed with the union when a supervisor failed to advise an employee she was entitled to a union representative during an interview in which a supervisor sought and received an admission that the employee had been drinking on a break.[211] Another arbitrator reduced discharges to suspensions when employees, observed skulking about in an area smelling of marijuana, refused to submit to searches while the union steward was prevented from meeting with them.[212]

Not all arbitrators will overturn discipline for a lack of union representation. One arbitrator rejected the claim that an employee with a previously known substance abuse problem was deprived of any process due her when the employer met with her, absent a union representative, to seek her consent to random testing as a condition for allowing her to keep her already endangered job.[213] Likewise, where an employer decided in good faith that the union representative need not be present at an interview with employees who admitted drug-related offenses on company property, an arbitrator declined to invalidate the company's decision to discipline.[214] An employer that begins a comprehensive, step-by-step testing policy, spelling out reasons to test, methods of sample-taking and chain of custody, and requirements that its laboratory must meet, is at the most risk of a procedural challenge. Until the employer can smooth out the mechanism, each procedural requirement is liable to result in errors that pop up like targets in a shooting gallery. Even the smallest target under such a policy may become barn-wide and irresistible if the drug testing policy itself provides that test results may not be relied upon unless the employer complies with the procedure. An employer normally must follow an established plant rule or procedure, such as a drug testing policy, about which employees have notice. Employees may be expected to rely on the fact that the published rule and program, and not some arbitrary creation, is the one to which they must attend.

Arbitrators have invalidated discipline where the chain of custody of the sample was broken, because the break made it unfair to conclusively attribute drug use to the employee tested.[215] They have likewise upheld grievances alleging that medical personnel did not follow procedures the parties agreed upon.[216] If the drug testing procedure does not provide for specific steps the employer and laboratory must follow to protect the chain of custody or the accuracy of the procedure, the employer probably must exercise "all due care" to secure the sample and properly identify it,[217] and the laboratory must likewise follow scientifically proper procedure to allow the arbitrator to find the test valid.

## Fundamental Fairness

Consistent with their duty to represent members fairly and to police the contract, unions usually will not tolerate management's decision to treat similarly situated employees differently. They will pursue challenges to a company's application of a drug testing policy that coddles some employees and bludgeons others. Arbitrators very frequently agree with them, particularly if the company tolerates alcohol abuse but punishes drug abuse. One arbitrator reinstated an employee discharged for sharing a joint on his break, finding no reasonable basis for the company's decision to discharge drug users immediately when it offered alcohol abusers progressive discipline.[218] Another reduced an employee's discharge to a suspension after the employee was found to have drugs in his clothes when he was examined after suffering a caustic burn. Discharge was too severe, the arbitrator said, when employees who drank on the job were only sent home.[219] In another case, employees who used alcohol were sent to a clinic and received progressive discipline. An arbitrator held that discharge without similar rehabilitative accommodations was too severe for marijuana users.[220]

It is not the case, however, that a union will automatically prevail if it takes an employer to task for unfairly denying drug using employees accommodations such as entry into employee assistance programs. Arbitrators have indeed held that employers who maintain these programs have an obligation to make them available to employees suspected of substance abuse.[221] They must also administer them reasonably. For instance, an arbitrator chastised one employer for refusing a rapid transit operator entrance into its employee assistance program by relying on the "enormous amount of damage" he caused in an accident.[222] The reasonableness requirement does not mean that management cannot use reasonable discretion to reject an employee for rehabilitation if the employee is a demonstrably bad candidate or a bad risk.[223] Where a drug testing procedure takes away this discretion by providing that employees who are observed to be under the influence or who test positive *shall* undergo rehabilitation, management's decision to discipline rather than rehabilitate a drug user is a shaky procedural proposition.[224] Employers can, of course, establish rules and qualifications necessary for entry into rehabilitation programs.[225]

When unions allege procedural unfairness, they have little chance of success if employees do not help themselves. Employers have no duty to go out of their way to encourage employees to seek rehabilitation.[226] One arbitrator upheld a company's decision to discharge a 26-year employee with an acknowledged alcohol problem, a 2-year record of absences, and exposure to progressive discipline, after the employee had failed to report when he called in to say he would be late. The employee refused treatment, and the arbitrator acknowledged that an employer has "no responsibility to force an employee with an alcohol problem into a rehabilitation program."[227]

Arbitrators also reject arguments of procedural unfairness when employees request participation in an employee assistance program only after they are disciplined.[228] It is not even necessary that an employer reinstate an employee to whom it offers reinstatement, one arbitrator has held.[229] Employees must at least substantially comply[230] with the program's requirements, as well. One arbitrator upheld the discharge of an employee who, while in a rehabilitation program, submitted another person's urine sample as her own.[231]

Unions likewise are intolerant of management decisions that punish employees for conduct the company has tolerated in the past,[232] and arbitrators have been persuaded to give relief. Arbitrators have reduced penalties when the union proved that other employees were treated less severely for similar drug-related infractions.[233] They have also reduced penalties imposed for types of conduct that were previously widespread[234] or even condoned.[235]

## Enforcement of Awards

Arbitral awards reinstating drug using employees because of failure to prove "impairment" or because of procedural flaws may send employers to court arguing that these awards adopt interpretations of the labor contract that are unenforceable as a matter of public policy. Most collective bargaining agreements provide that arbitration decisions are "final and binding," that is, conclusive to the exclusion of an employee's separate lawsuit raising the same issues or other issues arising out of the dispute.[236] At the same time, these agreements normally limit the arbitrator's power to the interpretation and application of the terms in the collective bargaining agreement. The Uniform Arbitration Act as it has been adopted, with variations, in many states,[237] and the Arbitration Act[238] in federal law provide that courts may set aside arbitration awards if the party seeking to set aside the award can show arbitral misconduct or incompetence such as fraud, refusing to hear material evidence, partiality, or materially exceeding the authority granted by the contract or the submission agreement. Similarly, courts may set aside arbitration awards violating " 'some explicit public policy' that is 'well defined and dominant, and is to be ascertained "by reference to the laws and legal precedents and not from general considerations of supposed public interests." ' "[239]

Understandably, arbitrators may hesitate to put an employee discharged for drug use back to work, but many do so if the employer's proof or procedures were faulty. The courts have not fully sorted out whether an arbitrator's award reinstating a drug using employee violates public policy.[240] Courts have found such a policy in state and federal criminal laws and federal regulations, but they have also increasingly recognized a public policy favoring personal privacy and restrictions on wide-ranging testing for drugs.[241] Those courts which have refused to enforce awards have done so on the grounds that the arbitrator's decision somehow stretched beyond the authority the contract gave him, usually because of his choice to change the company's disciplinary penalty.[242] Similarly, no court to date has decided whether a state statute regulating drug testing and limiting the uses of test results for disciplinary purposes creates an explicit public policy defining the scope of drug testing. While the new state laws may well give employers a new, more successful argument to advance against arbitration awards which reinstate drug users, they may also allow unions to challenge awards which uphold testing policies or discipline in violation of the statutes' requirements.

# —— NOTES

1. *Time,* September 15, 1986, p. 59.
2. *Vaca v. Sipes,* 386 U.S. 171, 177, 64 LRRM 2369 (1967) (implying from federal labor law a duty to "serve the interest of all members without hostility or discrimination toward any, to exercise its discretion with complete good faith and honesty, and to avoid arbitrary conduct.")
3. Sections 703(c) and (d) of Title VII of the Civil Rights Act of 1964, 42 U.S.C. §§2000 e-2(c) and (d) prohibit discrimination by labor organizations against

their members on the basis of protected status such as race, sex, national origin and religion.

4. A union's breach of its duty of fair representation to a member can be a violation of Sections 8(b)(1)(A), 8(b)(2), and 8(b)(3) of the NLRA. *See, e.g., Independent Metal Workers (Hughes Tool Co.)*, 147 NLRB 1573 (1964); *Bell & Howell Co.*, 230 NLRB 420, 95 LRRM 1333 (1977), *enforced*, 598 F.2d 136, 100 LRRM 2192 (D.C. Cir. 1979) (where the duty of fair representation included the duty not to discriminate on the basis of sex).

5. *See, e.g.,* Colorado: Anti-Discrimination Act, §24–34–401(6), §24–34–402(c), 1986; District of Columbia: Human Rights Act of 1977, §1–2502(15), (23); Illinois: Human Rights Act, §1–103(Q); Kansas: Act Against Discrimination, §44–1009(a)(2), 1986.

6. The Labor Management Reporting and Disclosure Act prohibits a union's actions with respect to internal union matters (such as formulating a policy regarding drug testing programs) which deprive members of rights including free speech. 29 U.S.C. §§411–15.

7. Since the 1970s, workers have increasingly opted to decertify their unions by means of NLRB decertification elections. The increase seems to stem in part from management efforts to go anti-union and in part from unions' inability to convince employees that their economic and job satisfaction needs are met. *See* the discussion in R. FREEMAN and J. MEDOFF, WHAT DO UNIONS DO?, 233–42 (Basic Books, 1984).

8. *Union Fights Drug Tests,* Jackson (Miss.) Citizen-Patriot, March 13, 1986.

9. *See, e.g.,* Risa Leiberwitz, Address, New York State School of Industrial and Labor Relations, November 15, 1986, *reported in* DAILY LABOR REPORT No. 225 A–5 (BNA, November 21, 1986).

10. *See Drug Testing in the Workplace on the Rise,* Employment Alert, February 19, 1987.

11. *Murray v. Brooklyn Gas Co.,* 122 LRRM 2057 (N.Y. Sup. Ct. 1986).

12. Section 301(a) allows both private employees and unions to file suit in federal court for violation of collective bargaining agreements. §29 U.S.C. §185(a). Private employees must demonstrate that they need the court's intervention to provide relief for a breach of contract because their union breached its duty to represent them fairly and thus deprived them of the benefit of contractual means to remedy the breach of contract. *Vaca v. Sipes,* 386 U.S. 171, 64 LRRM 2369 (1967). Before it files suit, the union must exhaust available contractual remedies for resolving the dispute, unless it has been frustrated in its attempts to do so, or the effort would be futile. *See, e.g., Macon v. Youngstown Sheet and Tube Co.,* 698 F.2d 858, 112 LRRM 2556 (7th Cir. 1983). Where the issue is whether a particular dispute is arbitrable, and thus whether the company breaches the contract by refusing to arbitrate, arbitrability is a question of contract interpretation for the courts. *See, e.g., Piggly Wiggly Operators' Warehouse, Inc. v. Piggly Wiggly Operators' Warehouse Independent Truck Drivers Union, Local No. 1,* 11 F.2d 580, 103 LRRM 2646 (5th Cir. 1980).

13. For a discussion of the union's resort to unfair labor practice charges, *see* text at notes 36–42.

14. 29 U.S.C. §104 (1970). The Act provides that "[n]o court of the United States shall have jurisdiction to issue any restraining order or temporary or permanent injunction in any case involving or growing out of any labor dispute . . ." when certain protected conduct is involved.

15. *Boys Markets, Inc. v. Retail Clerks Local 770*, 398 U.S. 235, 74 LRRM 2257 (1970); *Gateway Coal Co. v. Mine Workers*, 414 U.S. 368, 85 LRRM 2049 (1974).

16. A union may seek to file its suit in state court instead of federal court. Although the Supreme Court has not specifically addressed the issue of whether federal labor law applicable to private sector disputes must be applied in state court cases, at least one state court has followed the federal common law after *Boys Markets*. See *Manhattan-Walton Joint Venture v. Painters local 151*, 114 LRRM 2868 (Ala. Cir. Ct. 1982). *But see, Carter-Glogan Laboratories, Inc. v. Laborers Local 383*, 126 LRRM 2752 (Ariz. Ct. App. 1986) (Norris-LaGuardia's "clear proof standard" not applicable to damages suit in state court for violent strike activity).

Many states have passed versions of the Norris-LaGuardia Act, in any case, so the standards and results in a state court suit are likely to follow those in federal suits, where state laws survive claims that they are preempted by federal law. If a suit in state court raises questions of federal law, it may be removed to federal court, as may cases filed in state court to compel arbitration under §301 of the National Labor Relations Act. *Avco Corp. v. Aero Lodge 735 Machinists*, 390 U.S. 557, 67 LRRM 2881 (1968). *See also William E. Arnold Co. v. Carpenters*, 417 U.S. 12, 86 LRRM 2212 (1974) (state courts have jurisdiction under §301 to provide injunctive relief as well as damages). In the event a state court issues a temporary restraining order and a case is removed to federal court, the restraining order remains in force, but only as long as ten days, pursuant to Rule 65(b) of the Federal Rules of Civil Procedure. *Granny Goose Foods, Inc. v. Teamsters Local 70*, 415 U.S. 423, 85 LRRM 2481 (1974).

17. See *Lever Brothers Co. v. International Chemical Workers, Local 217*, 554 F.2d 115, 94 LRRM 2438 (4th Cir. 1976). These suits are proper only when the dispute over the employer's contract is in fact arbitrable. *Buffalo Forge Co. v. United Steelworkers*, 428 U.S. 397, 407–08 (1975).

Those private sector employees filing suits for injunctive relief rely entirely on claims that the collectively bargained for arbitration provision is in serious danger by virtue of the employer's action. Arguments that employees' constitutional rights will suffer from drug testing are inappropriate in private sector suits, and courts will reject them unless a state constitution creates these rights in the private sector. *Monroe v. Consolidated Freightways, Inc.*, 654 F. Supp. 661 (E.D. Mo. 1987) (dismissing suit for injunctive relief claiming drug testing violated employees' Fourth Amendment rights, filed by private corporations' employees in Missouri).

18. *Boys Markets, supra* note 15, at 254.

19. *Id.; Local Lodge No. 1266 v. Panoramic Corp.*, 668 F.2d 276, 283, 109 LRRM 2169 (7th Cir. 1981); *IBEW, System Council U-9 v. Metropolitan Edison Co.*, No. 86-4426, slip op. (E.D. Pa. August 14, 1986).

20. *See, e.g., Local Lodge No. 1266 v. Panoramic Corp., supra* note 19, at 283 ("a status quo injunction serves the salutary purpose of enforcing the parties' agreement to arbitrate by preserving an effective arbitral remedy for bargaining agreement breaches.")

21. *Lever Bros. Co. v. International Chemical Workers, Local 217, supra* note 17, at 123.

22. *Boys Markets, supra* note 15, at 254; *Local Lodge No. 1266 v. Panoramic Corp., supra* note 19, at 283.

23. *Local Lodge No. 1266, supra* note 19, at 284-85; *Amalgamated Transit Union Div. 1384 v. Greyhound Lines, Inc.*, 529 F.2d 1073, 1077-78, (9th Cir. 1976).

24. *IBEW Local 1900 v. PEPCO*, 634 F. Supp. 642, 121 LRRM 3287 (D.D.C. 1986). *See also Oil, Chemical and Atomic Workers Local 6-10 v. Amoco*, 635 F. Supp. 360, 123 LRRM 2934, 2936 (D.N.D. 1986); *Oil, Chemical and Atomic Workers Local 2-124 v. Amoco*, 651 F. Supp 1, 123 LRRM 3104, 3108 (D. Wyo. 1986); *IBEW, System Council U-9, supra* note 19 ("It is important to note that the Union does not argue that the employees will be irreparably harmed because they will be discharged if they refuse to take the test or because they may be discharged if they test positive. The union seems to agree that damages could remedy this type of injury."); *International Chemical Workers Union and Local 4 v. Olin Corp.*, No. 87 C 5745 (N.D. Ill. July 15, 1987) (Mem. order) (denying injunction where union did not show arbitrator could not remedy harms arising from discharge).

25. *Oil, Chemical and Atomic Workers Local 6-10, supra* note 24, at 2936.

26. *See, e.g., Oil, Chemical and Atomic Workers Local 2-124 v. Amoco, supra* note 24, 123 LRRM at 3107-08 (D. Wyo. 1986); *IBEW, Local 1900 v. PEPCO, supra* note 24 (enhancement of penalty under new drug testing policy did not materially change the stigma or humiliation suffered due to a drug-related disciplinary action; injunction denied).

27. *IBEW System Council U-9 v. Metropolitan Edison Co.*, No. 86-4426, slip op. (E.D. Pa. August 14, 1986).

28. *Id.*

29. *International Chemical Workers Union and Local 4 v. Olin Corp., supra* note 24, at 13.

30. *See, e.g., Graphic Communications Union Local 17(m) v. Stone Container Corp.*, ___ F. Supp. ___, 3 IER Cases 261 (S.D. Ind. 1988) (court characterized drug testing program with after-accident testing provisions as a violation of right of privacy, and granted union's motion for preliminary injunction) (appeal filed); *Local 185 v. Weyerhauser Paper Co.*, 650 F. Supp. 431 (S.D. Ill. 1986) (testing intrudes into personal life and invades privacy). *But see Greco v. Halliburton Co.*, 674 F. Supp. 1447, 2 IER Cases 1281 (D. Wyo. 1987) (court held that private employees' constitutional claims were meritless, because state and federal constitution applied only to "government or state action").

31. *IBEW, System Council U-9 v. Metropolitan Edison Co., supra* note 27.

32. *Id.*

33. *Murray v. Brooklyn Gas Co.,* 122 LRRM 2057 (N.Y. Sup.Ct. 1986).

34. For a discussion of the nature and scope of the constitutional issues, *see supra,* Chapter 2, text at notes 1–35. Cases granting injunctions include: *National Federation of Federal Employees v. Weinberger,* 818 F.2d 935, 2 IER Cases 145 (D.C. Cir. 1987); *Capua v. City of Plainfield,* 643 F. Supp. 1507, 1 IER Cases 625 (D.N.J. 1986); *National Treasury Employees Union v. Von Raab,* 649 F. Supp. 380, 1 IER Cases 945 (E.D. La. 1986), *rev'd,* 816 F.2d 170, 2 IER Cases 15 (5th Cir. 1987), *cert. granted,* ___ U.S. ___ (March 1, 1988); *Lovvorn v. City of Chattanooga,* 647 F. Supp. 875, 1 IER Cases 1041 (E.D. Tenn. 1986), *aff'd* 846 F.2d 1539 (6th Cir. 1988); *Penny v. Kennedy,* 648 F. Supp. 815, 1 IER Cases 1047 (E.D. Tenn. 1986), *aff'd* 846 F.2d 1563 (6th Cir. 1988); *American Federation of Government Employees v. Weinberger,* 651 F. Supp. 726, 1 IER cases 1137 (S.D. Ga. 1986). *But see, National Federation of Federal Employees v. Weinberger,* 640 F. Supp. 642 (D.D.C. 1986) (court dismissed suit for injunction on grounds of lack of jurisdiction held, Federal Labor Relations Authority and Merit Systems Protection Board provide review of federal drug testing directives); *Amalgamated Transit Union, Local 1277 v. Sunline Transit Agency,* 663 F. Supp. 1560, 125 LRRM 3154 (C.D. Cal. 1987); *Fraternal Order of Police, Newark Lodge No. 12 v. City of Newark,* 216 N.J. Super. 461, 524 A.2d 430, 2 IER Cases 437 (1986); *Caruso v. Ward,* 133 Misc. 2d 544, 506 N.Y.S.2d 789, 2 IER Cases 238 (N.Y. Sup. 1986), *aff'd,* 520 N.Y.S. 2d 551, 2 IER Cases 1057 (App. Div. 1987) (drug test properly enjoined); *Smith v. City of East Point,* 183 Ga. App. 659, 359 S.E.2d 692, 3 IER Cases 153 (1987) (drug test of fire fighter ruled unconstitutional search and seizure), *rev'd* 258 Ga. 111, 365 S.E.2d 432, 3 IER Cases 157 (1988).

35. For an example of the treatment of the "irreparable harm" issues at various stages of a suit for injunction in the private sector, *see IBEW, Local 1900 v. PEPCO,* 121 LRRM 3071 (D.D.C. 1986) (temporary restraining order granted); *IBEW, Local 1900 v. PEPCO, supra* note 24 (preliminary injunction denied).

36. 29 U.S.C. §158(d). The Act provides: " . . . to bargain collectively is the performance of the mutual obligation of the employer and the representative of the employees to meet at reasonable times and confer in good faith with respect to wages, hours and other terms and conditions of employment, or the negotiation of an agreement or any question arising thereunder . . ."

Many state labor relations acts now obligate public sector employers to bargain in the same way federal law requires private sector employers to do so. Some state labor boards have addressed drug testing issues. *See, e.g., Fraternal Order of Police, Miami Lodge 20 v. City of Miami,* 12 FPER ¶17029 (1985) (city wrongfully unilaterally required police officers to submit to urinalysis despite board management rights clause); *City of Atlantic City,* 11 NJPER ¶16185 (1985) (motion for order to cause city to require testing policy denied where union failed to demonstrate substantial likelihood of success on failure-to-bargain charge.

37. The duty to bargain the Railway Labor Act imposes is codified at 45 U.S.C.

§152: the rail or air transport employer must "exert every reasonable effort to make and maintain agreements concerning rates of pay, rules, and working conditions." The United States Supreme Court distinguished between "major disputes" arising under this Section, subject to bargaining and mediation, and "minor disputes," subject to final and binding arbitration. *Elgin, Joliet & Eastern Ry. v. Burley*, 325 U.S. 711, 722 (1945), *aff'd on rehearing*, 327 U.S. 661 (1946). Unless some provision of the contract arguably justifies drug testing, thus making its propriety a matter for an arbitrator to decide, the employer must bargain before implementing it.

The imposition of a new drug testing program requiring a train's entire crew to submit to drug testing after an accident involving a "human factor" has recently been held to create a "major dispute" requiring collective bargaining before the program may be implemented, despite the employer's enforcement of other anti-drug work rules for over 40 years. *Brotherhood of Locomotive Engineers v. Burlington Northern R.R. Co.*, 838 F.2d 1087, 127 LRRM 2812, 2816–17 (9th Cir. 1988). *See also Brotherhood of Locomotive Engineers v. Burlington Northern R.R. Co.*, 838 F.2d 1102 (9th Cir. 1988) (use of drug-detecting dogs is a "major dispute" requiring bargaining before implementation); *Railway Labor Executives' Association v. Consolidated Rail Corp.*, 845 F.2d 1187, 128 LRRM 2168 (3d Cir. 1988) (unilateral addition of drug screening to medical exams is not justified in the contract, and is thus a "major dispute" requiring bargaining); *International Brotherhood of Teamsters v. Southwest Airlines Co.*, 842 F.2d 794, 128 LRRM 2225 (5th Cir. 1988) (mandatory testing for drug and alcohol use is a "major" dispute not arguably justified by the contract, and must be bargained over prior to implementation); *Transport Workers' Union of Philadelphia, Local 234 v. Southeastern Pennsylvania Transportation Authority*, 678 F. Supp. 543, 127 LRRM 2835 (E.D. Pa. 1988) (implementation of random testing as to railway employees was a "major dispute" requiring bargaining). *But see Brotherhood of Maintenance of Way Employees, Lodge 16 v. Burlington Northern R.R. Co.*, 802 F.2d 1016, 123 LRRM 593 (8th Cir. 1986) (imposing urinalysis on individual crew member thought to have responsibility for triggering accident is a "minor dispute" for submission to arbitration, not bargaining; court divided on whether use of drug screen as part of periodic and return-to-work exam required bargaining); *Railway Labor Executives Association v. Norfolk & Western Ry. Co.*, 833 F.2d 700 (7th Cir. 1987) (drug screen added to routine urinalysis as part of medical exam does not require bargaining).

38. *Ford Motor Co. v. NLRB*, 441 U.S. 488, 498, 101 LRRM 2222 (1979), quoting from *Fibreboard Paper Products Corp. v. NLRB*, 379 U.S. 203, 222–23, 57 LRRM 2609 (1964) (Stewart, J. concurring).

39. 29 U.S.C. §158(a)(5) and (1).

40. See notes 53–64, *infra* and accompanying text, concerning waivers.

41. *NLRB v. Katz*, 369 U.S. 736, 738, 50 LRRM 2177 (1962); *Merrill & Ring, Inc.*, 262 NLRB 392, 110 LRRM 1309 (1982), *enforced*, 731 F.2d 605, 116 LRRM 2221 (9th Cir. 1984) (an employer's unilateral implementation of a work rule requiring day-shift employees to report to work prior to reporting

for jury duty was found to be a unilateral change of a mandatory subject of bargaining and, therefore, a violation of Section 8(a)(5)).

42. *Taft Broadcasting Co.*, 163 NLRB 475, 64 LRRM 1386 (1967), *aff'd*, 395 F.2d 622 (D.C. Cir. 1968); *NLRB v. Atlas Tack Corp.*, 226 NLRB 222, 227, 93 LRRM 1236 (1976), *enforced*, 559 F.2d 1201, 96 LRRM 2660 (1st Cir. 1977). No impasse can occur until the collective bargaining process has been exhausted and there appears no realistic possibility that a continuation of bargaining would be fruitful. *See Marriott In-Flite Services Div. of Marriott Corp.*, 258 NLRB 755, 108 LRRM 1287 (1981), *enforced*, 729 F.2d 1441, 113 LRRM 3528 (2d Cir.), *cert. denied*, 464 U.S. 829, 114 LRRM 2568 (1983). *Morco, Inc. d/b/a Towne Plaza Hotel*, 258 NLRB 69, 108 LRRM 1126 (1981); *J.D. Lunsford Plumbing, Heating & Air Conditioning, Inc.*, 254 NLRB 1360, 107 LRRM 1033 (1981), *aff'd*, 684 F.2d 1033, 110 LRRM 3367 (D.C. Cir. 1982); *Harry Sann, Jr. and Winton R. Wagner d/b/a/ Briarcliff Pavilion for Specialized Care*, 260 NLRB 1374, 109 LRRM 1383 (1982), *enforced*, 725 F.2d 669, 115 LRRM 2712 (3d Cir. 1983). For further discussion of impasse, *see* nn. 65–78, *infra* and accompanying text.

43. National Labor Relations Board, G.C. Mem 87–5 (September 8, 1987).

44. National Labor Relations Board, General Counsel Quarterly Report (April, 1988) (reported in No. 79 D.L.R. D-1, BNA, April 25, 1988).

45. *See, e.g., Continental Telephone Company of California*, 274 NLRB 1452, 118 LRRM 1598 (1986) (new unilaterally implemented Positive Disciplinary System not violative of Act where Union waived its right to bargain *via* management rights clause); *Harvard Folding Box Co., Inc.*, 273 NLRB 1031, 118 LRRM 1209 (1984); *Embossing Printers, Inc.*, 268 NLRB 710, 115 LRRM 1110 (1984); *Atlas Microfilming, Division of Sertafilm, Inc.*, 267 NLRB 682 (1983); *Truck Drivers Union Local 164, Teamsters (Bette Huey, an Individual)*, 267 NLRB 8, 114 LRRM 1006 (1983); *Ciba-Geigy Pharmaceuticals Div.*, 264 NLRB 1013, 111 LRRM 1460 (1982); *Tenneco Chemicals, Inc.*, 249 NLRB 1176, 104 LRRM 1347 (1980).

46. *See, e.g., LeRoy Machine Co.*, 147 NLRB 1431, 56 LRRM 1369 (1964).

47. *See, e.g., Holyoke Water Power Co.*, 273 NLRB 1369, 118 LRRM 1179 (1985) (health and safety conditions-noise level); *Armour Oil Company*, 253 NLRB 1104, 106 LRRM 1127 (1981) (noise level, safety equipment, and ease of handling of trucks).

48. *Lockheed Shipbuilding and Construction Co.*, 273 NLRB 171, 118 LRRM 1283 (1984) ("Lockheed I"). The Board found another violation of the Act on similar facts in *Lockheed Shipbuilding and Construction Co.*, 278 NLRB 18, 121 LRRM 1211 (1986).

49. *Lockheed I, supra* n. 48, 273 NLRB at 171.

50. *Medicenter, Mid-South Hospital*, 221 NLRB 670, 677–78, 90 LRRM 1576 (1975).

51. *Allied Chemical & Alkali Workers v. Pittsburgh Plate Glass Co.*, 404 U.S. 157, 179, 78 LRRM 2974 (1971).

52. *Lockheed Shipbuilding, supra* note 48, at 171. *Houston Chapter, Assoc. Gen'l Contractors*, 143 NLRB 409, 413, 53 LRRM 1299 (1963), *enforced*, 349 F.2d

449, 59 LRRM 3013 (5th Cir. 1965), *cert. denied,* 382 U.S. 1026, 61 LRRM 2244 (1966).

53. *See, e.g., Continental Telephone Co. of California,* 274 NLRB 1452, 118 LRRM 1598 (1985).

54. *Compare Suffolk Child Development Center, Inc.,* 277 NLRB 1345, 121 LRRM 1103 (1985) *with United States Postal Service,* 275 NLRB 360, 119 LRRM 1057 (1985).

55. *See, e.g., NLRB v. Henry Vogt Machine Co.,* 728 F.2d 802, 114 LRRM 2893 (6th Cir. 1983).

56. *See e.g., Ciba-Geigy Pharmaceuticals,* 264 NLRB 1013, 111 LRRM 1460 (1982).

57. *Exxon Company,* 253 NLRB No. 27, 105 LRRM 1514 (1980).

58. *Jacobs Mfg. Co.,* 94 NLRB 1214, 28 LRRM 1162 (1951), *aff'd,* 196 F.2d 680, 30 LRRM 2098 (2d Cir. 1952).

59. For an example of such a clause, *see* text at note 100, *infra.*

60. *See, e.g., Rockwell Int'l Corp.,* 260 NLRB 1346, 109 LRRM 1366 (1982).

61. *California Cedar Products Co.,* NLRB Advice Mem., 123 LRRM 1355 (October 10, 1986).

62. *Id.* at 1356.

63. *Bay Shipbuilding Corp.,* 251 NLRB 809, 811, 105 LRRM 1376 (1980) (NLRB deferred, under its doctrine in *Spielberg Mfg. Co.,* 112 NLRB 1080, 36 LRRM 1152 (1955), to an arbitrator's award finding unilateral change in insurance carriers did not violate the collective bargaining agreement).

64. *Id.*

65. NLRA §8(d) 29 U.S.C. §158(d).

66. For a comprehensive discussion of the myriad issues arising in bargaining situations, *see generally* MORRIS, ED., THE DEVELOPING LABOR LAW, 2d ed., 558–605 & First Supplement (1982).

67. *NLRB v. Insurance Agents Int'l Union,* 361 U.S. 477, 45 LRRM 2704 (1960); *General Electric Co.,* 150 NLRB 192, 57 LRRM 1491 (1964), *enforced,* 418 F.2d 736, 72 LRRM 2530 (2d Cir. 1969), *cert denied,* 397 U.S. 965, 73 LRRM 2600 (1970); *Tory Silk Mills, Inc. v. NLRB,* 185 F.2d 233 (D.C. Cir. 1950), *cert. denied,* 341 U.S. 914 (1951).

68. *See, e.g., NLRB v. Montgomery Ward & Co.,* 133 F.2d 676, 12 LRRM 508 (9th Cir. 1943).

69. *First National Maintenance Corp. v. NLRB,* 452 U.S. 666, 107 LRRM 2705 (1981); *NLRB v. Burns Int'l. Security Services, Inc.,* 409 U.S. 818, 80 LRRM 2225 (1972).

70. *See e.g., United States Gypsum Co. v. NLRB,* 484 F.2d 108, 84 LRRM 2129 (8th Cir. 1973).

71. For a full discussion of these factors, *see,* MORRIS, DEVELOPING LABOR LAW, *supra* note 66 at 579–606.

72. *NLRB v. Wright Motors, Inc.*, 603 F.2d 604, 102 LRRM 2021 (7th Cir. 1979); *Chevron Chemical Co.*, 261 NLRB 44, 110 LRRM 1005 (1982), *enforced sub nom Oil Workers, Local 4–447 v. NLRB*, 701 F.2d 172, 113 LRRM 2112 (5th Cir. 1983). *Compare NLRB v. Tomco Communications, Inc.*, 567 F.2d 871, 97 LRRM 2660 (9th Cir. 1978), *denying enforcement to* 220 NLRB 636, 90 LRRM 1321 (1975) (predictably unacceptable proposals, without other factors indicating bad faith in bargaining, are not sufficient to warrant a finding that the employer failed to bargain in good faith).

73. *Washington Steel Brass & Iron Foundry, Inc.*, 268 NLRB 338, 114 LRRM 1276 (1983); *Moore Drop Forging Co.*, 144 NLRB 165 (1963); *Schnelli Enterprises Inc., d/b/a/ Cellar Restaurant*, 262 NLRB 796, 110 LRRM 1362 (1982).

74. *General Electric Co.*, 150 NLRB 192, 57 LRRM 1491 (1964), *enforced*, 418 F.2d 736, 12 LRRM 2530 (2d Cir. 1969), *cert. denied*, 397 U.S. 965, 73 LRRM 2600 (1970).

75. *Crusader Lancer Corp.*, 144 NLRB 1309, 54 LRRM 1309 (1963) (requiring union to waive right to bargain during term of agreement).

76. *See NLRB v. Tonitt Mfg. Co.*, 351 U.S. 149 (1956).

77. *Penntech Papers, Inc.*, 263 NLRB 264, 111 LRRM 1622 (1982), *enforced*, 706 F.2d 18, 113 LRRM 2219 (1st Cir.), *cert. denied*, 464 U.S. 892, 114 LRRM 2648 (1983) (failing to provide negotiator with authority to conduct talks); *NLRB v. Cable Vision, Inc.*, 660 F.2d 1, 108 LRRM 2357 (1st Cir. 1981), *enforcing* 249 NLRB 412, 104 LRRM 1322 (1980) (employer bargained in bad faith when it caused delay, tended to defer union proposals for indefinite "study," and remained immovable in key areas without justification); *NLRB v. Industrial Use Products Corp.*, 455 F.2d 673 (9th Cir. 1972), *enforcing* 177 NLRB 328 (1969) (rejection of proposals previously accepted); *MRA Associates, Inc.*, 245 NLRB 676, 102 LRRM 1338 (1979) (introduction of new proposals after months of bargaining).

78. *Compare Inner City Broadcasting Corp.*, 281 NLRB No. 162, 124 LRRM 1313 (1986) *with Ashe Brick Co.*, 280 NLRB No. 162, 123 LRRM 1023 (1986).

79. *See, e.g.*, R. FREEMAN, J. MEDOFF, WHAT DO UNIONS DO? 104–09 (Basic Books, 1984) (grievance/arbitration reduces quits in unionized work forces).

80. *See* cases cited note 185, *infra* concerning the use of test results to support discipline.

81. *See Linde Co.*, 34 LA 1, 5–6 (Schmidt, 1959); *Altec Corp.*, 71 LA 1064, 1066 (Hays, 1978).

82. *Pacific Southwest Airlines*, 70 LA 833, 834–35 (E.A. Jones, Jr., 1978) (rejecting request for ruling on unilaterally adopted absenteeism policy without "evidence of specific applications"). The Ninth Circuit Court of Appeals found a similar grievance to be nonarbitrable. *Aluminum Co. of America v. U.A.W.*, 630 F.2d 1340, 105 LRRM 2390 (9th Cir. 1980).

83. *See, e.g.*, *Standard Products Co.*, 88 LA 1164 (Richard, 1987); *Albuquerque Publishing Co.*, 89 LA 333 (Fogelberg, 1987).

84. 29 U.S.C. §185. The statute reads:

"Suits for violation of contracts between an employer and a labor organization representing employees in an industry affecting commerce as defined in this Act, or between any such labor organizations, may be brought in any district court of the United States having jurisdiction of the parties, without respect to the amount in controversy or without regard to the citizenship of the parties."

85. *Textile Workers v. Lincoln Mills*, 353 U.S. 448, 445, 40 LRRM 2113 (1957).

86. *Sinclair Refining Co. v. Atkinson*, 370 U.S. 195, 50 LRRM 2433 (1962).

87. *General Electric Co. v. Local 205, Elec. Workers (UE)*, 353 U.S. 547, 40 LRRM 2119 (1957).

88. *Steelworkers v. Warrior & Gulf Navigation Co.*, 363 U.S. 574, 580–83, 46 LRRM 2416 (1960).

89. *See* notes 85–88, *supra*, and accompanying text and also Chapter 2 at notes 242–278 and accompanying text regarding preemption.

90. *Aluminum Co. of America v. U.A.W.*, 630 F.2d 1340, 105 LRRM 2390 (9th Cir. 1980).

91. *See, e.g., ARA Mfg. Co.*, 84 LA 856 (Lilly, 1985); *Budd Co., Trailer Div.*, 67 LA 130 (Howard, 1976); *United-Carr Tennessee*, 59 LA 883 (Cantor, 1972).

92. *Pacific Southwest Airlines, supra*, n. 79.

93. All cases involving issues other than drug testing: *see, e.g., Budd Co., Trailer Div.*, 67 LA 130 (Howard, 1976); *Trans World Airlines*, 47 LA 1127 (Platt, 1947); *United-Carr Tennessee*, 59 LA 883 (Cantor, 1972).

94. *Steelworkers v. Enterprise Wheel & Car Corp.*, 363 U.S. 593, 597, 46 LRRM 2423 (1960) (arbitration award is "legitimate only so long as it draws its essence from the collective bargaining agreement"). The arbitrator may look to external law to ascertain the sense of the contract language he interprets. *Id.*

95. *Faygo Beverages, Inc.*, 86 LA 1174 (Ellmann, 1986). *See also Boise Cascade Corp.*, (Kagel, 1986) (unreported).

96. *See, e.g., Bay Area Rapid Transit District*, 87–1 ARB ¶8084 (Concepcion, 1986). This is more likely to be the case where the contract gives an employer an *obligation* to ensure safety. *See e.g., York Water Co.*, 60 LA 90 (Tripp, 1972) (hard hat rule).

97. *Hobart Corp.*, 88 LA 905 (Feldman, 1987).

98. *Southern Extract Co., Inc.*, 59 LA 697 (Goodman, 1972). *Cf. Detroit Osteopathic Hospital*, 83 LA 1308 (Daniel, 1984).

99. *Southern Extract Co., Inc., supra* n. 98.

100. Reprinted in Collective Bargaining Negot. & Cont. (BNA) 36:421.

101. A zipper clause alone will not necessarily relieve management of the duty to bargain under the NLRA. *See* notes 97–99, and accompanying text *supra*. It means that management may, after bargaining over proposals if required to do so, implement the proposals at impasse without violating the agreement.

102. *See, e.g., Celanese Corp of America*, 24 LA 168, 172 (Dustin, 1954).

103. *See Union Oil Co. of California*, 88 LA 91 (Weiss, 1986) (invalidating discipline

taken based on drug tests, without posting a policy, even though work rule prohibiting drug use had existed for years).

104. *Bay Area Rapid Transit District, supra* n. 96; *Marathon Petroleum Co.,* 89 LA 717 (Grimes, 1987) (policy expanding work rule prohibiting drugs, to include off-duty conduct). In a suit for injunctive relief, courts reviewing the likelihood of the union's success on the merits and the degree of harm union members are likely to suffer if a company adopts a more severe drug testing program take the same position to deny unions injunctive relief. *See, e.g.,* cases cited in notes 24–26, *supra.*

105. ELKOURI & ELKOURI, HOW ARBITRATION WORKS, 4th ed. 555 (BNA Books, 1986), *citing Robert Shaw Controls Co.,* 55 LA 283, 286 (Block, 1970).

106. *See, e.g., Alabama Power Co.,* 88 LA 425 (Baroni, 1987); Brown & Williamson Tobacco Co., 62 LA 1211 (Davis 1974).

107. *See* this rule cited in *Foote & Davies, Inc.,* 88 LA 125, 127 (Wahl, 1986).

108. *See, e.g., Babcock & Wilcox Co.,* 60 LA 778 (Dworkin, 1972); *Capitol Area Transit Authority,* 69 LA 811 (Ellmann, 1977).

109. *Oil, Chemical and Atomic Workers Local 4-228 v. Union Oil Company of California,* 818 F.2d 437 (5th Cir. 1987).

110. *Id.*

111. An employer might not get away with the latter option in jurisdictions which prohibit employment discrimination against persons with mental or physical handicaps. Alcoholism is considered to be a disease. *See generally* Chapter 2 at notes 124–145 and accompanying text.

112. DENNENBERG AND DENNENBERG, ALCOHOL AND DRUGS—ISSUES IN THE WORKPLACE, 79–83 (BNA, 1983).

113. *See* text at note 184, *infra.*

114. AFL-CIO, *Drug and Alcohol Testing on the Job,* Publ. No. 177 (1987).

115. *See, e.g., W.E. Caldwell Co.,* 28 LA 434, 436–37 (Kesselman, 1957).

116. *See* Chapter 2, text at notes 123–145 for a discussion of legal prohibitions of discrimination against handicapped employees.

117. *Hoover Co.,* 77 LA 1287, 1290 (Strasshofer, Jr., 1982).

118. *See, e.g.,* the plan described in *International Chemical Workers and Local 4 v. Olin,* No. 87 c 5745 (N.D. Ill. June 15, 1987) (Mem. order).

119. *Bay Area Rapid Transit,* 87–1 ARB ¶8084 (Concepcion, 1986).

120. *Bath Iron Works Corp.* (Schmertz, 1986) (unreported).

121. *Faygo Beverages, Inc.,* 86 LA 1174 (Ellmann, 1986); *Bay Area Rapid Transit, supra,* note 119.

122. *Faygo, supra,* note 121.

123. *See* cases cited at notes 179–183, *infra,* and accompanying text.

124. *Bay Area Rapid Transit, supra,* note 119; *CFS Continental, Inc.,* 86–1 ARB ¶8070 (Lumbley, 1985).

125. *Bath Iron Works, supra,* note 120; *CFS Continental Inc., supra,* note 124.

126. *Hopeman Brothers, Inc.*, 88 LA 373 (Rothschild, 1986); *Bath Iron Works, supra,* note 120.

127. *Bay Area Rapid Transit, supra,* note 119.

128. The "reasonable grounds" requirement is particularly necessary where public employees are involved. Testing these employees constitutes a search under the 4th Amendment to the United States Constitution and a potential invasion of constitutional rights to privacy as well. *See* discussion in Chapter 2, notes 4–18.

129. *Indianapolis Power & Light Co.*, 87 LA 826 (Volz, 1986).

130. *Alabama Power Company*, 88 LA 425 (Baroni, 1987).

131. *See, e.g., Southern California Gas Co.*, 89 LA 393 (Alleyne, 1987) ("positive" test result did not prove employee used marijuana on the job); *Eastern Airlines, Inc.*, 89 LA 492 (Jedel, 1987) ("positive" result for ethanol insufficient as grounds for discharge when validity of test not established).

132. *City of Milwaukee*, 71 LA 329 (Maslanka, 1978) (supervision proper where equipment operator drank a glass of beer en route to other work); *Casting Engineers*, 71 LA 949 (Petersen, 1978) (discipline proper where employee admitted smoking marijuana on a previous shift); *BASF Wyandotte Corp.*, 72 LA 11 (Perry, 1978) (discharge proper for smoking away from work station).

133. *See, e.g., Lick Fish and Poultry*, 87 LA 1062 (Concepcion, 1986) (upheld summary discharge for drug-induced psychosis creating inability to work, despite employee's claim she kept drug use separate from work); *U.S. Plywood Corp.*, 88 LA 275 (Mathews, 1986) (discharge for absenteeism and failure to complete rehabilitation proper even though the substance-abusing conduct causing the problem was off-duty). *But see Union Oil Co. of California*, 88 LA 91 (Weiss, 1986) (discharge improper where tests positive only for off-duty use, and management made no claim that employees tested were unable to perform); *Southern California Gas Co., supra* n. 131. For a discussion of application of prohibitory rules to particular cases involving various approaches to accommodating addiction, *see* text at notes 218–231 *infra.*

134. *Browning-Ferris Industries of Ohio, Inc.*, 77 LA 289, (Shanker, 1981).

135. *General Telephone Co. of Calif.*, 77 LA 1052 (Schuster, 1981).

136. *Northwest Airlines*, 56 LA 837 (Wyckoff, 1971) (arbitrator reduced discharge to suspension for violating rule prohibiting drinking 24 hours prior to start of shift); *but see Trans World Airlines*, 38 LA 1221 (Waller, 1962) (arbitrator reinstated an employee who violated a rule prohibiting drinking 12 hours prior to start of shift, where there was no evidence she was affected by her drinking).

137. *Arco-Polymers, Inc.*, 69 LA 379, 386–87 (Milentz, 1977), citing *Wheaton Industries*, 64 LA 826 (Kenison, 1975). *But see, Brown & Williamson Tobacco Co.*, 62 LA 1211, 1212 (Davis, 1974) (finding unreasonable a rule allowing suspension for charges of off-duty criminal activities; the rule reverses the basic principle of "innocent until proven guilty").

138. For cases upholding discipline for conviction regarding off-duty involvement

with alcohol and other substances, *see Eastern Airlines, Inc.,* 76 LA 961 (Turkus, 1981) (discharge appropriate, stewardess apprehended while in uniform selling marijuana to another employee); *Safeway Stores, Inc.,* 78 LA 597 (Phelan, 1982) (summary suspension of employee charged with felony distribution of illegal drugs at job site); *New York Div. of Criminal Justice Services,* 79 LA 65 (Sabghir, 1982) (conviction for sale of methadone); *Group W Cable, Inc.,* 80 LA 205 (Chandler, 1983) (summary suspension justified when employee indicted after admitting using company vehicle to transport cocaine; company may presume an effect on its business); *Polk County, Iowa,* 80 LA 639 (Madden, 1983) (suspension of counselor who gave breathalyzer tests proper after DUI conviction; rule required employees to "refrain from conduct incompatible with employment and avoid willful violation of law"); *Martin-Marietta Aerospace, Baltimore Div.,* 81 LA 695 (Aronin, 1983) (discharge after conviction for sale of cocaine off-premises); *Pan Am World Services, Inc.,* 86 LA 891 (Ferguson, 1986) (discharge proper where employee lost license for 10 years after DUI conviction); *Lauter Co.,* 87 LA 1300 (Thornell, 1986) (just cause to suspend employee when arrested in drug raid and to convert to discharge upon conviction).

139. *Nugent Sand Co.,* 71 LA 585 (Kanner, 1978) (discharge improper where conviction was a result of employee's conduct while on sick leave); *McDonnell-Douglas Canada, Ltd.,* 74 LA 1103 (O'Shea, 1980) (discharge too severe after guilty plea to possession following in-plant police search; no notoriety, no impairment); *Vulcan Asphalt Refining Co.,* 78 LA 1311 (Welch, 1982) (discharge unjustified for conviction for sale of marijuana, despite employer arguments that report of arrest was bad publicity, and plant might be dangerous if employees were not attentive); *Pacific Bell,* 87 LA 313 (Schubert, 1986) (conviction for off-duty use or possession will not corroborate charges *re* on-premises use; discharge for on-premises use inferred from off-duty conviction unjustified); *General Telephone Co. of Cal.,* 87 LA 441 (Schubert, 1986) (suspension for conviction of misdemeanor possession without cause; no proof of connection between convictions and jobs); *Virginia Electric & Power Co.,* 87 LA 1261 (Jewett, 1986) (discharge for conviction of marijuana and cocaine possession improper where company did not prove "adverse effect" required under its own rules). *Cf. Nugent Sand Co.,* 81 LA 988 (Daniel, 1983) (discharge reduced for guilty plea to felony manufacture of controlled substance; rule notified employees of discipline *up to* discharge).

140. *See e.g., Capital Area Transit Authority,* 69 LA 811 (Ellman, 1977); *Bamberger's New Jersey,* 60 LA 960 (Trotta, 1973).

141. *Bamberger's New Jersey, supra* note 140.

142. *See* text under section "Application of Testing Policy," *infra.*

143. *See Faygo Beverages, Inc.,* 86 LA 1174 (Ellman, 1986).

144. *Signal Delivery,* 86 LA 75 (Wies, 1985).

145. *See Deaconess Medical Center,* 88 LA 44 (Robinson, 1986).

146. *Id.*

147. *But see Union Oil Co. of California,* 88 LA 91 (Weiss, 1986).

148. *Wheaton Industries,* 64 LA 826 (Kenison, 1975).

149. *General Telephone Co. of California,* 77 LA 1052 (Schuster, 1981).

150. *Capital Area Transit Authority, supra,* note 140.

151. *See San Diego Gas and Electric Co. v. National Health Laboratories, Inc.,* No. 4383 (San Diego Supreme Court, filed April 23, 1987, reported in 90 DAILY LAB. REP. A-3 (BNA, May 12, 1987) (reporting law suit filed by San Diego Gas and Electric Co. charging testing lab with negligence, fraud and deceit in urine screening).

152. For a listing of cases prior to 1983 involving grievances over workplace substance abuse, *see generally,* DENNENBERG & DENNENBERG, *supra* note 112.

153. Vt. Stat. Ann. 585.21 at 513(b); Iowa Code §730.5.2

154. *E.g.,* Vt. Stat. Ann. 585.21 at 513(b); Iowa Code §730.5–2; Minnesota Stat. §§181.93(13), 181.94(4); Montana Rev. Code Ann. §39–2–304; Utah Code Ann. §§34–38–9, 10, 11.

155. Arbitrators similarly rely on federal labor law to determine the parties' obligations under contract. *See, e.g., Laidlaw Transit,* 89 LA 1001 (D. Allen, 1987) (close reliance on NLRB law *re:* duty to bargain).

156. *White v. Davis,* 13 Cal. 3d 757, 533 P.2d 222 (1985); *Rulon-Miller v. IBM,* 162 Cal. App. 3d 241 (1984).

157. *Hopeman Brothers, Inc.,* 88 LA 373 (Rothschild, 1986) (In California, the union challenged the reasonableness of a unilaterally implemented substance-abuse plan which aimed at accident prevention through alcohol and drug screening programs; the arbitrator found the plan reasonable).

158. Arbitrators frequently cite federal cases on the implications of employee testing in the public sector, to justify imposing a "reasonable suspicion" requirement in private sector settings. *See, e.g., Faygo Beverages,* 86 LA 1174, 1177 n.1. (Ellmann, 1986).

159. *Faygo Beverages, supra* note 158, at 1177. *See also Capital Area Transit Authority,* 69 LA 811 (Ellmann, 1977); *Guiney v. Roach,* 654 F. Supp. 1287, 2 IER Cases 1225 (D. Mass. 1987); *Capua v. City of Plainfield,* 643 F. Supp. 1507, 1 IER Cases 625 (D.N.J. 1986); *Caruso v. Ward,* 133 Misc. 2d 544, 506 N.Y.S. 2d 789 (N.Y. Sup. Ct. 1986). Another source—or another way of discussing the "just cause" source—is some concept of a basic dose of fairness, or "industrial due process," an employer owes employees under the collective bargaining agreement. *See* discussion in text at notes 202–217.

160. *American Standard,* 77 LA 1085 (Katz, 1981).

161. *General Felt Industries, Inc.,* 74 LA 972 (Carnes, 1979).

162. *Texas Utilities Generating Co.,* 82 LA 6 (Edes, 1983).

163. *United States Steel Corp.,* 77 LA 854 (Hales, 1981) (employee sped past a stop sign when supervisor was on traffic control duty); *American Standard,* 77 LA 1085 (Katz, 1981) (employee was unsteady, staggering, swaying, disoriented, glassy-eyed, with slurred speech); *Pacific Motor Trucking,* 86 LA 497 (D'Spain, 1986) (odor of alcohol); *Roadway Express,* 87 LA 224 (Cooper, 1986) (disoriented, confused behavior); *Georgia Power Co.,* 87 LA 800 (Byars, 1986)

(violation of safety procedure, abusive language to foreman, inability to explain behavior); *Crown Zellerbach Corp.*, 87 LA 1145 (Cohen, 1986) (aberrant behavior, inability to perform, inability to reasonably explain conduct).

164. *Alcan Aluminum Co.*, 88 LA 386 (Kindig, 1986).

165. *Watauga Industries, Inc.*, 78 LA 697 (Galambos, 1982) (discharge was found too severe for employees smoking marijuana during lunch because the employee did not take affirmative action to "pass the word" that smoking of marijuana, which had been rampant in the plant, would no longer be tolerated); *Nabisco Brands, Inc.*, 86 LA 430 (Cox, 1985) (employer did not discriminate against employee by refusing him admittance to the employee assistance program as an alternative to discharge for sleeping on the job on a date he admittedly reported to work under the influence of alcohol); *Owens-Corning Fiberglass Corp.*, 86 LA 1026 (Nicholas, 1986) (company improperly discharged employee for allegedly violating rule against drug use on company property because action was based on former co-worker's admission that he had smoked marijuana with employee in the plant and rule was enforced disparately).

166. *Watauga Industries, Inc.*, 78 LA 697 (Galambos, 1982) (supervisor observed, from a roof-top, four employees smoking marijuana); *General Felt Industries, Inc.*, 74 LA 972 (Carnes, 1979); (discharge was improper because foreman's observation that employees were more boisterous than usual was insufficient evidence, as was his observation that employee's productivity was below its normal level).

167. For a discussion of the issues involved in identifying behavioral indications, *see* pp. text at notes 153–169, *supra*.

168. Arbitrator Concepcion found the inclusion of such a list in a policy to be reasonable. *Bay Area Rapid Transit*, 87-1 ARB ¶8084 (Concepcion, 1986).

169. Arbitrators seem to reject these arguments as long as companies substantially comply with the program's requirements and the employee is not prejudiced. *See, e.g., Union Oil of California*, 87 LA 297 (Boner, Azevedo, Totton, 1985). They may be more likely to agree with the union when the medical procedure is faulty. *See, e.g., Pacific Motor Trucking*, 86 LA 497 (D'Spain, 1986) (discharge improper on basis of test result where medical group did not follow procedure in letter of understanding).

170. *Division 241, Amalgamated Transit Union v. Sucsy*, 538 F.2d 1264 (7th Cir. 1976), *cert. denied*, 429 U.S. 1029 (1976); *Boise Cascade Corp.* (Kagel, January 8, 1987) (unreported).

171. *Division 241, Amalgamated Transit Union v. Sucsy, supra* note 170 (emphasis added). *See also Bi-State Development Agency*, 72 LA 198 (Newark, 1979); *Springfield Mass Transit District*, 80 LA 193 (Guenther, 1983); *Washington Metro Area Transit Authority*, 82 LA 150 (Bernhardt, 1983).

172. *Boise Cascade Corp.* (Kagel, January 8, 1987) (unreported).

173. *Id.*

174. *Deaconess Medical Center*, 88 LA 44 (Robinson, 1986); *Division 241, Amalgamated Transit Union v. Sucsy, supra* note 170. *Chicago Transit Authority* (Larney,

June 2, 1986) (unreported); *Chicago Transit Authority* (Goldberg, November 21, 1985) (unreported); *U.S. Air Force Logistics Command,* 78 LA 1092 (Feldman, 1982).

175. *Williams Pipeline Co.,* 78 LA 617 (Moore, 1982); *American Standard, WABCO Div.,* 77 LA 1085 (Katz, 1981); *See, generally,* ELKOURI & ELKOURI, HOW ARBITRATION WORKS, 4th Ed. 580–81 (BNA Books 1985).

176. *Id.*

177. *Chicago Transit Authority* (Larney, June 2, 1986) (unreported) (discounting union challenge to use of positive drug test obtained in return-to-work physical after layoff).

178. *Goodyear Tire & Rubber Co., Houston Chemical Plant,* 87–1 ARB ¶8231 (Fox, 1986).

179. *See* cases reported in ELKOURI & ELKOURI, *supra* note 175 at 695.

180. *See Michigan Consolidated Gas Co.,* 80 LA 693 (Keefe, 1983).

181. *Bi-State Development Agency,* 72 LA 198 (Newark, 1979); *Signal Delivery Service, Inc.,* 86 LA 75 (Weis, 1985) (refusal to submit to a blood alcohol test not insubordinate where employee was not forewarned that a refusal would be considered an admission and would result in discharge); *Gem City Chemicals, Inc.,* 86 LA 1023 (Warns, 1986) (discharge for refusal to submit to test during industrial physical improper); *Crown Zellerbach Corp.,* 87 LA 1145 (Cohen, 1986) (discharge too severe for refusal to take test; employer merely requested employee to take test and did not warn her refusal would be used against her); *Foote & Davies,* 88 LA 125 (Wahl, 1986) (discharge improper for refusal, where company had no enforced rule or policy on tests); *Pacific Gas & Electric,* 88 LA 194 (Koven, 1986) (discharge improper for refusal where settlement agreement did not explicitly require submission to testing); *Sanford Corp.,* 89 LA 968 (Wies, 1987) (discharge improper where employer failed to warn employee explicitly of consequences of refusal to take test); *General Industrial Contractors Co.,* 89 LA 1087 (Wolk, 1987) (discharge for refusal to take test improper, where employer failed to investigate employee's claim that he could not give sample due to "bashful kidney"). *Cf. Southern California Rapid Transit District,* 76 LA 144 (Sabo, 1980) (discharge too severe for employee who agreed to submit to test but refused to sign consent form).

182. *See, e.g., Fruehauf Corp.,* 88 LA 366 (Nathan, 1986) (employee given "last chance" unreasonably and without provocation to take test; discharge improper).

183. *American Standard,* 77 LA 1085 (Katz, 1981) (discharge upheld where employee was observed to be unsteady, swaying, disoriented, etc., and repeatedly refused test); *City of Milwaukee,* 78 LA 89 (Yaffee, 1982) (ten day suspension for failure to give a urine sample appropriate even where city employer failed to sustain false official report concerning probationary officer).

184. There is some question whether analyzing blood, where substances have not yet metabolized, may yield the possibility of determining the concentration of a substance in the human system at a given time, as existing analysis for blood alcohol content does. Still, there are few studies on human behavior

upon ingesting most chemical substances. Arbitrators have frequently been convinced that it is not yet possible to draw reasonable conclusions about the level of substance concentration necessary to conclude from a GC/MS result that a subject's behavior is affected. There are just as few studies to show particular effects on particular tasks, such as driving ability. One study does indicate that marijuana ingested 24 hours prior to performance will affect reaction time and thus the ability to perform a complex psychomotor task such as landing an airplane.

185. See, Union Oil Co. of California, 88 LA 91 (Weiss, 1986) (no claim employees were unable to perform their jobs); Chase Bag Co., 88 LA 441 (Strasshofer, 1986) (discharge for "under the influence" of alcohol improper when action was based on urine test results, which do not establish blood alcohol level to show "influence"); Faygo Beverages, Inc., 86 LA 1174 (Ellmann, 1986) (refusal to take test does not constitute proof of intoxication on the job); Georgia Pacific Corp., 86 LA 411 (Clarke, 1985) (discharge for "under the influence" improper where no expert testimony introduced re significance of presence of 280 ng/ml of THC in urine); Armstrong Rubber Co., 77 LA 775 (Koven, 1981) (discharge too severe for employee proven to be intoxicated but who had not damaged machine or threatened supervisor); Hayes-Albion Corp., 76 LA 1005 (Kahn, 1981) (discharge improper despite test's indication that employee had a substantial amount of alcohol in his blood; no proof he was unable to work); General Felt Industries, Inc., 74 LA 972 (Carnes, 1979) (discharge improper despite blood alcohol levels of .05 and .08; employees tested were only more boisterous than usual upon reporting for work).

186. Hayes-Albion Corp., 76 LA 1005 (Kahn, 1981).

187. Georgia-Pacific Corp., 86 LA 411 (Clarke, 1985).

188. Chicago Transit Authority and Local 241, A.T.U., (Goldberg, November 21, 1985) (unreported); Washington Metropolitan Transit Authority A.T.U. Local 689 (Fasser, 1984) (unreported); Greyhound Lines, Inc. and A.T.U. Division 1202, (Anderson, 1983) (unreported).

189. Union Oil Co. of California, 88 LA 91 (Weiss, 1986).

190. Chase Bag Co., 88 LA 441 (Strasshofer, Jr., 1986).

191. Durion Co., 85 LA 1127 (Coyne, 1985).

192. See, e.g., Eastern Airlines, 89 LA 492 (Tedel, 1987) (unconfirmed test "positive" for ethanol); Chase Bag Co., 88 LA 441 (Strasshofer, Jr., 1986) (urinalysis test, without blood test, did not establish blood alcohol level).

193. Thomas Steel Strip Corp., 87 LA 994 (Feldman, 1986) (discharge upheld after employee tested positive for a sufficient presence of THC to warrant a conclusion he was "under the influence"); Union Oil of California, 87 LA 297 (Boner, Azevedo, Totten, 1985) (suspension proper where employee's urine showed presence of a prohibited substance; arbitrator acknowledged that a positive test does not prove use on the job).

194. Alcan Aluminum Co., 88 LA 386 (Kindig, 1986).

195. Georgia-Pacific Corp., 86 LA 411 (Clarke, 1985).

196. *Roadway Express*, 87 LA 224 (Cooper, 1986); *Kroger Company*, 88 LA 463 (Wren, 1986).

197. *Roadway Express*, 87 LA 224 (Cooper, 1986).

198. *Kroger Company*, 88 LA 463 (Wren, 1986).

199. *Union Oil of California*, 87 LA 297 (Boner, Azevedo, Totten, 1985); *Roadway Express, Inc.*, 87 LA 1010 (D'Spain, 1986).

200. *Pacific Motor Trucking*, 86 LA 497 (D'Spain, 1986).

201. *Hussman Corp., Food Store Div.*, 87–2 ARB ¶8326 (Maniscalco, 1987); *Consolidated Coal Co.*, 87 LA 729 (Hoh, 1986) (Discharge of heavy equipment operator proper after two accidents; work rules prohibited negligent and careless performance, and "under the influence"); *Georgia Power Co.*, 87 LA 800 (Byars, 1986) (discharge of employee upheld where he engaged in abnormal behavior, admitted marijuana use); *Intermountain Rural Electric Assoc.*, 86 LA 540 (Watkins, 1985) (clear and convincing evidence employee was under the influence of alcohol: flushed, glazed eyes, odor, swaying); *Apcoa, Inc.*, 81 LA 449 (Hewitt, 1983) (discharge upheld where employee smelled of alcohol and could not work); *American Standard*, 77 LA 1085 (Katz, 1981) (discharge upheld when employee refused test; he was observed to be staggering, swaying, disoriented, unsteady, and glassy-eyed, with slurred speech; rule prohibits being under the influence of drugs); *Structurlite Plastics Corp.*, 73 LA 691 (Leach, 1979) (discharge proper where employees demonstrated "substantial symptoms" of being under the influence of some drug); *Porcelain Metals Corp.*, 73 LA 1133 (Roberts, 1979) (suspension proper where employee was under the influence of some prescribed drug, became disoriented, and had reduced motor control).

202. This section treats procedural issues with special importance in substance abuse cases. For the most part, it omits any general discussion of issues, such as the grievance's timeliness. For a discussion of these issues, *see generally*, ELKOURI & ELKOURI, HOW ARBITRATION WORKS, 4th ed. (BNA Books, 1986).

203. *See generally*, ELKOURI & ELKOURI, *supra* note 202, at 673–674.

204. These decisions are indexed in the BNA reporting system "Labor Arbitration" at key note 118.653.

205. *National Car Rental System, Inc.*, 75 LA 518 (Zumas, 1980).

206. *City of Kenosha*, 76 LA 758 (McCrary, 1981).

207. *Times Mirror Cable Television*, 87 LA 543 (Berns, 1986).

208. *Washington Metro Area Transit Authority*, 82 LA 150 (Bernhardt, 1983). See also, *Intermountain Rural Electric Assoc.*, 86 LA 540 (Watkins, 1985).

209. *Aeronca, Inc.*, 71 LA 452, 454 (Smith, 1978).

210. Federal law gives employees the right to have representation at an interview with management which an employee reasonably expects will lead to discipline. *NLRB v. Weingarten*, 420 U.S. 251 (1975). As a matter of federal labor law, the right appears to extend only to employees who are actually represented for purposes of bargaining over the terms and conditions of their employment. *Sears, Roebuck & Co.*, 274 NLRB 230, 118 LRRM 1329 (1985).

211. *General Telephone Co. of California,* 78 LA 793 (Roberts, 1982).

212. *Kraft, Inc.,* 82 LA 360 (Denson, 1984).

213. *Deaconess Medical Center,* 88 LA 44 (Robinson, 1986).

214. *Newport News Shipping & Drydock Co.,* 78 LA 921 (Garrett, 1982).

215. *Roadway Express, Inc.,* 87 LA 1010 (D'Spain, 1986).

216. *Pacific Motor Trucking,* 86 LA 497 (D'Spain, 1986).

217. *Union Oil of California,* 87 LA 297 (Boner, Azevedo, Totten, 1985); *Pacific Motor Trucking, supra* note 216.

218. *Mallinckrodt, Inc.,* 80 LA 1261 (Seidyan, 1983).

219. *Ethyl Corp.,* 74 LA 953 (Hart, 1980).

220. *Hooker Chemical Co.,* 74 LA 1032 (Grant, 1980).

221. *Weyerhauser Co.,* 86 LA 182 (Levin, 1985) (once an employer agrees to a rehabilitative approach without specifying limiting conditions, it must allow an employee suspected of prohibited off-duty drug use to complete a rehabilitation program before discharging him); *Indianapolis Rubber Co.,* 79 LA 529 (Gibson, 1982) (employee improperly discharged after alcoholism caused him to incur absentee "points," where company maintained an alcohol rehabilitation program).

222. *Chicago Transit Authority,* 80 LA 663 (Meyers, 1985). *See also, Springfield Mass Transit District,* 80 LA 193 (Guenther, 1983) (employer improperly discharged employee for failure to meet rehabilitation and aftercare requirements; letter suspending employee during rehabilitation had given him three months to comply, and time remained).

223. *See, e.g., Dresser Industries, Inc.,* 86 LA 1307 (Taylor, 1986) (employer not required to assist each employee through rehabilitation; in this case, employer reasonably decided the employee was a bad risk).

224. *Weyerhauser Co.,* 86 LA 182 (Levin, 1985) (once an employer agrees to a rehabilitative approach without specifying conditions, it must allow an employee suspected of prohibited off-duty drug use to complete a rehabilitation program before discharging him).

225. *Eastern Airlines, Inc.,* 74 LA 316 (Turkus, 1980).

226. *Pickhands Mather & Co.,* 80 LA 851 (Vernon, 1983).

227. *Pennwalt Corp.,* 86 LA 686 (Daniel, 1986). *See, also, Pacific Telephone & Telegraph Co.,* 81 LA 419 (Killion, 1983) (employee failed to cooperate with company medical department to enter rehabilitation program); *Continental Airlines, Inc.,* 75 LA 896 (Ross, 1980) (discharge would stand if employee fired for sleeping did not enroll in rehabilitation program); *National Gypsum Co.,* 73 LA 228 (Jacobs, 1979) (discharge proper where employee refused to continue treatment for a condition producing epilepsy-like trauma); *U.S. Plywood Corp.,* 88 LA 275 (Matthews, 1986) (discharge proper when employee failed to complete rehabilitation); *National Steel Corp.,* 88 LA 457 (Wolff, 1986) (employee failed to attend AA meetings).

228. *See, Preformed Line Products Co.,* 88 LA 340 (Strasshofer, 1986).

229. *Bemis Company, Inc.*, 81 LA 733 (Wright, 1983).

230. *Kerr-McGee Refining Co.*, 87 LA 737 (Caraway, 1986).

231. *Alta Bates Hospital*, 87 LA 719 (Rothstein, 1986).

232. For a brief discussion of the principles which make a past practice binding on management's conduct, see text accompanying notes 102–104, *supra.*

233. *See, Prescolite*, 71 LA 613 (Bridgewater, 1978) (discharge reduced when another employee had merely been sent home for working under the influence); *Browning-Ferris Industries of Ohio, Inc.*, 77 LA 289 (Shanker, 1981) (discharge reduced where the witness the employer presented to prove the grievant's drinking admitted he drank more, but was not disciplined); *American Meat Packing Co.*, 79 LA 1327 (Malinoski, 1982) (discharge for drinking and smoking marijuana too severe; undercover agent and supervisory leadman admitted everyone in the plant did it as well); *Western Paper Box*, 81 LA 917 (Concepcion, 1983) (discharge improper, even after employees had been warned, when other employees had violated rule and had not received warnings); *Owens-Corning Fiberglas Corp.*, 86 LA 1026 (Nicholas, 1986) (discharge proper for employee found in possession of marijuana on company lot even though his companion in the car was only suspended for refusal to stay).

234. *American Meat Packing Co.*, *supra*. n. 233.

235. *Navistar International Corp.*, 88 LA 179 (Archer, 1986) (suspension for drinking reduced where company had supplied beer for use on premises before). *Cf., Dresser Industries, Inc.*, 86 LA 1307 (Taylor, 1985) (discharge for fight at company picnic reduced; company did not provide sufficient supervision and had furnished beer and looked on as employees brought other alcohol).

236. This type of provision is a defense to a suit by either an employee who once again seeks redress for the employer's wrong, or by an employer seeking to overturn an arbitrator's award with which it disagrees. Employees' lawsuits under §301 of the NLRA raising arbitral claims before a grievance is processed will be dismissed for failure to exhaust the grievance/arbitration process, unless the employee also claims that his union did not fulfill its duty to represent him. *See, e.g., Sanders v. Washington Metropolitan Area Transit Authority*, 819 F.2d 1151, 125 LRRM 2772 (D.C. Cir. 1987), and cases cited in notes 4 and 12, *supra.*

Likewise, courts will dismiss suits in state and federal court which seek to avoid arbitration by alleging tortious wrongs or other state claims, on the grounds that federal law preempts these suits. *See, e.g., Utility Workers Local No. 246 v. Southern California Edison Co.*, ___ F.2d ___, 128 LRRM 2317 (9th Cir. May ___, 1988) (federal law preempts union's claim that random drug testing violates California state constitution's guarantees of privacy and freedom from unreasonable search and seizure).

237. Alaska: A.S. 09.43.010–09.43.180; Arizona: A.R.S. §§ 12–1501 to 12–1518; Arkansas: Ark. Stats. §§ 34–511 to 34–532; Colorado: C.R.S. 13–22–201 to 13–22–223; Delaware: 10 Del. C §§ 5701 to 5725; District of Columbia: D.C. Code 1981, §§ 16–4301 to 16–4319; Idaho: I.C. §§ 7–901 to 7–922; Illinois: S.H.A. ch. 10, ¶¶ 101 to 123; Indiana: West's A.I.C. §§ 34–4–2–1 to 34–4–

2-22; Iowa: I.C.A. §§ 679A.1 to 679A.19; Kansas: K.S.A. §§ 5-401 to 5-422; Maine: 14 M.R.S.A. §§ 5927-5949; Maryland: Code, Courts and Judicial Proceedings, §§ 3-201 to 3-234; Massachusetts: M.G.L.A. c. 251, §§ 1 to 19; Michigan: M.C.L.A. §§ 600.5001 to 600.5035; Minnesota: M.S.A. §§ 572.08 to 572.30; Missouri: V.A.M.S. §§ 435.350 to 435.470; Montana: MCA 27-5-111 to 27-5-324; Nevada: N.R.S. 38.015 to 38.205; New Mexico: NMSA 1978 §§ 44-7-1 to 44-7-22; North Carolina: G.S. §§ 1-567.1 to 1-567.20; Oklahoma: 15 Okl. St. Ann. §§ 801 to 818; Pennsylvania: 42 Pa. C. S.A. §§ 7301 to 7320; South Carolina: Code 1976, §§ 15-48-10 to 15-48-240; South Dakota: SDCL §§ 21-25A-1 to 21-25A-38; Tennessee: T.C.A. §§ 29-5-301 to 29-5-320; Texas: Vernon's Ann. Texas Civ. St. arts. 224 to 238-6; Utah: U.C.A. 1953, 78-31a-1 to 78-31a-18; Vermont: 12 V.S.A. §§ 5651 to 5681; Virginia: W.S. 1977, §§ 1-36-101 to 1-36-119; Wyoming: W.S. 1977, §§ 1-36-101 to 1-36-119.

238. 9 U.S.C. §1 *et. seq.* This Act does not apply to "contracts of employment of . . . workers engaged in foreign or interstate commerce," but federal courts frequently look to it to determine what constitutes the federal common law of labor relations concerning suits for violation of contract under §301 of the NLRA. *See, e.g., United Paperworkers International Union, AFL-CIO v. Misco, Inc.,* ___ U.S. ___, 126 LRRM 3113 (1987); *Ludwig Honold Mfg. Co. v. Fletcher,* 405 F.2d 1123 (3d Cir. 1969); *Pietro Scalzitti Co. v. Int'l Union of Operating Engineers, Local No. 150,* 351 F.2d 576 (7th Cir. 1965).

239. *Misco, supra* note 238, 126 LRRM at 3119, *quoting W. R. Grace & Co. v. Rubber Workers,* 461 U.S. 757, 766 (1983), *quoting in turn Muschany v. United States,* 324 U.S. 49, 66 (1945).

240. The Supreme Court in *Misco* expressly refused to decide whether a court could determine "public policy" from a source other than statutes, regulation, or other positive indicia of law. *Misco, supra* n. 238, 126 LRRM at 3120 n. 12. *See also Equitable Gas Company, Div. of Equitable Resources, Inc. v. United Steelworkers of America,* 676 F. Supp. 648, 127 LRRM 2264, 2269 (W.D.Pa. 1987) (court upheld arbitrator's award finding that employer had insufficient indicia of drug use to order test, and reinstating employee terminated for refusing test. Court remanded for reconsideration of all factors involved in employer's refusal of an economic security allowance to the employee); *Northwest Airlines, Inc. v. Airline Pilots Association, International,* 808 F.2d 76, 124 LRRM 2300 (D.C. Cir. 1987) (court refuses to overturn airline's board of adjustment's decision to reinstate alcoholic pilot upon certification by Federal Air Surgeon that pilot was free from effects of alcoholism); *S. D. Warren Co. v. United Paperworkers' International Union,* 815 F.2d 178, 125 LRRM 2086 (1st Cir. 1987) (holding that arbitrator exceeded authority by reducing discharge of employee who used, possessed, or sold drugs on company property, and that award violated public policy), *vacated and remanded,* ___ U.S. ___, 126 LRRM 3360 (1987), *on remand,* 845 F.2d 3, 128 LRRM 2175 (1988) (holding: award vacated on grounds of arbitrator's act in excess of authority under contract, but not on public policy grounds); *Amalgamated Transit Union Div. 1300 v. Mass Transit Administration,* 504 A.2d 1132, ___ N.E.2d ___, 121 LRRM 2894 (Md. Ct. App. Feb. 25, 1986).

241. *Equitable Gas Co.*, *supra* note 225, 127 LRRM at 2269; *Greco v. Halliburton Co.*, 674 F. Supp. 1447, 2 IER Cases 1281, 1283 (D. Wyo. 1987) (federal court dismissed a suit arguing that termination for refusal to submit to urinalysis violated the state's public policy favoring privacy; court could not say that termination was not in furtherance of policy in favor of drug testing).

242. *See, e.g., S. D. Warren Co.*, *supra* note 240.

# —7—

# THE NIDA GUIDELINES

*The National Institute on Drug Abuse and Department of Health and Human Services published these guidelines in the Federal Register, Vol. 53, No. 69, 11 April 1988.*

These Final Mandatory Guidelines are hereby adopted in accordance with Executive Order 12564 and section 503 of Pub. L. 100-71 as set forth below:

MANDATORY GUIDELINES FOR FEDERAL WORKPLACE DRUG TESTING PROGRAMS

Authority: E.O. 12564 and sec. 503 of Pub. L. 100-71.

## Subpart A—General

1.1 Applicability.

(a) These mandatory guidelines apply to:
   (1) Executive Agencies as defined in 5 U.S.C. 105(2);
   (2) The Uniformed Services, as defined in 5 U.S.C. 2101 (3) (but excluding the Armed Forces as defined in 5 U.S.C. 2101(2);
   (3) And any other employing unit or authority of the Federal Government except the United States Postal Service, the Postal Rate Commission, and employing units or authorities in the Judicial and Legislative Branches.

(b) Any agency or component of an agency with a drug testing program in existence as of September 15, 1986, and the Departments of Transportation and Energy shall take such action as may be necessary to ensure that the agency is brought into compliance with these Guidelines no later than 90 days after they take effect, except that any judicial challenge that affects these Guidelines shall not affect drug testing programs subject to this paragraph.

(c) Except as provided in 2.6, Subpart C of these Guidelines (which establishes laboratory certification standards) applies to any laboratory which has or seeks certification to perform urine drug testing for

Federal agencies under a drug testing program conducted under E.O. 12564. Only laboratories certified under these standards are authorized to perform urine drug testing for Federal agencies.

(d) The Intelligence Community, as defined by Executive Order No. 12333, shall be subject to these Guidelines only to the extent agreed to by the head of the affected agency.

(e) These Guidelines do not apply to drug testing conducted under legal authority other than E.O. 12564, including testing of persons in the criminal justice system, such as arrestees, detainees, probationers, incarcerated persons, or parolees.

(f) Agencies may not deviate from the provisions of these Guidelines without the written approval of the Secretary. In requesting approval for a deviation, an agency must petition the Secretary in writing and describe the specific provision or provisions for which a deviation is sought and the rationale therefore. The Secretary may approve the request upon a finding of good cause as determined by the Secretary.

1.2 Definitions.

For purposes of these Guidelines the following definitions are adopted:

*Aliquot.* A portion of a specimen used for testing.

*Chain of Custody.* Procedures to account for the integrity of each urine specimen by tracking its handling and storage from point of specimen collection to final disposition of the specimen. These procedures shall require that an approved agency chain of custody form be used from time of collection to receipt by the laboratory and that upon receipt of the laboratory an appropriate laboratory chain of custody form(s) account for the sample or sample aliquots within the laboratory. Chain of custody forms shall, at a minimum, include an entry documenting date and purpose each time a specimen or aliquot is handled or transferred and identifying every individual in the chain of custody.

*Collection Site.* A place designated by the agency where individuals present themselves for the purpose of providing a specimen of their urine to be analyzed for the presence of drugs.

*Collection Site Person.* A person who instructs and assists individuals at a collection site and who receives and makes an initial examination of the urine specimen provided by those individuals. A collection site person shall have successfully completed training to carry out this function.

*Confirmatory Test.* A second analytical procedure to identify the presence of a specific drug or metabolite which is independent of the initial test and which uses a different technique and chemical principle from that of the initial test in order to ensure reliability and accuracy. (At this time gas chromatography/mass spectrometry (GC/MS) is the only authorized confirmation method for cocaine, marijuana, opiates, amphetamines, and phencyclidine.)

*Initial Test (also known as Screening Test).* An immunoassay screen to eliminate "negative" urine specimens from further consideration.

*Medical Review Officer.* A licensed physician responsible for receiving laboratory results generated by an agency's drug testing program who has knowledge of substance abuse disorders and has appropriate medical training to interpret and evaluate an individual's positive test result together with his or her medical history and any other relevant biomedical information.

*Permanent Record Book.* A permanently bound book in which identifying data on each specimen collected at a collection site are permanently recorded in the sequence of collection.

*Reason to Believe.* Reason to believe that a particular individual may alter or substitute the urine specimen as provided in section 4(c) of E.O. 12564.

*Secretary.* The Secretary of Health and Human Services or the Secretary's designee. The Secretary's designee may be contractor or other recognized organization which acts on behalf of the Secretary in implementing these Guidelines.

1.3 Future Revisions.

In order to ensure the full reliability and accuracy of drug assays, the accurate reporting of test results, and the integrity and efficacy of Federal drug testing programs, the Secretary may make changes to these Guidelines to reflect improvements in the available science and technology. These changes will be published in final as a notice in the **Federal Register.**

## Subpart B—Scientific and Technical Requirements

2.1 The Drugs.

(a) The President's Executive Order 12564 defines "illegal drugs" as those included in Schedule I or II of the Controlled Substances Act (CSA), but not when used pursuant to a valid prescription or when used as otherwise authorized by law. Hundreds of drugs are covered under Schedule I and II and while it is not feasible to test routinely for all of them, Federal drug testing programs shall test for drugs as follows:
   (1) Federal agency applicant and random drug testing programs shall at a minimum test for marijuana and cocaine;
   (2) Federal agency applicant and random drug testing programs are also authorized to test for opiates, amphetamines, and phencyclidine; and

(3) When conducting reasonable suspicion, accident, or unsafe practice testing, a Federal agency may test for any drug listed in Schedule I or II of the CSA.

(b) Any agency covered by these guidelines shall petition the Secretary in writing for approval to include in its testing protocols any drugs (or classes of drugs) not listed for Federal agency testing in paragraph (a) of this section. Such approval shall be limited to the use of the appropriate science and technology and shall not otherwise limit agency discretion to test for any drugs covered under Schedule I or II of the CSA.

(c) Urine specimens collected pursuant to Executive Order 12564, Pub. L. 100-71, and these Guidelines shall be used only to test for those drugs included in agency drug-free workplace plans and may not be used to conduct any other analysis or test unless otherwise authorized by law.

(d) These Guidelines are not intended to limit any agency which is specifically authorized by law to include additional categories of drugs in the drug testing of its own employees or employees in its regulated industries.

2.2 Specimen Collection Procedures.

(a) *Designation of Collection Site.* Each agency drug testing program shall have one or more designated collection sites which have all necessary personnel, materials, equipment, facilities, and supervision to provide for the collection, security, temporary storage, and shipping or transportation of urine specimens to a certified drug testing laboratory.

(b) *Security.* Procedures shall provide for the designated collection site to be secure. If a collection site facility is dedicated solely to urine collection, it shall be secure at all times. If a facility cannot be dedicated solely to drug testing, the portion of the facility used for testing shall be secured during drug testing.

(c) *Chain of Custody.* Chain of custody standardized forms shall be properly executed by authorized collection site personnel upon receipt of specimens. Handling and transportation of urine specimens from one authorized individual or place to another shall always be accomplished through chain of custody procedures. Every effort shall be made to minimize the number of persons handling specimens.

(d) *Access to Authorized Personnel Only.* No unauthorized personnel shall be permitted in any part of the designated collection site when urine specimens are collected or stored.

(e) *Privacy.* Procedures for collecting urine specimens shall allow individual privacy unless there is reason to believe that a particular individual may alter or substitute the specimen to be provided.

(f) *Integrity and Identity of Specimen.* Agencies shall take precautions to ensure that a urine specimen not be adulterated or diluted during the collection procedure and that information on the urine bottle and in the record book can identify the individual from whom the specimen was collected. The following minimum precautions shall be taken to ensure that unadulterated specimens are obtained and correctly identified:

(1) To deter the dilution of specimens at the collection site, toilet bluing agents shall be placed in toilet tanks wherever possible, so the reservoir of water in the toilet bowl always remains blue. There shall be no other source of water (e.g., no shower or sink) in the enclosure where urination occurs.

(2) When an individual arrives at the collection site, the collection site person shall request the individual to present photo identification. If the individual does not have proper photo identification, the collection site person shall contact the supervisor of the individual, the coordinator of the drug testing program, or any other agency official who can positively identify the individual. If the individual's identity cannot be established, the collection site person shall not proceed with the collection.

(3) If the individual fails to arrive at the assigned time, the collection site person shall contact the appropriate authority to obtain guidance on the action to be taken.

(4) The collection site person shall ask the individual to remove any unnecessary outer garments such as a coat or jacket that might conceal items or substances that could be used to tamper with or adulterate the individual's urine specimen. The collection site person shall ensure that all personal belongings such as a purse or briefcase remain with the outer garments. The individual may retain his or her wallet.

(5) The individual shall be instructed to wash and dry his or her hands prior to urination.

(6) After washing hands, the individual shall remain in the presence of the collection site person and shall not have access to any water fountain, faucet, soap dispenser, cleaning agent or any other materials which could be used to adulterate the specimen.

(7) The individual may provide his/her specimen in the privacy of a stall or otherwise partitioned area that allows for individual privacy.

(8) The collection site person shall note any unusual behavior or appearance in the permanent record book.

(9) In the exceptional event that an agency-designated collection site is not accessible and there is an immediate requirement for specimen collection (e.g., an accident investigation), a public rest room

may be used according to the following procedures: A collection site person of the same gender as the individual shall accompany the individual into the public rest room which shall be made secure during the collection procedure. If possible, a toilet bluing agent shall be placed in the bowl and any accessible toilet tank. The collection site person shall remain in the rest room, but outside the stall, until the specimen is collected. If no bluing agent is available to deter specimen dilution, the collection site person shall instruct the individual not to flush the toilet until the specimen is delivered to the collection site person. After the collection site person has possession of the specimen, the individual will be instructed to flush the toilet and to participate with the collection site person in completing the chain of custody procedures.

(10) Upon receiving the specimen from the individual, the collection site person shall determine that it contains at least 60 milliliters of urine. If there is less than 60 milliliters of urine in the container, additional urine shall be collected in a separate container to reach a total of 60 milliliters. (The temperature of the partial specimen in each separate container shall be measured in accordance with paragraph (f)(12) of this section, and the partial specimens shall be combined in one container.) The individual may be given a reasonable amount of liquid to drink for this purpose (e.g., a glass of water). If the individual fails for any reason to provide 60 milliliters of urine, the collection site person shall contact the appropriate authority to obtain guidance on the action to be taken.

(11) After the specimen has been provided and submitted to the collection site person, the individual shall be allowed to wash his or her hands.

(12) Immediately after the specimen is collected, the collection site person shall measure the temperature of the specimen. The temperature measuring device used must accurately reflect the temperature of the specimen and not contaminate the specimen. The time from urination to temperature measurement is critical and in no case shall exceed 4 minutes.

(13) If the temperature of a specimen is outside the range of 32.5°–37.7°C/90.5°–99.8°F, that is a reason to believe that the individual may have altered or substituted the specimen, and another specimen shall be collected under direct observation of a same gender collection site person and both specimens shall be forwarded to the laboratory for testing. An individual may volunteer to have his or her oral temperature taken to provide evidence to counter the reason to believe the individual may have altered or substituted the specimen caused by the specimen's temperature falling outside the prescribed range.

(14) Immediately after the specimen is collected, the collection site person shall also inspect the specimen to determine its color and look for any signs of contaminants. Any unusual findings shall be noted in the permanent record book.

(15) All specimens suspected of being adulterated shall be forwarded to the laboratory for testing.

(16) Whenever there is reason to believe that a particular individual may alter or substitute the specimen to be provided, a second specimen shall be obtained as soon as possible under the direct observation of a same gender collection site person.

(17) Both the individual being tested and the collection site person shall keep the specimen in view at all times prior to its being sealed and labeled. If the specimen is transferred to a second bottle, the collection site person shall request the individual to observe the transfer of the specimen and the placement of the tamperproof seal over the bottle cap and down the sides of the bottle.

(18) The collection site person and the individual shall be present at the same time during procedures outlined in paragraphs (f)(19)-(f)(22) of this section.

(19) The collection site person shall place securely on the bottle an identification label which contains the date, the individual's specimen number, and any other identifying information provided or required by the agency.

(20) The individual shall initial the identification label on the specimen bottle for the purpose of certifying that it is the specimen collected from him or her.

(21) The collection site person shall enter in the permanent record book all information identifying the specimen. The collection site person shall sign the permanent record book next to the identifying information.

(22) The individual shall be asked to read and sign a statement in the permanent record book certifying that the specimen identified as having been collected from him or her is in fact that specimen he or she provided.

(23) A higher level supervisor shall review and concur in advance with any decision by a collection site person to obtain a specimen under the direct observation of a same gender collection site person based on a reason to believe that the individual may alter or substitute the specimen to be provided.

(24) The collection site person shall complete the chain of custody form.

(25) The urine specimen and chain of custody form are now ready for shipment. If the specimen is not immediately prepared for shipment, it shall be appropriately safeguarded during temporary storage.

(26) While any part of the above chain of custody procedures is being performed, it is essential that the urine specimen and custody documents be under the control of the involved collection site person. If the involved collection site person leaves his or her work station momentarily, the specimen and custody form shall be taken with him or her or shall be secured. After the collection site person returns to the work station, the custody process will continue. If the collection site person is leaving for an extended period of time, the specimen shall be packaged for mailing before he or she leaves the site.

(g) *Collection Control.* To the maximum extent possible, collection site personnel shall keep the individual's specimen bottle within sight both before and after the individual has urinated. After the specimen is collected, it shall be properly sealed and labeled. An approved chain of custody form shall be used for maintaining control and accountability of each specimen from the point of collection to final disposition of the specimen. The date and purpose shall be documented on an approved chain of custody form each time a specimen is handled or transferred and every individual in the chain shall be identified. Every effort shall be made to minimize the number of persons handling specimens.

(h) *Transportation to Laboratory.* Collection site personnel shall arrange to ship the collected specimens to the drug testing laboratory. The specimens shall be placed in containers designed to minimize the possibility of damage during shipment, for example, specimen boxes or padded mailers; and those containers shall be securely sealed to eliminate the possibility of undetected tampering. On the tape sealing the container, the collection site supervisor shall sign and enter the date specimens were sealed in the containers for shipment. The collection site personnel shall ensure that the chain of custody documentation is attached to each container sealed for shipment to the drug testing laboratory.

2.3 Laboratory Personnel.

(a) *Day-to-Day Management.*
   (1) The laboratory shall have a qualified individual to assume professional, organizational, educational, and administrative responsibility for the laboratory's urine drug testing facility.
   (2) This individual shall have documented scientific qualifications in analytical forensic toxicology. Minimum qualifications are:
      (i) Certification as a laboratory director by the State in forensic or clinical laboratory toxicology; or
      (ii) A Ph.D. in one of the natural sciences with an adequate undergraduate and graduate education in biology, chemistry, and pharmacology or toxicology, or

(iii) Training and experience comparable to a Ph.D. in one of the natural sciences, such as a medical or scientific degree with additional training and laboratory/research experience in biology, chemistry, and pharmacology or toxicology; and

(iv) In addition to the requirements in (i), (ii), and (iii) above, minimum qualifications also require:

(A) Appropriate experience in analytical forensic toxicology including experience with the analysis of biological material for drugs of abuse, and

(B) Appropriate training and/or experience in forensic applications of analytical toxicology, e.g., publications, court testimony, research concerning analytical toxicology of drugs of abuse, or other factors which qualify the individual as an expert witness in forensic toxicology.

(3) This individual shall be engaged in and responsible for the day-to-day management of the drug testing laboratory even where another individual has overall responsibility for an entire multi-specialty laboratory.

(4) This individual shall be responsible for ensuring that there are enough personnel with adequate training and experience to supervise and conduct the work of the drug testing laboratory. He or she shall assure the continued competency of laboratory personnel by documenting their inservice training, reviewing their work performance, and verifying their skills.

(5) This individual shall be responsible for the laboratory's having a procedure manual which is complete, up-to-date, available for personnel performing tests, and followed by those personnel. The procedure manual shall be reviewed, signed, and dated by this responsible individual whenever procedures are first placed into use or changed or when a new individual assumes responsibility for management of the drug testing laboratory. Copies of all procedures and dates on which they are in effect shall be maintained. (Specific contents of the procedure manual are described in 2.4(n)(1).)

(6) This individual shall be responsible for maintaining a quality assurance program to assure the proper performance and reporting of all test results; for maintaining acceptable analytical performance for all controls and standards; for maintaining qualify control testing; and for assuring and documenting the validity, reliability, accuracy, precision, and performance characteristics of each test and test system.

(7) This individual shall be responsible for taking all remedial actions necessary to maintain satisfactory operation and performance of the laboratory in response to quality control systems not being

within performance specifications, errors in result reporting or in analysis of performance testing results. This individual shall ensure that sample results are not reported until all corrective actions have been taken and he or she can assure that the test results provided are accurate and reliable.

(b) *Test Validation.* The laboratory's urine drug testing facility shall have a qualified individual(s) who reviews all pertinent data and quality control results in order to attest to the validity of the laboratory's test reports. A laboratory may designate more than one person to perform this function. This individual(s) may be any employee who is qualified to be responsible for day-to-day management or operation of the drug testing laboratory.

(c) *Day-to-Day Operations and Supervision of Analysts.* The laboratory's urine drug testing facility shall have an individual to be responsible for day-to-day operations and to supervise the technical analysts. This individual(s) shall have at least a bachelor's degree in the chemical or biological sciences or medical technology or equivalent. He or she shall have training and experience in the theory and practice of the procedures used in the laboratory, resulting in his or her thorough understanding of quality control practices and procedures; the review, interpretation, and reporting of test results; maintenance of chain of custody; and proper remedial actions to be taken in response to test systems being out of control limits or detecting aberrant test or quality control results.

(d) *Other Personnel.* Other technicians or nontechnical staff shall have the necessary training and skills for the tasks assigned.

(e) *Training.* The laboratory's urine drug testing program shall make available continuing education programs to meet the needs of laboratory personnel.

(f) *Files.* Laboratory personnel files shall include: resume of training and experience; certification or license, if any; references; job descriptions; records of performance evaluation and advancement; incident reports; and results of tests which establish employee competency for the position he or she holds, such as a test for color blindness, if appropriate.

2.4 Laboratory Analysis Procedures.

(a) *Security and Chain of Custody.*
   (1) Drug testing laboratories shall be secure at all times. They shall have in place sufficient security measures to control access to the premises and to ensure that no unauthorized personnel handle specimens or gain access to the laboratory processes or to areas where records are stored. Access to these secured areas shall be limited to specifically authorized individuals whose authorization

is documented. With the exception of personnel authorized to conduct inspections on behalf of Federal agencies for which the laboratory is engaged in urine testing or on behalf of the Secretary, all authorized visitors and maintenance and service personnel shall be escorted at all times. Documentation of individuals accessing these areas, dates, and time of entry and purpose of entry must be maintained.

(2) Laboratories shall use chain of custody procedures to maintain control and accountability of specimens from receipt through completion of testing, reporting of results, during storage, and continuing until final disposition of specimens. The date and purpose shall be documented on an appropriate chain of custody form each time a specimen is handled or transferred, and every individual in the chain shall be identified. Accordingly, authorized technicians shall be responsible for each urine specimen or aliquot in their possession and shall sign and complete chain of custody forms for those specimens or aliquots as they are received.

(b) *Receiving.*

(1) When a shipment of specimens is received laboratory personnel shall inspect each package for evidence of possible tampering and compare information on specimen bottles within each package to the information on the accompanying chain of custody forms. Any direct evidence of tampering or discrepancies in the information on specimen bottles and the agency's chain of custody forms attached to the shipment shall be immediately reported to the agency and shall be noted on the laboratory's chain of custody form which shall accompany the specimens while they are in the laboratory's possession.

(2) Specimen bottles will normally be retained within the laboratory's accession area until all analyses have been completed. Aliquots and the laboratory's chain of custody forms shall be used by laboratory personnel for conducting initial and confirmatory tests.

(c) *Short-Term Refrigerated Storage.* Specimens that do not receive an initial test within 7 days of arrival at the laboratory shall be placed in secure refrigeration units. Temperatures shall not exceed 6°C. Emergency power equipment shall be available in case of prolonged power failure.

(d) *Specimen Processing.* Laboratory facilities for urine drug testing will normally process specimens by grouping them into batches. The number of specimens in each batch may vary significantly depending on the size of the laboratory and its workload. When conducting either initial or confirmatory tests, every batch shall contain an appropriate number of standards for calibrating the instrumentation and a minimum of 10 percent controls. Both quality control and blind performance test samples shall appear as ordinary samples to laboratory analysts.

(e) *Initial Test.*

(1) The initial test shall use an immunoassay which meets the requirements of the Food and Drug Administration for commercial distribution. The following initial cutoff levels shall be used when screening specimens to determine whether they are negative for these five drugs or classes of drugs:

|  | Initial test level (ng/ml) |
|---|---|
| Marijuana metabolites ........................................................... | 100 |
| Cocaine metabolites ............................................................. | 300 |
| Opiate metabolites ............................................................... | 300 |
| Phencyclidine ....................................................................... | 25 |
| Amphetamines ...................................................................... | 1,000 |

[1]25ng/ml if immunoassay specific for free morphine.

(2) These test levels are subject to change by the Department of Health and Human Services as advances in technology or other considerations warrant identification of these substances at other concentrations. Initial test methods and testing levels for other drugs shall be submitted in writing by the agency for the written approval of the Secretary.

(f) *Confirmatory Test.*

(1) All specimens identified as positive on the initial test shall be confirmed using gas chromatography/mass spectrometry (GC/MS) techniques at the cutoff values listed in this paragraph for each drug. All confirmations shall be by quantitative analysis. Concentrations which exceed the linear region of the standard curve shall be documented in the laboratory record as "greater than highest standard curve value."

| | Confirmatory test level (ng/ml) |
|---|---|
| Marijuana metabolite[1] ........................................................ | 15 |
| Cocaine metabolite[2] ........................................................... | 150 |
| Opiates: | |
| Morphine ........................................................................ | *300 |
| Codeine ......................................................................... | *300 |
| Phencyclidine ................................................................... | 25 |
| Amphetamines: | |
| Amphetamine ................................................................... | 500 |
| Methamphetamine .............................................................. | 500 |

[1]Delta-9-tetrahydrocannabinol-9-carboxylic acid.
[2]Benzolylecgonine.

(2) These test levels are subject to change by the Department of Health and Human Services as advances in technology or other considerations warrant identification of these substances at other concentrations. Confirmatory test methods and testing levels for other drugs shall be submitted in writing by the agency for the written approval of the Secretary.

(g) *Reporting Results.*
(1) The laboratory shall report test results to the agency's Medical Review Officer within an average of 5 working days after receipt of the specimen by the laboratory. Before any test result is reported (the results of initial tests, confirmatory tests, or quality control) it shall be reviewed and the test certified as an accurate report by the responsible individual. The report shall identify the drugs/metabolite tested for, whether positive or negative, and the cutoff for each, the specimen number assigned by the agency, and the drug testing laboratory specimen identification number. The results (positive and negative) for all specimens submitted at the same time to the laboratory shall be reported back to the Medical Review Officer at the same time.

(2) The laboratory *shall report as negative* all specimens which are negative on the initial test or negative on the confirmatory test. Only specimens confirmed positive shall be reported positive for a specific drug.

(3) The Medical Review Officer may request from the laboratory and the laboratory shall provide quantitation of test results. The Medical Review Officer may not disclose quantitation of test results to the agency but shall report only whether the test was positive or negative.

(4) The laboratory may transmit results to the Medical Review Officer by various electronic means (for example, teleprinters, facsimile, or computer) in a manner designed to ensure confidentiality of the information. Results may not be provided verbally by telephone. The laboratory must ensure the security of the data transmission and limit access to any data transmission, storage, and retrieval system.

(5) The laboratory shall send only to the Medical Review Officer a certified copy of the original chain of custody form signed by the individual responsible for day-to-day management of the drug testing laboratory or the individual responsible for attesting to the validity of the test reports.

(6) The laboratory shall provide to the agency official responsible for coordination of the drug-free workplace program a monthly statistical summary of urinalysis testing of Federal employees and shall not include in the summary any personal identifying information. Initial and confirmation data shall be included from test results reported within that month. Normally this summary shall be forwarded by registered or certified mail not more than 14 calendar days after the end of the month covered by the summary. The summary shall contain the following information:

(i) Initial Testing:
   (A) Number of specimens received;
   (B) Number of specimens reported out; and
   (C) Number of specimens screened positive for:
       Marijuana metabolites
       Cocaine metabolites
       Opiate metabolites
       Phencyclidine
       Amphetamines

(ii) Confirmatory Testing:
   (A) Number of specimens received for confirmation;
   (B) Number of specimens confirmed positive for:
       Marijuana metabolite
       Cocaine metabolite

Morphine, codeine
Phencyclidine
Amphetamine
Methamphetamine

(7) The laboratory shall make available copies of all analytical results for Federal drug testing programs when requested by DHHS or any Federal agency for which the laboratory is performing drug testing services.

(8) Unless otherwise instructed by the agency in writing, all records pertaining to a given urine specimen shall be retained by the drug testing laboratory for a minimum of 2 years.

(h) *Long-Term Storage.* Long-term frozen storage ($-20°C$ or less) ensures that positive urine specimens will be available for any necessary retest during administrative or disciplinary proceedings. Unless otherwise authorized in writing by the agency, drug testing laboratories shall retain and place in properly secured long-term frozen storage for a minimum of 1 year all specimens confirmed positive. Within this 1 year period an agency may request the laboratory to retain the specimen for an additional period of time, but if no such request is received the laboratory may discard the specimen after the end of 1 year, except that the laboratory shall be required to maintain any specimen under legal challenge for an indefinite period.

(i) *Retesting Specimens.* Because some analytes deteriorate or are lost during freezing and/or storage, quantitation for a retest is not subject to a specific cutoff requirement but must provide data sufficient to confirm the presence of the drug or metabolite.

(j) *Subcontracting.* Drug testing laboratories shall not subcontract and shall perform all work with their own personnel and equipment unless otherwise authorized by the agency. The laboratory must be capable of performing testing for the five classes of drugs (marijuana, cocaine, opiates, phencyclidine, and amphetamines) using the initial immunoassay and confirmatory GC/MS methods specified in these Guidelines.

(k) *Laboratory Facilities.*

(1) Laboratory facilities shall comply with applicable provisions of any State licensure requirements.

(2) Laboratories certified in accordance with Subpart C of these Guidelines shall have the capability, at the same laboratory premises, of performing initial and confirmatory tests for each drug or metabolite for which service is offered.

(l) *Inspections.* The Secretary, any Federal agency utilizing the laboratory, or any organization performing laboratory certification on behalf of the Secretary shall reserve the right to inspect the laboratory at any time. Agency contracts with laboratories for drug testing, as well as contracts for collection site services, shall permit the agency to conduct unannounced inspections. In addition, prior to the award of a contract the agency shall carry out preaward inspections and evaluation of the procedural aspects of the laboratory's drug testing operation.

(m) *Documentation.* The drug testing laboratories shall maintain and make available for at least 2 years documentation of all aspects of the testing process. This 2-year period may be extended upon written notification by DHHS or by any Federal agency for which laboratory services are being provided. The required station shall include personnel files on all individuals authorized to have access to specimens; chain of custody documents; quality assurance/quality control records; procedure manuals; all test data (including calibration curves and any calculations used in determining test results); reports; performance records on performance testing; performance on certification inspections; and hard copies of computer-generated data. The laboratory shall be required to maintain documents for any specimen under legal challenge for an indefinite period.

(n) *Additional Requirements for Certified Laboratories.*
   (1) *Procedure Manual.* Each laboratory shall have a procedure manual which includes the principles of each test, preparation of reagents, standards and controls, calibration procedures, derivation of results, linearity of methods, sensitivity of the methods, cutoff values, mechanisms for reporting results, controls, criteria for unacceptable specimens and results, remedial actions to be taken when the test systems are outside of acceptable limits, reagents and expiration dates, and references. Copies of all procedures and dates on which they are in effect shall be maintained as part of the manual.
   (2) *Standards and Controls.* Laboratory standards shall be prepared with pure drug standards which are properly labeled as to content and concentration. The standards shall be labeled with the following dates: when received; when prepared or opened; when placed in services; and expiration date.
   (3) *Instruments and Equipment.*
      (i) Volumetric pipettes and measuring devices shall be certified for accuracy or be checked by gravimetric, colorimetric, or other verification procedure. Automatic pipettes and dilutors shall be checked for accuracy and reproducibility before being placed in service and checked periodically thereafter.
      (ii) There shall be written procedures for instrument set-up and normal operation, a schedule for checking critical operating

characteristics for all instrument tolerance limits for acceptable function checks and instructions for major trouble shooting and repair. Records shall be available on preventive maintenance.

(4) *Remedial Actions.* There shall be written procedures for the actions to be taken when systems are out of acceptable limits or errors are detected. There shall be documentation that these procedures are followed and that all necessary corrective actions are taken. There shall also be in place systems to verify all stages of testing and reporting and documentation that these procedures are followed.

(5) *Personnel Available To Testify at Proceedings.* A laboratory shall have qualified personnel available to testify in an administrative or disciplinary proceeding against a Federal employee when that proceeding is based on positive urinalysis results reported by the laboratory.

2.5 Quality Assurance and Quality Control.

(a) *General.* Drug testing laboratories shall have a quality assurance program which encompasses all aspects of the testing process including but not limited to specimen acquisition, chain of custody, security and reporting of results, initial and confirmatory testing, and validation of analytical procedures. Quality assurance procedures shall be designed, implemented, and reviewed to monitor the conduct of each step of the process of testing for drugs.

(b) *Laboratory Quality Control Requirements for Initial Tests.* Each analytical run of specimens to be screened shall include:

(1) Urine specimens certified to contain no drug;

(2) Urine specimens fortified with known standards; and

(3) Positive controls with the drug or metabolite at or near the threshold (cutoff). In addition, with each batch of samples a sufficient number of standards shall be included to ensure and document the linearity of the assay method over time in the concentration area of the cutoff. After acceptable values are obtained for the known standards, those values will be used to calculate sample data. Implementation of procedures to ensure that carryover does not contaminate the testing of an individual's specimen shall be documented. A minimum of 10 percent of all test samples shall be quality control specimens. Laboratory quality control samples prepared from spiked urine samples of determined concentration shall be included in the run and should appear as normal samples to laboratory analysts. One percent of each run, with a minimum of at least one sample, shall be the laboratory's own quality control samples.

(c) *Laboratory Quality Control Requirements for Confirmation Tests.* Each analytical run of specimens to be confirmed shall include:

   (1) Urine specimens certified to contain no drug;

   (2) Urine specimens fortified with known standards; and

   (3) Positive controls with the drug or metabolite at or near the threshold (cutoff). The linearity and precision of the method shall be periodically documented. Implementation of procedures to ensure that carryover does not contaminate the testing of an individual's specimen shall also be documented.

(d) *Agency Blind Performance Test Procedures.*

   (1) Agencies shall purchase drug testing services only from laboratories certified by DHHS or a DHHS-recognized certification program in accordance with these Guidelines. Laboratory participation is encouraged in other performance testing surveys by which the laboratory's performance is compared with peers and reference laboratories.

   (2) During the initial 90-day period of any new drug testing program, each agency shall submit blind performance test specimens to each laboratory it contracts with in the amount of at least 50 percent of the total number of samples submitted (up to a maximum of 500 samples) and thereafter a minimum of 10 percent of all samples (to a maximum of 250) submitted per quarter.

   (3) Approximately 80 percent of the blind performance test samples shall be blank (i.e., certified to contain no drug) and the remaining samples shall be positive for one or more drugs per sample in a distribution such that all the drugs to be tested are included in approximately equal frequencies of challenge. The positive samples shall be spiked only with those drugs for which the agency is testing.

   (4) The Secretary shall investigate any unsatisfactory performance testing result and, based on this investigation, the laboratory shall take action to correct the cause of the unsatisfactory performance test result. A record shall be made of the Secretary's investigative findings and the corrective action taken by the laboratory, and that record shall be dated and signed by the individuals responsible for the day-to-day management and operation of the drug testing laboratory. Then the Secretary shall send the document to the agency contracting officer as a report of the unsatisfactory performance testing incident. The Secretary shall ensure notification of the finding to all other Federal agencies for which the laboratory is engaged in urine drug testing and coordinate any necessary action.

   (5) Should a false positive error occur on a blind performance test

specimen and the error is determined to be an administrative error (clerical, sample mixup, etc.), the Secretary shall require the laboratory to take corrective action to minimize the occurrence of the particular error in the future, and, if there is reason to believe the error could have been systematic, the Secretary may also require review and reanalysis of previously run specimens.

(6) Should a false positive error occur on a blind performance test specimen and the error is determined to be a technical or methodological error, the laboratory shall submit all quality control data from the batch of specimens which included the false positive specimen. In addition, the laboratory shall retest all specimens analyzed positive for that drug or metabolite from the time of final resolution of the error back to the time of the last satisfactory performance test cycle. This retesting shall be documented by a statement signed by the individual responsible for day-to-day management of the laboratory's urine drug testing. The Secretary may require an on-site review of the laboratory which may be conducted unannounced during any hours of operations of the laboratory. The Secretary has the option of revoking (3.13) or suspending (3.14) the laboratory's certification or recommending that no further action be taken if the case is one of less serious error in which corrective action has already been taken, thus reasonably assuring that the error will not occur again.

2.6 Interim Certification Procedures.

During the interim certification period as determined under paragraph (c), agencies shall ensure laboratory competence by one of the following methods:

(a) Agencies may use agency or contract laboratories, that have been certified for urinalysis testing by the Department of Defense; or

(b) Agencies may develop interim self-certification procedures by establishing preaward inspections and performance testing plans approved by DHHS.

(c) The period during which these interim certification procedures will apply shall be determined by the Secretary. Upon notice by the Secretary that these interim certification procedures are no longer available, all Federal agencies subject to these Guidelines shall only use laboratories that have been certified in accordance with Subpart C of these Guidelines and all laboratories approved for interim certification under paragraphs (a) and (b) of this section shall become certified in accordance with Subpart C within 120 days of the date of this notice.

2.7 Reporting and Review of Results.

(a) *Medical Review Officer Shall Review Results.* An essential part of the drug testing program is the final review of results. A positive test result does not automatically identify an employee/applicant as an illegal drug user. An individual with a detailed knowledge of possible alternate medical explanations is essential to the review of results. This review shall be performed by the Medical Review Officer prior to the transmission of results to agency administrative officials.

(b) *Medical Review Officer—Qualifications and Responsibilities.* The Medical Review Officer shall be a licensed physician with knowledge of substance abuse disorders and may be an agency or contract employee. The role of the Medical Review Officer is to review and interpret positive test results obtained through the agency's testing program. In carrying out this responsibility, the Medical Review Officer shall examine alternate medical explanations for any positive test result. This action could include conducting a medical interview with the individual, review of the individual's medical history, or review of any other relevant biomedical factors. The Medical Review Officer shall review all medical records made available by the tested individual when a confirmed positive test could have resulted from legally prescribed medication. The Medical Review Officer shall not, however, consider the results of urine samples that are not obtained or processed in accordance with these Guidelines.

(c) *Positive Test Result.* Prior to making a final decision to verify a positive test result, the Medical Review Officer shall give the individual an opportunity to discuss the test result with him or her. Following verification of a positive test result, the Medical Review Officer shall refer the case to the agency Employee Assistance Program and to the management official empowered to recommend or take administrative action.

(d) *Verification for opiates; review for prescription medication.* Before the Medical Review Officer verifies a confirmed positive result for opiates, he or she shall determine that there is clinical evidence—in addition to the urine test—of illegal use of any opium, opiate, or opium derivative (e.g., morphine/ codeine) listed in Schedule I or II of the Controlled Substances Act. (This requirement does not apply if the agency's GC/ MS confirmation testing for opiates confirms the presence of 6-monoacetylmorphine.)

(e) *Reanalysis Authorized.* Should any question arise as to the accuracy or validity of a positive test result, only the Medical Review Officer is authorized to order a reanalysis of the original sample and such retests are authorized only at laboratories certified under these Guidelines.

(f) *Result Consistent with Legal Drug Use.* If the Medical Review Officer determines there is a legitimate medical explanation for the positive test result, he or she shall determine that the result is consistent with legal drug use and take no further action.

(g) *Result Scientifically Insufficient.* Additionally, the Medical Review Officer, based on review of inspection reports, quality control data, multiple samples, and other pertinent results, may determine that the result is scientifically insufficient for further action and declare the test specimen negative. In this situation the Medical Review Officer may request reanalysis of the original sample before making this decision. (The Medical Review Officer may request that reanalysis be performed by the same laboratory or, as provided in 2.7(e), that an aliquot of the original specimen be sent for reanalysis to an alternate laboratory which is certified in accordance with these Guidelines.) The laboratory shall assist in this review process as requested by the Medical Review Officer by making available the individual responsible for day-to-day management of the urine drug testing laboratory or other employee who is a forensic toxicologist or who has equivalent forensic experience in urine drug testing, to provide specific consultation as required by the agency. The Medical Review Officer shall report to the Secretary all negative findings based on scientific insufficiency but shall not include any personal identifying information in such reports.

2.8 Protection of Employee Records.

Consistent with 5 U.S.C. 522a(m) and 48 CFR 24.101-24.104, all laboratory contracts shall require that the contractor comply with the Privacy Act, 5 U.S.C. 552a. In addition, laboratory contracts shall require compliance with the patient access and confidentiality provisions of section 503 of Pub. L. 100-71. The agency shall establish a Privacy Act System of Records or modify an existing system, or use any applicable Government-wide system of records to cover both the agency's and the laboratory's records of employee urinalysis results. The contract and the Privacy Act System shall specifically require that employee records be maintained and used with the highest regard for employee privacy.

2.9 Individual Access to Test and Laboratory Certification Results.

In accordance with section 503 of Pub. L. 100-71, any Federal employee who is the subject of a drug test shall, upon written request, have access to any records relating to his or her drug test and any records relating to the results of any relevant certification, review, or revocation-of-certification proceedings.

## Subpart C—Certification of Laboratories Engaged in Urine Drug Testing for Federal Agencies

3.1 Introduction.

Urine drug testing is a critical component of efforts to combat drug abuse in our society. Many laboratories are familiar with good laboratory practices but may be unfamiliar with the special procedures required when drug test results are used in the employment context. Accordingly, the following are minimum standards to certify laboratories engaged in urine drug testing for Federal agencies. Certification, even at the highest level, does not guarantee accuracy of each result reported by a laboratory conducting urine drug testing for Federal agencies. Therefore, results from laboratories certified under these Guidelines must be interpreted with a complete understanding of the total collection, analysis, and reporting process before a final conclusion is made.

3.2 Goals and Objectives of Certification.

(a) *Uses of Urine Drug Testing.* Urine drug testing is an important tool to identify drug users in a variety of settings. In the proper context, urine drug testing can be used to deter drug abuse in general. To be a useful tool, the testing procedure must be capable of detecting drugs or their metabolites at concentrations indicated in 2.4 (e) and (f).

(b) *Need to Set Standards; Inspections.* Reliable discrimination between the presence, or absence, of specific drugs or their metabolites is critical, not only to achieve the goals of the testing program but to protect the rights of the Federal employees being tested. Thus, standards have been set which laboratories engaged in Federal employee urine drug testing must meet in order to achieve maximum accuracy of test results. These laboratories will be evaluated by the Secretary or the Secretary's designee as defined in 1.2 in accordance with these Guidelines. The qualifying evaluation will involve three rounds of performance testing plus on-site inspection. Maintenance of certification requires participation in an every-other-month performance testing program plus periodic, on-site inspections. One inspection following successful completion of a performance testing regimen is required for initial certification. This must be followed by a second inspection within 3 months, after which biannual inspections will be required to maintain certification.

(c) *Urine Drug Testing Applies Analytical Forensic Toxicology.* The possible impact of a positive test result on an individual's livelihood or rights, together with the possibility of a legal challenge of the result, sets this type of test apart from most clinical laboratory testing. In fact, urine drug testing should be considered a special application of analytical forensic toxicology. That is, in addition to the application of appropriate analytical methodology, the specimen must be treated as evidence, and all aspects of the testing procedure must be documented and available for possible court testimony. Laboratories engaged in urine drug testing for Federal agencies will require the services and advice of a qualified forensic toxicologist, or individual with equivalent qualifications (both training and experience) to address the specific needs of the Federal drug testing program, including the demands of chain of custody of specimens, security, property documentation of all records, storage of positive specimens for later or independent testing, presentation of evidence in court, and expert witness testimony.

3.3 General Certification Requirements.

A laboratory must meet all the pertinent provisions of these Guidelines in order to qualify for certification under these standards.

3.4 Capability to Test for Five Classes of Drugs.

To be certified, a laboratory must be capable of testing for at least the following five classes of drugs: Marijuana, cocaine, opiates, amphetamines, and phencyclidine, using the initial immunoassay and quantitative confirmatory GC/MS methods specified in these Guidelines. The certification program will be limited to the five classes of drugs (2.1(a) (1) and (2)) and the methods (2.4 (e) and (f)) specified in these Guidelines. The laboratory will be surveyed and performance tested only for these methods and drugs. Certification of a laboratory indicates that any test result reported by the laboratory for the Federal Government meets the standards in these Guidelines for the five classes of drugs using the methods specified. Certified laboratories must clearly inform non-Federal clients when procedures followed for those clients conform to the standards specified in these Guidelines.

3.5 Initial and Confirmatory Capability at Same Site.

Certified laboratories shall have the capability, at the same laboratory site, of performing both initial immunoassays and confirmatory GC/MS tests (2.4(e) and (f)) for marijuana, cocaine, opiates, amphetamines, and phencyclidine and for any other drug or metabolite for which agency drug testing is authorized (2.1(a) (1) and (2)). All positive initial test results shall be confirmed prior to reporting them.

3.6 Personnel.

Laboratory personnel shall meet the requirements specified in 2.3 of these Guidelines. These Guidelines establish the exclusive standards for qualifying or certifying those laboratory personnel involved in urinalysis testing whose functions are prescribed by these Guidelines. A certification of a laboratory under these Guidelines shall be a determination that these qualification requirements have been met.

3.7 Quality Assurance and Quality Control.

Drug testing laboratories shall have a quality assurance program which encompasses all aspects of the testing process, including but not limited to specimen acquisition, chain of custody, security and reporting of results, initial and confirmatory testing, and validation of analytical procedures. Quality control procedures shall be designed, implemented and reviewed to monitor the conduct of each step of the process of testing for drugs as specified in 2.5 of these Guidelines.

3.8 Security and Chain of Custody.

Laboratories shall meet the security and chain of custody requirements provided in 2.4(a).

3.9 One-Year Storage for Confirmed Positives.

All confirmed positive specimens shall be retained in accordance with the provisions of 2.4(h) of these Guidelines.

3.10 Documentation.

The laboratory shall maintain and make available for at least 2 years documentation in accordance with the specifications in 2.4(m).

3.11 Reports.

The laboratory shall report test results in accordance with the specifications in 2.4(g).

3.12 Certification.

(a) *General.* The Secretary may certify any laboratory that meets the standards in these Guidelines to conduct urine drug testing. In addition, the Secretary may consider to be certified any laboratory that is certified by a DHHS-recognized certification program in accordance with these Guidelines.

(b) *Criteria.* In determining whether to certify a laboratory or to accept the certification of a DHHS-recognized certification program in accordance with these Guidelines, the Secretary shall consider the following criteria:

   (1) The adequacy of the laboratory facilities;
   (2) The expertise and experience of the laboratory personnel;
   (3) The excellence of the laboratory's quality assurance/quality control program;
   (4) The performance of the laboratory on any performance tests;
   (5) The laboratory's compliance with standards as reflected in any laboratory inspections; and
   (6) Any other factors affecting the reliability and accuracy of drug tests and reporting done by the laboratory.

3.13 Revocation.

(a) *General.* The Secretary shall revoke certification of any laboratory certified under these provisions or accept revocation by a DHHS-recognized certification program in accordance with these Guidelines if the Secretary determines that revocation is necessary to ensure the full reliability and accuracy of drug tests and the accurate reporting of test results.

(b) *Factors to Consider.* The Secretary shall consider the following factors in determining whether revocation is necessary:
   (1) Unsatisfactory performance in analyzing and reporting the results of drug tests; for example, a false positive error in reporting the results of an employee's drug test;
   (2) Unsatisfactory participation in performance evaluations or laboratory inspections;
   (3) A material violation of a certification standard or a contract term or other condition imposed on the laboratory by a Federal agency using the laboratory's services;
   (4) Conviction for any criminal offense committed as an incident to operation of the laboratory; or
   (5) Any other cause which materially affects the ability of the laboratory to ensure the full reliability and accuracy of drug tests and the accurate reporting of results.

(c) *Period and Terms.* The period and terms of revocation shall be determined by the Secretary and shall depend upon the facts and circumstances of the revocation and the need to ensure accurate and reliable drug testing of Federal employees.

3.14 Suspension.

(a) *Criteria.* Whenever the Secretary has reason to believe that revocation may be required and that immediate action is necessary in order to protect the interests of the United States and its employees, the Secretary may immediately suspend a laboratory's certification to conduct urine drug testing for Federal agencies. The Secretary may also accept suspension of certification by a DHHS-recognized certification program in accordance with these Guidelines.

(b) *Period and Terms.* The period and terms of suspension shall be determined by the Secretary and shall depend upon the facts and circumstances of the suspension and the need to ensure accurate and reliable drug testing of Federal employees.

3.15 Notice: Opportunity for Review.

(a) *Written Notice.* When a laboratory is suspended or the Secretary seeks to revoke certification, the Secretary shall immediately serve the laboratory with written notice of the suspension or proposed revocation by personal service or registered or certified mail, return receipt requested. This notice shall state the following:

(1) The reasons for the suspension or proposed revocation;

(2) The terms of the suspension or proposed revocation; and

(3) The period of suspension or proposed revocation.

(b) *Opportunity for Informal Review.* The written notice shall state that the laboratory will be afforded an opportunity for an informal review of the suspension or proposed revocation if it so requests in writing within 30 days of the date of mailing or service of the notice. The review shall be by a person or persons designated by the Secretary and shall be based on written submissions by the laboratory and the Department of Health and Human Services and, at the Secretary's discretion, may include an opportunity for an oral presentation. Formal rules of evidence and procedures applicable to proceedings in a court of law shall not apply. The decision of the reviewing official shall be final.

(c) *Effective Date.* A suspension shall be effective immediately. A proposed revocation shall be effective 30 days after written notice is given or, if review is requested, upon the reviewing official's decision to uphold the proposed revocation. If the reviewing official decides not to uphold the suspension or proposed revocation, the suspension shall terminate immediately and any proposed revocation shall not take effect.

(d) *DHHS-Recognized Certification Program.* The Secretary's responsibility under this section may be carried out by a DHHS-recognized certification program in accordance with these Guidelines.

3.16 Recertification.

Following the termination or expiration of any suspension or revocation, a laboratory may apply for recertification. Upon the submission of evidence satisfactory to the Secretary that the laboratory is in compliance with these Guidelines or any DHHS-recognized certification program in accordance with these Guidelines, and any other conditions imposed as part of the suspension or revocation, the Secretary may recertify the laboratory or accept the recertification of the laboratory by a DHHS-recognized certification program.

3.17 Performance Test Requirement for Certification.

(a) *An Initial and Continuing Requirement.* The performance test program is a part of the initial evaluation of a laboratory seeking certification (both performance testing and laboratory inspection are required) and of the continuing assessment of laboratory performance necessary to maintain this certification.

(b) *Three Initial Cycles Required.* Successful participation in three cycles of testing shall be required before a laboratory is eligible to be considered for inspection and certification. These initial three cycles and any required for recertification) can be compressed into a 3-month period (one per month).

(c) *Six Challenges Per Year.* After certification, laboratories shall be challenged every other month with one set of at least 10 specimens a total of six cycles per year.

(d) *Laboratory Procedures Identical for Performance Test and Routine Employee Specimens.* All procedures associated with the handling and testing of the performance test specimens by the laboratory shall to the greatest extent possible be carried out in a manner identical to that applied to routine laboratory specimen, unless otherwise specified.

(e) *Blind Performance Test.* Any certified laboratory shall be subject to blind performance testing (see 2.5(d)). Performance on blind test specimens shall be at the same level as for the open or non-blind performance testing.

(f) *Reporting—Open Performance Test.* The laboratory shall report results of open performance tests to the certifying organization in the same manner as specified in 2.4(g)(2) for routine laboratory specimens.

3.18 Performance Test Specimen Composition.

(a) *Description of the Drugs.* Performance test specimens shall contain those drugs and metabolites which each certified laboratory must be prepared to assay in concentration ranges that allow detection of the analyte by commonly used immunoassay screening techniques. These levels are generally in the range of concentrations which might be expected in the urine of recent drug users. For some drug analytes the specimen composition will consist of the parent drug as well as major metabolites. In some cases, more than one drug class may be included in one specimen container, but generally no more than two drugs will be present in any one specimen in order to imitate the type of specimen which a laboratory normally encounters. For any particular performance testing cycle, the actual composition of kits going to different laboratories will vary but, within any annual period, all laboratories participating will have analyzed the same total set of specimens.

(b) *Concentrations.* Performance test specimens shall be spiked with the drug classes and their metabolites which are required for certifications: marijuana, cocaine, opiates, amphetamines, and phencyclidine, with concentration levels set at least 20 percent above the cutoff limit for either the initial assay or the confirmatory test, depending on which is to be evaluated. Some performance test specimens may be identified for GC/MS assay only. Blanks shall contain less than 2 ng/ml of any of the target drugs. These concentration and drug types may be changed periodically in response to factors such as changes in detection technology and patterns of drug use.

3.19 Evaluation of Performance Testing.

(a) *Initial Certification.*
   (1) An applicant laboratory shall not report any false positive result during performance testing for initial certification. Any false positive will automatically disqualify a laboratory from further consideration.
   (2) An applicant laboratory shall maintain an overall grade level of 90 percent for the three cycles of performance testing required for initial certification, i.e., it must correctly identify and confirm 90 percent of the total drug challenges for each shipment. Any laboratory which achieves a score on any one cycle of the initial certification such that it can no longer achieve a total grade of 90 percent over the three cycles will be immediately disqualified from further consideration.
   (3) An applicant laboratory shall obtain quantitative values for at least 80 percent of the total drug challenges which are ±20 percent or ±2 standard deviations of the calculated reference group mean (whichever is larger). Failure to achieve 80 percent will result in disqualification.
   (4) An applicant laboratory shall not obtain any quantitative values that differ by more than 50 percent from the calculated reference group mean. Any quantitative values that differ by more than 50 percent will result in disqualification.
   (5) For any individual drug, an applicant laboratory shall successfully detect and quantitate in accordance with paragraphs (a)(2), (a)(3), and (a)(4) of this section at least 50 percent of the total drug challenges. Failure to successfully quantitate at least 50 percent of the challenges for any individual drug will result in disqualification.

(b) *Ongoing Testing of Certified Laboratories.*
   (1) *False Positives and Procedures for Dealing With Them.* No false drug identifications are acceptable for any drugs for which a laboratory offers service. Under some circumstances a false positive test may result in suspension or revocation of certification. The most serious false positives are by drug class, such as reporting THC in a blank specimen or reporting cocaine in a specimen known to contain only opiates. Misidentifications within a class (e.g., codeine for morphine) are also false positives which are unacceptable in an appropriately controlled laboratory, but they are clearly less serious errors than misidentification of a class. The following procedures shall be followed when dealing with a false positive:

(i) The agency detecting a false positive error shall immediately notify the laboratory and the Secretary of any such error.

(ii) The laboratory shall provide the Secretary with a written explanation of the reasons for the error within 5 working days. If required by paragraph (b)(1)(v) below, this explanation shall include the submission of all quality control data from the batch of specimens that included the false positive specimen.

(iii) The Secretary shall review the laboratory's explanation within 5 working days and decide what further action, if any, to take.

(iv) If the error is determined to be an administrative error (clerical, sample mixup, etc.), the Secretary may direct the laboratory to take corrective action to minimize the occurrence of the particular error in the future and, if there is reason to believe the error could have been systematic, may require the laboratory to review and reanalyze previously run specimens.

(v) If the error is determined to be technical or methodological error, the laboratory shall submit to the Secretary all quality control data from the batch of specimens which included the false positive specimen. In addition, the laboratory shall retest all specimens analyzed positive by the laboratory from the time of final resolution of the error back to the time of the last satisfactory performance test cycle. This retesting shall be documented by a statement signed by the individual responsible for the day-to-day management of the laboratory's urine drug testing. Depending on the type of error which caused the false positive, this retesting may be limited to one analyte or may include any drugs a laboratory certified under these Guidelines must be prepared to assay. The laboratory shall immediately notify the agency if any result on a retest sample must be corrected because the criteria for a positive are not satisfied. The Secretary may suspend or revoke the laboratory's certification for all drugs or for only the drug or drug class in which the error occurred. However, if the case is one of a less serious error for which effective corrections have already been made, thus reasonably assuring that the error will not occur again, the Secretary may decide to take no further action.

(vi) During the time required to resolve the error, the laboratory shall remain certified but shall have a designation indicating that a false positive result is pending resolution. If the Secretary determines that the laboratory's certification must be suspended or revoked, the laboratory's official status will become "Suspended" or "Revoked" until the suspension or revocation is lifted or any recertification process is completed.

(2) *Requirement to Identify and Confirm 90 Percent of Total Drug Challenges.* In order to remain certified, laboratories must successfully complete six cycles of performance testing per year. Failure of a certified laboratory to maintain a grade of 90 percent on any required performance test cycle, i.e., to identify 90 percent of the total drug challenges and to correctly confirm 90 percent of the total drug challenges, may result in suspension or revocation of certification.

(3) *Requirements to Quantitate 80 Percent of Total Drug Challenges at ±20 Percent or ±2 standard deviations.* Quantitative values obtained by a certified laboratory for at least 80 percent of the total drug challenges must be ±20 percent or ±2 standard deviations of the calculated reference group mean (whichever is larger).

(4) *Requirement to Quantitate within 50 Percent of Calculated Reference Group Mean.* No quantitative values obtained by a certified laboratory may differ by more than 50 percent from the calculated reference group mean.

(5) *Requirement to Successfully Detect and Quantitate 50 Percent of the Total Drug Challenges for Any Individual Drug.* For any individual drug, a certified laboratory must successfully detect and quantitate in accordance with paragraphs (b)(2), (b)(3), and (b)(4) of this section at least 50 percent of the total drug challenges.

(6) *Procedures When Requirements in Paragraphs (b)(2)-(b)(5) of this Section Are Not Met.* If a certified laboratory fails to maintain a grade of 90 percent per test cycle after initial certification as required by paragraph (b)(2) of this section or if it fails to successfully quantitate results as required by paragraphs (b)(3), (b)(4), or (b)(5) of this section, the laboratory shall be immediately informed that its performance fell under the 90 percent level or that it failed to successfully quantitate test results and how it failed to successfully quantitate. The laboratory shall be allowed 5 working days in which to provide any explanation for its unsuccessful performance, including administrative error or methodological error, and evidence that the source of the poor performance has been corrected. The Secretary may revoke or suspend the laboratory's certification or take no further action, depending on the seriousness of the errors and whether there is evidence that the source of the poor performance has been corrected and that current performance meets the requirements for a certified laboratory under these Guidelines. The Secretary may require that additional performance tests be carried out to determine whether the source of the poor performance has been removed. If the Secretary determines to suspend or revoke the laboratory's certification, the laboratory's official status will become "Suspended" or "Revoked" until the

suspension or revocation is lifted or until any recertification process is complete.

(c) *80 Percent of Participating Laboratories Must Detect Drug.* A laboratory's performance shall be evaluated for all samples for which drugs were spiked at concentrations above the specified performance test level unless the overall response from participating laboratories indicates that less than 80 percent of them were able to detect a drug.

(d) *Participation Required.* Failure to participate in a performance test or to participate satisfactorily may result in suspension or revocation of certification.

3.20 Inspections.

Prior to laboratory certification under these Guidelines and at least twice a year after certification, a team of three qualified inspectors, at least two of whom have been trained as laboratory inspectors, shall conduct an on-site inspection of laboratory premises. Inspections shall document the overall quality of the laboratory setting for the purposes of certification to conduct urine drug testing. Inspection reports may also contain recommendations to the laboratory to correct deficiencies noted during the inspection.

3.21 Results of Inadequate Performance.

Failure of a laboratory to comply with any aspect of these Guidelines may lead to revocation or suspension of certification as provided in 3.13 and 3.14 of these Guidelines.

# TABLE OF CASES

Cases are referenced to chapter and footnote number(s), e.g., 2:21 indicates the case is cited in chapter 2, footnote 21. Names of cases discussed in text are italicized; the corresponding footnote number indicating the location of the discussion in text also is italicized, to distinguish the discussion from other footnotes which merely cite the case.

*The following lists the parallel citation services that are used within the case citations and are published as part of the *Labor Relations Reporter* by The Bureau of National Affairs, Inc.: FEP Cases indicates Fair Employment Practice Cases; IER Cases indicates Individual Employment Rights Cases; LA indicates Labor Arbitration and Dispute Settlements Decisions; and LRRM indicates Labor Relations Reference Manual.

I
IBEW v. Hechler, ___ U.S. ___, 2
IER Cases 129, *on remand*,
834 F.2d 942, 3 IER Cases
331 (11th Cir. 1987)

IBEW, Local 1900 v. PEPCO
—634 F. Supp. 642, 121 LRRM
3287 (D.D.C. 1986) 5:11,
12, 25; 6:24, 26

—___ F. Supp. ___, 121 LRRM
3071 (D.D.C. 1986) 5:25;
6:35

IBEW, System Council U-9 v. Metropolitan Edison Co., No. 86–
4426, slip op. (E.D. Pa.
August 14, 1986) 5:11, 12;
6:19, 24, 27, 31

Independent Metal Workers (Hughes
Tool Co.), 147 NLRB 1573
(1964) 6:4

Indianapolis Power & Light Co., 87
LA 826 (Volz, 1986) 6:129

Indianapolis Rubber Co., 79 LA 529
(Gibson, 1982) 6:221

Inner City Broadcasting Corp., 281
NLRB No. 162 (1986) 6:75

Intermountain Rural Electric Ass'n,
86 LA 540 (Watkins, 1985)
6:201, 208

International Brotherhood of Teamsters v. Southwest Airlines
Co., 842 F.2d 794, 128
LRRM 2225, (5th Cir.
1988) 2:211; 6:37

International Chemical Workers
Union and Local 4 v. Olin
Corp., No. 87 C 5745 (N.D.
Ill. June 15, 1987) (Mem.
order) 5:21, 31; 6:24, 29,
118

J
Jackson
—v. Consolidated Rail Corp.,
717 F.2d 1045, 114 LRRM
2682 (7th Cir. 1983) 2:242

—v. Minidoka Irrigation District,
98 Idaho 330, 563 P.2d 54,
115 LRRM 5040 (1977)
5:76

Jacobs Mfg. Co., 94 NLRB 1214
(1951), *enforced*, 196 F.2d
680 (2d Cir. 1951) 6:55

J.D. Lunsford Plumbing, Heating &
Air Conditioning, Inc., 254
NLRB 1360, 107 LRRM
1033 (1981), *aff'd*, 684 F.2d
1033, 110 LRRM 3367
(D.C. Dir. 1982) 6:42

Joftus v. Kaufman, 324 F. Supp. 660
(D.C. Cir. 1971) 2:155

Johnson
—v. Hydraulic Research Mfg.
Co., 96 LRRM 2466 (Cal.
Ct. App. 1977) 2:248

—v. Railway Express Agency,
Inc., 421 U.S. 454 (1975)
2:111

—v. World Color Press, Inc.,
147 Ill. App. 3d 746, 498
N.E.2d 575, 1 IER Cases
1446 (5th Dist. 1986) 2:199

Jones v. McKenzie, 628 F. Supp.
1500, 1 IER Cases 1076
(D.D.C. 1986), *rev'd in part,
vacated in part*, 833 F.2d
335, 2 IER Cases 1121
(D.C. Cir. 1987) 2:14, 23;
5:4, 21, 43

K
Kay Fries, Inc., 265 NLRB 1077,
112 LRRM 1377 (1982)
2:218

Keehr v. Consolidated Freightways
of Delaware, Inc., 825 F.2d
133, 2 IER Cases 565 (7th
Cir. 1987) 2:250, 252

Kelsay v. Motorola, 74 Ill. 2d 172,
384 N.E.2d 353, 115
LRRM 4371 (1982) 2:194,
195

Magers v. U.S. Air, Inc., 525 F. Supp. 853 (D. Md. 1981) 2:189

Mallinkrodt, Inc., 80 LA 1261 (Seidyan, 1983) 6:218

Manhattan-Walton Joint Venture v. Painters Local 151, 144 LRRM 2868 (Ala. Civ. Ct. 1982) 6:16

Marathon Petroleum Co., 89 LA 717 (Grimes, 1987) 6:104

Marriott In-Flite Services Div. of Marriott Corp., 258 NLRB 755, 108 LRRM 1287 (1981), enforced, 729 F.2d 1441, 113 LRRM 3528 (2d Cir.), cert. denied, 464 U.S. 829, 114 LRRM 2568 (1983) 6:42

Martin-Marietta Aerospace, Baltimore Div., 81 LA 695 (Aronin, 1983) 6:138

M.B.M. Co. v. Ounce, 268 Ark. 269, 596 S.W.2d 681 (1980) 2:185

McDonnell v. Hunter, 809 F.2d 1302, 1 IER Cases 1297 (8th Cir. 1987) 2:16, 22; 5:21, 27

McDonnell-Douglas Canada, Ltd., 74 LA 1103 (O'Shea, 1980) 6:139

McKinney v. County of Santa Clara, 110 Cal. App. 3d 787, 167 Cal. Rptr. 89 (1980) 2:164

McLeod v. City of Detroit, 39 FEP Cases 225 (E.D. Mich. 1985) 2:133, 138

MediCenter, Mid-South Hospital, 221 NLRB 670 (1975) 2:212; 6:47

Merrill & Ring, Inc., 262 NLRB 392, 110 LRRM 1309 (1982), enforced, 731 F.2d

605, 116 LRRM 2221 (9th Cir. 1984) 6:41

Merritt v. Detroit Memorial Hosp., 265 N.W.2d 124 (Mich. Ct. App. 1978) 2:153

Metropolitan Edison Co.
—AAA Case No. 14 300 093886 (Aarons, Oct. 9, 1986) 5:27
—V. NLRB, 460 U.S. 693 (1983) 2:216

Meyer v. Nebraska, 262 U.S. 390 (1928) 2:30

Michigan Consolidated Gas Co., 80 LA 693 (Keefe, 1983) 5:63; 6:180

Milwaukee, City of, 71 LA 329 (Maslanka, 1978) 6:132, 183

Mobil Coal Producing, Inc. v. Parks, 704 P.2d 702, 1 IER Cases 1341 (Wyo. 1985) 5:76

Moniodis v. Cook, 64 Md. App. 1, 494 A.2d 212, 1 IER Cases 441 (Md. Ct. Spec. App. 1985), cert. denied, 304 Md. 631 (1985) 2:186; 202

Monroe v. Consolidated Freightways, Inc., 654 F. Supp. 661 (E.D. Mo. 1987) 6:17

Moore Drop Forging Co., 144 NLRB 165 (1963) 2:232; 6:70

Morco, Inc. d/b/a Towne Plaza Hotel, 258 NLRB 69, 108 LRRM 1126 (1981) 6:42

Morris v. Lutheran Medical Center, 215 Neb. 677, 340 N.W.2d 388, 115 LRRM 4966 (1983) 5:76

MRA Assoc., Inc., 245 NLRB 676, 102 LRRM 1023 (1979) 2:238; 6:77

Mulholland v. Department of Army, 660 F. Supp. 1565, 2 IER Cases 868 (E.D. Va. 1987) 2:17

Redmond v. GAF Corp., 574 F.2d 897 (7th Cir. 1978) 2:129

Rendell & Baker v. Kohn, 457 U.S. 830 (1982) 2:1

Roadway Express, 87 LA 224 (Cooper, 1986) 5:34, 44; 6:163, 196, 197, 199, 216

Robert Shaw Controls Co., 55 LA 283 (Block, 1970) 6:102

Robinson v. Devine, 37 FEP Cases 728 (D.D.C. 1985) 2:143

Rochester Inst. of Technology, 264 NLRB 1020 (1982), *enforcement denied*, 724 F.2d 9 (2d Cir. 1983) 2:217

Rockwell International Corp., 260 NLRB No. 153, 109 LRRM 1366 (1982) 2:225; 6:60

Roe v. Wade, 410 U.S. 113 (1973) 2:24, 27

*Rosemond v. National Railroad Passenger Corp.*, No. 85 Civ. 5661 (S.D.N.Y. 1986) 2:*150, 180*

Rulon-Miller v. IBM, 162 Cal. App. 3d 241 (1984) 2:3; 6:156

Rushton v. Nebraska Public Power Dist., No. 87–1441, slip op., 3 IER Cases 25 (8th Cir., April 14, 1988) 2:2, 17, 22; 5:19

Rust Engineering Co., 85 LA 407 (1985) 5:62

**S**

Safeway Stores, Inc., 78 LA 597 (Phelan, 1982) 6:138

Salimi v. Farmers Ins. Group, 684 P.2d 264, 1 IER Cases 1403 (Colo. App. 1984) 5:76

Sanders v. Washington Metropolitan Transit Authority, 819 F.2d 1151, 125 LRRM 2772 (D.C. Cir. 1987) 6:236

San Diego Building Trades Council v. Garmon, 359 U.S. 236 (1959) 2:243

San Diego Gas and Electric Co. v. National Health Laboratories, Inc., No. 4383 (San Diego Supreme Court, filed April 23, 1987) (reported in 90 Daily Lab. Rep. A-3 May 12 (1987)) 5:52; 6:151

Sanford Corp., 89 LA 968 (Wies, 1987) 6:81

Scalzitti Co., Pietro, v. International Union of Operating Engineers, Local No. 150, 351 F.2d 576 (7th Cir. 1965) 6:238

Schnelli Enterprises, Inc., d/b/a Cellar Restaurant, 262 NLRB 796 (1982) 6:73

Seattle-First National Bank v. NLRB, 638 F.2d 1221 (9th Cir. 1980), *denying enforcement to* 241 NLRB 753 (1979) 2:230

Shell Oil Co.
—81 LA 1205 (Brisco, 1983) 5:63
—Deer Park, 84 LA 562 (Milentz, 1985) 5:63

*Shoemaker v. Handel*, 795 F.2d 1136, 1 IER Cases 814 (3d Cir.), *cert. denied*, ___ U.S. ___, 1 IER Cases 1136 (1986) 2:2, 15, *35*

Signal Delivery, 86 LA 75 (Wies, 1985) 6:144, 181

Simpson v. Reynolds Metal Co., 629 F.2d 126 (7th Cir. 1978) 2:130

Sinclair Refining Co. v. Atkinson, 370 U.S. 195 (1962) 6:86

Skinner v. Oklahoma ex. rel. Williamson, 316 U.S. 535 (1942) 2:27

Smith v. American Service Co. of
Atlanta, 611 F. Supp. 321
(N.D. Ga. 1984) 2:117

Smith v. Evening News Ass'n, 371
U.S. 195 (1962) 2:256

Smith v. Teledyne Industries, Inc.,
578 F. Supp. 353, 115
LRRM 2901 (E.D. Mich.
1984) 5:76

Southern California Gas Co., 89 LA
393 (Alleyne, 1987) 6:131,
133

Southern California Rapid Transit
Dist., 76 LA 144 (Sabo,
1979) 5:57, 6:181

Southern Extract Co., Inc., 59 LA
697 (Goodman, 1972) 6:98,
99

Southwest Gas Corp. v. Ahmad, 99
Nev. 594, 668 P.2d 261,
114 LRRM 2633 (1983)
5:76

Spielberg Mfg. Co., 112 NLRB 1080
(1985) 6:63

Springfield Mass Transit Dist., 80 LA
193 (Guenther, 1983)
6:171, 222

Staggs v. Blue Cross of Maryland,
Inc., 61 Md. App. 381, 486
A.2d 798 (1985) 5:76

Standard Products Co., 88 LA 1164
(Richard, 1987) 6:80

Steelworkers v. Enterprise Wheel &
Car Corp. 363 U.S. 593, 46
LRRM 2423 (1960) 5:7;
6:97

Steelworkers v. Warrier & Gulf Navigation Co., 363 U.S. 574,
46 LRRM 2416 (1960) 5:7;
6:88

St. Francis College v. Al-Khazraji, ___
U.S. ___, 41 FEP Cases
1712 (1986) 2:111

Storms v. Caughlin, 600 F. Supp.
1214 (S.D.N.Y. 1984) 5:43

*Strachan v. Union Oil Co.,* 768 F.2d
703, 1 IER Cases 1844 (5th
Cir. 1985) 2:190, 262, *263–
64*

Structurlite Plastics Corp., 73 LA
691 (Leach, 1979) 6:201

Suffolk Child Development Center,
Inc., 277 NLRB 1345
(1985) 6:51

**T**

Taft Broadcasting Co., 163 NLRB
475, 64 LRRM 1386
(1967), *aff'd,* 395 F.2d 622
(D.C. Cir. 1968) 6:42

*Tandy Corp. v. Bone,* 283 Ark. 399,
678 S.W.2d 312 (1984)
2:*184*

Tenneco Chemicals, Inc., 249 NLRB
No. 171 (1980) 6:42

Texas Dept. of Community Affairs v.
Burdine, 450 U.S. 248
(1981) 2:118

Texas Utilities Generating Co., 82
LA 6 (Edes, 1983) 5:14;
6:162

Textile Workers v. Lincoln Mills, 353
U.S. 448 (1957) 2:259; 6:82

Thompson v. St. Regis Paper Co.,
102 Wash. 2d 219, 685
P.2d 1081, 1 IER Cases
392 (1984) 5:76

Thomson v. Weinberger, 682 F.
Supp. 829, 3 IER Cases 7
(D. Md. 1988) 2:18

Times Mirror Cable Television, 87
LA 543 (Berns, 1986) 6:207

Todd v. South Carolina Farm Bureau Mutual Ins. Co., 283
S.C. 155, 328 S.E.2d 602
(1984) 2:183

Tomco Communications, Inc., 220
NLRB 636 (1975), *enforced,*

# INDEX

Number in *italics* refer to pages on which illustrations appear.